The Governor and His Lady

The Governor and His Lady

THE STORY
OF WILLIAM HENRY SEWARD
AND HIS WIFE FRANCES

Earl Conrad

G. P. Putnam's Sons   New York

For

MILDRED AND HY

with love

ACKNOWLEDGMENTS

No WRITER is a creator entirely unto himself, to paraphrase the old John Donne expression, and so I have a handful of grateful acknowledgments to many kind people:

Dr. Lewis A. Scheuer, of New York, placed at my disposal his invaluable Lincoln library, and with this, excellent suggestions on Lincoln-Seward literature.

Margaret Butterfield, curator of special collections of the Rochester University Library, in charge of the Seward letters, was helpful in making available the vital letters of Frances Seward, and other resources of the library.

Betty Lewis, curator of the Seward House at Auburn, New York, and Richard C. S. Drummond and Herman Cohen, also of Auburn, very helpfully provided special books and bibliographical information. So too did the Reverend Byron Higgon of Jaffrey, New Hampshire, and Myron G. Conn of Auburn.

My appreciation also to Mrs. Ella Joyce Schoonmaker, of Sennett, Cayuga County, for her research in connection with the chapter, "The Mystic Chords of Memory."

Harold E. Beyea, of the law firm of Cravath, Swaine and Moore, the descendant law firm of the original Miller-Seward law office in Auburn, made a gift to me of Robert Swaine's book, *The Cravath Firm.*

Ida M. Cohen, Assistant Librarian of the New York State Library at Albany, assisted by the loan of many special Seward books and county histories. Worden Gilboy of Rochester, New York, extended research help.

The work was begun several years ago at the New York Public Library. It was completed there early this year, in the newly set up Frederick Lewis Allen Author's Room, where the courtesy was provided of a sustaining membership. My thanks to the N.Y.P.L.

3

Special thanks to the administrators of the McDowell Colony, at Peter-boro, New Hampshire, where, for a time, I worked on this story.

My son, Michael, aided in researches at Rochester University, and in other ways.

Yet, as with all my books, the final expression of appreciation and reliance goes to my critical and stimulating wife, Alyse.

E. C.

CONTENTS

5

Part *Three*   THE GOVERNOR AND HIS MISTRESS

THE cannon sound of the late 1780s hardly ceased rolling when the advance rumblings of the Civil War could, by some, be faintly heard, and when William Henry Seward was born, in the young year of 1801, in the bright morning of America, it was for him to come up almost literally within the echoes of the first great event, only to sense a more tragic cannonading not long distant.

He of all the American statesmen was the one nearest to span in public life and office the coaxial conflicts of our birth and growth, the American Revolution and the Civil War.

The primeval forest that swam green for ages from one coast to the other, like a third ocean, still rolled in its own floral tides when he was a boy living in the remote little settlement of Florida, in Orange County, in southeastern New York. The Indians were still a live force on all sides, and they had not been pushed far westward. In the hamlet of Florida, with only a dozen two-story houses, they still feared that the red men might lurk, and wolves were not uncommon; deer were everywhere and caught quick for meat; and a little boy was warned against going too deeply into the woods.

The pre-Columbian green of our land stretched like a great tent top everywhere, the forests unlumbered, the scent of the air everywhere like swords of sweetness in the nostrils, unsullied by oils and gases, all emerald and yellow-green were the mountains, mass on mass of taut hills, tensed with the closeness of the bush, the evergreen fighting ever for ascendancy, and the thick trunks crushing the lean, all bark-gianted land through which the Indian trails only cut their way. Veterans still young told how they froze hard and hungry in a Pennsylvania valley, how they knew or talked with Washington, or saw the general close and high on his horse;

9

and they still owned the rifles that they carried into battle and went with them hunting deer and wildcat.

This was a time to be born, to be nourished on the nation's roots, to live in a magnificent new lost world that had only recently been found; to be nurtured on Sam Adams' word, and Tom Paine's bugle and Washington's deeds: a time to hear fresh new stories of Benjamin Franklin. In the log cabins our earliest inventors were tinkering with handwrought nails and moving toward engines: toward steamboats soon to run on the Hudson, toward better ways of gathering cotton, toward turning wheels faster; and on all sides most of the actual founders of the country still lived. They had woven a new spirit out of the primordial world, literally cut the amendments out of the forest; and the villages formed everywhere, life sparking; huge colorful coaches crowded the roadways, oxen and horses and mules and men, working, carving the American turkey.

William Henry Seward came into all of this inheritance in the early-hood of the nation. Much is known about him. But very little, almost nothing, has been told—not until this story—of the remarkable invalid woman, Frances Adeline Miller Seward, who loved him and contended with him from his young manhood onward.

REVEILLE

ALL through the 1870s, a fierce battle raged in the parlors, saloons, the debating areas of American society. Who was the greater man, Lincoln or Seward? Who ran the Government during the war, Lincoln or Seward? Who made the policy, and who was the master mind? Wasn't it really William H. Seward of Auburn, New York? Wasn't the Secretary of State the real Prime Minister, and didn't Lincoln take his advice most of the time and do what Seward said?

It was a senseless debate, a kind of side encounter to the main argument, the talk over the North-South war itself. It was a stupid and inane debate but it went on for years, it went on for a generation, until about the year 1900, when it seemed to be settled in favor of Lincoln. Perhaps it was settled in favor of Lincoln from the outset; nonetheless it was one of the postscripts to the great war.

Once, in the village of Auburn, New York, in the early summer of 1874, when the debate was hottest, there was a bad fist fight on Genesee Street, right in the center of the town, between a Seward man and a Lincoln man: one of the last battles of the Civil War.

It was noontime, the sun obliqued in the sky, giving off just enough warmth to make it desirable for a couple hundred people to stand there and watch the way these two battered each other, and between punches saying, "Lincoln, I said!" "Seward, goddamit!"

Then a punch and a swipe, with, on the sidelines, the populace cheering one or the other.

"Come on, Lincoln man, knock him out!"

"The Lincoln man can't do it. This Seward fellow'll take him."

Work was suspended in the nearby stores; the grocery emptied and the clerks and the employer came outside and watched. The crowd in the restaurant left their tables and hustled out to join the circle around the two fighters. They came from down the street and up the street. The officer didn't try to stop this fight. "Let it go. This thing has got to be fought out. Let 'em fight awhile. 'Taint goin' to settle nothin' anyway."

On the sidelines the villagers were saying, "It's that speech Charles Francis Adams made. There ain't been no peace in the state since he told the State Legislature Seward saved the Union and was a greater man than Lincoln."

"Adams don't know. He was in England while the war was on here. He just wouldn't know. He was minister to England and he wasn't around to know. He was Seward's friend, that's all."

The two fighters were veterans of the Civil War, and both members of the New York State Ninth Regiment, founded by Seward. They had known each other since childhood, and fought, one at Antietam and the other at Gettysburg, and now, nine years after the war, they were out here on the cobbled street bloodying each other over this side issue which had loomed as a large one—in the North anyway. The early summer breeze brought soft Indian winds down the main street, and the townsmen forgot the smell of brier and oak and hickory and maple in their nostrils as the fight went on. It was too balmy really for a fight, yet the knuckles cracked against soft flesh and bones, amid the murmurs, "Seward!" "No goddamit, Lincoln!"

The two men were dragging and weary by now and some were saying, "Ought to stop it. It's a stupid fight. They won't settle nothin' except who's the better street fighter."

The academic talk went on in the crowd. "Gideon Welles sure straightened that out. You read his book? Book just come out."

"No, what's it say?"

"Says Seward wasn't no executive at all. Says Seward had no principles. Says Seward just represented the money power in Albany. Says Seward had a lot of gifts, but he never influenced Lincoln any more than anyone else. Says Lincoln was his own boss and it says Charles Francis Adams don't know what the hell he's talking about. Besides, the damn fool went and spent our good money on them icebergs up in Alaska."

"Well, you can't make me believe Seward didn't have principles and no ability and no influence on the war and on Lincoln."

"I ain't a-sayin' that. I'm just sayin' what Welles says, that Lincoln ran the policy, and Seward didn't have no more say than anyone else in the Cabinet."

"You got to admit, if Seward hadda died when Booth's friends tried to kill him, along with Lincoln, the both of 'em would be standin' together in heaven now as twin arms of the wagin' of the war."

Just then the fighter defending Lincoln as the great man of the war fell to the ground. The Seward man hovered over him weak and panting and perspiring, and himself ready to fall.

For the time being the matter was settled. Seward was a greater man than Lincoln—at least to some folks. After all this was Auburn, where Seward had lived, and they ought to fight for one of their own.

Part One

THE GOVERNOR AND HIS FATHER

Chapter One

"LET ME INTRODUCE TO YOU
MY SON...."

THE quiet of the campus life was suddenly awakened. Ordinarily, on the day when the students returned to Union College, at Schenectady, and walked across the big green lawn of the one-hundred-acre site, not much happened but the greetings they gave one another after the summer's absence. But on this day there was a buzz of interest among the seniors and the juniors.

"Look at the freshman," they murmured, and they stared at the figure of a fifteen-year-old shorty, with a flame of red hair and a big nose, who shambled across the green paths, startled at the look of the high buildings and the sartorial appearance of the student body.

They stopped and they congregated and they pointed at him. They could afford to do so. They were dressed in a silken, velvety, even slightly feminine way. It was the year 1816, and the styles were special and still determined by England; the young dudes wore locks of hair down over their foreheads, one or two were tough-bearded, and others wore mutton-chop whiskers. They were tradesmen's sons and their trousers were of cashmere, beige and black; their overcoats were velvet-lined, with tab fasteners in front that gave the effect of narrow waistlines; they wore brass buckles on lustrous black shoes; and to top off that, a few had natty beaver hats, and one or two, with all the *élan* of distinguished statesmen, carried canes.

Naturally they looked askance at the new comic figure who strolled among them wearing the rustic clothes that had been crudely cut for him by an unconcerned tailor in the distant town from which he came. He looked appositely green as he gawked and scuffled over the pathways, and he became more and more self-conscious about the long styleless coat he wore, and the mud-spattered shoes still covered with farm soil; and his gray cotton pants certainly looked different from what the other fellows wore.

He could stand it no longer. They must stop turning to look at him, to laugh and call him bumpkin, hillbilly and "small carrot." He walked up to the boldest and most foppishly dressed upperclassman: "Say, is there a tailor near the campus?"

"Mist-er! Is there? And do you need him badly!"

The newcomer got his directions and then the informant inquired, "Do they give names to fellows like you where you come from?"

"My name is William Henry Seward, sir, and I'll have you know my father is a magistrate and a member of the State Assembly."

"Now I know why we have such sloppy state government."

A group of upperclassmen collected. The senior who administered the impromptu initiation of the new arrival said, "You understand you have to answer all questions put to you by seniors?"

"I shall try to conform."

"Been hunting lately?"

"I hunt."

"Caught yourself some polecat?"

William Henry didn't answer. The older boy grabbed and removed the redhead's fur hat, and he put it up to his nostrils. "Smells like polecat, by gods!"

"It is polecat," William Henry said.

"Polecat hell, we're realists at this college and around here we call a skunk a skunk." He threw the hat far down the field and said, "You don't have to wait till you get to the tailors to get rid of that, do you?"

"The accomplished fact seems to be an accomplished fact," William Henry answered, keeping his patience.

Another senior examined the redhead's long coat. "Is this a hand-me-down from the great man after he arrived in the State Legislature?" It chanced that it was.

"It was especially designed for me—look, gentlemen, I told you I wanted to get to a tailor's."

"Let's take him to the tailor, hey fellows?"

Three or four of the huskiest upperclassmen lifted William Henry to their shoulders and carried him across the campus, while a crowd joked, looked on, followed.

William Henry felt that it was a long way to the tailor's, and as he looked at the building, askew, from his position atop a few broad shoulders, feeling curiously vested with importance and popularity, he thought it a strange-appearing tailoring shop; for it was an ivy-covered green-painted structure not very high, and the main door was adorned with little half-moons.

As they carried the reluctant freshman tenderly into the main privy of Union College, they gently lowered him, as one of the students in solemn tones lectured him on the virtues of scholarship no matter where and how humbly and in what circumstances true education begins; and he would, it was suggested, be eternally grateful for the regal way in which he was carried to his first seat of learning.

After he saw the registrar and found out where he would be rooming, and who with, he headed off campus into the little sprinkling of houses nearby known as Schenectady, and found several tailor shops all in one area. He entered one of them, introduced himself as a new student, identified himself as the son of a wealthy judge, asked about cash and credit arrangements, what they could do for him. The tailor turned him around, looked him up and down, pointed to the stylish things they did, and said, "I can fix you up." The tailor did.

So did other tailors in the coming months. William Henry rolled up accounts that he couldn't pay. The bills went on to his stern father in a village a hundred miles south of Union College.

Dr. Samuel S. Seward stamped about the parlor of his comfortable one-story attic-ed house in the little hamlet of Florida, which is in Orange County, in the southeast of New York State. He was in a rage over the bills sent to him by the Schenectady tailors. It was easy for him to lose his temper; he was an irritable man; he already had two sons leave him because of his outbursts over economy, but this one at Union College, his fourth child, exasperated him completely. He was afraid William Henry would bring disgrace to him and the family. That would be bad for Dr. Seward, because he was the town magistrate, politician, physician, grocer and whatnot, and he had position to maintain, so that an ornery son had to be dealt with in an ornery way.

He wasn't a tall man himself, but he had more height than his boy.

Facially they bore a remarkable resemblance to each other, except that the parent's hair was graying; and now this most honored citizen of the small community paced about loudly asking Mrs. Seward what kind of a son they had. "Now what do *you* think of him, Mary?" he stormed. Who'd ever suppose their farm-born offspring would turn out to be a dude the minute he got away from home! Imagine three suits, seven shirts, four neckcloths, two new pairs of shoes, two hats, three pairs of gloves, a stick-pin, a gold ring, twelve pocket handkerchiefs—And God knows what he bought with the cash! That's what the tailors billed me for. Well, by heavens, I shan't pay those bills. Let *him* pay the tailors—see how far he gets!

And Father Seward never did pay the bills; so that William Henry went from one tailor to the other over a period of time, discovering the world of fashion along with Latin, English composition, and Euclid. He had come to the school well educated already, by prevailing college standards, and at fifteen he had qualified as a sophomore.

Scholastically he moved ahead with a fair share of the highest possible marks, and he set for himself the goal of becoming a member of the newly organized fraternity known as Phi Beta Kappa. In this object good tailor-ing was to play a part, he felt, but the bills that went to his father remained unpaid. His credit went bad. The tailors were looking for him. He was still only seventeen and the senior year was to begin when William Henry, feeling in some disgrace, and not wanting to walk the streets of Schenec-tady for fear of bumping into any of the several cloakmakers he was indebted to, decided suddenly to quit college, make his own way in the world, and shed himself of a difficult and unreasonable father.

Impetuous and independent by nature, he now acted—as poets have been known to act, as rebels have almost universally acted in their youths—prematurely, with a will of their own—and a plunge into adventure.

Someone snitched on William Henry. It may have been the president of Union College, or a professor, or a schoolmate, but one day, early in Janu-ary of 1819, Dr. Seward received a letter saying that his son had quit col-lege, that he was leaving this very day—January 1st—that he was on his way to New York, and then bound by boat down the coast to Georgia. There was talk of a job as a schoolmaster near Eatonton, and he and an-other school chum had already gone. Perhaps, the informant suggested, you can head them off in New York.

That was exactly what Dr. Seward set out to do. Imagine, he said to Mrs. Seward, "having to hunt for him in the hotels of Mannahatta [the original Indian name which was what they sometimes called it then]. When I find him, I may very well test his strength against mine. I haven't done it in years and I'm itching for the chance."

"Now, now," said Mrs. Seward, "you'll do nothing of the sort. Just get him back to school where he belongs."

Mrs. Seward was an unobtrusive, very maternal, religious and conventional person. She was shocked by news of the flight; she may have feared, like Dr. Seward, that they had spawned a troublesome son. In the Florida home there was a scene of true anguish, while the slaves hitched a fast horse to a swift, lean, two-seater sleigh. Mrs. Seward hurried about, rustling up extra sweaters, extra long drawers, extra blankets, and food for the doctor to nibble on as he went over the roads.

Two days of hard driving, out of the curved hills of the Ramapo Mountains, soon reaching the village of Tuxedo, then the grueling drive down alongside the Hudson; all day long moving in the winter bite, whipping the horse from time to time, once or twice stopping off at a tavern to get warm; and at last the doctor reached the wharves of New York.

He stopped at a hotel, the first one he saw, and he asked the clerk, "Sir, do you know where I can find some private agents?"

"What do you mean?" the clerk said.

"Detectives—investigators. I need help."

The judge was sent to an office on Bowling Green, the quarters of an early-day "private eye." When the doctor described his mission, the investigator said, "This is a big city, mister. If we're going to head off that rip-snorting son of yourn before he takes ship, we'll need help." He then made a deal with the judge whereby he and two other agents would be paid by the day, while they hunted in saloons, boarding houses and hotels along the waterfront. "This is a job," the investigator said, "that'll have to get done in about twenty-four hours. If we don't find him then, we'll have to take a trip south."

"I shan't send you south," the judge snapped. "Find him here."

For the next two or three days Dr. Seward and the three private agents went into every saloon, tavern and whorehouse along the waterfront. The judge remonstrated with the investigators about entering the bawdyhouses. "My son won't bother with any of that, just look in the hotels and the taverns, see where he's registered." The investigator said, "Look, mister, you got a runaway. A guy that'll do that 'll do anything. You hired us to look and we'll find 'im."

Dr. Seward bit his lip, admitted to himself the possibility that his errant son might be capable of anything.

William Henry was only a few hundred yards away all of the time that they searched. He was on board the schooner *Tybee,* which waited for the right wind so as to take off for the South. He had boarded the schooner immediately upon his arrival in Manhattan—much as he wanted to see the city. He and his companion had been referred to it by a longshoreman who gave them a small poster.

For New York

The Schooner *Tybee.*

A regular trader, & a good substantial vessel. She will be dispatched with all possible expedition. For freight or passage apply on board, at Harvey's wharf, or to

Capt. Israel Beeman

who offers for sale at very reduced prices Georgia Products, South Carolina Products: Peanuts, Cotton, Rice, Tobacco Cane, Indigo, 3 Mandingos.

Every time Dr. Seward passed by the schooner he said to himself, "Imagine him taking ship on a tub like that." But the judge never thought of going aboard the vessel.

One morning the wind was right, and the schooner slid out of the harbor.

When the judge returned to Florida minus his son, the gentle Mrs. Seward put down the tasks of household, sat quietly on the edge of a couch and began to dab a handkerchief over her eyes. Then she lay down on the couch and she wept.

That angered the judge all the more with his young errant. Oh, if he could lay his hands on the one who had driven his mother to prostration! Yet he howled around the house that there was nothing to worry about, not a thing. "That madcap knows how to take care of himself, you can see that," he shouted. "We'll hear from him, just watch for the mail coach, mark my word!"

But Mrs. Seward wasn't easily consoled. She had a special fondness for the redhead; something of her mother's Irish quality was in this boy, in his features, his waving carrot top, a lyrical something that made him do things like this; he was frail too, he had often been sick, and now he was on the high seas somewhere, perhaps in the bottom of some creaking and groaning ship, seasick, and headed God knows where! She cried repeatedly . . . and they settled down to waiting for the mail.

Mrs. Seward's fears were quite right. William Henry was on board the rickety schooner, below deck, seasick; the weather cold, the incoast voyage rough. Occasionally he went upstairs, staggered out on deck and grabbed the rail, then returned into the interior of the schooner, in his inner eye still seeing the white aprons above, blown full of the wind, carrying him southward: and in another bunk his friend was just as miserable. Occasionally he ate some codfish, hard biscuit, and from time to time drank the schooner's coffee. "Never mind," he soothed his friend, "we'll get better coffee than this at our academies." Seven days later the ship anchored at Savannah.

From here William Henry and his schoolmate made an inland voyage by stage to Augusta. They started by night, through cotton country, and the warm smell of Georgia in midwinter was in William Henry's nostrils, startling him by the contrast with the cold New York State regions he had just "graduated" from. The land was dry, the verdure looking burnt in the moonlight, the whole terrain different.

His friend had a job waiting for him in Augusta; and he expected to find work a few counties farther on in the neighborhood of a place called Eatonton, the capital of Putnam County: there a new academy was being built.

At Augusta he parted with his friend, and he hired a gig and went on alone; but his money was low, and when he wasn't fascinated by the field scene, the spectacle of the slaves at the roadside and deep in the cotton rows, he was worried about how it would all end. He had an inward fear that his father might be schoonering south himself.

For two days he rested at a spot called Mount Zion. Immigrants from Orange County lived there and the Sewards were known to them. It was a breathing spell in his impetuous getaway; then, refreshed, he moved on, this time by foot, with thirty miles remaining to reach Eatonton.

He was tired, his clothes shaggy; still he absorbed the new countryside. Squirrels, jaybirds, woodpeckers livened the roadway. Occasionally he looked, in small streams, for the wildlife of the South he had heard of, alligators and crocodiles, but he saw no more than minnows. Farmers gave him a lift in their cotton trucks, fed him, brought him to Eatonton; and he spent a night there . . . still ten miles away from the new unnamed settlement.

Now for the last lap . . . his shirt was soiled, and the rest of his clothes looked beaten from the ocean travel, the stage journey and the hiking; it was no way for a new schoolmaster to make much of an impression. But he still had a few cents; so he bought a flagrantly colorful neckcloth big enough to cover the front of the dirty shirt; then he pushed on, his shoes clod-clodding in the warm earth. At length he came into an area where he heard the sound of woodchopping, America building. He hurried along, saw new log houses going up, heard the crash of a high tree, watched the

23

lumberers lay low the shortleaf pine; and he knew he was at last in the environment where the new academy was being built.

He had an address, and he went to see a man named Andrew Ward. Ward and his family lived in a log house (a double, they called it, for it had two rooms and an attic), and William Henry was greeted with all good welcome, and taken to the academy a few hundred feet away. It was a rambling clapboard structure, the roof of the main building not on yet, but an office was complete; and when the school was finished they would be able to seat a hundred students.

Ward brought the young schoolmaster to the academy and introduced him to William Turner, owner of the big plantation called Turnwold, on which the settlement was being organized. Turner was also Secretary of the Treasury of the State of Georgia, a principal proponent of the academy idea; and, by way of an examination, he asked the newcomer some general questions. The applicant flourished his intellect and his erudition, and the Georgian was impressed. He assured William Henry that they meant to do things the right way in the new school. "We have just sent to Philadelphia for three dozen lead pencils," he said proudly.

Later, while William Henry waited outside the wooden building, Turner and four other trustees of the academy met inside and discussed the qualifications of the puckish fellow from the far North, with the manner of voluble self-ease. Turner strongly recommended William Henry. There was no question about the scholarship of the applicant— but—how old was he?

"I'd say he was fifteen," one elder said.

"Oh, no," said Turner, who wanted William Henry to stay. "He must be close to twenty-five."

Somebody else said, "Twenty'd be nearer it, but what's it matter if he can teach our farmers and our children how to cypher?"

Another said, "I'd say he was just about seventeen—but he's here—he's come all the way from the other side of the world—so let's hire him anyway."

William Henry was haled before the trustees, and he heard Turner make a solemn and eloquent speech of approval. It was not they who were fitted to examine him or his attainments, the State Treasurer said, but it was he, with his gifts, who was fit to question them. . . . He would get eight hundred dollars a year, he could lodge with any of the villagers he chose, pay a hundred a year for his board; but during the next six weeks while they finished building the school, he could have a vacation, see the countryside; they would outfit him with a horse and buggy, and he could travel about Georgia, and stay board-free with the trustees.

24

this to her and to his father? We have been plunged into shame and grief by this 'principal' you have hired, and what I am writing about, Sir, is simply to say this: Let me warn you, Major Alexander, and the trustees of your academy, and all others whom it may concern, that if you continue to harbor this delinquent, I will prosecute you to the utmost rigor of the law.—Respectfully yours, Dr. Samuel Seward, Magistrate."

Major Alexander called at the Wards and found William Henry at a table littered with papers and books, industriously working out an ancient and modern history course. The head trustee glanced at the first sheet:

1. *The Creation.* The earth a chaotic mass. Creation of light. Separation of land and water. 2. Vegetable life. The heavenly bodies. Animal life. 3. God's blessing on His works. Creation of man. Dominion given to him.

And so on, through Biblical, Greek and Roman history—which he intended continuing right on up to the current controversies among the Jeffersonian Republicans.

Silently, a little sadly, the president of the Union Academy handed the schoolmaster the threatening letter. As William Henry read, and the pen slipped out of his fingers, the major hastened to rally the redhead's spirits. He put it squarely to the boy: he could either go back north, or, if he wanted to, stay, and let the old codger sue and be damned.

But William Henry was much chastened. His sister had written saying that their mother was near to distraction, and only his return home would restore her calm and health. And Mrs. Seward wrote to her son and begged his return.

The trustees felt badly when he told them he would be taking a ship back up the coast. For he was a charmer: still a boy, he was already interesting as a personality. He had endeared himself to the school elders, to the people of the settlement, and even to the slaves of the neighborhood. But the compromise he suggested was that he would stay until a successor arrived. And he did remain until the academy opened and until another Union College man reached there. William Henry even taught school for a few days; but at last, in May, after a five months' adventure, he bid good-by, with real sadness, to Georgia, to his patrons, to his sixty students.

When he returned to Florida, he was, in the little town, a controversial fellow. Some believed he had guts and verve and resolve, and they liked him for what he had; but others, friends and relatives, said he had a delinquent streak, there was a devil inside him, and he would come to no good.

Dr. Seward didn't conceal his dislike for what his son did. He regarded

27

William Henry as being impenitent, not at all cured, and capable of further deviltry; and thereafter, even when they were together and silent, there was war between them. . . .

That caustic attitude continued after William Henry returned to Union College, the father constantly expecting to face some new distress with this jouncy, unpredictable son with the big intellect, an uncertain ambition and a tendency to jump the traces.

William Henry, after he graduated college, went to New York to serve an apprenticeship in a law office. But he failed somehow, and he once more returned home.

He stayed about the house for months, reading, moping, not knowing exactly which way to turn and what to do about himself. His father didn't like having him about in so aimless a way, doing no work on the farm, disinterested in their grocery store. The young law student seemed only to dream and drift and prowl from one room to another, and he always had a book in his hands.

Actually curiosity and revolt still worked in him. There was a frontier—the biggest thing in America.

Then he learned of a job in a small town two hundred and fifty miles into the wilderness. Now, if Pa only underwrote his expenses westward . . .

Chapter Two

THE GIRL AT THE FRONTIER

ONE wintry day in the year 1822, William Henry argued violently
with his father. He had asked the doctor for enough farewell
money to get himself started in a certain little New York hamlet
named Auburn, but Dr. Seward, who regarded his son by now as an out-
right burden, snapped, "You'll be back!"

"Not if I can help it," the son answered. Inwardly he knew there was
some justification for his father's harshness.

"You won't be able to help it," the doctor nagged. "It's your nature."
He fixed a harsh finger the younger one's way, reminding him, "So far
you've failed at everything." Failed at what? the son asked. "We put you
out to a music master to teach you to sing, and you sound like a crow."
Thank you, Father, said the patient son, anxious to get going. He was
packed and ready to coach westward to the frontier country, Central New
York. "We tried to teach you to dance, and paid a dancing master so
you'd be able to make your way among decent people, but you get about
on the meeting-hall floor like a toad." *Thank* you, Father, said William
Henry, and the old gentleman caught the sarcasm. "We hired a French
teacher for you and you learned French quite as well as you did dancing
and singing. . . ."

But here the son, who was interested in law, attempted to make a point.
"I should like to remind you that my real problem has been in mastering
Coke on Lyttleton, and mastering Lilly's Entries."

The idea that his son dared to deny his unprofitable behavior moved
the doctor to a freshet of abuse. "Don't you think I know what you did
the whole time in New York with that wastrel, David Berdan?"

William Henry was penniless, dependent, and thought he should be
careful how much and how far he opposed the disgusted parent. "What
did I do, Father?"

The opportunity to tell his son what he had done in New York made
the angered Dr. Seward literally pour: "Why, you finabbled the whole
year away! I sent you to John Anthon's to learn law and you made of

29

Beekman Street, you and your friends, a playground for your whimsy and your wantonness. You idled with plain girls, you and Berdan—I know—all of you. You played—and spent my money. You monkeyed around with that dawdling literary society you call the New York Forum, and it was nothing but a waste and a wine-guzzling opportunity. Berdan! Berdan! That's all I've heard. Berdan and his poetry and his literary aims— and *you* may wish to follow him! That's what's in your mind. You can't make up your mind *what* you want to do!"

William Henry, in a quiet tone, said that that wasn't true at all; he wanted the law, he was going to practice it, too; but what if he had grounded himself a bit in life and letters and in a few of the simpler enjoyments of youth?

"There you go!" the doctor shouted. "You've admitted it! You'll be back, I know you'll be back. You'll spend this money too, you'll write home, and I'll have to send you coach money, and you'll be hanging around the farm again reading books and chewing apples—and you a full-grown man!"

"No sir, Father, not this time. I tell you I am now ready for the practice of law. I was simply not ready till now."

The judge was skeptical; he had set and definitive ideas about what should happen when a boy became a man. "I shouldn't be too well disposed toward you if you were to argue a case before me—I pity your clients."

William Henry had his mouth tight shut and he absorbed dutifully.

The judge didn't want his sons to take advantage of him because he had money. Money, he believed, unwisely spent on his children, could ruin them. Let them get out and make their fortunes as he had made his. The practice of medicine, farming, being a merchant, and a magistrate, arriving at last even in the State Legislature, had given Dr. Seward a confidence as a parent and citizen which he worked to the limit. Moreover, he was especially disgusted with this son because he had lavished more time and money upon him than the others. William Henry had been smaller, weaker than his brothers; so, let him get the education while the stronger ones did the manual labor about the farm. As a result, William Henry had got that kind of background, and what did he do with it? He'd gone to New York and turned Beekman Street, he and Berdan, into a regular playground: student princes they were, dawdling over wine in cafés, talking books and theatre, dreaming of walking across Europe, and doing Godknowswhat at night! The judge felt that real moral deterioration was on in the big city. He'd been there not long before, and he saw two young men standing in front of a house with a girl, and both men had on their hats and one was smoking.

William Henry didn't make complete denials, for he had just spent the most enjoyable year of his life in the largeness of New York, already peopled by a quarter of a million, lost in the rooming-house life of Lower Manhattan, where Beekman Street, off Park Row, was an anticipation of the later Greenwich Village.

William Henry and Berdan had a kind landlady; she understood their need for fun, romance, adventure. "Now, don't come in too late, William and David," she said to them, and winked; and the two went jauntily off to their evening hangouts, the taverns, the Forum—and their girls. The younger, Berdan, a law student, was an aesthetic fellow who was switching over to literature, an American Bohemian-in-the-making; he and William Henry, who had met at Union College, tramped the streets of the city, blocking their ears when the horsetruck-traffic sound was heavy, marveling at the waterfront and market sights, dazzled by the number of buildings four and even five stories high, attending the theatre, dating girls—till young Seward's money ran out.

Dr. Seward reminded him, "I got the reports on you, Son, I know what you were doing. You were having one deuce of a fine time."

"Father," said William Henry softly, "I didn't do so much. The time had come for me to be a man."

"Good! That's what I want to hear! Now get out and try not to write me for money!"

"I won't, you can be sure."

"You will! You'll be back—too soon."

He took the fifty dollars that his father gave to him.

For the next five days, biting December days, he traveled over the rutted, snow-sprinkled roads of the southern counties of the state, headed for the settlement of Auburn, in the heart of what was not yet called the Finger Lakes Region. The village had all the then-current aspects of the frontier. But small as the place was, there was an intellectual life, a political circle or two, printing was a heavy local industry, and a class of mechanics who worked in small factories were talking of "workingmen's rights."

Yet little of that was the young lawyer's interest, as his coach trailed along the Owasco River road, and entered the town on Christmas Day. From this place he had received recently two offers of legal employment, and one interested him much. It was a job in the office of Judge Elijah Miller, a man with as much status in Auburn as Dr. Samuel Seward had in Orange County. The judge had a seventeen-year-old daughter, Frances.

She and William Henry had met at the Seward home a year and a half earlier. At that time, William Henry's sister, Cornelia, brought Frances there on a vacation from the girl's school they attended together. The boyish law student, at the time only nineteen, was drawn to Frances. She was cheerful, with a lightness of talk, gentle, feminine, she laughed much, did not seem very deep; she was a kind of indulged girl, well-bred at a number of schools, taking easily to languages and the arts, but only really interested in strictly girlish things. Yet William Henry recognized her as a product of the gentility of their time.

They corresponded while William Henry had his errant period, revolting from school, frisking in New York, not making out too well as a law apprentice.

The big orange-colored coach pulled up in front of Eleazer Hunter's tavern on East Genesee Street, and young Seward felt frozen as he exited from the stage. The slight chap with the large nose, with his bright hair concealed by a bulky fur-lined hat, stepped from the carriage and walked up on the porch of the tavern, then entered.

William Henry and Frances Miller greeted each other cautiously, because there was a big man standing at her side. She curtsied, extended her hand, and called him by his middle name, Henry.

Judge Miller had a courtroom voice, darkly modulated. "So, young Mr. Seward, you've really come to help relieve me of my legal pressures?"

"I certainly hope so, sir." William Henry had agreed to a partnership with Judge Miller which stipulated that if, at the end of a year, his earnings fell short of five hundred dollars, the judge would make up the deficiency.

"I suspect you'll be the youngest member of the bar in our community."

They walked outside, into the stinging Christmas morning air, and entered Elijah Miller's red-colored two-seater sleigh. They piled into the front, Frances in the middle. A speckled gray horse snapped forward with the load, and they slid along the main street, the horse cantering, the bells on the shaft jangling.

William Henry remarked on the frontier look of the business section, so raw, so new, so unbuilt, with the appearance of a place cropping up out of the earth, as if made of its own stones and timber.

That started the judge reminiscing. He'd first seen this region exactly a generation earlier when it was only an Indian trail, a few feet wide, he said; he'd been only twenty-two then, and he'd come here from the East, on foot, over the Indian paths of New York through the Mohawk Valley. That was less than thirty years before, he recollected, and the route wasn't even clearly marked. He too had come here as a lawyer. "Like you, Mr.

Seward, the same age, and when I got here the only cabin that was built was John Hardenbergh's."

This was a good town, the judge murmured, in a hushed, loving voice; it had been good to him; he'd made money here and helped build it ever since he'd settled here in 1808; there were mighty fine people here and a man could make a good life for himself in just this spot; it was drab and cold in the winter, but it was God's heaven in the summer months; young Seward was welcome, an ambitious fellow could get into things and make a name for himself, and a fortune, and have anything else he wanted.

The runners on the sleigh made a sloshy music along Genesee Street, turned into South Street, and the vehicle smoothed along till they came to the Miller property. Elijah Miller rambled on of the home he'd built just five or six years before, and the work that still had to be done on the property.

He thought it was only proper for the young newcomer to put up at Mrs. Brittan's. She had a fine rooming house for lawyers, merchants, bankers. He'd be young as to most of the men there now, but he'd meet gentlemen.

"But first," said the judge, "let's have Christmas dinner at our place."

They arrived in front of a big natural-stone colored house sheltered in the center of five acres of primeval wood. Bits of snow lodged in the stone-colored brick. Tall gray snow-specked trees, except for a few green, long-fingered pine, surrounded the dwelling, and the bare limbs and the leafless branches stretched over the rooftop of the home that still stands, big and sturdy as ever, a hundred and fifty years later.

Chapter Three

"THE RELATIONSHIP BETWEEN JUSTICE AND LAW IS ONLY INCIDENTAL"

FOR several months he moved about the village making collections for merchants, burying deep in himself a growing distaste for the work and his disgust with himself for being good at it. His room in the rear of the Widow Brittan's house was his office, and he came and went from that place.

The settlement in winter appealed to him. Auburn, borrowing its name from "sweet Auburn, loveliest village of the plain," of Goldsmith's poem, *The Deserted Village,* was literally a cradle still rocking in the American Revolution. The place had been founded by Colonel John Hardenbergh, who, for his services to the Revolutionary cause, was awarded a tract of land. He'd settled, cleared the land, and Hardenbergh's Corners had become re-named Auburn, so the place was therefore a direct flowering from the war against the English.

But in the center of the town there was a great gray cemetery-like disfigurement: the Auburn State Prison. It had been built and opened only a few years earlier to absorb an overflow of the crowded jails of New York. The swampy streets, the weed-covered open fields, stretched away from the gray-walled tomb, and the residential areas sprang up irregularly all about for a radius of a mile.

One day in the spring, when the thaw had struck, and the town was running like a pool, and the spring winds brought green tips to the maple trees, a convict was let out of prison, having served his term for burglary. Discharged prisoners didn't have much money when they left the prison, only a few dollars they might have earned in the prison shops, and a new suit of clothes provided by the state. They had to get out of town at once and they were expected to walk out or leave by coach going somewhere, but they mustn't settle in the village.

This convict, a man of about thirty, went out East Genesee Street early in the morning, moving up and down the tree-lined hills. The community

34

looked to him fresh, prosperous, growing; and as he reached the outskirts, he saw a lonely house. He noticed that the front door was open, and no one seemed to be about. The petty thief entered the dwelling and looked over its comforts. Ah, the crockery, the silverware: he found a flour bag into which to pour the items, and he started packing. He filled the bag with trinkets and baubles, then his eyes fell on a knitted scarf and a color-ful cloth that might make a shirt. He started to take these. "What are you doing here?" someone sharply asked him, having entered on the soft-carpeted floor.

The burglar decided to run for it; but in line with his early training he didn't care to leave empty-handed; and as the bag of silver and crockery was too heavy, he grabbed up a hunk of cloth and another item and he sped from the house.

The owner and his sons soon captured the offender, and they brought him, by wagon, to the constable's office in the village center. The arrested man was jailed and indicted—and the incident was assigned to William Henry to handle: his first trial case.

He went to the primitive courthouse where justice was served on the second floor. The lower floor was a jailhouse built of upright logs.

The lawyer had never been in a cell before, and he'd never spoken with a professional thief either. Curious, he entered the lockup and asked, "How could you commit a theft immediately after serving a term in that place?"

"Never entered my mind."

"You mean you just had to go into that house?"

"Had to have some help to get to New York. Had to do something."

"Is this the way you intend resuming life? Didn't you learn a trade in prison?"

"A trade?" The answer meant nothing to Seward.

"Didn't you ever have any schooling?"

"School?" The same kind of meaningless echo.

"You are guilty of the theft, you know."

"I ain't said no."

"I don't know how to get you out of this—can you suggest something?"

"You suggest something, you're the lawyer."

"This is a second offense for you. If you're found guilty you'll go back into state prison again. I'd hate to see that."

"I'd hate to see it."

"Everybody'd hate to see that," said the lawyer.

William Henry held in his hand the indictment which described the

35

stolen items as "one quilted holder of the value of six cents and one piece of calico of the same value."

"You stole twelve cents' worth of stuff, it says here."

"I did a bad job."

"Real bad. Nothing you can tell me that will help?"

The man shrugged. "I done it," he said. "It's up to you."

He looked at the very white face, with its prison pallor, a kind of heart-trouble whiteness to it: the man had small gray eyes, a nondescript set of features; he was a dead soul; he had stolen all through childhood, didn't know his parents. William Henry had heard of this type when he studied law as an apprentice in New York a year earlier. They called them "juvenile delinquents." This one had grown to maturity.

"I'll do whatever I can," the young attorney promised.

He strolled out of the jailhouse and walked along broad, tree-spaced Genesee Street wondering what to do. He was a stranger and he looked with interest at the forty or so sprung-up shops of the tiny community. He passed the firearms shop of H. B. Hawley, and he noted the small sign in the window: PISTOLS, BULLETS, POWDER, HORNS, PARTS, DUELING CASE WITH PISTOLS.

Next door was the ironworks of Halls Tobias, and that spot seemed especially busy, because the place was filled with tools, kitchen utensils, broilers, griddles, every kind of metal object. He peeked inside at a couple of counters covered with iron items, scythes and iron shovels in one corner, axes, hammers and smith's vises in another; and on the door was the neatly printed sign, a forerunner of twentieth-century business practice: PURCHASERS WILL FIND STRICT ADHERENCE TO THE PRINCIPLE OF SMALL PROFITS AND FREQUENT SALES. Also another sign: that iron would be cut or bent free of expense to the purchaser. He glanced at the proprietor but his eyes were mainly full of what he'd seen in jail, and he turned and walked on.

Still thoughtful about the case assigned to him, he passed, half-interestedly, Howland's Hat Shop, the tannery, the silversmith's shop, the goldsmith's shop, and he reached as far as Lumber Lane, a south turn off Genesee Street where a young cabinetmaker named Brigham Young was busy inside a woodworking shop designing items for house interiors.

At Samuel Cumpston's store he idly looked over some of the more popular commodities of the time, managing also to chat a moment with the proprietor, and buying from him a bottle of Wistar's Balsam. He read the advertised items: Log Cabin Sarsaparilla, Nervura Old Homestead Tonic (will cure most cases of the hypos), Sage Hair Tonic, Oxygenated Butter, Calf Shoes $3. A busy, growing town, he mused, people making money; and the bottled items, how the inventive mind of the period was at work—

Gold Bond Java Coffee, Utica Spring Water, Seneca Head Powder, Worm Powder, and Seneca Hoof Packing, described as Nature's Own Remedy.

He sauntered past an open spot about thirty feet wide; it was weedy and muddy in there, and no building constructed yet, somebody holding the half-acre for a good price; and then he came to the quiet wooden Indian, all a-feather in front of Blaisdell's Barber Shop. It was a narrow store only a few feet wide, and you could look through the door and see the shelves of shaving mugs, and the smart-looking barber chair, with its gadgetry for leverage, folding backward, rising up, a leather headrest for the head. He glanced briefly at the incidental sign that read, TEETH PULLED HERE—20 CENTS A TOOTH," and drifted to the next establishment.

That was the Fast Horse Tavern, and the whiff of liquors floated out into the street over the slate sidewalk on which the lawyer strolled.

He came to Canley and Smith's Apothecary, and it was evident that the state of medicine was advancing, men were experimenting and manufacturers were packaging the latest cures: gold-thread root, pulverized cinch powder, Lobelia Soap, Scabish, Bloodroot, Spearmint, Snake Root, sweet basil, sugar of lead, soda-mint tablets, and the jars with their cures, leach and ointment jars, bleeding cups, salves, infinite mysterious-looking jars of herbs in ochre and beige and green colors, hinting at mystic curative properties; and people got them by prescription or by word-of-mouth recommendation. It was a good town to practice in, he thought, there was commercial activity here, the people buying, the stores much occupied.

It was the little establishment next door to the apothecary's that gave him his best thought, the tailor shop of Thomas Finn. This was a one-story wooden structure, and the tailor sat at his window close to the slate-wood sidewalk. As he stitched he could look up and say hello to any passer-by.

He entered the shop, introduced himself as a lawyer associated with Judge Miller, and the tailor acknowledged, "I've seen you about."

The lawyer asked Finn if he could tell one cloth from another and one kind of stitchwork from another.

"I ought to. I been tailoring twenty years."

William Henry said, "I'll be back."

In a half hour he returned to the shop bearing with him the quilted holder and the piece of calico.

The lawyer said, "This is a quilted holder. Look at it, will you?"

"It is not a quilted holder," the tailor promptly denied, fingering the item. "This holder is sewed, an ordinary sewing stitch."

"Yes?" William Henry's eyes lighted. It was a minor point, it might mean something. "And this piece of calico—"

"Calico?" the tailor promptly said. "Who told you that was calico? That's a material we call white jean. That never was near calico."

"Are you sure?"

"Sure I'm sure. Unless you think you know my business better than I do."

"I certainly do not." Then William Henry asked, "Would you go into court and swear to it that this holder is sewed and that cloth is white jean?"

"I certainly would. I wouldn't want to see that poor devil sent back in there for stealing a shilling's worth of nothing."

Only William Henry knew that inside himself he wasn't as confident as he outwardly appeared when he arose in court before all the older men to plead his first case. He said to himself that he'd be willing to pay twice the fee he was getting for this to have one of the others handle it; but still, something in him, drive or need or bravado, pell-melled him into doing a distasteful thing.

In the wooden-walled, whitewashed court of the log-and-frame building with that temporary look that belonged to the frontier—"We'll build this courthouse now and have a bigger one later when we get bigger"—he entered the dock and at once broke a precedent. The rule of that period, for most cases, was that beginners had older men address jury and judge; the beginners were supposed to watch the courtroom champs as they pirouetted in the docks, waved their arms and made their points. But he hadn't gone to any older man with his marshaled facts and offered, "Here, for this part fee, present the case for me." He jumped in himself.

Nervousness and an ailment that hung over from early respiratory trouble gave his voice a hoarseness that aroused attention from two or three lawyers in court. They heard someone with a grating voice asking vital questions of the tailor.

The Honorable John Hurlburt was there, standing off to the side, and next to him was another star of the judiciary, William Brown. Lawyer Brown said to Hurlburt, "Who's that boy with the foghorn sound asking all those questions?" Hurlburt answered, "Miller took him in. He's full of vinegar, isn't he?"

Other attorneys looked on while William Henry, after his examination, gave the judge a meaningful look, as though to say, "See, this man never stole a quilted holder nor a piece of calico."

All of a sudden the judge dismissed the case. He turned wrathfully on the district attorney and said, "Hereafter, be careful how you formulate the indictments and make sure of your facts. We have to let this culprit go free now."

So, rather miraculously and swiftly, William Henry won his first case—and got a fee from the county. Off to the side of the room stood the Athletes of the bar, as the old pros were called, they who outdistanced others, won cases, and made money. One remarked, "Little Bill turned a neat one, didn't he? Looks like we may have some minor competition in the courthouse."

Inwardly William Henry crowed like a rooster. He could bring something back to the Miller office, boast of his success to Frances, and dash off a note to that disbeliever in the southern part of the state, Dr. Seward. Yet because he was William Henry Seward, destined to become something bigger than a village lawyer, he had a curious thought on his way out of court. He remembered something that he'd learned very early in his legal training, one of the axioms of the business which he was always baffled over, something that lawyers all over the world knew and were taught, and something that was inwardly disturbing to him: *The relationship between justice and law is only incidental.* He learned that in this first instance when he won a case for a man who was properly guilty as charged.

Chapter Four

A POLITICIAN PROPOSES MARRIAGE

WILLIAM HENRY and Frances Miller strolled southward over the slate sidewalks of South Street. This was the "nice street" of the village, in the making, where the manufacturers and store proprietors and real-estate people lived. A few fine houses were going up on either side of the road, for it was still a road, and not yet a "Macadamized" pavement.

He was speaking of his small triumphs at the bar, and his certainty of earning more than the five-hundred-dollar minimum he had been assured of by Frances' father. They chatted of mutual friends, of the trellises on the side of a wooden porch, and they admired the iron-bar figurines of cherubs and angels on an ornate iron fence that went along the sidewalk in front of the rich Willard house.

Frances, gently at William Henry's side, was slightly taller than he. She was reedish of build actually, though it wasn't easy to see how she was built because of the long, outflaring ankle-length dress she wore. She had a vague irregularity of feature, a quality that made its appearance when she talked: then her oval-shaped face had a way of lengthening into a sudden seriousness.

To him that was one of her principal attractions, her fluency, her literacy, her charm and chatter in conversation, the sudden bursts of earnestness. He listened as she indulged in the lightest and seemingly most meaningless chatter: of her married sister Lazette whom she admired and adored, of her father who was a kind of giant to her in a kindness and watchfulness that was almost maternal; and she murmured, like music, of her schooldays, her teachers and their idiosyncrasies; her schoolmates and the funny things they said and did; and she wandered from amusing comment about people in her father's circle to chitchat of church life and Sunday-school routine.

But William Henry was intuitive, and a judge of people, and it was in this very lightness of her chatter that he detected her true character and her values. She was well brought up, with something of the Quaker way about her, even though the Millers were Episcopalians; she had respect for people, she believed in honor, respectability, virtue—which William Henry believed in. He surmised this from her interests, from the incidents that struck her as amusing or wrong. He saw no sign of brilliance in her, no intellectuality such as he had been exposed to, and such as he had developed, but her brain was alert, she thought nimbly, and she had humor and empathy. She could grow.

Then there was this silence. They walked, they observed, and they were silent.

No one ever knows exactly what is in another person's mind; and Frances didn't know the goings-on in her suitor's brain. He glanced through the trees at the vague green distance that was the north side of the village, thinking of another young lady he'd been visiting ever since his arrival in town, and glad now that he was done with her. Today he was making his choice of Frances, if she would have him.

The other girl—Edna Kasson—had been a kind of trouble and problem. He'd never been certain of her affections; sometimes she seemed to love him, sometimes not; he was confused by her, and it had hurt his pride and his self-respect. He wasn't sure he wanted to be attached to a personality like that, he was afraid of it. True, her father, Arthur Kasson, was very rich, one of the weathiest men in the town. But he was a hard man, he'd made his money, they said, by extortionate and oppressive means, and he was unsure of Mr. Kasson as a father-in-law. A son-in-law who was also a lawyer might fall into the clutches of such a man, and be used by him in his moneymaking schemes. Then where would he be? If Mr. Kasson lived on he'd become a very rich man, if he kept making money as he did now, and yet—Mr. Kasson had seven children, and would probably divide his money among all seven.

There was no such problem at the Millers. There were only two girls by Judge Miller, and one was married, and besides, the judge was almost as well-to-do as Mr. Kasson. Beyond that, Frances Miller was a nicer girl, he thought; more unaffected, more candid, more comprehensible, more manageable. He'd been thinking about these matters for weeks; his father was after him to get married and settled and have done with frittering about; and so, with these pressures upon him and these uncertainties to be resolved, he ventured a proposal to Frances. There, quietly, along the avenue, she happily accepted his offer, and she told him that all that remained was her father's consent.

"That," he said, "is a bigger problem than you may imagine, Frances."

"Why?"

"Because it is."

"But Father likes you."

"That's not enough. I shall have a hard time with him."

"What makes you say so?"

"I think you don't know how deeply attached he is to you, Frances. I think you don't know as well as I that he is loath to allow you to leave him."

She was astonished, unbelieving. How could Henry think such a thing? Girls got married, her sister Lazette had wed; everyone got married, Father expected her to marry.

"All that may be, but I shan't have it easy with him."

She protested, enumerating the points in his favor, how her father liked the way he conducted himself about the village, at the church, at the town meetings, at the courthouse, his promise as a lawyer.

"Still," said William Henry, astutely, full of practicality and designs, "there is something that I wish you would do which will make it easier for us."

He told her that when he went to her father it would be best for her not to be in the village. Would she be willing to go to her cousin in Ludlowville while he approached the judge? She said she would. "Very well," said William Henry, "I'll take you there, then return by myself."

He felt better. His head lifted up. His large nose looked impressive and a little proud. He drew a small black cigar out of an inside coat pocket and he lighted it. The cigar looked a bit out of place in the mouth of so young and so small a man.

There was one other thing he must do, and this he did, after he took Frances to Ludlowville, and upon his return to Auburn. It was a letter he wrote to his father.

The letter was dated August 12th and it opened, "Dear Father."

If there was one thing that he had ever acted deliberately upon or thought about seriously, he began, it was upon the subject his father had recently prodded him about—marriage. He had studied character and consulted circumstances, he said, opening his letter not unlike a legal paper, and then he stated the heart of the matter.

1. My first principle was that I would never unite my fortune with another unless there was a strong and devoted attachment mutually existing between us.

2. My next principle was that I would not unite myself to one who did not possess a strong mind, together with a proper respect for me.

3. And lastly I resolved that I would not unite myself to any person where poverty would be the result of the union.

With this platform of personal principles as the springboard from which he'd thereafter live, he proceeded in a few paragraphs to demolish Mr. Kasson—even though Dr. Seward preferred him because of his wealth—and he then removed Miss Kasson from the picture for the reason of her uncertain character and the fact that she'd already hurt his pride.

"These are arguments to the head. There are others of the heart," he went on. Frances was of undissembling mind, and she had a proper respect for him. She returned his affections; she loved him. That settled it. "I therefore think that if there be any person to whom on acquaintance you would be willing to join your errant son, it is she...." Then he announced to his father that he'd made an accomplished fact of it. He'd proposed to her and she had accepted him. He was vain enough to think that Judge Miller would take him as a son-in-law, and finally, without giving his father all the reasons, he mentioned, "I have taken Frances to her cousin in Ludlowville that she might not be at home when the hard tale was told to her father." He would let Dr. Seward know the outcome the following week. Would Father be so kind as to make Mother acquainted with what was going on?

He finished his note with a comment that may have been as close to his heart, or closer, than all the matters "aforementioned," as he might have professionally put it:

"Politics here are at a dead stand. . . . Yours affectionately, William Henry."

One evening, with the background all set, as he imagined, with Frances safely away and the judge reclining in his big leather chair, William Henry called; and, when he was seated respectfully opposite, with his clasped fingers over a crossed knee, he asked the judge for his daughter.

The judge, at fifty, was a big man, full and rounded, yet not a fat man. He was of English stock, and he had a John Bull look, a jowly face with an underchin, and his nose was sharp-edged and aquiline. His hair was graying and not too thick, and he wore it brushed close to the skull. The judge had no beard or mustache or sideburns, like many of the men of that time, but was close-shaven; and he had noticeable bushy eyebrows, like spider's legs, darker than the hair on his head. His eyes were light blue, not large, and the skin of his lids hung heavily over the blueness; his ears seemed smaller than was right for his head, and they were closely pinned to the sides of his head, tautly, economically. He was a strong-looking man and his face was a projection of Puritanism, virtue, will.

His parents had been Quakers and he had generally a Quaker's morality; so that beneath his forceful exterior he had an inner benevolence and religiosity. He was proprietary toward what he owned, and possessive of his daughter, as William Henry knew.

He was much of a man to approach, and the suitor wasn't surprised when the judge amiably answered, "Henry, let me congratulate you on your happy thought of sending Frances to Ludlowville—"

They were two politicians, and the younger one let his blue eyes fall, with no expression of guilt.

The judge sparred. "I'm glad you decided that this was a matter just between us—"

William Henry nodded.

"We are happy, Frances and I, that you wish to marry her. We are really happy."

William Henry's eyes lighted. Success.

"But there is, of course, a preference of mine—in this matter."

It was about what the young man waited for, yet he didn't know the form it would take.

The judge beamed. "Here is a fine ready-made house and home and property, Henry. Why don't you just come and live with us? You and Frances can just *have* the house—"

There, it had been said, expected, yet unexpected.

It wasn't, to William Henry, quite the gift it might have been to many young men. He was embarrassed by it.

With all the pride he could muster, he stutteringly, raspingly replied that it didn't become a young man to move into such a ready-made situation as this, appreciative as he was. What about the two of them setting up housekeeping in some small place in the village? Rent? And buy something later—of their own?

The old judge's face went as cold as if he were passing sentence on a hardened offender.

"No, Mr. Seward. My daughter stays with me as long as I live!"

"As long ... as long ... as ... you ... live?" The whole proposal seemed collapsing, the marriage simmering out. It was one thing to marry well, to get a bride with a good dowry ... but this ... this was too obvious, he'd be a laughingstock.

"Just—as—long—as—I—live." The father paused and stared at the suitor. Then, "Do you think Frances will go with you if I forbid it?" There was no malevolence in the question. Only certainty and pride.

"Probably not."

"Well, son, love isn't enough in this situation. It's love my daughter, love my house. And if I must say, I don't think you'll be doing too badly."

"Do you know what they'll say in the town, at court?"

"Certainly, they'll say you married into a flower bed and they'll wish they were you!"

"It isn't a situation I can like, sir. I can support a wife—now or later—certainly a little later."

"If you waited five years and she waited five years, and then if she waited ten years and you waited ten years—and you had a fortune and you owned everything here that I don't own—she still doesn't leave this house while I'm alive!"

"I understand."

"Now we're making headway." The judge was definitive, and yet he was full of friendliness for this young man. In a warmer tone, he said, "Henry, why don't you lay down your cards?"

"There isn't much alternative—except give her up—and I'll not do that."

"Of course you'll not do that." The judge warmed to the job. "Now listen, son, if you're going to start life worrying too much about what people say—when you're doing yourself good—you'll begin with a handicap." He argued, "Do you realize how many law papers I had to write by hand before I could buy the land to build this place? I'm saving you all that pain and all those years. I'm offering you a ready-made home—and servants—"

"I appreciate it all." William Henry was humble, still didn't like it. He had bright hair, independence, manhood, ability—and he'd rather wait a year or two, save money, take a small house somewhere in the village, and go it his own way. A dowry yes, but not this....

The judge tried another softening-up approach. "Henry, do you know what it is to get old and be lonely and have no wife and no children around?"

William Henry made a lawyer's reply: "I've had no such experience, sir, so I can't answer."

"Well, believe me, I'm having the experience. Frances' mother died eleven years ago. When the girl was only six or seven. She looks like her mother looked. Lazette is married and no longer lives here, and I even have to go and see her; and if Frances left me—here I'd be, with this house I built only six years ago, and the servants—and you and Frances'd be living somewhere in a . . . a log cabin."

"No sir, Mr. Miller. It'd be better than that."

"Henry, do you know—after hearing you ask for my daughter the way you're doing, and demanding the right to set up in a place of your own—after I hear you go at me like this, do you know, son, I want you more than anything else in the world to be *my* son! You're not with your father any more. You've left him. You'll never go back there! But you're here,

Henry, and I've never had a son, and what the dickens is wrong with being a son-in-fact as well as a son-in-law? Come to your senses, lad!"

"You make it sound difficult to resist!"

"I tell you, there's no other way you can marry my daughter! You've *got* to marry this house and you've *got* to marry me and you've *got* to marry my servants and you *can't* ever take her away from this house! Those are my terms!" The judge hammered on doggedly with warmth and love and want, but with an immovable finality.

Young Seward had felt it would be something like this; he'd seen the hand of the father ever since the day he arrived in the village—such a love for a daughter as would arouse this religious parent to clubs, gunfire and warfare. He'd seen it on those winter evenings a few months earlier when he came to the judge's house and watched the way the corpulent fellow mothered his little girl, and brooded over her like a male hen. He'd seen it and Frances didn't know a thing about it. Just that she was under his thumb and obeyed him like a chickling in a nest with its flapping parent. She always called him Pa, but he was Ma too.

The big man looked down literally on the small fellow with the anxious look and the helpless manner. Once more the judge went benevolent. It seemed that *he* was proposing, rather than the young lawyer. He *was* proposing, too, a strange deal that invited a young fellow into the bosom shelter of an established home, and he knew what it meant to a youth's pride and a man's pride, and it was much to overcome; and he was proud of the way the young fellow went about trying to snatch this little girl out of the big cosy house away from the substantial green-blooded property.

"Why, do you know how that girl'd miss this house and this back yard, son?"

"She'd get used to another house and another back yard. They all do."

"Oh, no, son. Not a chance. This is the *only* house she knows. She watched each board when it was hammered on. She helped plant the trees and the rosebushes. She had her own little playhouse down in back of the property for years. She's spent hours with her dolls in that grape arbor—" He motioned outside through a window. "It wasn't easy to send her off to school. No, sir! She just wanted to get back here. This is the only home she's ever had, and she probably never will have another one!"

William Henry absorbed it all, torrents of it, the old man was swept with it, and the lawyer felt shorter than ever. Yet he'd found out one thing, that Judge Miller really, deeply wanted him for a son-in-law. The gray-haired judge, with the spectacles on his forehead, gushed with affection: all the Millers were affectionate, the suitor noted, but there was this condition—immutable, and he couldn't temporize with it, or sunder it.

He said, "Mr. Miller, I love your daughter. I guess I'd better get to love this house."

"Henry, I adopt you as my own son!"

"Thank you, sir!"

"—As my own son, Henry!"

They were shaking hands fervently. But deep within, the young lawyer was uncertain, although he knew there was no alternative. He'd have to face the sling shots, the arrows, the catcries of the men at the bar, the sly glances of store proprietors who'd joke about how he fell in so soft. He'd meet with the jealousy of other young men who might have imagined themselves eligible for the judge's daughter. There'd be gossip when the engagement was announced ... and when they married, sooner or later ... and he took up residence in the new six-room South Street home, he knew there would be a regular waterfall of talk.

He hurried over the streets, through the intersections, to his room. He had told "the hard tale" to Judge Miller. He wouldn't give all the details of the deal to his father—not now—but he let him know—frenetically—with dashes between his thoughts—

August 15th, 1823

MY DEAR FATHER—

I have to claim your congratulations—the question is proposed and answered in the affirmative. This ends the negotiations—I am anxious to see you here and introduce to you your daughter Frances.

Judge Miller has adopted me as a son.

Yours sincerely,

WILLIAM HENRY

He had gone about the business of making marriage as a politician might do it. He had planned strategy, he knew what to expect, he had considered an alternative; these procedures bore all the earmarks of the careful strategist.

For the time being he had won half the battle: an engagement was agreed on; as for whether or not he'd live in the house, or have Frances in a place of his own, that could be handled later.

Each man to his own method. A politician loves as much as another one loves, but he loves in his own way. A politician has to have a long eye.

Chapter Five

THE "EMINENT ADVOCATE"
AT AUBURN

POLITICS may have been at a dead stand, but William Henry wasn't. He scudded about the village of two thousand like a sailboat on its way. He was a joiner and an organizer, and when there wasn't anything else to join, he'd organize something himself—like dances. He couldn't dance, and that upset Frances because she enjoyed dancing; but he could organize dances, and make money from them, which he did. He had joined the Episcopal Church soon after his arrival, yet told himself he'd never be so confirmed in any religious view as to be parochially bound to it, if he ever felt that, for conscience reasons, he needed to leave it. He enrolled in the militia and drilled with the men in an open spot on the edge of Fort Hill, the big hump of waving hill just off the center of the town.

He made occasional visits to the hangouts where men gathered. He lolled before the Old Bank House, and watched the stagecoach horses snort and claw to a stop in front of the tavern. The stage lines were privately owned, the coaches named the Pilot and the Eagle, and, rattling over the highways, if the roads were dry, they threw up a blanket of dust. He halted at the two-story wooden hotel called the Center House. Public meetings and dances went on there in the evening, and on Sundays there were religious services and Sunday school. Villagers looking for someone to see or talk to drifted toward this place naturally, and the talk would be apt to be about politics. (Everything turned on politics, or religion, perhaps money talk.)

"I hear you came out against the Regency," businessman Wicks Tuttle, a Democrat, an older man, told him in front of the Center House. "Yes, I've lined up with the Cayuga Republicans." Tuttle said that's what he'd heard. "And I hear you gave a talk the other night at this place and said the judges were buying their jobs from the Regency." William Henry acknowledged that, and added, "I also said that the Regency was selling the jobs." Could he prove that? Tuttle wanted to know. William Henry answered it was common knowledge. The Democrat asked, "Young fellow, you got a lot of red hair, and a nice big nose and a lot of spunk, but how do you expect to get anywhere in politics if you're going to fight the Regency?" The young fellow replied, "I'm just saying what I think the public ought to know. Do you think I'm the only one opposed to the Regency?"

He'd been educated by his father to be a Jeffersonian Democrat, but party labels didn't mean much to him. He was interested in the content of political labels, parties, groups—what they stood for, and what they did, and not who they said they philosophically followed. He doubted that the Democrats, nationally, would ever relinquish slavery, and he opposed the Democratic Party leadership in Albany on the simple ground that it wasn't democratic at all, and was, in fact, a very personal government by a clique of a dozen men. They'd gotten into office three years earlier as a result of a people's protest against certain dissatisfactions with the State Constitution. Now an opposition was rising that said the Regency ruled worse than the gang that preceded them. William Henry charged in an address before the Republican Convention of Cayuga County (his first political speech) that the Regency was a statewide phalanx run from the top of the Hudson River. Each county, he said, was dominated by a small group of justices and politicians who were bound with the Albany men by political ties; that this group wasn't interested in internal improvements, that they ruled independently of the people's will, that the justices had too much power in property matters. The Regency was also opposed to a change in the State Constitution that would give the common citizen a chance to name presidential electors, for the Regency wanted Martin Van Buren for President.

It was a man-size dragon for a novice to go out and slay—and he was the first in the county to attempt it.

"You don't want to see Van Buren get to be President, hey?"

He answered, "No. I'm for John Quincy Adams—and better government."

Tuttle ended, "Well, we'll see."

One evening in midwinter, early in the year 1824, William Henry visited in the parlor of the Miller home. He and Frances, her father, and the judge's old mother, Paulina Titus Miller, who was in her seventies, crowded about the brick fireplace whose hearth went three feet deep into the room. The old lady was white-haired, her face a map of ruddy, rural lines. The parlor itself was twelve feet high, so that the flames, yipping

49

from a half-dozen logs, still failed to heat the quarters. Grandma Miller's spinning wheel was against a wall a few feet away, for she hadn't been able to work at it in days, the weather had been so cold. The flames lighted the few fixtures: a picture or two on the oak-paneled walls, a tall grandfather clock that ticked noisily so that it could be heard when the flames didn't loudly crackle; there was a leather-covered sofa against the south wall, a rocker and three or four plain maple chairs, and in a corner of the room a small writing table of mahogany. It wasn't lavishly done, even if it was Judge Miller's entertaining room. They hadn't lived in the place long enough for it to acquire the knickknacks, the aging and the wear that gives a room its character. Yet possibly the presence of the talkative William Henry helped; for he brought books and newspapers into the house; his black boots were standing in the hallway by the door, the ashes from his cigars were heaped in a clay tray on the long mantelpiece; and he regaled them with his latest story of the court...

"I am assigning to your defense," the county judge began, "an eminent advocate...."

The offender stood in the dock gratefully. He glanced at the slight William Henry with the eager look, for the new lawyer alerted at the judge's kind description of his talents.

"In the meantime," His Honor continued, "I'm remanding you to the county jail where you'll be in the custody of the sheriff until your case is tried. You can tell your story to this accomplished attorney at the jail."

The judge wasn't exactly joking. He had watched the beginning lawyer handle a few criminal cases, and besides, he wanted to assure the wandering wayfarer who had fallen into trouble that justice was alive in this village.

A gavel plopped on the bench, and William Henry walked with his new client, his new fee, and the sheriff, downstairs to the lockup.

"Did you attempt to rape this woman, as they charge?" he asked in the cell.

"Look," said the defendant, not replying to that question, "I myself am a lawyer. I had a practice at the Philadelphia bar...."

"Why aren't you there now?"

"It became unremunerative. Besides, I make a better lecturer."

"Yes, about that lecture. Why didn't you give the lecture?"

The prisoner lowered his head.

William Henry wanted to understand his man. "You posted placards all over, you left the tickets at the bookstore, the people paid twenty-five cents apiece for them—and I'm informed they sold nearly all the tickets. Instead of giving the talk, you ran off with the money...."

The middle-aged, bright-eyed, well-dressed defendant bristled. "Don't you think that people could learn something from that too, as well as from the views I might have expressed?"

"That seems like a strange answer," the lawyer murmured. A thought came to him how this man might be defended.

"I decided that there wouldn't be enough of an audience—so I took my departure."

"All right, now we're making headway. You took your departure—and on your way, on one of our out-of-the-way roads, along the banks of the river, you saw this light on in the farmhouse—?"

The prisoner listened. The attorney completed the picture, as a constable and farmer had described it, asking for confirmation or denial. "You figured out that the woman had the light on while her husband was away, and you entered the house. She was in her bedroom. There you made a forcible attempt on her?"

Silence.

"Why did you enter the house?"

"I wanted food."

"Food? The constable says you saw this pretty woman—and you tried to attack her. She says so too. Her husband claims so. That's what I shall have to contend with when we plead...."

"Look," said the adventurer, "if you were the 'eminent advocate' that the judge said you were you would find a defense for me, instead of persecuting me."

That did it. William Henry decided the man was a genuine eccentric. The human mind interested him: the strange beings who found their way into the dock, the curious, the queer, the characters, the miscreants who landed in cells: he read what there was to read about their nature, but the meaning of sanity and insanity was vague to him, unclear to medicine and to the courts—and he saw here an opportunity.

"I have a defense," he ventured. "The one defense that can possibly get you out of this scrape...."

"What is it?"

"Insanity."

A large rounding of the eyes occurred in the accused; he stared at the attorney, he was silent, and the lawyer thought that the man accepted this defense.

"I'll be in touch with you." The attorney walked out.

A few days later, in court, William Henry listened while the district attorney pictured the offense. The woman testified, the husband came to the stand, the constable had things to say. The jury listened.

William Henry addressed the court briefly. Here was, he said, a picture of irrationality from its inceptions to its end: a lawyer who didn't practice law, a lecturer who didn't lecture, a well-dressed man who was actually impoverished, an irresponsible who, fresh upon one set of senseless actions, followed through with the sheerly unbalanced idea of entering a farmhouse in a lonely place and undertaking what he had. He wound up, "I therefore plead insanity in behalf of my client."

That ended the pleading, and the judge strongly urged the jury to free the prisoner on the defense offered by William Henry.

Still, the jury decided that the smart-looking, well-dressed fellow in the dock knew what he was doing. He was a swindler and an adventurer, they decided. They didn't like to have this type coming through their village. "Guilty!"

The next morning the prisoner was brought in for sentence.

"You know, of course, that you've been tried for a heinous crime," the judge began. "Because you are a poor man and a stranger here I assigned to you a youthful but highly able counsel. This lawyer did such an excellent job in your behalf that I personally am convinced that you are not in your right senses. But the jury thinks otherwise, and the jurors decide, so I have to sentence you." He paused a minute on this note of regret, then asked, "Have you anything to say before the sentence of the court is pronounced?"

"I certainly do!" The man leaped to his feet. "I got enough to say to prevent *any* court from punishing me as a felon."

He turned a contemptuous glance at his defender, and motioned him aside with his hand. "This boy here doesn't understand my case. He betrayed me!"

The judge rapped his gavel. "Here, now ..." he tried to interrupt.

But the garrulous, queer and probably disturbed prisoner tore into the "eminent advocate." William Henry fidgeted at his counsel table. He looked helplessly from the judge to his client.

The prisoner roared, "He defended me on false grounds!"

"You wish now to deny the insanity plea?"

"Certainly. I'm as sound as you, Your Honor!"

"My soundness is not at issue here. Finish what you have to say—"

"He should have defended me on the ground I attempted no violence!"

The judge half stood with anger. "Stop that, sir," he hollered. "Stop it right now!"

The defendant halted, his mouth partially open.

"For what you've done you can either be sent to the county jail for a short term, as for a misdemeanor, or receive seven years in the state prison for commission of a felony.... I now believe the jury have not been unjust in their verdict. *Start talking again ... if you will, sir ... but at your risk!*"

The stranger with the restless tongue fell silent.

William Henry got him off with ten days in jail.

Afterward the judge approached the lawyer. "Did this fellow unsettle you, after the fine work you did for him?"

"I didn't exactly expect his outburst. I think he was not convinced of the 'eminence' of my advocacy."

The judge said, "The plea you entered for this man was as true as that ... over there."

He pointed to an oak pedestal in a corner of the room. On the stand rested a two-foot-high sculpture in gray clay, the robed figure of Lady Justice. The scales were in her left hand, balanced subtly, precisely, in the measurement of absolute truth.

It was getting late, the time when he usually returned to his room at the Widow Brittan's, but this night the snowfall already reached up to the windows. They could no longer see through the tall windows, and the glass was a white stain full of wintry design. Outside there were no longer any sidewalks or roads, only huge wastes of white; the village all bedecked, and so with the entire frontier. The long winters of this locality were a dread, to the women in particular. The season lasted eight or nine months, and four or five of these were invariably bitter. The sting and bite from the Canadian country moved in, gathered strength over Lake Ontario, then seemed to settle over Western New York for long, unrelieved weeks. Then came colds, sickness, deaths. It was no wonder that the cemeteries of the time carried so many gravestones with notations of the death of infants and of young people.

Tonight, in the Miller home, they suffered from the lack of stoves, and they huddled by the hot logs in robes, cloaks and buffalo blankets. In front they burned, their faces were hot, yet on the hearth a pan of water swiftly turned to ice. The judge complained that he'd tried to write during the day but the ink froze in his well. The floors were cold, no one wanted to walk about the house or get away from the fire. They dreaded going to their rooms where it would be even colder.

William Henry noticed how Frances shivered at the hearth, how she stayed close and trembled. She seemed fragile, almost fluttering in the cold. She had a high, wide forehead, a thin, very delicate nose, and a kind of full-throated shaping of her neck. Now she seemed indrawn, somehow

53

suffering, and it detracted from her prettiness. She had a frail hyper-feminine constitution. She loved this house, and in the summer she liked her village better than any place she had ever seen, but when the autumn turned sour and the sleet came, and hail turned to snow, and icicles started to form at the eaves, and the snow packed down on the sloped roofs, and when the whiteness became deeper and deeper, and the temperatures fell far down toward zero and stayed there for long periods, and the winds blew, something inside her shriveled. She went through each of these cold seasons as others did, complaining, sometimes sick for a few days, then rising again. She was still very young, yet inwardly she was already wounded by the incessant cold and the endless gray, and the seemingly ever-falling snow.

William Henry placed another blanket about her, shielding her still more from the icy room interior whose temperature remained untouched by the snapping yellow and orange tongues.

Chapter Six

THE BROKEN LINCHPIN THAT ALTERED
THE POLITICS OF THE CENTURY

TEN months later the two families took a get-acquainted trip to Niagara Falls. They traveled in a large velvet-lined barouche owned by Judge Miller and driven by his colored man, William Johnson. For a week and a half they rode westward and stayed about the neighborhood of the Falls; they picnicked in the nearby groves, and they stayed and dined at the neighborhood inns, so that both families came to know each other.

It wasn't until they reached Buffalo, on their way back, that there was mention of the marriage plans of Frances and William Henry, and then it occurred casually in the Benjamin Rathbun restaurant.

This was the fashionable and talked-of place, and the Easterners had been told they must dine here. They sat about a large linen-covered table lunching on a new kind of fish, and the two judges were absorbed in tasting a drink hitherto unknown to them and recommended by Rathbun himself as "the cock-tail." While the judges savored the drink, William Henry's mother, Mary Seward, and his sister Cornelia, munched and talked of the place. William Henry and Frances sat side by side; and they remarked on the strange fruit or vegetable, those shiny red balls in the bowl in the center of the table. Three young women were busy carrying hard drinks, mugs of beer and plates of food to a quiet patronage. A bar in a far corner, with a curious overhanging gate characteristic of the taverns of that time, was the busiest spot in the place; a sign crocheted in color read *Mind Your P's and Q's,* and pictures of horse racing and sailboat racing, on the walls, livened the mood. Round tables were arranged irregularly, and straw-bottom chairs were about each table.

Rathbun, the fashionably dressed proprietor, a man in his late thirties, approached them. He wore an air of prosperity, and in the little wildcat settlement of Buffalo he rated as one of the most popular citizens. He was big, with an expansion about his front as if he ate his own food heartily, drank his own beverages liberally, and didn't worry overly. His path would cross William Henry's many years later in a tragic kind of way, but at this instant, as he approached their table, for it was his genial habit to spend a moment or two with each of his customers, Judge Miller complained, "This is a very bony fish, Mr. Rathbun. What is it?"

The tavern keeper answered, "It's a fish I'm trying to introduce around here. It's called whitefish—it's plentiful in Lake Ontario, and I think a real delicacy, but you're not the first to complain about the bones."

The judge passed judgment. "It is a tasty fish, but it keeps my fingers too busy."

"They're small bones, sir," Rathbun said, "but I believe the taste is worth finding your way around those bones."

William Henry had the most pressing curiosity. "Sir, what are these things?" and he pointed at the red balls in the white bowl. "A table decoration or a food?"

"Believe me, sir," the tavernkeeper answered, "it's a food, a very fine food—if I could only make people believe this."

"What's it called?"

"Hereabouts some call them 'love apples.' The right name is 'the tomato.' Botanists call it a berry. Cut it open, put salt on it ..."

That did it. Instantly the tomato level of the bowl was lowered as each reached, and there was a hungry scramble to slice up the berry and possess the single saltcellar.

Love apples! Tomatoes! Awful! Full of seeds! Squashy! Sour! How can you eat them?

Rathbun laughed. This party had the usual reaction. "If you once get used to them you won't want to do without them."

"Where do these pitted bombs come from?" William Henry asked.

"It's a southern product. Someone brought seeds here recently and a few people in town planted them. I think we have to learn what to do with them."

Everyone volunteered suggestions: send them back south, use them for unpopular speakers at political meetings....

"Just the same, Mr. Rathbun," Judge Miller said, "I can understand why your tavern is so celebrated. Do you have anything else as exotic as this 'cock-tail'?"

"I did have, only recently—something so delicious you wouldn't believe it possible. It was a fruit as large as a cocoanut, with thorns on the outside, called a pineapple. They were brought here by Conestoga wagon, and unfortunately they were spoiled when they arrived. Believe me, beneath this thorn lies a fruit as sweet as the world has ever seen."

"Where do they come from?"

"From New York. Where or how they grow I wouldn't know. Next year when the Erie Canal reaches Buffalo I expect to serve all the new things that the New Yorkers are importing from everywhere." Rathbun's eyes darted with a thought. Abruptly he said, "I'll be back."

He went through a door into the kitchen.

In a minute he returned, and in a confidential way re-approached the table. He placed a plate containing a gold-skinned, stiffened fish before them. "Taste that," he said. "Just take the skin off and taste what's inside."

William Henry's mother volunteered to pry off the skin; she stripped it away until there was an ochre-colored meat. She passed bits of it around to each. What is this? they wanted to know, with delight. What kind of fish is this?

"The same as the other," Rathbun said. "Only it's smoked. Smoked whitefish. That we can export. When the canal touches our village I'll ship this fish off to New York all through the cold months and show *them* something."

Judge Miller remarked, "That's one of the astonishing facts of our growth—the new things we come upon, new foods, new places, new know-how, new ..."

"—New marriages too," Rathbun presumed lightly, glancing at Frances and William Henry.

Judge Miller adopted a mock-judicial tone. "Exception. Your statement is intended as a prima facie observation, but it is a conclusion drawn from only circumstantial evidence."

"Lawyers!"

"A lawyer and two judges," Dr. Seward corrected.

Rathbun asked, "You mean you have all been to Niagara—and this couple have been there—and they're not yet married?"

After the flick of laughter Rathbun walked off to another table. William Henry mentioned that this was as good a time as any to set a marriage date. Frances thought the ceremony should be within a few months, and they settled upon October 20th.

Two days later, the homegoing party passed over the warped and mud-jammed highway called Buffalo Street that led into Rochester. It had rained, the road was shoddy with unevenness, and in poor repair. In front of the Miller coach and behind it there stretched for miles an intermittent line of vehicles: Conestoga wagons drawing five and six tons of freight, buggies, rigs, democrat wagons, mail coaches; for this was the main route across the state and through the frontier. Mud spattered their carriage, spotting the border trimmings and discoloring the gold-leaf scrolls on the doors; the iron rims looked wet and caked, the spokes splotched, the hubs corrugated with drying and new-wet earth. The little log houses of the village came into view. The road was so uneven that tree timbers and flat boards were laid together in the improvisation of a pavement so as to prevent vehicles from sliding into the ditches on either side. Their coach was weary and ill used from taking the ruts, the bumps, the hills, the hard miles over the dirt roads; and a linchpin in the front axle, vital to the wheel and to the safety of the passengers, was strained and ready to crack.

At the instant their wagon went over the rude wooden supports, the linchpin gave way, the wheel slid off the axle, the coach crashed to its base, and the shafts tore away from the flanks of the horses. The animals reared and jammed against each other. Their fright increased, and in their excitement, trying to break away, they hitched the coach about so that it lost balance and careened sideways. There were feminine screams. For an instant the vehicle was half-angled over the embankment. Then all the passengers except one, as if poured from a funnel, streamed out, tumbling down the side of a muddy ravine six or seven feet deep. The carriage, as if waiting for its cargo to get clear, came down with a scrawsh on its side into the mud and logs, most of the box remaining on the road but part hanging over the abrupt dip. One horse broke loose, galloped down the road neighing and free, and the other, grappled to the shafts by the powerful leather harness, pawed the air and beat on the muddy timbers.

That was all that the watching villagers could see; then they ran, some toward the thrown passengers while a few young men chased after the runaway.

Only William Henry escaped being tossed into the ditch. He had somehow landed on the road edge. He hurried to the others; he scrounged in the hollow from one to another, in ankle-deep mud, helping them to right-side positions. To his surprise, to everyone's, no one was hurt; but they were prone, rueful or at some askew angle.

He heard a warm voice and he looked up. Someone came down the gully, with one long foot sliding not too cautiously ahead of the other. "Here, let me help you."

It was a tall man in his late twenties, a figure with a rough, muscular look. Whoever he was, he took command, and he aided the Millers and the Sewards, one at a time, back up to the road.

The travelers tested their limbs, brushed themselves, praised their luck. Two young men returned with the runaway horse. A group of village men helped turn the coach right side up, and an expert or two examined the wheel and axle damage.

The Millers and the Sewards gathered around the tall man who had entered the ravine, for he still assumed an informal direction. They listened as he sent someone to get help from the wagon shopkeeper in the village; and then he remarked smilingly that he thought the repairs to the coach could be made in a few hours. He was a rapid-motioned figure, with a ruddy complexion, and he had deeply set gray eyes beneath a high forehead. He had a rather long face, his nose was powerful and straight, and he had a strong, pleasant chin. Women could easily regard him as vigorous and handsome. But he was dressed shabbily, and he looked a little lean and even hungry.

"Who," asked William Henry, his hand extended, "are we indebted to?"

The big man with the easy air and the commanding manner crooked his elbow. "No indebtedness whatever. My name is Weed, sir—Thurlow Weed."

So the trip to Niagara had been eventful, the marriage date set, and as a curious coincidence of the journey, the consequence of a broken linchpin, two principal politicians of the Civil War century got acquainted.

William Henry Seward and Thurlow Weed met in mud, and they would stick through thicker than this in the next half-century as, together, they formed political movements, picked and guided Presidents, and determined and channeled in enormous measure, toward its dramatic outcome, the antislavery sentiment of their time.

Their relationship was to begin shortly . . . in an abduction and a probable murder, and a mystery that has never been solved.

Chapter Seven

POLITICS NO LONGER AT A
DEAD STAND

EARLY in the summer of 1826, Thurlow Weed's next-door neighbor, Russel Dyer, walked into the office of the Rochester *Daily Telegraph,* which Weed edited. Weed was at work setting type, his editorials having been written, the news stories done, the advertising notes set up. Soon the press would yield up the latest issue of the little political journal that provided a scant living for himself, his wife and three children.

"May I speak with you privately?" Dyer asked.

"Of course." Weed locked the door. They were alone.

"Are you a Freemason, Weed?"

"No."

"Well, I have something to tell you. It's an explosive powder—"

Weed bent his head forward.

"Promise me you won't tell anyone of this—take an oath?"

"I can't take any oath—but I don't give away secrets once I give my word."

Dyer decided to talk. "You know Captain Morgan who boards with me?"

"I have seen him."

"He is a Mason, you know—"

"I didn't know. What of it?"

"He's taken me into his confidence—" Then Dyer hushedly breathed into Weed's wide-open ears, "He wishes to expose the Masons. He has written a complete revelation of the first three degrees of Masonry—"

"No!"

"Yes...I have seen it!...And he wants a publisher."

"He wants to publish this?"

"Would you be willing to print it?"

Weed wanted to hear more. Dyer went on—that it would have to be

60

printed secretly, there would be a suitable division of the earnings, perhaps publication might be necessary under a pseudonym, as, if the authorship became known, the life of the writer might not be worth a font of that type. . . .

Whatever Weed thought of the idea he had a perfect out, and he declared it. "My partner, Bob Martin, is a Mason. We couldn't touch it."

Dyer's face clouded. "I think it certainly does let you out." He paused, hemmed. ". . . I think we'll have to look elsewhere."

Weed said, "Why don't you stay out of it, Dyer? It looks too hot for anyone to be hooked up with."

Dyer didn't answer that. He did say, "Weed, you promised you'd keep this secret?"

"I certainly shall. I'm even afraid to breathe it to myself. After all, most of the businessmen in Rochester are Masons."

Dyer left, and Weed forgot about the incident.

Captain William Morgan was born in Culpepper County, Virginia, in the fireworks year of 1776, and he earned his military title in the War of 1812. He was a man of bearing, of some education, and he had an intelligent face: he had a very high forehead; that, or he was balding at the front, and he had a habit of lifting his glasses to his forehead and letting them rest there when his eyes smarted and he wanted relief from the lenses. He was stockily built, of medium height, and he was forty-five when he decided upon his strange career of "exposing" the Masonic Order. His partisans said he was a man of honor and uprightness, and his enemies swore that he was an idler, a drinker, and unreliable. In 1822 he settled in the hamlet of Le Roy, in Western New York. That was in Genesee County, where the Masons were well established. In that community he joined the society, and stayed active in it for about two years. Somehow he ran afoul of his fraternal brothers; no one knows quite how or why, except that the Masons described him as being a swindler, an idler and intemperate. It became unpleasant enough for him in that small place so that he moved to Batavia. But the rumor of his reputed unreliability was relayed to the Order in Batavia, and he was as unpopular there—with the Masons—as he had been in the other little village.

Feeling pressed and persecuted by the Order, or angered, or having other emotions known only to himself—and definitely motivated by the possibility of earning some quick money—he developed the idea of revealing to the world the secrets of the Masons. He moved to the larger town of Rochester, and for two months worked on a book; and here he heard from his friend Dyer that Thurlow Weed wouldn't publish it.

61

Yet the handwritten description of the first three degrees of Masonry known as the Blue Lodge were complete and in his possession and they already bore the title *Illustrations of Masonry*. He knew that there was an impression in non-Masonic circles that the interior workings of the Order were special to some extraordinary extent, that a revelation of them might find a large market, and, full of resolve, he persisted in the hunt for a printer.

He found one. It was another Mason, Colonel David C. Miller, editor of the Batavia *Advocate,* and himself an "entered apprentice" in the Order. Miller was a prominent support in his dubious venture.

They worked nights and Sundays on the typesetting, Miller doing the work, Morgan standing by to guard his literary product. But the word was already abroad in Masonic circles: rumors of the impending publication passed from one lodge to another.

On August 9th, a notice appeared in a Canandaigua newspaper:

NOTICE AND CAUTION

If a man calling himself William Morgan should intrude himself upon the community, they should be on their guard, particularly the Masonic fraternity. Any information in relation to Morgan can be obtained by calling at the Masonic Lodge in this village. Brethren and companions are particularly requested to observe, mark and govern themselves accordingly. Morgan is considered a swindler and a dangerous man. There are people in this village who would be glad to see this Captain Morgan.

The same announcement appeared in the newspapers of Batavia and the close-by village of Black Rock.

The Cayuga Bridge, a few miles west of Auburn, was a demarcation between the more explored area of New York State and the frontier. As westbound travelers moved off the long bridge on the far side, they entered true wilderness, broken only by a scattering of about two dozen settlements that strung out for the remaining 150-mile distance to Buffalo. There were a half-dozen towns between Rochester and Buffalo. This was a flat region, compared with the hilly and mountainous country to the east. The towns were of less size and population than Auburn, and they looked about like the place where William Henry settled. The people lived, thought and acted similarly: the more ambitious read a lot, a few entered politics, most farmed, but they were fair-play Americans who liked to have a plot of land, privacy and their civil rights; and only a few aspired to extraordinary wealth. They had been living quietly since the War of 1812. Everyone was busy accumulating land, a house, a livelihood. Live and let live was the spirit among them; education and culture were objectives, and the church was a social center. They had values to live by and they believed that in living you had to have working values.

All this was about to be violently upset, from Cayuga Bridge all the way to Buffalo inside the deep frontier, because the Masons were influential in the administrative life of the settlements. They had in official locations judges, constables, sheriffs, Assemblymen and Senators. All were worried.

The fraternalists of Batavia received visits from their lodge brothers in Stafford, Le Roy, Rochester, Canandaigua, Gaines. They convened. How suppress the book that was being stamped out, in the silence of night, in the offices of the Batavia *Advocate*? For days they made reasonable efforts, and latterly, some of a more forceful sort, to persuade Captain Morgan and Colonel Miller to abandon their unprecedented project.

At first they tried intimidation. See if he scares, they decided. Debt was a serious offense then, if a creditor wanted to press an action to recover money; so Morgan was brought into court for a small debt. He was jailed, but Colonel Miller bailed him out. The incident roused Morgan all the more; he had some deep-seated hatred for his former fraternalists and he was determined to defy them.

But his troubles increased.

On Saturday afternoon, August 18th, four Batavians, including a constable with the latest legal paper, rushed into his home, seized him and all the papers they could find, and once more hurried him off to the lockup.

For the next two weeks, among Masons in all these towns, there was a ferment, a fear and a resolve. Rumor and threat passed among them. Some whisperings even reached outside of Masonic ranks. What to do about William Morgan? The frontier was restive. How protect the great name of Masonry? How rid themselves of the traitor, and forestall the publication of the "secrets"?

Ideas were not lacking how this was to be done. . . .

One night, when the moon was a big red cent tossed high in the sky, when the people all through the frontier slept so that they could rise with the sun again and go into their fields, Captain Morgan was abducted from jail. That was the night of September 12th. The next day Morgan was moved westward. Men and horses and coaches went on a furtive journey through the small towns that led toward Fort Niagara: all day, on the 13th, a fast coach, reeling and rumbling, went through the frontier.

In the village of Lewiston, straggling along the Niagara River, townsmen saw a party that they described later as certainly the abduction group, taking the captain into a large gray-stone three-story structure known as

63

the Frontier House. Here, James Fenimore Cooper not long before wrote *The Spy*.

For days there was mystery along the frontier. Where was Morgan? Was it true that inside Fort Niagara, the ancient stone pile that four nations had at different times occupied, Captain Morgan was held behind walls four feet deep? ... Was he in the Castle, in the northwest corner of the fort? ... Was he imprisoned in the inner blockhouse or the outer blockhouse? ... Was he behind the great oak doors weighing 1,400 pounds, doors that opened and closed silently, easily? ... Was he in darkness or was he in light? ... Did they keep him near the gun ports on the second story where the heavy shutters concealed all that was within? ... Was he confined in the great hall, the council room where Sir William Johnson in 1764 signed a treaty with the Indians? ... Was he anywhere near the Poisoned Well, whose water was poisoned by some demon in human shape, as legend whispered? ... How many men guarded him? ... What was in store for him—if he was held there at all? ... Was he alive? ... Was he dead? ... Where was Morgan?

No one exactly knew. No one that would tell. No one else that would give away a secret of the Order.

To all these questions there was only silence.

Late September in Batavia is a leaf-turning time, and as a mood of russet and orange, ochre and burnt sienna enveloped the community, Mrs. Morgan spent tearful days wondering where her husband was, whether he was still alive. Citizens came to her house hourly, and revealed their concern and sympathy. Something alien to the civil procedure had occurred. There was a widespread sentiment that private men, working apart from judicial processes, or in defiance of them, had taken the law into their own hands; and this touched the deepest nerve in the community life, for the people respected law and order, they liked the republican system of courts, the method of due process, and they disliked to see this operable structure unbalanced.

Trumbull Cary, an early settler who had prospered, paced up and down the parlor of his gray-painted colonial-type brick house in the village center at Main and Bank streets. He walked out on his front porch, beneath the two-story Ionic-columned porches; he stood in the elliptical arched doorway and looked beyond into the village of small timbered dwellings. He had built this place nine years earlier, saw a happy town growing up around him ... and now this. He didn't like it. He decided to call a meeting of other town leaders like himself, invite the attendance of the general public, and appeal to Governor De Witt Clinton for help.

The villagers met, and the facts of Morgan's disappearance were given to the public. The men who presided were as prominent in the life of Batavia as any of the Masons; and in fact, among the most determined dissenters demanding an investigation were high, conscience-stricken Masons themselves. The proceedings of the meeting were sent to Governor De Witt Clinton, and they asked his help in finding Morgan.

The governor was himself the highest-ranking Mason in the Union.

He replied that he had asked Canadian authorities for their help in recovering the missing man if he were there and alive. He was careful, however, to portray the Masons as a body which did not and could not countenance the action that purportedly had occurred: "I know that Freemasonry, properly understood and faithfully attended to, is friendly to religion, morality, liberty and good government; and I shall never shrink, under any state of excitement, or any extent of misrepresentation, from bearing testimony in favor of an institution which can boast of a Washington, a Franklin and a LaFayette as distinguished members, and which inculcates no principles, and authorizes no acts, that are not in accordance with good morals, civil liberty, and entire obedience to government and laws. It is no more responsible for the acts of unworthy members than any other association or institution."

That was about how the Masonic order had been reputed until these events, and that is its reputation today. But the unfortunate fact of that particular moment was that a few individuals, zealous over the Masonic vows, taking perhaps too literally the threats of retribution for traitors to these vows, acted as they did; and launched, inadvertently, on the political scene of New York State, a whole new stable of public personalities.

In Rochester, Thurlow Weed carefully read the accounts of the missing Captain Morgan in Colonel Miller's Batavia *Advocate*.

He had no sympathy with Morgan's disavowal of his pledge to secrecy and no particular attitude toward Masonry as an association and credo. He was well aware that many of the honored men of that time were Masons. He did have a minor objection to the Order for the fact that it excluded women, but his real position until now was merely neutral. Yet here was an act of violence, a news break, he was a journalist, and he published this editorial in his paper:

Excitement at Batavia

Much excitement exists at Batavia in consequence of the mysterious and protracted absence of Captain William Morgan, who, several weeks ago, seems to have been spirited away from his family and his home by Freemasons, with a view, it is alleged, of preventing his publication of the secrets of their Order. The persons engaged in this violation of law must have been over-zealous members of the fraternity. It is incumbent, however, upon better-informed Freemasons to take the laboring oar in discovering the whereabouts of the absent man, and in restoring him to liberty.

Weed learned at once the depth of the sensitivity of the issues that had been struck: for the Masons of Rochester instantly and en masse withdrew their support. Subscribers and advertisers rushed into his offices, and, forgetting all prior manifestations of friendship, they withdrew their ads and dropped their subscriptions.

Not more than twenty-four hours after the publication of that brief editorial, the business of the *Telegraph* fell away to almost nothing. Weed had, in a stroke, and in a few words, brought disaster to his fortunes, and he had also involved his partner, Robert Martin.

"What in hell is this, Bob?" he asked.

The Mason showed Weed a little book that contained an oath administered to those who joined the Order. The pledge indicated that a violation of secrecy invited a violent retribution.

"Now," said Martin, "what do you think of a man who takes an oath like that, binds himself to people who are bound in all good faith to one another—and then violates it?"

Weed gave a snap judgment. "By gods, I think he deserved the punishment he called down on his own head."

Yet that was a quick pronouncement which he reversed very soon. Driven to think about Masonry, law and order, the number and distinction of Masons in national life, matters of civil rights, he recalled that George Washington, in his Farewell Address (though himself a Mason) warned his fellow Americans against secret associations.

But the damage was done. The *Telegraph* was finished as a source of livelihood—for him. Weed turned over to his partner his own share in the assets of the publication, and, feeling that he was washed up in Rochester, he decided to look for work elsewhere.

He wrote to Utica where he heard of a certain opening, the letter going to an old and influential friend, but he received a curt reply saying nothing doing. The friend turned out to be a Mason. The same thing happened when he wrote to a newspaper associate at Troy.

It was only then that he realized how far, how seriously he had run afoul of a real power in the land.

Weed was broke; he had a wife and three children to feed. He was angered and a little desperate. But Thurlow Weed had resilience. He'd

66

had as humble an origin as any frontiersman of that time, and the hard-
ships of his earliest days had taught him to bounce back and plug and
fight and slug. He knew what it was to have to walk three miles in the
snow, barefooted, to get a copy of *A History of the French Revolution*.
When he returned to his father's log cabin with the book, he had to read
it lying down on the floor of a shed called a "sugar house," and, with his
body inside the shed, and his head outside of it, he read by the light of a
flaming pine knot. At eight he blew a blacksmith's bellows for a smith
in the village of Acra, in Greene County, where he was born; and he was
so small that he had to stand on a box to reach the handle of the bellows.
He grew big and tough, and he could handle his mitts with anyone who
crossed him. In his teens, he drifted into printing. For ten years he roved
from one village to another across New York State, setting type, writing
news, penning editorials, and he got to know the state—and the state of
mind in the whole frontier. He was a kind of boy wonder about politics,
the way he turned his journalism into political meaning. By the time he
and William Henry met, Weed had already been in the State Legislature.

Weed was still in his twenties, he was important in Western New York
politics—and now this thing broke, and the Order was giving him the old
boycott.

He liked opposition. Very well, the Masons were that god-awful powerful? Well, that was too powerful!

There was an old printing press that lay idle in the village of Rochester,
a Ramage press, it was called. There was a battered font of type to go with
it. It'd be slow work printing with this apparatus, but a man could get out
a newspaper.

Weed, as the most astute politician at the frontier, sensed an issue that
could rouse people. Civil rights and opposition to secret societies—these
were at the core of American sympathies: a man was missing, the Order
was displaying its power too fearfully....

He went to three friends who floated the money with which to buy the
primitive printing materials ... and, driven to the wall, he founded the
most controversial publication of that hour, *The Anti-Masonic Inquirer*.

A long lake and dreary Montezuma Marsh lay in the path of westward
travelers through frontier New York back in the Revolutionary War
period; and, in 1799, they built the great Cayuga Bridge, a narrow wooden
trestle more than a mile long. It was regarded as an engineering marvel
and some thought it was worth a trip into the western wilderness just to
see and move on the long walk over water. When you reached the other
side, the big forbidding marsh country opened, with its denseness of alder,

willow and cattails, the incessant loon sounds. The armies of the War of 1812 moved over Cayuga Lake via this overhang, and all westward-headed stages made a drumlike *bu-da-dum, bu-da-dum* as they rolled across the boards.

The bridge and the lake and the swamp were a kind of barrier between the unknown hinterland and the ground that had been broken as far west as Auburn.

The whole region was lake-ridden, forest-laden; it was known that resisting Indians were not far west of the bridge; and news from Western New York had to pass by letter, newspaper and coach or horseback eastward across this span.

One of the earliest copies of Weed's new publication, addressed to Seward, arrived at the home of Judge Miller in Auburn. Other, later copies arrived, and William Henry read them. "News from across the bridge," they called letters and papers that came from that direction; and they read eagerly, for it was as from some distant country.

William Henry wondered how Weed could found a new periodical in the name of opposition to such a privileged institution. He and the Rochester man had seen each other a half-dozen times since the stagecoach incident; occasionally he went west on legal business, and four or five times when Weed passed through Auburn, eastbound, he stopped to visit the Sewards and the Millers. A friendship had developed between the tall man with the drive and the political intuition, and the short man with the vision and the ambition.

"What's happened out there?" William Henry asked his father-in-law.

"I can't decipher it," the judge answered. "I expect odd things to happen over that way where they have to fear thieves hiding out in the marsh, but this—"

William Henry wondered. "You don't suppose Weed has gone off on some tangent?"

"I suppose they've all gone haywire, the way this fever is spreading; it's like an infected district out there."

William Henry, who knew that Weed was a totally political man, asked himself: What can Weed have in mind? He'd soon have a talk with him.

In October, November and December the stages rumbled quicker, the Cayuga Bridge timbers shook with a great tremoring: for in the western counties the villages were a-surge, like one of the Finger Lakes after an electric storm. The newspapers wagon-wheeled in from the west were packed with developments: small newssheets a foot high, eight or nine inches wide, in minute print, with the unobtrusive, understated headlines:

GOVERNOR CLINTON'S ALARM

He Has Offered a New Reward for
Morgan's Abductors

There Are Now Five Counties
Involved

Whole communities were split with dissension; within families, the members took sides—for or against Masonry and secret societies. Churches, primarily the Baptist, Methodist and Presbyterian, were sundered: pastors who were Masons or sympathetic to the Order were discharged. Masons were resigning from the association in groups. Everyone in each town seemed somehow involved. In any hamlet men put one another on the spot: "Are you for or against secret societies?"

Although, by January, realignments were at work inside the political force at the frontier, no actual new party was yet in the field. Still, the ferment that might lead to something like that was there. In a few villages citizens held public rallies where they resolved not to vote for Masons who ran for office.

Then, early in that month, at Canandaigua, the three men who took Morgan from his cell pleaded guilty to charges of abduction, and they received jail sentences ranging from one month to two years. As a result of that there poured over the frontier a fresh mood of anti-Masonry. Judge Enos Throop, who later became Governor of New York State, in sentencing, stated the issue this way: men had disturbed the public peace, they had dared to raise parricidal arms against the laws and the constitution of the government, they had assumed a power that was not compatible with a due subordination to the laws and the public authority of the state. He said, "We think we see in this public sensation the spirit which brought us into existence as a nation, and a pledge that our rights and liberties are destined to endure."

At the close of President James Monroe's administration in 1824, federal politics had become largely reduced to a mere personal contest for possession of the White House and rule from Washington. The various sections and states had their contenders: John Quincy Adams, from Massachusetts; William H. Crawford, for Georgia; Andrew Jackson, the Tennesseean; John C. Calhoun, of South Carolina; and Henry Clay, Kentuckian.

Adams was chosen President by the House of Representatives in 1824, and the political aspirants continued their competition for Executive succession; but the interest of the people was in other matters, closer to home, like buying and running farms, opening businesses, getting jobs, creating new arts and industries, founding a bank in town, building bridges and roads, getting a school going, and then a college. It was important to put a big tall spire on the church and let them see the cross miles away before the coach got into town.

It was steamboat time, canalboat time, stagecoach time, and horseback time. The time of the building of homesteads also had begun; and around the frontier cabins there was a great bustle of activity involving the whole family: shooting the deer so as to have venison, and keeping it underground, frozen, for steady eating in the winter; raising chickens so as to have plenty of eggs; chinking clay earth between the log timbers to keep out the cold; making a little shed for the dog to sleep in; maple sugaring in the spring, for the whole north was covered with maples, the grand tree of the nation, prior even to the pine. There was peace in rural America—relative peace at least, perhaps a longer peace than this nation has ever seen, the breeding of sheep and hogs going on, the milking of cows, and stay out of range of the wild bulls and build fences about them. Haying time, when the ox drew to the meetinghouse the two-wheeled cart with the family in it. It was a rude, even a harsh idyllicism, free of the discord of any profound political fever. Everywhere peace, save in the South, perhaps, where there was always a steady slow-burning tragedy; and in these push-west settlements of Western New York, Ohio and Michigan they didn't have any gnawing concern about politics—just so long as neither the English nor anyone else attempted another invasion.

But now, behind the Cayuga Bridge, a strange seed pod opened. A mere social issue was exploding into an unprecedented pattern; the present static party alignments, at least in the North, faced upset; the decelerated period was at an end.

As William Henry might have written to his father, "Politics is no longer at a dead stand."

Chapter Eight

WILLIAM HENRY TAKES A MISTRESS

IN THE spring of 1825, a few months after William Henry and Frances were married, there was a stillness in the home of Judge Miller. The bridegroom was ill.

He was in his room, upstairs, in the fourposter bed that he shared with Frances, and he seemed to have something more than a springtime illness. He lay asleep much of the time, beneath the satin canopy, and he was without appetite and without strength. Frances was in his room when he was awake. She sat on the Hitchcock chair at his bedside much of the time. A few feet away there was a portable writing desk, with places on a backboard for ink and writing paper; and sometimes Frances wrote a letter to a friend or a relative. She placed wood in the fireplace on the north side of the room; and from time to time she gave him a spoonful of a thick red syrupy tonic. She listened to the grandfather clock out in the corridor, with its loud manly tick-tock, tocking the days away; and occasionally she floated down the spiral staircase on some errand to the house below, but as quickly returned to her husband's side. In the evening she lighted the candle in the silver holder on the small maple table near the bed; and late each evening she crawled into bed at his side. Whatever he had, it wasn't contagious.

This quietness had gone on for weeks, this silent scene, the young man ill, no one quite knowing for sure what held him to the bed. Occasionally the judge poked his head inside and asked how the son-in-law felt; and sometimes Grandma Miller looked in and asked if there was anything she could do. Now and then William Henry was visited by another member of the household, Aunt Clara. This was Clarinda McHugh, the sister of Judge Miller. There'd be a word or two of kind inquiry, and then William Henry was left alone again with Frances. Once, William Johnson, who spent most of his time in and around the stone stables in the rear of the acreage, went upstairs, at Frances' invitation, and said a few words of cheer to the sick one. William Henry, who was sensitive to the presence and the feelings of the colored, seemed grateful.

71

While he was abed a letter arrived from his mother, who didn't know that he was sick. Perhaps because she understood something of the impetuosity of her son, or perhaps simply from a maternal instinct, to give him a bit of advice, she wrote:

May 6, 1825

MY DEAR SON:

You are now the head of a family and many duties devolve upon you. I hope you will be a kind and tender and affectionate husband and may a kind providence grant to help your union in life. Read your Bible. Go to the House of Worship, that is the place God prays with His people.

Your loving mother,

MARY

But that was the whole trouble—that he wasn't the head of a family. And it was this over which he was ill.

He had found the household, dominated by the presence of his father-in-law, constricting to his independent spirit, and therefore unpleasant to him, as he had anticipated. It was a big house for the time and the community, yet for the number of people within, the newness of the marital experience, the intimacy with a whole new family, all this was much for him to make an adjustment to, and he couldn't easily make it. He kept dreaming of a little house of his own.

The attitude he had feared among his fellow pros at the bar had developed, right on time. Once, when he won a small case that might have gone either way, in the disposition of a judge who was no Solomon, his colleague representing the losing client said to him outside of court, with full double meaning, "You get all the breaks, don't you?" That had cut him deeply.

Others, like poor shopkeepers, treated him with an attitude that he, subjectively, felt to be close to contempt; and he resented the light in the eye of some of them, which he, perhaps too sensitively, read as: "Here comes the well-married young Seward, a good customer to have, he's in the money." They knew that the stranger, whoever he was, whatever his gifts, was ensconced in the No. One house of the town, and while there was no scandal to it, nothing really wrong with it—there it was, in the snide, or knowing or even the admiring glances, the rare remarks made to him. Inwardly he wanted to get out, to show these people he could support a wife in a home of his own buying, that he could be as proper as any, that he didn't need the help that he had fallen into by right of his marriage; and when the matter became a source of argument between himself and Frances, she tried to placate him. "They are just a little envious of you, Henry. You should ignore them. If you love me it shouldn't matter what they are saying about you." He'd murmur that he loved her, but wished they had their

72

own home. She reminded him that he had promised her father he would live in the house, and he hadn't been deceived. He said he knew that, but a man had his self-respect to think of. Then he'd get hard about it. "One of these days, when I get the money, I want to buy a place of our own." She answered, "Whatever you say, Henry," figuring he hadn't the money yet to do anything of the sort, and there was nothing to do but drift with the situation.

Now he had become ill over it all.

One day he said he was ready to get up. He dressed; he looked out of the window; the sky was clear and blue, and the sunlight shone in from a low horizon; it illuminated the slush-cloaked neighborhood; beyond and about lay the thawing village, and he wished to go for a walk.

For two or three days more he went carefully, regaining his strength, eating better, cheering up.

Then, one evening, he said, "Frances, I'm going to the meeting of the Cayuga Republicans—"

"It's too cold, Henry. You'll have a relapse. Stay in—by the fire—with me."

He went.

He resumed work at his law office; he labored days and nights; he didn't show up at home very much, only at noon and in the evenings, to eat, and to sleep at night.

In fact, he had a new attitude, Frances thought.

This went on into early summer.

His step picked up. He became hearty and energetic again. His capacity for work and study appeared to intensify. He pored over law books late into the night. He'd be by himself, reading, profoundly absorbed, so that often Frances hovered about his shoulder trying to pry him loose.

Something had happened to him and she couldn't reach him.

She was pregnant, and he was much interested that he was going to be a father, and she a mother, but he seemed to be pursuing something else, something that was beyond her understanding.

She was puzzled. She didn't yet grasp that William Henry had a Mistress, and that he had gone to her.

His Mistress was Lady Politics. She had been his first love from as early an age as five. Politics and public service. Government, Justice, Society. These had seemed to him to be supremely important ever since the day when, as a very small boy, his father stood him up on the counter of the Seward store, and said, "Now recite the poem you have learned." Small William Henry, posed on the maple counter, overseeing the room with

73

its barrels of flour, sugar, salt, lard, crackers and prunes, and looking over the listening villagers, rattled off some rhymed lines. The townsmen applauded. One of them asked, "What you going to be when you grow up?"

"Going to be a justice of the peace—like my pa," William Henry promptly said; for he had noticed that accused persons, when they were arraigned before Judge Seward, treated him with very great respect.

But when the neighbors left, Dr. Seward rebuked his son.

"Don't you know you get an office like that because people give it to you—for your worth?"

"No."

"You don't just go out, like a bear, and say, 'I'm going to be a judge,' and then put your paws around the office."

"How, then?"

"Like I say. It comes to you, or it don't. It comes to you by the favor of others."

That hadn't frightened off William Henry. He would be a judge some day, he decided, anyway; and now, recovered from his illness, he chased after his judicial and political aims.

Mainly his law practice became a means for widening his acquaintance, for mingling with the community administrators and politicians. He gave more time to the work of building the local militia, perhaps because he understood, without even having to think about it, that a community's defense was the first principle of its existence, and this was a front line of civic occupation.

So that there was nothing surprising, perhaps, that a few months after he got out of his sickbed, on July 4th, 1825, he was one of the speakers at the Independence Day observance in front of the primitive courthouse.

An intermittent mist, not quite a rainfall, came down as William Henry, hatless, dressed in light summery clothes, spoke from the stairtop of the two-story, white-painted structure. In front of the building and over the grass lawn there were gathered several hundred townsmen; they spread across the wooden sidewalks, and into the curbless, unpaved, earthen street. A flag with a few stars flew from a high pole in the side yard, and the cloth fluttered weakly in the summertime drizzle.

Frances were there, a few feet distant from him; so was Judge Miller, Aunt Clara, and even Grandma Miller, and he didn't seem nervous as he made his remarks. Frances observed him, young, spirited, lean, seeming almost out of place among the older men beside him on the courthouse veranda. She, as the others, listened intently as he spoke, in a not very loud voice, with a certain rasp to it, how the nation had become firmly based and truly secure since the wars with England.

The Union was still unshaken, he told them, and he doubted that political parties would ever rise again upon cardinal principles. New parties might come and go every year or so, but this only served to keep political waters in healthy motion. There was domestic peace, and peace would prevail for a long time to come, it seemed to him.

Moreover, if there were sullen spirits who believed that the North and South could ever separate, they were wrong. "The North will not willingly give up the power they now have in the national councils, of gradually completing a work in which, whether united or separate, from closeness of territory, we shall ever be interested—the emancipation of slaves."

And the South, he went on, wouldn't likely ever expose itself to a war with the North while they had so many slaves ready to revolt, to become free and find revenge.

No, he saw no such developments.

If there were to be separation on the basis of sections, it might be the East from the West, at the Alleghenies or the Mississippi, but never the North from the South.

It was a groping start toward a credo; he had made his political beginnings by revealing a particularly ignorant awareness of the main problem of the nineteenth century.

The best way to have a public life was to be able to afford it, he told himself. Never have to rely on the salary obtained from a political organization or by holding a government job. For a career in the community eye, first get the money that would make him independent of any need to rely on the public treasury; become free of all pressure, all possible corrupting influence. Make money.

Criminal cases of a minor sort came his way: small actions and small fees, but he handled them:—the three young men who wrecked Daball's Tavern on West Genesee Street after they drank too much; the defense of the farmer who slugged a neighbor in a dispute over a fence that overlapped the farmer's property; an abduction, the robbing of the post-office till. But he had his eyes on civil suits: the fees were larger, the field more remunerative. Occasionally he asked his father-in-law for advice in matters of real property. Judge Miller was the local authority on real property law.

Nobody suspected that he detested the technicalities of law work, the uncertainties as to results, the waiting upon what a judge would do; the ulcerous nature of contention between lawyers, the way in which lawyers had to raise their voices to make a point, to win a case. Young men started out in law, he knew, perhaps thinking they were subserving the ends of justice, but they soon found themselves in endless cockfights with other lawyers fighting for money. Fighting to win for a client—and get a fee.

Outwardly he carried himself with a cheerfulness and a good nature that belied what he felt inside. Not even Judge Miller suspected his son-in-law's distaste for practice at the bar. When they stoptalked in the evening, the rare evenings when William Henry stayed around the house, the young lawyer recounted his experiences with all the zeal of one who loved his work. Actually that was because William Henry was a story-teller, and he was willing to spin a tale at any time about anything worth telling.

He wrote his papers carefully, peculiarly neat and accurate, and the court clerks liked to see them. He picked up law business in all the villages of Cayuga County; he was out often, driving by horse and buggy from one place to another, handling the criminal and civil cases that came his way; and merchants in Albany and New York, who had debtors in this region, employed him to make collections. That work, in particular, upset him. Calling at a man's place of business, or having to write him a stern little note, demanding payment—this wasn't pleasant. It wasn't what he envisioned for himself. It wasn't the kind of law he wanted to handle. There were large litigations in the land, at all times, and if he had to practice law, he hoped somehow in some way to reach the level of the most meaningful law—perhaps even a practice that had something to do with justice.

Chapter Nine

THE POWER OF THE OBLIQUE
APPROACH

I FAIL to conceive," said William Henry to Thurlow Weed, "how a mere act of violence can be the basis of a political movement." He was in Rochester on a law call and he stopped at his friend's newspaper office. Letters had gone between them; Weed followed the reports of Seward's activity with the Cayuga Republicans.

"The political movement is already a fact," Weed replied, "while you fail to see it."

"I see a hysteria about Morgan's disappearance—but where is the public philosophy, the wounded interest that makes this matter vital enough to lead into any wide-scale political action?"

"My dear Seward," Weed answered, as they blew an acrid cigar smoke at each other, "it isn't merely the abduction—not even murder, if the Masons have done away with him—but the idea of a secret and powerful organization imposing its will on the community does violence to our growing national tradition."

Seward wanted to be convinced before he threw in his lot with anti-Masonry, before he helped make this the central issue among Cayuga Republicans or any others. "But Weed, nobody's pocketbook is threatened—"

"Wrong! Ultimately it *is* an issue of the pocketbook. Secret organizations banded together by dubious oaths for private help can only be economic. This is the symbol of unknown power. Unknown power is something to fear. We can't allow our country, at this seeding time, to grow up with a root of fear in it—"

"All right," William Henry conceded, "supposing you're right, and I agree with you—Masonry is wrong, secret societies are inimical to the genius of our country—still, where is the political cause? How rouse people on this mere social principle? How make this into a platform? What can you do with it?"

"Nothing," said Weed, "unless we organize on the basis of anti-Masonry.

77

Support our August convention, Seward. Swing the Cayugans to the State Convention—"

"It's a possibility. I wish I was convinced that this was a right course. I fear it's premature to abandon the National Republicans right now—"

"It *is* the course. And that's where you come in, Seward—you and others like Granger, Fillmore, Whittlesey, Spencer, Wadsworth. Work for the movement in your county as they're working in theirs." Leading figures in each western county had already combined in an anti-Masonic convention held in February of 1827, and they had planned the Anti-Masonic State Convention of which Weed now spoke.

William Henry puffed on a thin black cigar, and he seemed reflective. He stared out of the second-story news office into the square below where there moved the millers, the merchants, the artisans. Weed's place was near the Four Corners, where Main and State streets met. Not far away, the River of Many Falls, as the red men called it, the Genesee, ran fast, and the village set along both sides of it. All through this region there raged the anti-Masonic ferment. He had Weed's word for it that the counties of Genesee, Chautauqua, Erie, Niagara and Monroe were hot over the absent Morgan. He heard Weed murmuring some hushed prophecy that within a year or so the State Legislature would be receiving anti-Masonic members.

The journalist, though he was alone with William Henry, bent forward toward the redhead, his most characteristic gesture, and whispered, as if they were not alone and as if they might be overheard. "Look, this is what we've been waiting for. An issue, Seward, an issue! The country has been quiet as a cemetery for years, ever since Monroe. This is a break in the thread, the peace era is over—with this very matter. We can take a principled position and we can climb on the back of this uprising into office and power. There isn't another thing we can use to unseat the Regency. Not another thing. We need this fight, Seward, and we must ride with it!"

That was different. That was tactics. William Henry knew the importance of *the approach*.

Being opposed to the principle of secret organizations wasn't enough to convince him of itself that in this lay a political course. But what other domestic battle point was there? What else was rousing the people anywhere? Nothing. All was quiet—all but the spreading doubt and the increasing fear of private power, secret power.

"When I get back to Auburn," William Henry said, "I'll talk it over with my friends."

It was true Americana, this expanding imbroglio between Masons and anti-Masons, ripping up homes, towns, churches—and, pretty soon, political parties—like a small, local civil war, principles battering each other on the head, private and group interest colliding with public and national policy. It was a strange issue, too, peculiarly American, especially native. No issue here of rich against poor, no matter of oppressive government or undue taxation, but a curious moral-philosophic point, the simple undesirability of oath-ridden secret societies in a free land—and the spirit that had bored deep into the national consciousness in 1776, the spirit of *the cause,* was touched; so that questions of honor and social credo and philosophic outlook were ripped into the open.

The continuing mystery played into the hands of the leaders of the Western New York ferment. Weed and others steered and channeled the rising as the fear of Masonry spread from state to state.

William Henry was convinced that Masonry was wrong, and that it ought to be combated, but he believed that there was a question of timing, that the launching of an Anti-Masonic Party then might be premature, so he lingered on through 1828 with the National Republicans.

Late in the year he attended a convention of this party at Utica. Frances was there with him, and she stayed at a hotel, while William Henry took part. On the evening before the assemblage there was a caucus between forty New York and up-State delegates to determine whether an up-Stater or a New Yorker would preside. The row that blew up nearly ended the convention before it began. It went on for about two hours.

William Henry sat quietly all through the argument, saying little, and the less he said and the more heated the dispute became, the more he worked himself into a pacifying eloquence. His law practice had taught him that when two clients were at each other's throats, postpone the meeting, try again later—compromise.

When he got the floor he said that while he favored the up-State candidate for the presidency of the convention, the city candidate was also a helluva good fellow, and they oughtn't to fight like a bunch of kids, but act like grown men and politicians and realize what was at stake. He suggested that they just sleep on it overnight, and in the morning take a vote, and abide by it. There was almost a tear in his eye as he finished, and they all went out sober.

Overnight they fell in love with William Henry.

The next morning, before the convention began, the two rival candidates for presiding honors grabbed hold of him and begged him to be president of the convention. Reluctantly, but in tremendous haste, he accepted.

He had begun practical inner party life on the hallowed ground of being a unifier.

From then on, as often as William Henry could get away from his law practice and resist his wife's urgings to stay at home, he went over the state helping the Anti-Masonic Party to take form. He had become literally a political organizer. That was a different role from his principal talent as a speechmaker and as the writer of eloquent addresses for himself and others to deliver. In the circles of the new movement he became admired largely because of his well-organized orations; they had style, power, and an imagery that was comprehensible to his audience, and although he had no distinguished speaking manner, what he had to say, and how he shaped it, arrested attention. Beyond all this he had a sunniness of personality, friendliness, and a lack of personal animosity. "Did you hear what the red-head had to say?" "The redhead told me this story." "The redhead was the life of the meeting." "The redhead had them all laughing." "The redhead made more sense than the others."

He discovered that much had to be accomplished in an oblique way. Actually this knowledge may have been first nature to him, as was the manner in which he had proposed marriage, yet he became more and more adept at learning to work through others. Somewhere he had discovered the tactic of having his own purposes appear to result from the decisions of others. This facility may have stemmed from the advice he had received in childhood from his father not to expect ever to become a judge or mag-istrate except by the favor of others.

He had, recently, an instructive experience along that line. He tried to get an appointment to the post of Surrogate of Cayuga County because a friend of his, then holding the office, was resigning. He went to Albany and saw Governor De Witt Clinton, carrying with him a letter of recommenda-tion from the retiring office holder. The governor recommended him to the Senate. While Seward was waiting for the Senate to act, an unexpected development in state affairs placed him in a political position opposed to that of Clinton and to the party that ruled in the Senate, so that the State Senators rejected his nomination. He learned from this humiliation that it was a mistake to place himself in the hands of the executive, that it was wrong to compromise his own independence and rely on appointive power —that perhaps it was far better to secure office "by the favor of others," as his father had put it—by the will of the voting populace.

William Henry was in Albany, and he had a room at the Eagle Hotel. He was on his way to Philadelphia. A national anti-Masonic convention was opening there in mid-September. Weed had only recently opened shop with the Albany *Evening Journal,* in the shadow of the Capitol buildings. Prominent anti-Masons had urged him to leave Rochester, and in the capi-tal he occupied an old structure that had been built around the time of the

Revolution. He made the rounds of the news sources himself, he gathered the advertisements, he wrote the editorials, he set the type. In a short time the paper acquired a circulation in a half dozen nearby states.

William Henry and Weed were together one evening at the hotel, and in the course of their talk, Weed asked, "By the way, Seward, I have a personal question."

"Certainly."

"How are you doing financially?"

That rather surprised the lawyer, and for an instant he seemed to hesitate, though he had no reservation about telling his friend exactly what he was worth—so that Weed swiftly followed up: "...What I mean is, are you making enough so you can give part of your time to public office?"

William Henry relaxed into a picture of what his status was and how he felt. Sure, he had a bank account now, but of late he hadn't been thinking of being in Government. It was the action of political life generally that interested him, and whether in office or not, he would probably always be in politics. Moreover, since he experienced the statewide rebuff on the Surrogate's job, and the whole political community knew about it—well ... holding office simply wasn't part of his current thinking.

That's what he said.

Weed listened sympathetically. "One rebuff, and you're through? That doesn't sound like you, Seward."

"It isn't me. It's just that I wouldn't ever go hunting public office by myself, like the way I ran to Governor Clinton. That cured me of being pushy about being a public servant."

"You're not asking for office—I'm the one that's asking you whether you'd like it."

"Weed, I just haven't been thinking that way lately."

The newspaper man reflected a few seconds. "I think I know you better than that. There's more politics in your veins than there is—well, I was going to say ... blood, but the figure isn't right."

"Maybe the figure *is* right. What did you have in mind?"

"Only that I've learned enough from your district to believe it possible that the party apparatus there might want to nominate you for the State Senate."

William Henry shrugged it off. Or so it seemed to Weed.

During the next few days, in Philadelphia, William Henry presented the Anti-Masonic Party creed to an assemblage of ninety-six delegates from eleven states. He debated the policies with those who asked for clarification, and he offered the resolutions that gave life to a new national political force. They talked of how they would throw their weight in coming local and national elections.

Back in Auburn, unknown to William Henry, the county Anti-Masonic Party leaders received a short note from Thurlow Weed saying, "Go ahead with Seward in your locality."

Chapter Ten

YOUR OWN FRANCES...

SOON after the birth of Augustus, their first child, Frances moved into a chronic and apparently inevitable illness. It was a malaise that was no one thing. There was rheumatism and that was very real, for the bitter winters of the vicinity affected all, and killed many. Perhaps there hung over Frances the shadow of the memory of how blizzardy weathers, and the frozen little house that Judge Miller first lived in, in Auburn, killed her mother. Sometimes the judge spoke of it, sometimes Grandma Miller recalled it, and Frances listened, virtually unable to remember her mother. The judge's wife had been Hannah Foote, of Williamstown, Massachusetts, and she had gone west to be Mrs. Elijah Miller. Hannah Miller birthed the two girls, and then she went into a series of "colds" and emerged with tuberculosis. Late in the summer of 1809, in her twenty-fifth year, she returned to Williamstown to spend her last days with her mother. Elijah Miller had never married again. His mother and his sister, Clarinda, came to live with him, and they had raised Frances and Lazette. Now there was the ghost of a threat over the Miller house of some kind of repetition of the first tragedy. Or so it seemed, for Frances ailed, and the job of nursing Augustus, and trying to keep warm her own frail body, seemed almost too much for her.

When these physical factors combined with the emotional one of frustration through having a much-absent husband, something inside of her turned: she became what would be called today neurotic, though then her complaint was always that she had "the hypos" or she felt faint and had "the vapors." She was depressed, a little wretched and a little confused. To be young, only twenty-one or so, and to need a husband about, and yet to have to bid good-by to him every few days while he went off politicking or taking care of his legal business was too much for her affectionate nature.

More, from the start there was another source of household conflict: it was subtle, never out in the open. It was Frances' attachment to her father, and his continuing guardianship over her even though she had a husband.

This father-daughter relationship was deep, familial, tender, and William Henry sensed it, and it gave him the feeling that he never fully possessed a wife. If he was partly married to public life, Frances, from the outset, couldn't break the original family tie with her father and the house on South Street.

So a curious battle of three personalities opened, William Henry seeking domestic independence and the justification of his manhood; Frances requiring love from two men, albeit two different kinds of love; and the third, the incessantly paternal judge, retaining, with the grasp of a miser, his daughter's closeness and affection, seeing in her features the face of the wife who had died early in his marriage.

As a result there had been a train of swift postmarital developments, first William Henry's illness and recovery, followed by his revolt into an immitigable public life; then from Frances came a reaction of illness and discovery and upset that was in direct proportion and reversal to her husband's literal escape, or to his oblique new adjustment to matrimonial life. As for Judge Miller, he knew very well what was happening, and there wasn't anything going on that couldn't be remedied by the expenditure of a few well-placed bucks. Obviously the house was too small. "Let's have more rooms here," he said, "make this the biggest place in Auburn. You'll be having more children and we'll need more space."

The carpenters and the bricklayers went to work, adding a new section to the rear of the house, making a larger, more expansive cellar, and new upper rooms two stories high. A new coat of paint went on too: the last paint job had been done by the journeyman painter, Brigham Young, who was, at the moment, raising a lot of hob over a religious creed to become known as Mormonism.

All day Frances listened to the pounding, the sawing, and to the hoarse calls of the workingmen; and the sounds and the smell of paint didn't add to her happiness. Even this, she felt, wasn't going to restore to her the ever ambulant Henry.

Occasionally she placed Augustus in the carriage and strolled with him up East Genesee Street. "East Hill" they called it, a swoop of elm and maple trees that leveled off and led eastward. Partway up the incline she turned south on Owasco Street, a winding road that went alongside an outlet from the Owasco Lake. She walked a half mile, past flour and woolen mills and residences, to the little garden-surrounded home of her older sister, Lazette Maria Worden. They had been close in childhood; now marriage drew them even nearer. Lazette was married to Alvah Worden, a young businessman who had studied for the law. Judge Miller had put Alvah into business running a cotton mill, after he had married

84

Lazette. (Apparently the judge believed that the best way to take care of his daughters was to be sure to set up their husbands.) Lazette was shorter than Frances, brown-haired and pretty, and she was also a mother.

On this summer day Frances talked of her husband's restlessness; he didn't seem as close to her now as before he had been ill, she complained; he was pleasant, kind, full of devoted sentiment, yet he had acquired a certain detachment, like someone who was going somewhere—she didn't know where. "Half of him is somewhere else, not at home, and not with me," she said. He'd stay in his office till the oil in the lamp burned out; or he'd be away all day at some nearby village on some legal matter; sometimes he was away two and three days if he had to go to Rochester or Syracuse. Cases and courts and political rallies. "They're like girls he's chasing, Lazette, really."

"Be happy he isn't really chasing girls."

"I am—but the way he comes home, grabs a meal, rushes off!"

He was tender to her, she told her sister, and he dawdled with Augustus like any father; he was solicitous of her health, but these attentions lasted just so long . . . then he'd get animated about something he was doing; a good civil action had fallen his way, or he was chairmaning tonight's Republican meeting, or they had made him captain of the artillery.

Then she reached what she had to say—that Henry wasn't happy in the judge's house.

Lazette asked how Henry and their father got along.

"Splendidly—but Henry simply doesn't feel at home." They had the law in common, Frances said, and common political interest, but her husband, in the privacy of their room, kept talking about buying a place for themselves.

"Can he afford to?" Lazette asked.

"He has banked a thousand dollars."

"Isn't he satisfied with the enlargement of the house?"

"It doesn't touch him. He wants his own place."

"You have to think about it. You may have to do it."

"But how can I leave Father? You know how lost he'd be."

"Frances, a wife *has* to go with her husband."

"I know, but Father—"

"You are not married to Father, Frances!"

Lazette went on that William Henry was spirited, that he was ambitious; he wasn't likely to allow another man, even a father-in-law he liked, to run his matrimonial affairs.

"He knew when he married me how Father felt—"

85

"Henry has about him a terrific independence. You have to understand his feelings."

Frances said she did understand; in a way it was a handicap for a man beginning a public career to have it said of him that all had been easy, that he had fallen into a property.

"Now he's full of anti-Masonic politics," she went on. "He's got to help Thurlow Weed, he says. That keeps him away. If that linchpin hadn't broken, we'd have never met the man—"

"No, Frances. Henry is a born public man. They'd have met somewhere else. You'll simply have to keep up with his politics."

That thought interested Frances. "I've never had any interest in politics—"

"Well, darling, *get* interested."

Lazette tried to comfort her sister; it would straighten out, she predicted, marriage adjustments took time; and meanwhile Frances mustn't make herself sick over these matters.

Yet that was what had happened; Frances was bewilderingly ill over the situation. Sharing a husband with such a relentless rival as the public and the political community seemed an impossible competition, and the realization had become converted to an unexpected and irreparable emotional hurt.

It was a development that hadn't been anticipated by anyone in the deal Henry worked out with her father when he became "adopted" as a son-in-law.

During the summer and autumn of 1828, when William Henry was away for weeks at a time, Frances began the writing of her long long letters. In these she kept William Henry informed of every detail of family life, an hour-by-hour account of what happened in the home and in the town. She wrote on folded double-sheet paper, each sheet of which was ten inches square. If she sent just the one double sheet of writing, it meant that there were four full pages in a very minute hand, many many words to each line, the lines close-packed, so that by the time William Henry finished a letter—it might take fifteen minutes to read—he had absorbed two thousand, perhaps three thousand words of a diarylike report on the life of the house. Sometimes when the four pages were filled, she simply reversed the paper and wrote crosswise over the other writing, and though it was more laborious to make out the wording, her letter could still be read, both the horizontal and the vertical writing. She wrote with a quill dipped into a gray-black ink, and her hand worked tremulously, nervously, the lines often rising in the center of the page and declining toward the right, like emotional waves, these outpourings showing openly her unhappy condition, and that the long letters were a poignant effort to overcome her longing for a husband she loved very much.

When the autumn set in and she must look forward to a new long season of gray and cold, she wrote to William Henry. He was then in Albany engaged in organizational work of a more or less private nature, for it had to do with his need to quietly make certain important connections in the development of the Anti-Masonic Party. Frances wished he were at home this rainy night, she was so lonely. "... Little Gus has gone to sleep— Aunt Clary is writing— Grandma meditating.—I went to church this afternoon and heard a good sermon from Dr. Rudd—many inquiries are made about you sometimes. I say you have gone to Syracuse—sometimes beyond this— Aunt Clary says you have gone for a drove of sheep— I have heard so much said on the subject that it is almost impossible for me to refrain from laughter when the question is asked— I should not know what to do with myself, you are absent so much, if it were not for little Gus— One cannot be very lonely when he is about, he has many diverting little tricks— My rheumatism is much better and Augustus has not coughed since you left him— He says Pa gone leave Ma all alone— Ma cry cry cry— Goodnight, darling, and take care of yourself— Your own Frances."

So her letter began, between each clause or sentence that inevitable dash. She knew where to place commas and periods—but there was a haste and a frenzy in her writing and in her thinking—and she must get on with what she had to say; and while William Henry was away, these letters arrived for him about once a week. The mails went out that infrequently, and it took seven days for a letter to reach Albany, so what Frances did was to start a letter, and every few hours note on the letter the time when she resumed writing the latest events in the house, who said what and to whom, and what happened:

"3 o'clock— The rain keeps falling— I have had the hypos all day— Eliza is watching Gus at the moment— Grandpa is in the library held to the house by the rain—" Then after dinner at night, she resumed with a few more paragraphs, and before retiring she might take up the quill again, noting the hour when she wrote. The next morning, the same: "Tuesday, after breakfast," and what happened, two or three paragraphs. Then again at noon, all that had occurred during the morning, who came to the door, what Peter said about the sick horse, the excitement by the kitchen window where a wounded sparrow had trapped itself and kept flapping its wings against the pane, and the branch blown by the strong wind so that it struck heavily against the house, and Father's decision that he must saw off this branch.

So that the young politician in Albany, with the anti-Masons, building his career, got a blow-by-blow account of every breath that wafted through the Miller house. He was having a domestic life by proxy. This would go on, intermittently, for the next twenty years, the long letters—when he was away—the detail separated only by the dashes—and out of this writing and loneliness Frances fashioned a strange personal document of the small details of day-by-day living in a genteel house of that time.

Not that William Henry was always away. He would be about the house and the town for weeks; but then, with a relentlessness that was necessary in the life of an ambitious man, one who had to build fences and bridges into his own future, an absence occurred. It might last for days, weeks, and later even for months: but he always came back to the family and country life he preferred, only to be drawn away again and soon by his ambition to the public life that he craved—and the dash-ridden letters to him during his absence—and his replies to her—they too had begun.

Even the purchase of Bill Brown's small house, of four rooms, painted white with green trimmings, and the pretty yard all about it, located across the street from Judge Miller's, didn't change the situation as much as Frances hoped it might. The judge had consented to Henry's purchase of the place—a thousand down and five years to pay off a mortgage—and the move occurred. "You really want to do this, don't you, Henry?" the judge said to his son-in-law. William Henry, with his usual bland and oblique approach, never mentioned that the purpose of the move was to show the town, his family and his friends that he could stand on his own legs. "It's a matter of Frances' health, Judge. The hammering that they're doing on the new part of the house is hard for her to take."

But it didn't keep him home much more than when he lived at the Millers'. In fact, now he had to pay off the mortgage, and his family (the Orange County kin) borrowed from him heavily so that he must work at his practice even harder than before.

Most of the day Frances was alone in the little house with Gus, unless her father or Aunt Clary or Lazette or some other relative came to see her; and she continued to have the "hypos," and it didn't take much for her to get the faint vapory feeling. She had only to think of Henry not being around to experience that reaction.

Man of the world or not, absent from home or not, he was as involved in the minute particulars of household life as anyone else. She saw to that. It was a way she secured attentions from him, though he be away for weeks: she made him buy things, send things for her and Augustus.

"...Do not think me selfish, my dear Henry, if I was sorely disappointed about the portrait— I wished you to have a miniature painted for me alone —one that I could always have with me when absent from you— When you are away from home your time is always occupied by yourself or society—the case is different with me—at home or abroad I always have some solitary hours and then you cannot imagine how dear to me would be a likeness of the kind I wish—" So she courted her absent husband and made him think of her, in case he ever got so busy he might not think of her, and to make sure he was occupied with her, "—will you get me three or four dozen corset rings— I would not trouble you with so trifling a commission but there is none in the village at present and you know these things are indispensable—do not forget Augustus' cap—and remember the skein of white worsted at Flints—" So that Henry, in Albany, or anywhere, had to push about in the drygoods stores to get things needed back home, and to send them, or return with them, and she kept reminding him of the feminine things she wore and the baby things Augustus needed. "—When may we expect you home— I think it will be more than four weeks—"

In the winter she was in this cold house, trying hard to keep herself and Augustus warm. She put logs on the fire, staying in the parlor where it was pleasanter and then, often, she just picked up Augustus and skipped across the road, and ensconced herself with her father, grandmother and aunt, and the familiar colored help.

At other times when she was inside the little white house, and when the snow covered its shingled roof, and the place looked forlorn, the judge stood at his front window, and he peeked out, from behind the lace curtains, to see what was going on across the street. Occasionally Frances pushed the curtain away from her front window and looked over at the big place, the mammoth lawn, and it looked warmer and sounder and surer; even the huge trees, though they were barren of leaves, seemed sheltering. It was the place she loved most of all.

"Let's wave to Gramps," she would say to Augustus, and they would wave wildly for a minute.

Chapter Eleven

... OF THE DIVIDED HEART

EARLY in June of the following year, Frances and Augustus went by stagecoach and boat to Florida to visit William Henry's family. William Henry thought it might be nice if she got to know them better; he would be busy all summer going between Western New York and Albany, and such a trip might be good for her health. So she set out in a stage, she and Augustus, with Henry's new law partner, Nelson Beardsley, Beardsley's young wife, and one other passenger.

Beardsley, who was only twenty-two, was paymaster of the local Thirty-Third Regiment of Cavalry, and William Henry was the colonel; they were close friends as well as partners, and civically active together, so that the Sewards and the Beardsleys saw each other socially. Beardsley was tall, lean, with a rather long face, a high forehead, dark eyes, and an aquiline nose; he was full of charm and kindness and conversational ease. Beardsley was to take her as far as Newburgh, far down the Hudson, so that the fragile, the delicate Frances wouldn't have to go alone and handle by herself the difficulties and the dangers of a long journey.

That evening, at seven o'clock, the stage rolled into Baggs Square, at Utica, the village that was growing rapidly since the Erie Canal had been built through there. They stayed till the following afternoon, putting up at the Baggs Hotel overnight. In the morning they watched the traffic on the canal for a time and then went to a place called the Garden. There they bought ice cream, which Frances said wasn't as good as what they got in Auburn; but Gus was amused at the crackerlike cone in which the cream was served. They hadn't seen a thing like that before; you ate the cone and all.

In the afternoon they boarded a carriage on the new fast stage line, the Eclipse. Very speedy. The horses were changed each eight miles, and they rode all night: through the Mohawk Valley, alongside the Erie Canal. Sometimes they could see the steady line of canal traffic, barges and freights and passenger boats all alight, moving east and west alongside them, but they, on wheels, moved much faster than the canal traffic. Though they couldn't sleep much, Frances told the Beardsleys she much preferred this kind of passage to riding in a canal cabin with its small dirty berths and its mosquitoes.

She must reach the Sewards in Orange County looking well-dressed and fashionable, and nothing *mauvaise* about her, as she Frenchly put it to herself. Not because she herself required fashionable dress, but Henry wanted her that way, presentable, ladylike, smart. Naturally she must be a help to him, so she gave styling more attention than she would have out of her own interest. In the State Street area of the capital, she became a busy girl. She bought materials to make Gus a red velvet spencer, some "plain" for William Henry, and four rolls of "plain" for herself (that was cloth that might be made into anything one needed for the summer). She had brought along a special and expensive white dress, and it had to be repatterned overnight so as to accord with the latest mode. Meantime she carried an ill-looking hat, so frayed that she was almost ashamed to be seen with it—and the coach travel hadn't improved its appearance.

At the milliner's she has been shown two pattern hats and she combined the moderate aspects of each as her own design: it was styled of white ariphone crape trimmed with lilac ribbon and lilac flowers, the whole pattern molded in cap fashion, with blond laces running beneath the chin from cap edge to cap edge. "Now, you will have this ready in the morning?" she asked. The milliner answered, "Yes, that will be six dollars." Yet when she called for it in the morning, the milliner, knowing that she was leaving by boat, said, "That will be eight dollars." Frances' brows lifted slightly. "My dear woman, you take advantage of me." But the milliner said, "Madam, there were many tricky catches in your chapeau that I hadn't counted on. If I do not charge you the eight, I have not only lost the better portion of a night's sleep—for I worked late on this—but also I make no profit." Frances was reasonable. "In that case ..." Yet the minute she walked out of the shop she had no regrets, for the ladies in the street obviously admired it.

At the mantuamakers (robes, negligées) she was told that they made silk frocks mostly with plain waists, trimmed them with a broad bias piece around the bottom with any kind of beading that the fancy dictated, and either one or two small ruffles or rolls; and, of course, more simply patterned slips had to be worn beneath the manteau.

The white dress was ready on time, in the morning, and she wore it, changing into it at the dressmaker's. It was full-waisted, equally full at the top and bottom and before and behind, with full shoulder straps, the bottom plain with as many tucks as the cloth allowed, berrage drapes trimmed with two-folds and rolls: for the more handwork there appeared on a dress the more styled it was. So she had learned much of what was new in fashions, what had just been inferred from styles in Paris—and late in the morning, when the sun was high, like a yellow pillow over the river banks, she and the Beardsleys boarded the steamer for Newburgh.

She must have looked pretty and all would have been very well, but when they got on the boat the first person she met was a political colleague of William Henry's, a man she didn't like. It was Julius Rhodes, a married man of Albany and an anti-Mason, and he held his arms wide as if he expected Frances to run right into them. He yowled, "My, my, aren't we the sweetest . . . !" He clamped his hands around her shoulders, pressing in the big bustly new shoulder tops, and he plumped a buss straight on her lips, and held an instant—while a whole cabinful of passengers looked on, and she and the Beardsleys were embarrassed. ("I do think he is the most intolerably impudent man I ever knew!" she wrote to Lazette.)

Seven hours later, in the evening, they reached Newburgh, where she had to part with the Beardsleys. From there she must go on alone through sparse Orange County with only Gus. All of her defensive and frail instincts were up; she was nervous, and she felt ill about having to jar along in another coach without a male escort. Gus cried because Nelson Beardsley wasn't around any more to pat and fondle and entertain him and help take some of the pressure off the young mother. ("Lazette, you must know I have a wonderful regard for Beardsley, he couldn't have been more attentive to me had I been his sister.") It was a huge coach, and in it, she noted, there was one Irish girl, probably going to work for someone, somewhere, and the remainder of the party were men. Fortunately the stage proprietor himself was in the coach, seated next to her, so she had nothing to fear, and the proprietor was very polite to her. Beardsley had even taken care of the bill for lodging at Albany and paid the stage fare, and he had put the baggage on the coach, and she had nothing to do but ride to Goshen. She arrived at this place at midnight where she had to stay at "a strange publick house." She couldn't sleep, and it was all so upsetting that toward daylight she had the vapors.

But she went on, in the morning, and arrived at Florida later in the day, almost exhausted.

She was in a bedroom of the Seward house now, with Augustus, somehow recovering, and writing this tale, detail by detail, to her sister—with the characteristic dashes between the clauses—her feverish young mind full of girlish wonder and impression. "—hope I shall never be under the necessity of making another journey of 24 miles alone—it rains today and is rather gloomy— Cornelia, I understand, is joining the Methodist Church."

She concluded in a master stroke of feminine impulse, "—Do write soon and tell me every little thing you do or say— Your own sister Frances."

It was her first visit to the Seward place since her schooldays when she and Cornelia Seward had passed a Christmas vacation there, and she had first met William Henry. Since then Judge Seward had built extra rooms, so that now there were seven. It was a one-story place, low, with a gambrel roof, painted white, and the construction sprawled in an irregular way as if rooms had been added from time to time. Yet it was well-built, with oak floors and a straight oaken staircase that went upstairs to a low attic. The windowing and shuttering were stanch. In the winter the insulation might be as good as that of the Miller home, she supposed. Outside, a huge American sycamore tree, with variegated trunks and an upper portion that was wonderfully rhythmic and green, spread its branches over the house and cooled it.

The big general store up front seemed to be the center of everything. As you entered the door, a bell clanged your arrival; a stove was in the center, and beyond, in back of the heater, was a counter, and to its rear were shelves that went almost to the ceiling. On the shelves were boxes, cans, jars: horse liniment, clocks, scissors, hats, needles, wearing glasses, kettles, most everything anyone in the community might need. Sometimes Mrs. Seward waited on the trade, and at other times other members of the Seward family handled the business, but mostly—when he was around, and not in court, and not attending to his affairs as postmaster, and not off to the bank in Goshen, and not out riding, and not in the barn—Dr. Seward was there, selling to the townsmen, engaging them with his philosophy and his judgments, and standing bravely next to a sign that read:

The Price is Marked Clearly
on All the Goods
In Plain and Simple Figures

Some villagers brought barter and goods in exchange for coffee, tea, or some leather item, but others had cash. This might be a large yellow coin called a penny, or a nickle big as a cracker, and occasionally a wafer-sized coin showed up with a hole in it where somebody had run a string through it in order to hang onto it a little more tenaciously or so as not to lose it.

In an important corner of the room there were several shelves stocked with supplies of the prevalent drugs, including a row of bottles of the popular Mrs. E. G. Brown's Metaphysical Discovery for Women's Frequent Complaints. But this corner was official by its possession of a tall pinewood doctor's bureau; the upper part of the fixture was built with a series of large

93

pigeonholes containing pharmaceutical mugs and jars, and below were three small, narrow pigeonholes for more concentrated and specialized medicaments, an impressive printed apothecary's symbol over each compartment: Sugar of Lead, Soda Mint Tablets, Tannin, and all the other herbs, seeds and nostrums of the day—for the merchant was also a doctor. In a final faraway corner there was an imposing solid hickory desk, with appropriate tools at its backboard; these were a glass inkwell shaped like a rowboat, and a green glass filled with sharpened quills, the feather ends sticking up in a plume like something on a woman's hat; and above this desk there were three shelves of fat law books—for the doctor was also a lawyer, when he wasn't a judge...or was not away, taking part in the affairs of the State Legislature.

You went through this many-purposed room into a lively sitting room; beyond it was a small dining room and off that, in the rear, was the kitchen. Bedrooms opened on the right and left of the parlor and dining rooms. The whole place was constructed of joined wood, one beam locked tightly into another. The interior walls were decorated with religious symbols, sketches, pictures of the Lord on the Cross. In the parlor, occupying a conspicuous place, there was a two-leveled mahogany table; on the top rested a huge family Bible, and on the lower board there were other religious books. Yet in the bedrooms Frances found that there were many general books, although not the novels that she liked to read.

Now about the money, she wrote to William Henry who was then at Auburn—she was letting him know because he had asked to be kept informed of what she spent and she shouldn't run out of cash and have to ask anybody for anything—and she told him she had left Auburn with thirty-eight dollars and she had twenty-four left, and she wouldn't need any more, she was sure, until he arrived in Florida. She told him how she had been taken advantage of in Albany by the milliner, besides which the hatbox cost eight shillings, "so you see how they impose on me," and then she wrote her impressions of villagers she had met.

As she wasn't the politician he was, and she was inclined to speak her mind, expecially in her notes to family members, she always said exactly what she thought about people. William Henry would become almost unique in history for having a record unblemished by any known public or private statement against even his most serious rivals; but not so the naïve and honest and sensitive Frances. If she disliked someone she might not say so to that person's face—she wouldn't because she was groomed and bred in mildness and Christianity, and she tried to make a living matter out of the precepts of the Christian Church—but still she laid on heavily what she thought in her letters to anyone in the family. As it happened, these letters would remain in people's houses for a hundred and fifty years before they would be looked over by any outsiders and her honest opinions become known. Moreover, she didn't hesitate to disagree with William Henry about a great many matters, political, philosophic and domestic, and she regularly let him hear her opinions.

The village of Florida seemed to her to be somewhat less than a one-horse place, as the expression went; she had a hard time getting to understand the simple ways of a simple farm folk, and she said some things to William Henry that distressed him. He was a patriot, fundamentally, and that included his love for the humble villagers of Florida and Orange County. He had once mentioned to Frances that the town name was from the Latin *Floridus,* covered or red with flowers, and that was what it was to him, a village of crimson beauty. So it upset him to hear Frances say she was a little bored at having to make calls at the homes of friends and farmers of the neighborhood. He wrote to her, a little sharply, to please try to be helpful about things, and not to do anything to offend his ma and pa, to which she answered by saying she hadn't meant anything unkindly and she would be content to stay here as long as he desired it, "and will try to be everything you wish." But she managed to mention in the same letter that it was cold, cold, cold, and she had a fire in her room and that helped her to take the cold weather in spite of headache and rheumatism; she spent the previous evening reading to his ma, going to bed with a headache; and she hadn't written the day before because she was a little homesick and there wasn't much doing about the house, just that they sat moping in the sitting room there most of the day, and she read occasionally in Hannah More's works on morality and religion—she had found the book in the room of his brother, Jennings, while rummaging around from one room to another for want of anything better to do; and as a matter of fact she hadn't had such a bad case of the hypos since she had left Auburn as she had right this minute.

And this was Frances, beginning a life with one who she knew was remarkable in many ways and a man she must get to understand. So she was by herself reading much, trying to develop herself, looking into history books that hadn't really interested her ever before. Nothing much had profoundly interested her as a schoolgirl, even though she got passing marks without difficulty; but it had dawned on her more recently that she had a husband who was growing, politically growing; what with his having been chairman of a statewide political convention in Utica, and becoming known for writing the best expressions of anti-Masonic sentiment—anything could happen, living with a man like that. So perhaps

95

Lazette was right, she would have to get to talk his kind of talk. If she didn't he might find some other woman who would talk his talk, and so now she exchanged ideas with the Sewards as she had discussed politics and philosophy with her sister, father, and with everyone; she read what they told her to read, and she had reached a point where she agreed with Henry that Masonry was a bad principle, secret orders dangerous, and, of course, she had always held that slavery was wrong. "You know how my Quaker grandparents would have felt about that, and how Pa feels about it. I can't bear to think of it, and I never never wish to see the South as you've done, I couldn't stand it."

Perhaps she had headaches, in part, because she was trying to stretch her understanding. She spent hours and hours by herself (while servants took care of Gus) reading whatever she could pick up, and she began to suspect that she must look into stronger fare than the novels that she and Lazette had been gobbling up since the age of ten or eleven. William Henry was traveling with high company, and she must keep up with it. This Thurlow Weed, with the eyes like steel magnets and the voice that just told people what to do and think, right while he was seeming only to suggest viewpoints—this Weed and her husband were together so much these days, in a special kind of friendship that was part politics but also just plain personally friendly. Perhaps that was why she had political dreams. To Lazette, the one to whom she really confided her inmost heart, she wrote: "I dreamed all night about the Governor and his Lady—thought they were all at our house attending a dinner party—you were home and did the honours of the table—for my part I was spellbound as we so often are in dreams and could not get any clothes to put on—at last I put on my winter hat and made my curtsy to her ladyship— Gus very kindly woke me just at that time so I was saved from the interesting and instructive conversation that must have followed— Your own Frances."

Perhaps the dream just about symbolized her own problem—that she couldn't quite put on the necessary political clothes, possibly couldn't keep up with the circle her husband was moving into, so she went for her winter hat—the dark cold interior of her spirit, where all of this was somehow shriveling her, yet challenging her, where she brooded, tried to grow, learned to reason politically, against the day when such a circle might be her own.

So Frances moiled onward, in this youthful, delicate, aching way, having fallen into a marriage with an intellectual power of some sort, and having awakened somehow to the discovery, as a consequence, that she had a ponderous domestic and personal situation. She hadn't anticipated or conceived of such before marriage, and she had the sensation sometimes when William Henry was speaking to her that he was whirling far around and over her head; and she had the job of lifting herself to this mind's level, so it was no wonder that she often had "the vapors" and was faint with the size of the problem she had married. All this potential in this small man who wasn't even as tall as she, who didn't weigh as much as she did; yet his hair was like a flag flying before her eyes all day and all night, and he was on his way somewhere, moving faster by the week and month—himself and four or five other men already running a political party—so her brain fevered, and she suffered as the very young perplexed wife of a very precocious figure.

The outlet, in this predicament, was Lazette, beloved Lazette:—"My dearest Sister— Your letter, although accompanied by three from Henry, was the first opened and shall be the first answered because it is a long time since I have had a letter from my own Sis— After all, my dear Sis, I find I write with more freedom to you than anyone else in the world— we grew up together when you were Zetty and I was Fanny— I think you know my heart and can make more allowances for the waywardness of my disposition than anyone else— Did you see me behave very naughty every day of my life I should still retain the same place in your affection, should I not, dearest— At least I have the vanity to imagine so— It is the easiest thing in the world for me to write you a letter, only see how much I have written already and the letter cannot be sent until Thursday and it will be a whole week going to you— Why, Lazette, when we were eleven years old we used to read and to say the least comprehend the plot of every novel that fell our way—perhaps I have saved myself from the hypos by this means—"

She rambled on, in the gray-black ink, in the small hand, fifteen or twenty words to a line, of all that she did and saw and felt here in Florida, how she did not object so much any more to the unceremonious visits that they sometimes made to the neighbors, for this appeared to be the fashion of the country, and as the visits were to plain people who made no pretensions to gentility, she found it much pleasanter than she had anticipated.

Had the two men in her early life, her father and her husband, somehow divided her heart, split it so that it could never fully belong to one more than the other? Had this violence done to her emotions made it possible for her to belong, piecemeal, to each of her close ones—to whichever welled up in her thoughts and feelings at a given time? It seemed as though something like this had happened. Nursed in a house interior and a family interior where there were always older ones to shelter her, each

97

claiming something from her, she had been perhaps cut up in a way that a husband couldn't easily undo. Was it a result of the strange marriage deal whereby the father hung onto the daughter "so long as I live"?

To her sister she had become, as she revealed in her letters and in her signature, "Your own sister, Frances," as if Lazette and only Lazette held her inmost affections. With her father, whose house and presence she couldn't leave, it was "Your own daughter, Frances." And to her husband, for the love of whom she was ill, she was "Your own Frances." Later, when she wrote to her sons, it would be, at the close, "Your own mother, Frances."

So each had a powerful claim upon her, and she seemed to allow herself to be possessed in part by each of those vital to her. It was as if family had overwhelmed her and fragmented her, and given her an affectional character that went out fully to each while she dealt with each. Perhaps that is not an uncommon condition among women who love who are deeply involved in family.

Whatever else, it was a family sense that was inordinate in its density and fervor. And was there one who owned her more than any other? Was it William Henry? Or would she always be Frances Seward of the divided heart?

Chapter Twelve

THE JUDGE RESERVES JUDGMENT

JUDGE SAMUEL SEWARD, the esquire of Orange County, was in
the recesses of the green barn located thirty yards behind his house.
There were two horses in a stable that had four stalls. Straw was kept
in one, hay in another, and the horses were in the other compartments. At
the far end of the walkway there were large wooden bins that contained
oats and grain; and upon nails in the walls there hung leather straps and
harnesses. Here, wearing special barn clothes, a buckskin coat, leather
gloves, and old corduroys, the portly judge spent occasional hours groom-
ing his horses and shoveling the horse stools from the stalls through the
open stable door onto the dungheap outside. The exercise was good for
him; he didn't mind the acrid fume that lifted into his nostrils. He liked
the sound of the whinnying horses, and when he went by the animals or
entered their stalls to water them he uttered whoops of good cheer and
slapped their flanks.

The barn was where he did his best political thinking and where he
nursed the bruises of family life.

The judge felt, at the moment, a little whirled up, like the iron racing-
horse weathervane that spun on top of his barn. For his dissatisfaction
with his son had simmered along even after William Henry married: he
always stayed in wait, like an officer of the law, wondering what unpleasant thing his son was going to do next.

That feeling was even alive now as the young politician moved up,
higher, into public life. The judge couldn't quite believe it.

Yet an air of surprise had come over the doctor of late. It seemed to
him that since William Henry had settled down, sired two sons (Frederick, the second infant, had been born on July 8th, 1830), was making
money at the bar, and had even bought himself a small home of his own,
why, possibly he was straightening out. Maybe he wouldn't disgrace the
Seward name after all. Can it be, he asked himself, my son in the State
Senate of New York—and he still in his twenties?

It was hard for him to believe, considering how much trouble the red-haired one had been only a few years earlier. Why, said the middle-aged judge to himself, when I sent him to Union College, the disgrace was awful! At that time the judge had been so angered at his son's rebellion that he had warned him, "If you don't look out you'll wind up like Claudius Smith!" Smith was a horse thief who took cows and horses from Whigs during the Revolutionary War period and sold them to the British. He was hanged later at Goshen, New York.

At the recollection of his early troubles with his son, and still hurt by the memory, the judge picked up his shovel, filled it full of horse leavings, and angrily hurled the steaming product far outside the door, then watched the fertilizer fly and fall on the other side of the pile....

"How did this happen?" the judge murmured to himself as he shoveled away, in his barn, in unbelief, late in the year of 1830, after the elections. "My son in the State Senate! Not the Assembly, but the higher body, the Senate!"

He was incredulous.

Inside he ticked off the counties represented in the seventh senatorial district: Onondaga, Cayuga, Seneca, Ontario, Wayne and Yates: the whole frontier, practically.

Then he shouted aloud to his horses, "I hope he doesn't make a fool of himself!"

Part Two

THE GOVERNOR AND HIS LADY

Chapter Thirteen

STRANGE CASE OF THE
LOCKED KNEES

SO, AS a result of the incident at the frontier, the Morgan episode, he was in Albany, early in January of 1831, ready to take his seat in the State Senate. He put up at the Eagle Hotel, the principal rendezvous of the politicians and the people in the State Government. While he was wandering around the lobby, in the company of several anti-Masons, Martin Van Buren, the leader of the Regency force, who lived in Albany, happened into the hotel. William Henry was pointed out to him as one of the new anti-Masonic representatives sent there to fight the Regency. Van Buren, who had held many offices and even been Governor for a short time, and was headed for the Presidency, was nearly fifty years old. He looked over the slight William Henry and asked of another Regency man, "How old is he?" When he was told that the Cayuga County representative was only twenty-nine, Van Buren remarked that he didn't look to be more than twenty-two or three. "You can't tell about little fellows like that," Van Buren said. "Sometimes their size pushes them in a terrible way—they want to prove something." The other Regency man said, "He wants to prove that the Regency rule is no good. Think he can do it?" Van Buren shrugged his shoulders.

It might seem strange that a man destined to become a most considerable statesman and a major contributor to his nation's progress would begin political life with a bad case of *lock-knee*—but it happened.

Days went by before the Legislature convened, and William Henry, waiting around Albany, worked himself up into a ball of tension.

On the fifth of January, the session opened, and the young senator entered the legislative chamber utterly frightened about having to take his seat among so many older men. They looked at his small frame, his youngness, and he knew what they were thinking. He certainly wasn't as qualified as most of these might be, he told himself, and he secretly believed that the voters of the six counties of the seventh district who had sent him here must have been terribly thoughtless to have done so. Voters sure can be ignorant of whom they send to office, he said to himself, with a self-deflation that he didn't even have to muster. If they only knew that he was too scared to get up on the floor and speak; if they knew that his knees were actually locked and that he sat there trembling while the business of the Senate went on....

Once, when he voted "Aye" on some resolution, and he heard his own guttural voice leap out of his mouth, he was jolted by it. The more he sat still and realized his petrification the more he understood that sooner or later he had to do something about it.

But the feeling of being weightless, as if he floated meaninglessly in space, stayed with him. Once he reached his hands down along his thighs and ran his palms forward to the locked knees. They were really taut with incapacity. He looked about to see whether anyone suspected how paralyzed he was. He decided that nobody knew this but himself. How did this happen? he asked himself. What am I doing here? I'll have to write Frances about this.

This went on for ten days—desolate, blowy, wintry, Albany days. It was now January fifteenth, and he hadn't said anything but "Aye," and that only once.

Each day he walked from the Eagle Hotel up the long hill that led to the capitol building. Snow was six inches deep in the streets and for a few days the wind, sweeping in from the west, blasted through the small busy city. State Street was loaded with white, the store fronts covered with a packing of powder, the sidewalks slippery, the edge of it all piercing the young senator in a cheerless way. Going uphill he glanced backward at the Hudson River, frozen and blocked up for the winter—frozen, that was it. Everything frozen, including William Henry. If he could only get up and speak to his colleagues of the Legislature. He had been in courtrooms for years; he had addressed conventions and public rallies, and had caused spectators to stir and even cheer when he made a strong point; but now, on this day, as he went alone up the hill, he denounced himself harshly: "William Henry, you're a fool to be afraid of your shadow. Show them your mettle. Bring up the salt business."

He had been telling himself that for days, ever since the first Senate session, since the state had furnished him with two quires of beautiful pink paper, a dozen Holland quills, a neat pearl-handled knife—and three dollars a day for representing his district.

But going after the Regency wasn't a small matter. The Regency ruled the state; it was a gathering of politicians representing banded business interests in the Albany district. They had run the state for years, they passed out patronage, the paying jobs. Because of this, there was a constant murmur of dissent all over about "the Albany dynasty."

It was an opportunity for a young man with guts, but if he got up to speak they would see his big nose, his flopping red hair, and his knees might snap.

As the days advanced and as he watched the senators go through the processes of proposing laws and making debate, he saw that he wasn't on Mount Olympus, that it was a routine, and some of his compatriots were definitely mediocre.

That realization strengthened him.

These were only local politicians wrangling with each other and revealing varying degrees of incapacity. He ought to get up there and really say something. "Get after the salt business, Henry!" He talked to himself, saying what he imagined Frances might say to him. "Go on," she'd say, "go after the salt business."

The salt business was only a fifty-thousand-dollar graft that the Regency was involved with. In Syracuse there were salt mines; it was the pride and the big business of the place, and out at Split Rock, a few miles from Syracuse, miners were carting bushels and tons of the white stuff away each day and shipping it everywhere. But the state was supposed to get a duty on each bushel, and private contractors, working with politicians, were defrauding the state of its due, and a few of the Regency men were understood to be getting a rake-off instead of the bushel tax being paid into the treasury. It was big scandal around Syracuse, and in that part of the state they expected Seward to defend them. It was dynamite, there would be a furor in the Senate, the newspapers would have something big if he exploded the thing; and yet, he wondered whether that was the way to begin political life.

It was the fright of a nonswimmer who has to make his first plunge into water over his head.

At last he found himself working with that pink paper and the quill supplied by the state, and drawing a resolution demanding a Senate investigation of the fraudulence in the State Treasury.

His paper was in his hand finally, ready to read.

But then he had an excellent idea. Why not postpone it till Monday?

His heart felt faint; he could feel the beats hitting his shirt front. On all sides older and wiser men had the good sense to stay in their seats; why should he stand—and go after the biggest sore point in the state at that moment?

Go on, Henry, get up! Show 'em!

Suddenly he unlocked his knees. He was on his feet, aware that what he was saying wasn't coming out very loudly, but they could see him standing, waving a paper, and calling, "Mr. President—Mr. President—I want to offer a resolution...."

The President of the Senate had a voice with a factory whistle depth and the strength of it was like a breeze that William Henry, thirty feet away, thought he could feel. *The President will receive the resolution from the Senator from the Seventh District—"*

A page boy carried it forward while William Henry stood watching the boy move up front.

Then he sat.

An instant later the President's voice boomed again. He would read the resolution just proposed by the young Senator from Auburn....

"Resolved: That fraudulence at the salt springs in Syracuse, whereby the State of New York is being defrauded of fifty thousand dollars annually, through abuses in the Treasury Department, be investigated...."

The President of the Senate got that far, and there was an outcry from all parts of the chamber. The Regency men were on their feet demanding the tabling of the resolution. (And the investigation never did thereafter get off the ground.)

The President malleted for order. He finished reading the resolution. But murmurs, almost surly, spread through the room ... Who the hell is that redhead? What's ailing this juvenile from the seventh? How did he get in here? ...

The Regency men carried their motion to have the move tabled. This thing had to be handled behind locked doors if it could be. They would have to go and see this whippersnapper from the west and find out what he wanted.

William Henry was delighted at the tabling of the motion. He wouldn't have to debate at once anyway. It was good he wouldn't have to debate because his knees had locked again, hard, with nervous fright, and he could never have risen from his seat.

Chapter Fourteen

THE WHISPER THAT RISES FROM
THE EARTH

THE street where Thurlow Weed lived was filled primarily with private houses, but it also harbored a theatre, a couple of taverns, and Mrs. Dole's rooming house, where an artist named Ichabod Wood carved profiles in metal and leather, and called his product a physiognotrace. Once this had been known as Van Driessen Street, after a Dutch pastor, but the needs of metropolitan simplification resulted in the new and snappier Green Street; Thurlow and Catherine Weed and their children lived at No. 104, in a plain two-story house.

Catherine had Weed pretty well tamed. They had a romance of their own, a three-year separation before marriage, as Thurlow went out over the state in search of his fortune. He returned, with no fortune, but they married, the children came, and now Mrs. Weed knew just about everything that her husband did. Or most everything. This came about through a wonderful feminine ruse.

Weed once told her that he had a faulty memory, and in the early days of their marriage it seemed to her that he did have a poor faculty for recollection. "You must train yourself to remember names of people and places and be able to recall what you do and what people say," she warned him, "or you'll never be a success in journalism or politics." He could see the sense of that and wondered what he could do. "I have an idea," she said. "We must work at it. You must train your memory; each night, when you come home, tell me everything that you did all day, whom you met, what they said, what they looked like. Let's start that way and see whether your memory improves."

So he began telling his wife of all his moves, whom he talked to, men and women, what he and she said. "Now, Thurlow, tell me what she looked like. Can you remember what her features were?" In that way she learned just what women crossed her handsome husband's path, how good-looking they were, what he said and what she said, and so she kept tabs on him. Meanwhile his memory improved. Through recalling details he implanted them, and his memory became excellent ... and Catherine Weed got so that she could tell when he was holding back any detail. Yet she kept quiet, figuring she had brought off a remarkable achievement in any case to get this big masculine treasury of confidential information on every politician and political process in the East to ungush it for her each night. Sometimes when he was really tired she'd say (because where *he* was concerned, *she* was the politician), "Now, Thurlow, you're too weary tonight, but tell me the first thing tomorrow morning at breakfast." By then he might be omitting a few details, but he kept up the habit most of his life because he discovered that it was an excellent way to become a good storyteller.

"Now whom did you give a cigar to?" she prodded, knowing that this was one of the keys to his reservoir of memory. Once he recollected who he benefited with a smoke, he was able to follow through with what had been said. "Oh, yes, Birdsall asked me for a cigar...." Oh, he did? Catherine responded, well, what did he have to say?

And he gave a cigar to Schoolcraft, the Albany banker. "And Schoolcraft?" she prompted. "He's doing well, isn't he?" Yes, Thurlow agreed, he's making money and like so many men that make money, he wants to go to the State Senate or to Congress. "Can you do anything for him?" He answered that, well, perhaps a little later he might be able to put Schoolcraft into Congress. Then he had to give a physical description of Mrs. Schoolcraft, and how she helped her husband, and how she dressed, and what she believed, and whether she opposed her husband or agreed with him or was independent of him, or whether she was a clinging vine.

So that actually, Catherine knew much about everybody in the political swim, and their family, but she kept it all to herself. She just plodded ahead with her baking, sewing, and cleaning, and raising the three children, and batting the dust out of the carpets hanging on the clothesline, and seeing that no bedbugs got into the crevices of the bed, and cooking and doing dishes, throwing tattered clothes into the closet to use for dusting, and getting down on her hands and knees and scrubbing the oilcloth-covered floor, and keeping a little leather pouch filled with pennies and nickels for emergencies (because they always occurred, Thurlow not making much money as yet), and she was busy some of the time washing and pressing his clothes. Lately he was dressing a little better; he'd dressed in sheer rags for years, and occasionally, at Christmastime, Weed welcomed from his friends a pair of boots, a shirt, neckcloths, any practical gift whatever.

Catherine had a lean and drawn face, and there were simple lines of hardship in her features. She looked years older than Weed, but she wasn't, she was a year younger; she had just had so many hungry days when whatever food there was went to the children first, and what was left was for her. All through Weed's itinerant journalist period, when the living was rough and poor, Catherine had done the managing, taking in wash, and sewing for other women, and scrounging about in the garden outside for vegetables before it was time for them to be ready and ripe and edible.

At about the time when Weed's power was becoming widely known, though he was as yet no political legend, he would say to Catherine, "Now Catherine, you saved me from being shipwrecked many times in the last ten or twelve years, many times." She absorbed that proudly and happily; it was true, and she felt he was worth the way she slaved. For she was the only one who really knew the man's power and drive in full, for she felt it. She was certain that he was going to be an even bigger and more important man some day than he was now; for it was already predicted for him by such a gifted man as Seward, she said to herself, that some day her husband would rule political life in America.

After the Senate sessions, if the air was crisp and not too cold and not too damp, Weed called for the Senator at the Eagle, or William Henry dropped around to his friend's house on Green Street. They liked to walk, they liked Albany, and William Henry, because he was having his first success here, even had a love for the place.

Now, in the 1830s, politics was all but an industry here, and there might be the tremendous population of 20,000 any day. Babbitry was born and the business men urged: Welcome the settlers. Welcome industry. Erect big three- and four-story buildings. Let's have more canals leading to and from Albany. Two thousand horses and wagons went through the main street daily, making an almost deafening clatter on the cobblestone, so that they were right, in Western New York, who viewed this eastern center as a true cosmopolis, with its vital theatre, its commerce, its lively journalism, its culture—this center where politicians spawned intrigues that placed men in the White House.

After tonight's walk, they and a party of anti-Masons intended going to the museum, a local cultural center, to see a performance by the Fire King, but that was two hours away, so they sloughed through the snow that covered the wooden sidewalks, wandering from State Street through Pearl to Columbia, then riverward toward Dock Street and Quay Street where it edged the Hudson. The white river spread; the wind came in hard and reddened their faces, and they liked the ruddy feel; and most of the time they didn't talk politics. The friendship between them was already way beyond mere political alliance. The tall man didn't have to slow his pace, for William Henry moved fast, and walking kept him well. A chronic nature lover, and a starer of the skies, he looked upward and studied how the evening twinkled, and he murmured, "You know, Weed, I believe millions of people may inhabit those planets."

Weed answered with a feigned abstractedness. "Millions, millions... yes, but it's a hard vote to get hold of."

Later they and their colleagues, Albert Tracy, William Maynard and Francis Granger, all Western New York anti-Masons, started from the Eagle Hotel to the museum. This was a new marble building at State and Market streets where art works and natural science objects were exhibited. Here, performers from New York and abroad sometimes appeared; and this was the place which was first in the town to be illuminated by gas-light about fourteen years earlier. There was talk all over the capital of the latest sensation, the Fire King.

When the anti-Masons arrived they found that the place was already occupied by senators and assemblymen and their wives, and the benches were well filled. The anti-Masonic clique sat midway down the room, and they at once noticed that the room was warming.

For on the stage there was a specially installed stove on which were several kettles that contained liquids. Steam arose from them so that metallic fumes spread through the room.

A fanfare of drums announced the entrance of the Fire King, and he pranced on stage from the wings, a tall man dressed in red simulating flames, and wearing a hat that swirled up yellow and red, like a man afire. He opened with a swift, self-confident speech announcing that he was about to perform the most miraculous feats of fire magic, and he defied the intelligence of the audience to prove any chicanery. As he spoke an assistant, a pretty young woman colorfully dressed, moved onstage and took a place beside the oven.

The performer tossed his red gloves to the side of the stage, and then, holding a piece of paper in his hands close to a lighted candle, he said that he would put the paper in the blaze and hold it there for five minutes, and by blowing on the paper, prevent it from burning....

So he did.

The Fire King bowed to the applause, motioned for attention: he would eat some hot liquid melted sealing wax. Would anyone come forward and confirm that it was scalding wax? He swallowed the substance, smacking his lips and dabbing his fingertips to his tongue as if to exact the last delicious relish.

Next, he would place molten lead on his tongue. Spectators were free to examine it, and he invited a few from the audience. The Fire King said to one inspector, "Here, touch it if you don't believe it." The man touched, and snapped his hand back, burned. Then the magician put the liquid on his tongue, pouring from a teaspoon, and he held it there while the appreciative audience in the steaming room wildly applauded.

"And now," he said augustly, "for the *pièce de résistance*...I shall swallow boiling oil."

While the Fire King busied himself about his stove, stirring a kettle of liquid, half dancing as he capered about, the fumes from the stage drifted into every crevice of the room. The spectators were sweated as if in a steambath; their senses were dulled; they wiped their necks, their foreheads.

They saw boiling oil poured from a bottle into a kettle; they watched it heat up and heard it bubble. The Fire King brought the product forward to the edge of the stage so as to add further conviction to his stunt; they watched him pour the smoking fuel into a tall glass, and he drank the contents as if it were tea. The handclapping came to the stage a little damp and strained, as if it had to filter through steam to reach him.

"You have been so generous to me tonight," said the Fire King, "that I shall cook you all a beefsteak—while I myself remain inside the oven to watch that it becomes well done!"

It would be a good trick even today, perhaps even a hundred years from now.

The Fire King crawled into the hot oven of the stove that had heated up the whole museum, and before he disappeared inside he waved a very red porterhouse steak at the audience, then drew it inside with him. "Stick around now," he said before he closed the door. "I'll have this steak for you soon."

The oven roared with heat. The assistant wandered around the stove tending the oven, stoked more coal; and the whole room stifled, for all the heat onstage drifted into the benches; yet they waited on, wearily hoping to see two beefsteaks instead of one.

The Fire King leaped out exactly ten minutes later, chipper as ever, and he held aloft a well-done porterhouse, waving it about like a gonfalon of victory; he wiped his own steaming face with his red banners and handkerchiefs, and he bowed to the even warmer audience response.

Only William Henry was unmoved. He didn't believe in magic, luck, superstition: he was convinced that man was full of designs and plans, ways and schemes. Unmasking trickery was a professional virtue of his. It was the earnest side of him and it could make him at times momentarily humorless.

"Nothing to it," he said. "The secret is in the substances which he uses to counteract the heat."

"That's the precise substance," Weed said, "that we fellows in practical politics have never been able to find."

It was too early to retire, so the anti-Masons went to William Henry's room at the Eagle. His quarters were their regular hangout. There, in a plain room, gathered around a coal stove, the politicians talked shop and often went into the deeper meanings of their time and world. The evening moonlight poured into the east window. William Henry moved about restlessly, looking once or twice out of the window at the frozen Hudson; Weed, smoking a cigar, sat by the stove, his long legs resting on a coal scuttle; and the others lounged in rockers.

William Henry studied the associates who had helped raise to this state level the offbeat issue of opposition to the Masonic Order. Francis Granger, a big, handsome man who had run for governor as an anti-Mason, had been whipped, but he was in Albany to confer with the others and live up to his role as one of the two or three principal leaders of the movement. He knew state politics, and William Henry thought of him as being not exactly a great man, but having the faculty of being successful. He preferred, as a personality, William Maynard, a senator; he thought of Maynard as a gigantic intellect, an industrious man, a democrat with an aristocratic manner, a man of method and originality, yet a little cold and not likely to be as successful as Granger. The other big wheel of the anti-Masons, Albert Tracy, also a senator, was literary, with aesthetic tastes, eloquent, and anxious to hold high office, but he had an ulcerous stomach and a tendency toward depression and fitfulness.

Tracy, Maynard and Granger were eager for public advancement and they all responded to the behind-the-scenes leadership of Thurlow Weed. Maynard and Tracy now toyed with the youngest aspirant.

"You'll never want to be a lawyer again after this, Seward," Maynard remarked.

"Why not?"

"This is the big time. Government rules, Government is power. Next to it, handling the average law case is baby milk."

"I find the Senate sessions pretty darned dull a good part of the time."

"Dull sometimes, but when Government boils and orders and drives and moves, everything else is nothing. After this you'll never want to defend another petty thief."

"I'll be glad to get back to Auburn."

"And when you get there you'll be glad to return to Albany...then you'll have your eye on the governor's job . . . then Christknowswhat. It's in most of the men that are here in the State Senate. It's in every Assemblyman. Each one wants to be the great man."

William Henry at this time had a deep ambivalence about his directions. He wanted to be in Government, but an active part of his brain constantly visualized Auburn, his wife and children, and the slower tempo of small-town life. He wasn't convinced that office-holding was going to be a permanent mode of life for him. In fact, a few weeks around Albany had already stripped away some of the veneer of the official life: he sensed an unending competition among the politicians that was unpleasant; he saw coarseness, incompetency and inadequacy among many of his senatorial colleagues. Voters down below, as it were, might conceive of this as "life upstairs," but often it was chilling, lonesome, unrewarding. These were his thoughts, but he didn't know how overwhelmingly he was the victim of his public ambitions. Actually he was bitten by a bug bigger than anything in his backyard. In the face of the real drive that possessed him, he argued that he had a family to support, that he couldn't afford to hold office.

"None of us can," Maynard said, "but we do—and you will."

"How do you know what I'll do?"

"You've got the bug, Seward. You've got it worse than some folks have got the cholera."

"Worse than you?"

"No, I've got it worse than anybody." They laughed because Maynard could laugh at himself. He went on, "It's a damnsight easier to sit in the Senate—even the State Senate—and draw a salary and maybe even be famous one day, than it is to handle some of those nasty law cases."

"For three dollars a day?" William Henry asked.

"Governors get more," Tracy suggested. "Congressmen and United States Senators get more. Presidents sometimes go down in history." Tracy pointed to Weed. "Look at the boss. He wants to quit writing gossip for newspapers and do bigger things. He'll do it too, some day when he can name a President, wait and see."

Weed said he doubted that he would ever lay aside the quill. "I still have to learn how to write, you know. They say I murder the English language. . . ."

"Yes, sometimes you do," Seward said, "—but also the opposition."

They moved in, sharply, after the young redhead. They knew him well; they saw intellect and ambition, and a covert kind of wonderful personal physical energy that they couldn't keep up with. It was as if the strength of a very big man was stored in his small frame. They sensed the advantage of his youth, how he moved from one calculated position to another—as they all tried to do—and they knew his inmost secret. His real inner strength was that he was a historian, in love with his country and its tradition. Moreover, he was already concerned about his place in history, even a little worried about immortality; that was part of the religious quandary of the time: "Do you believe in the immortality of the soul?" There was this big debate as to what happened to a man's soul, what happened to his works and his name, after he was dead. It was debated in every church, over cracker barrels, and by politicians in these early smoke-filled rooms in hotels like the Eagle.

"Seward," said Tracy, "you've got it worse than most of us. You're damnfool enough to think that posterity's opinion and its remembrance of you is important."

"Of course it is. Posterity is your children, and their grandchildren. It's your country. There's nothing but the future and what it says and what it'll be."

"You think I'm worried about what they say about me after I'm gone?" Tracy asked.

"You ought to be, everybody ought to be." William Henry could be a little righteous.

"Just as soon as they flop the clods on my chest I'm willing to be forgotten. All I want is what I see and feel and get now, because I can't be sure there's anything after this life."

They were all looking at William Henry now; he was much on the spot. They had touched his core feelings, his desire to be well thought of, to become useful and great. Granger just listened; Maynard stared, like a bird ready to swoop. Tracy waited for an answer.

The smoke circled around the stove. The cigar smell permeated the little room.

"I don't know, Tracy, I don't know," Seward said, thoughtfully. "Sometimes I think that what they say about a man after he dies may be faintly heard by him, like a whisper that rises from the earth."

Tracy was irritated. "Boy, have you got it!" He turned to Weed. "Thurlow, there's your man. He wants immortality. Stake everything on him. He'll try not to let you down. The rest of us'll make more mistakes than he. Put him up there, Thurlow."

Weed laughed. "I like Seward's views. I like everything he says. I learn from him, even about novels, what to read, what to think."

Tracy turned snappishly on William Henry. Actually they were good friends, they confided closely. "Get over that idea, you redheaded fool! Live today, forget about the monuments after you're gone. They may put

112

a stone on you after you're dead that's so heavy it'll keep you buried for an eternity."

William Henry heard, but his listening was like sails listening to a wind that carried the boat onward; for a man on his course could only go the way the winds in his soul drove him.

"Make a big enough mistake and you'll be remembered by posterity too," said Weed, who couldn't be persuaded to run for office.

"That gives us all a chance," William Henry said.

Only a few days later an incident occurred that reminded him of the truth of Weed's observation.

He received a note, delivered to his seat in the Senate Chamber, and, for an instant after he read, he stared in astonishment at the signature. He half rose, then he sat back and he reread:

My Dear Sir:
Would you be so kind as to call to see me at the Merchants' Exchange? I have been retained as counsel in the George Crowder case.
Respectfully yours,
Aaron Burr

Burr! Was he still alive?

William Henry had been connected with the Crowder case ever since 1823. It was the first civil suit that came his way after he joined up with Judge Miller; the case involved a title to a large property, originally a military lot, in Cayuga County; he represented the defendant, and he had got the case ruled out of court twice. Now, nine years later, Burr was employed by Crowder to reopen it. So he had no alternative but to call on the man who had once been aide to Washington, and almost an American President.

Late that afternoon, after the session adjourned, when it was still daylight and the snow in the streets and over the buildings appeared to make the day linger on a little longer, he headed for the Merchants' Exchange, an old run-down, weatherbeaten hotel, the most obscure lodging in the capital.

He climbed an ill-kept, odorous and narrow staircase, and he groped in a gray corridor to Burr's quarters. As he trod in the dark a feeling of unreality deepened inside him; it happened every once in a while this way: the Revolutionary War had ended nearly a half century earlier, and yet it echoed from time to time through some participant who was still alive.

He knocked. A shriveled, dwarflike figure came to the door and a voice creaked, "Come in, Mr. Seward."

Burr extended his hand in a gesture of the finest grace, and William Henry was momentarily jarred, curiously smitten to realize that he grasped the hand that had fired the bullet into Alexander Hamilton. He hoped that Burr would not notice his intense gaze.

The old man's face and head looked worked upon, scrubbed and curried, as if he tried to prevent the ravages of the years. A patch of gray hair decked out his head, and a powder thick as paste was over it; the ancient face was withered, as if there were a wrinkle in it for every day of distress he had lived since the days of his glory.

William Henry watched the ancient relic of the past bustle about, drawing a long, close-fitting cloak over him, a robe that they called a surtout, apparently to conceal his withered frame. The Senator, still trying not to be caught studying the other one, couldn't help but notice the poor cotton shirt and how the tie, loud of color, barked bravely in the current fashion.

The whole aspect of the old man was steadily arousing in William Henry a sense of pathos. It seemed to the young lawyer that there was a kind of undying light and life in Burr's eyes; as if the uncontrolled ambition of the man, that which had brought him into his final disrepute, had projected onward doomedly, but as if it were now converted into a simple dogged design of longevity and personal wretchedness.

They sat, a few feet apart, close to a coal stove.

Burr took the initiative, trying to place his young guest at his ease, speaking as if he were not the deteriorated statesman, but just another attorney in practice at the bar, and he opened by professions of sympathy for the anti-Masonry that had brought William Henry into the Senate Chamber. It was the voice that mostly intrigued the young politician: like hinges creaking in a door ready to fall off. Was this the voice that once stirred to fervor the colonial revolutionists? William Henry wondered. And this the same throat that barked the commands of a lieutenant colonel in the war itself? The tongue and lips that spoke as Vice President to Jefferson? Could this be the proud statesman who vied with Alexander Hamilton for the nation's favor in the Presidential seat? It really was, he knew, but weakened and deteriorated; and yet this was the voice that once, in Burr's early manhood, dominated the political life of New York State; and later, much later, it had become the expression of an unbridled ambition that stretched out for rule and power over Mexico. Now the years had melted this stentorian throat to its present pathetic, pleading squeak.

The old man knew this mood of wonder and chagrin that he aroused in sensitive people, and he entered into soothing explanations as to how he happened to be engaged in the practice of law. He had returned to this country after his long years of exile in Europe, and, in New York City, he had resumed at the bar. He mentioned several clients and cases he had represented. William Henry nodded his head politely; but Burr continued to stay away from the Crowder case. It is frequently a fashion of attorneys everywhere and in all times to parry before getting down to business, to try to strike a lighter mood so as to prepare a gentler quality in the inevitable dispute they will have, so that Burr continued to drift about with a certain volubility, passing from Albany politics into reminiscence of the Revolution.

William Henry listened, fascinated, as Burr remarked, "You know Washington was a talentless man—for high office? You know that?"

William Henry answered that he didn't know it.

"Yes, he was completely dominated by Hamilton." The voice crackled and burred.

"Completely?"

"Of course completely. Washington wouldn't write a note of invitation or an acceptance to a dinner without having Hamilton take care of every detail."

The frontier lawyer parried that he had read Marshall's *Life of Washington,* which pictured the general in a different and a much more favorable light. Burr dismissed that. "The histories are partial, interested, unreliable, and false." He continued, "Washington was cold, haughty, formal. It was Franklin who was the man of the age. Franklin was kind, suave, gentle."

"I don't doubt the fine things you say of Franklin."

Burr laughed. "Only what I say of Washington and Hamilton, eh?" Then he resumed, "Franklin was a wit, a humorist of high facility, great as Talleyrand."

There was a pause. Burr might have turned to the business of the moment, but Hamilton was on his mind. "I know you will think I am prejudiced in anything I say of Hamilton ... owing to ..."

"I go with Voltaire as to freedom of expression."

"In that case, and since I never conceal my thoughts about Hamilton— he was a parasite on Washington. He was an unfriendly man, most unamiable, and there was not the slightest generosity in him."

Burr hesitated. William Henry sensed that the old man was on the verge of telling of the duel itself.

The old man's eyes glistened, and they rolled inside of his crow's feet and his wrinkles; for he knew he had once been mighty, and this run-down of great names and great events was all that he could offer to the young man seated beside him, a Senator he needed. But he didn't speak of the duel, he drifted back to the Revolutionary War battles, the failure at Quebec, the Battle of Monmouth. "You mentioned historians. ... I was present myself with the army at a skirmish which it had with the enemy at Monmouth, in New Jersey. I know what happened there, but I've read a dozen accounts of that battle in as many histories, and if it weren't for the date and the place of the battle which they all agree on, I shouldn't recognize from the descriptions that it was Monmouth at all."

At last Burr moved in on his purposes. He should like to revive the Crowder case, twice thrown out of court, and would not Seward help him in his application to reinstate the case in chancery?

William Henry wanted no part of the revival of this case—a suit destined to drift on until nearly the middle of the century, and then to be won by William Henry's client.

"Offhand, sir," said the State Senator, parrying for time, "I would say no, but give me a day or two to think of this."

He backed out of the old man's presence; the room and the light and the shriveled figure dimmed; he tracked down the stairs, thinking, thinking, and each step on the brittle steps sounded to him like a gunshot returning to him out of a past that he had known—until today—only from hearsay and history books.

Chapter Fifteen

THE LEATH....FACTURERS'....ANK

NOT long afterward, William Henry was in his hotel room, holding in his fingers a crumpled note, and he swore. He could swear like a "canaller," one of the tough breed of ex-farmer boys who steered craft on the Erie Canal, and reputedly outcussed all men who had ever gone before, blasting away at mosquitoes, slow horses, complaining passengers, bad weather, and the lack of something to drink. William Henry reserved his profanity for special occasions worthy of his finest cuss forensics. He had heard the conventional oaths that are characteristic of all the generations of man, as a farm lad, but he didn't swear then, unless secretly perhaps at his father for his great severity. In fact a whole substream inside his consciousness was reserved for knocking down, in the plainest language, the things that displeased. But only more recently, as he dipped deeply into politics, had he taken to dropping connected sequences of oaths in the presence of his closest associates. He had discovered that there was vernacular of the street, the grocery store, and the farm field that a politician needed to have. Even in the State Senate there were two languages: one was the serious, formal, sometimes classic language of an important speech, and the other was the easy, colloquial talk of the members when the Senate life moved routinely and when there was no one listening in the gallery.

Mostly he kept this cussing to himself and he tried not to let the language flow through his mind when he sat in church; but in practical politics, when he was frustrated, and in law practice, with clients who didn't do what he asked them to do, he stared with amiable and understanding eyes, while within, the wordage flooded as it did around steamboats, boxing matches, saloons, and in the privacy of many a fine American home. He never used that language when he was with his family, but in the smoke-filled rooms it rose from him, as black smoke from a chimney, and the darkest sex-tinted and most bowel-ridden terms exited from him like players in a drama, who go offstage, then return a little later. For two minutes he unreeled, like a fisherman, his whole repertoire. Suddenly missing was the classic language of which he was capable, and in its place, all the vernacular of the curbside, the cracker barrel and the backwoods awoke and glowed like a devil's valedictory.

He had a reason to swear.

The letter that excited his profanity was on fine stationery, and it was scented; Seward even put the note to his big nose and smelled it before he crumpled it:

DEAR SENATOR SEWARD:

Doubtless you know the merit in the bill favored for passage by the Leather Manufacturers' Bank. It will be of interest to the writer of this letter if you vote for it and I respectfully urge you to do so. I also cherish the thought of making your acquaintance soon.

Most sincerely yours,

H_____ R. L_____, EsQ.

THE LEATHER MANUFACTURERS' BANK

The audacity of the leather gang, he said to himself, as he began to recover. Aloud he muttered to the paunchy red-hot stove, "The lobby is becoming corrupt and impudent." The letter had fallen to the floor. He picked it up and tossed it into the stove. He wanted to talk to someone about this but no one was at hand. He paced the room, thinking of the arrogance of the leather industry, which was a major financial force of the day....

For it was a leather time then, before plastics and synthetics, and everywhere in the country hard and thick leather snapped and cracked and held things together; the fur trade and leatherworking and tanning had emerged from the animal abundance, and its mark was everywhere, in the thongs that bound six-team horses to the Conestoga on which William Henry had ridden; in the genuine, long-lasting boots and shoes and leggings that he and others wore; leather trappings on the furniture, leather over the seats, and thick cowhide to hold for generations; leatherworking shops in each village, next door to the ironmaster's shop perhaps, and leather and iron went together in the fixtures that were entering the houses in the towns all the way from New England into William Henry's Western New York, and beyond the Cayuga Bridge. Leather and iron on the freight coaches; heavy fur covering on the grips, suitcases and trunks that he packed with him wherever he went; tan and black and ochre strappings around the baggage. And horses, which figured in everyone's lives, literally dwelt in a leather kingdom; their kingdom the blacksmith shops, with leather harnesses and reins and whips hanging off the wall sides to catch the eye of the farmer or coachman bringing in his horse to be shod. In every store leather odds and ends, calf and cow, pig and steer hide, buffalo hide, deerskin for moccasins that William Henry wore at home and here in Albany at the hotel; leather-lined lounging robes, but a light, a gossamer leather; and the surface of so many items in the shops bearing the sheen of cropped animal hair, bison and elk and whatever else was trapped or shot, skinned and stretched and tanned, and strung out for carpets, or couch covering, all with beads upon it, and colors painted around the beads: so that he went browsing in the little shops of the tiny villages where the stage stopped, to get things for Frances and the boys, and he might pick up a leather-handled jacknife, a leather-covered pencil holder, and leather cases for almost anything that anyone used or bought or carried or didn't even need: but the trappers kept bringing leather into the villages, and the farmers carefully saved every skin of every pig and cow and cat they killed, and there was always a few cents to be had for the skin, any skin. Lasting leather too, not yet diluted, not yet mixed with pulp, but real, off of the doomed beast, clean and pure leather as thick as nature had protected the beast with; double and treble thicknesses of this, because leather was plentiful, and these dualities and triads then sewed into a firmness to last half a lifetime or a whole lifetime, taking hard weather and serious wear and constant irritation, but holding: thongs around things; horse collars hard as iron but transmuted from cowskin; a man's hat fur-lined, and heavy leather around it to keep mountain wintertime cold and wind from freezing the ears or frosting the skull. That was how the nation could come up, because it was wilderness living and a body needed to be bound in strong stuff so as to hold, and leather did it while you built a log cabin, or made a track through woods, or scuffed out a new road, or worked on a canalboat on the Barge Line, or built the two-story houses that sprang up everywhere, from nothing, like suddenly appearing beehives. Skin and leather workers, hide experts everywhere, at their benches, with keen-steeled knife and chemical, flattening and straightning fur, skin, and hide, scissoring it into the varied shapes, making an art of leather: a peculiar American product picked up from the Indian, developed by the colonial American, and now, in the time of the leather lobby, permeating the furniture, the clothes, the walls. Leather frames and even pretty pictures painted by local artists on large irregular slabs of tanned hardness; the people literally skinning the countryside. And William Henry liked his leather-handled cane, his leather case for his spectacles, his leather pouch for the extra cigars he kept in an inside pocket, his fur-lined coat for winter going, and, even when he watched America unraveling from the woods, as he rolled along on the extension tops of the rainbow-hued coaches, it was as one who was aware of the leather time, the industrial and artistic meaning of it. "Here, let me have the leather a minute," he said to the driver often; then he took the long leather whip that thinned down to a needle-fine waving end, and he snapped it over the horses—*nyip-nyip*—and they spurted to a raucous wheel-rumbling over the rutted roadways. So close was leather to him in each day's living....

Yet when the powerful Leather Manufacturers' Bank tried to tell him how to vote on a bill in their interest, that was something else again.

Albert Tracy entered. "What do you think, Tracy?—" Excitedly he told his colleague of the letter he just tossed into the stove, and he plucked it out so that a charred bit of the printing—*The Leath ....facturers' ....ank* —was still visible. Tracy held it in his hand and he listened while the Auburnian stormed and cussed and ended up saying, "I had made up my mind to vote for that bill, Tracy, now I'm disposed to vote against the bank."

Tracy agreed that the leather lobby apparently halted at nothing. He pulled a letter from an interior pocket. It was the same note, addressed to him. "I thought I'd show it to you. I'd supposed I was the only one that got it." And his letter went into the stove.

Meanwhile, because William Henry chanced to favor this particular bill for his own reasons, from political-philosophic motives of strengthening the state's economy, he voted in favor of the measure, but with a certain reluctance.

He believed the matter was ended, and then one day, when he was in his room on a weekend, he heard a knock at the door. He opened it and admitted a well-dressed, confident, middle-aged man who handed him a card and murmured, "May I introduce myself ... ?"

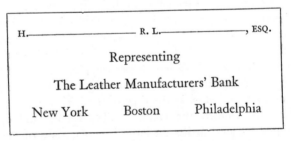

H.———————— R. L.————————, ESQ.

Representing

The Leather Manufacturers' Bank

New York   Boston   Philadelphia

"Come in," said William Henry.

After a comment on the weather, the visitor said, "Sir, in gratitude for the passage of the bill, and your vote in favor of it, you may have any amount of stock in the bank at ten per cent."

William Henry murmured that he wanted no stock. Neither did he want a scene. The bank representative didn't seem to hear, and he resumed, "You see, I couldn't offer it to you until the bill passed."

Just a little louder, but still patiently, William Henry remarked, "It's useless to offer it to me before or after the bill's passage. I—just—don't—want—it."

The visitor seemed puzzled, as if he weren't used to such a reaction. "I'm offering you money, mister. What's the matter with you?"

"That isn't why I voted for the bill. The state pays me to make decisions for or against measures. When I'm not here in the Senate I make my living from the practice of law."

The leather lobbyist acted dismayed. "I don't understand turning down money."

"It's the kind of money, sir."

"You seem pretty young to me. I guess you don't know how it works."

"I know how it works." The Senator moved toward the door.

"If you knew how it works you wouldn't take such a cavalier attitude toward the Leather Manufacturers' Bank!"

"Still, you notice that I have—and now, will you ... ?" William Henry held the door open.

"You'll never be more than a piddling State Senator with an attitude like that."

"The Senate Chamber is not the one that should be piddled in ... !"

"I think I'm in the wrong room—"

William Henry twisted the knob, welcoming the visitor out.

The lobbyist left, with a jerk, as if he expected the redhead to boot him in the rear.

Chapter Sixteen

THE VIEW FROM THE WEEPING ROOM

FRANCES was back in her father's house. She wasn't well, and much of the time she was upstairs in her room, the same one where William Henry had his bad illness several years earlier. From this retreat she more or less ran the house, except when the judge overruled her. From here she sent word to the kitchen help, here she received occasional calls from her aunt and grandmother, and it was in this room principally that she passed her hours with Baby Frederick. Young Gus ran in and out, up and down the spiral staircase, and sometimes farther down to the kitchen in the basement, then back up through the house to his mother's side. She was trying to make up her mind whether to cut his hair—it had grown so as to entirely cover his neck behind—and she decided she wouldn't cut it in front. He might as well look like a girl for a year or two, his hair was so soft and fine that she would feel remorse in cutting it at all. Occasionally she went downstairs for a few hours, at mealtimes, or into the library, or the parlor, but the room upstairs inevitably drew her: there she could reread the letters from Henry, weep when she felt like it, absorb all kinds of reading matter, and nurse her deep psychological wounds.

One of the first results of Henry's election to the Senate was the family decision that she give up the new little house, that they sell it altogether, and she return to the judge's. There, with so many to help out, now that she had two little ones, she would be happier. William Henry himself had proposed it before he went east. After all, he had vindicated himself; he had succeeded after a fashion, and he was a halfway successful man: he had proved his independence to the town and the family. Now he could return to the Miller house and live in it gracefully. And so Frances was home, in the big nest, for the rest of her life—except when she would be away with her husband—and the old judge re-won the point that had been agreed upon in the marriage deal that she was to stay in this house as long as he lived. The judge was happy over it all; now there were two grandchildren to liven the place.

But the situation cut Frances a little deeper. She was more than ever intimately involved in the life of her father and his family, more than ever united to her clan, but more than before split in her affections. She knew that a return to the judge's house, while it had its comforts, could never make up for the missing husband; and he had no sooner left Auburn for the Capitol than he got her first complaint: "Happy New Year to you, dearest," she wrote, "for you have run away and left me alone with the two tiny ones—they are dear creatures and I have no right to complain for as Gus says, 'Ma, you are not all alone when I am with you!'" Still, it was a lonely New Year, she told him, and four months would seem like such a long time. She wound up that note by mentioning that the night before they had been up to see Lazette and she had returned with a headache. Headaches and toothaches. All one week, the first week of William Henry's absence, she nursed a bad toothache; and sometimes, as a result, she went to bed during the daytime and let the others handle the children. One dark morning, at six o'clock, when the roosters hadn't even crowed yet, her candle burned out and no Henry to help her, she arose, with the hurt in her mouth unbearable, and she went downstairs to get some laudanum and brandy to relieve herself. She lit a candle, she stumbled about in the dim light, and the judge, also upstairs, hearing the motion below, thought the house might have a burglar in it. He got up, slowly sneaked downstairs, and saw that it was only his unsettled daughter moving about, and neither fire nor candle, laudanum nor brandy could help her, and her teeth ached till daybreak.

Nights when she couldn't sleep, she looked out of the window, saw the beautiful moon yellowing the white village, and she drifted into long thoughts of life: "Thinking of the evanescence of all human happiness in the shortness of our existence in this world," she wrote him, "—of the uncertainty of destiny in the next—until my heart has almost blinded my eyes—I feel melancholy—my only refuge from such feelings is in writing to you now you are not here to cheer me with your kind voice...."

Something in her needed sympathy badly, but it wasn't forthcoming from anyone, not the way Henry could provide it; and she had, it seemed, acquired a way of stumbling from one injury and ill to another; little accidents about the house, as on the night when she was putting the children to bed and she hit her elbow against the bedpost. She wrote to him that she never had anything so trifling occasion so much pain: "I think it must have touched a nerve, the chords become contracted and the veins swollen instantly— It continued to pain me until I went to bed, my wrist was so weak I could not write any more that evening— I still feel a weakness when I write but I do not apprehend any other ill effects from the blow...."

123

Sensitive, lonely, deeply hurt Frances: she retired frequently to her room, to be alone, to weep, and to read. William Henry knew just what it all meant, and he proposed that she pack up the children and come to Albany and spend the session there with him; other senators had their wives and families along with them, why not they? They could stay at the Eagle or some rooming house close to the Capitol. He was as lonely for her as she for him. But the divided nature of Frances asserted itself. She was now wrapped up in her children, for she had become to them "your own mother," and she told him that it gratified her to know that he thought he might be happier if she were with him—"But it cannot be because it would be almost cruel to take my little ones from a home where they are so comfortable and happy this cold cold weather— I am too foolish a mother to leave them—so it cannot be— I think you will become a little less lonely when you become more accustomed to your new mode of spending your time."

As a result, life tore at both, with its own distending tugs. He had to have his politics and his absences, and with these, his longings for home; and Frances wanted the snug house of her father, the warmth of her children, the closeness of blazing logs in the fireplace of her own room; so she couldn't always have her husband, and in his place she did have the unending headaches, toothaches, rheumatism, minor accidents.

But this time, at her writing table in the privacy of her room, studying his latest letter from Albany, she was more upset than usual. Distance had its dangers. He filled his letters with the gossip of Albany, of his political colleagues, the meeting with Burr, seeing the Fire King; whom he saw, where he went, what he thought; and he had been writing eloquently of one of his anti-Masonic associates, Albert Tracy, who represented western counties in the Senate. Tracy impressed William Henry as being brilliant, eloquent, a gifted conversationalist; but he feared he might be losing Tracy's friendship, and he wondered why; Tracy had been acting queerly. But Frances knew why, for in a recent letter William Henry mentioned he had been to the Tracys' and he had seen a beauty. That was Mrs. Tracy.

There it was, Frances was thinking, William Henry's bright eye, which was worth worrying about.

She had learned that even at the time William Henry proposed to her, he had been seeing the Kasson girl, and she didn't forget the fact that her husband was thinking of someone else all the time he courted her. Now, in Albany, he had seen a beauty, and her husband had sensed William Henry's interest, whatever it might be, and Tracy was properly a little disturbed. William Henry went to church with the Tracys, he visited their home, he went on a shopping trip with her. Frances wrote to him: "So, you have been to Tracy and seen a beauty—well I should like to see her, to look at her that is, for I never yet found any woman that I thought perfectly beautiful—this is because I have been so foolish as to form my ideas of beauty, I may say all human excellence, from books—how many disappointments I might have spared myself had I never seen a work of fiction, how many I might yet escape would I efface these romantic impressions." She wound up saying, "Seriously I am glad you have found friends who make your time pass so pleasantly—you know I have two little boys with me to love and be loved by while you are away from us—so I will not quarrel with anyone who makes love to you—"

The novel, from its earliest days, exerted a special appeal for young women and, in particular, girls of the genteel class from which Frances issued—for they could afford to buy them. She had read one entertainment after another, stories of emotional hassles, ecstatic love matches, triangular intrigues, with happy or unhappy endings, noble heroes—the conventional "romances" of the early novel. Young, sheltered, not knowing what really went on in the world outside, she apparently couldn't judge the real from the fanciful; and instead, she learned to expect something fiery, passionate, exalted, out of life and marriage, which wasn't there in the sober relationship she had with an ambitious husband who was off to his own wars, his own Mistress Politics, so much of the time. Dimly she was beginning to understand that she had acquired a distorted view of the real world from the fictions she had read.

Now, in her private tower in the judge's house, she sat at her writing table, tapping the quill end thoughtfully on the wood. Around her were the things she loved. The rocking chair that was fifty years old and had been in Grandma Miller's house a long time before, in Bedford, New York. An intricate and pleasing wallpaper design enlivened the room, a design of spring flowers and sunlight; the fourposter bed was made, and it was clean and white, the flames snapped in her private fireplace, the activity of the house came faintly to her ears from below, and Frederick gurgled in a crib a few feet away. This was a more serious matter, she thought. She didn't question William Henry's fidelity. She deduced that he had answered his loneliness and his incessant need for female company by an intense cultivation of the Tracys' friendship. It might be, it probably was, perfectly platonic, perhaps a little upsetting to Albert Tracy, flattering to his wife, and halfway satisfying to William Henry. But it only went to show what would go on in a man's mind when he was away from his wife and home. She recalled a note he had sent before, how, for two weeks after he arrived in Albany, he hadn't talked with a single woman and he felt bad about that. Oh yes, Henry had corrected himself, he had talked with one: it was Amy, the ancient housekeeper at the Eagle, and after being so long away from women, he decided she wasn't bad-looking at all.

That was William Henry, she thought; the congenitally heterosexual man, who felt more like a man when women were about. She probably would have to put up with that roving eye of his. What to do? How keep pace with this strangely vivid man who was her husband?

Lost in the depths of her room, reading his letters carefully, weeping easily, torn by all the compulsions that held her to this house, yet wanting very much to be with this magnetic little fellow who loved people, women, life—she could see him, oh so clearly: there was that peculiar feature which was to her of singular interest, a curious thing that made it impossible for his face ever to be out of her mind for very long. In speaking or smiling his upper lip had a nervous and tremulous motion that was independent of its action in articulation. It was an involuntary motion, and it leaped to life frequently, for he spoke or smiled frequently.

In the quiet of the upper-story room, William Henry was alive to her and close. She saw this animated face, with the streak of lightning in the upper lip; she heard always his entrancing talk; and when she read his letters, his voice came into her eyes—and she decided then and there that in the subsequent sessions of the State Legislature, William Henry would have his whole family with him in the capital.

Chapter Seventeen

THE BREAKERS OF THE HEADS OF THE DRAGONS IN THE WATERS

ON a day late in the summer of 1832, twenty plain men, working-men of Albany, moved northward on foot out of the capital, in the direction of the Champlain Canal. They were close together, silent, a mood of anger upon them as they strode ahead, some carrying knotty sticks just torn from trees, others bearing homemade clubs and a few holding axe handles. Probably no more determined band marched out of the city since the War of 1812. These went forward to beat out the brains of the cholera monster if they saw him coming. Him or Her or It—this contingent was out to smash the cholera with their bare hands, with the weapons of earliest man—for nothing else seemed to help. The disease had entered New York State from Canada, and thousands were sick and dying. Doctors couldn't check it, nothing could halt the scourge.

Each weaponed man had lost a child or two children, or a wife, or a mother, or some other kinsman. They moved in the roadway through the avenues of Albany, headed outward to the line where the "Northern Canal," as they called it, came closest to their city. The canal led north-ward; over it went commerce between New York State and Canada, and because of this, these early-day cholera fighters bore a temporary animus toward their neighbor to the north. For Quebec and Montreal were rav-aged by the disease. About 25,000 immigrants had arrived there from Europe this year, and apparently they had brought the Asiatic malaise into this continent. England was in the throes of cholera, so were other Euro-pean countries; and now Albany appeared to be one of the earliest Ameri-can cities affected.

Perhaps, the band of cholera warriors reasoned, the affliction had come down the Champlain Canal from Montreal: stop it! fight it at the banks of the canal! drive it backward! And nobody laughed. Nobody, because it was well understood that medical science was helpless to stop the invader. The disease came on insidiously; the warm, sunny weather seemed to cozen it, to bear it into communities on the most unsuspecting breezes; it seemed also to travel by water routes. It came on with stomach upset, with an uncontrollable diarrhea. The victim began to vomit, to weaken, all in a few hours; in a day the skin lost its elasticity, the eyes sank, the patient was already in bed, the voice enfeebled. The pulse became rapid and weak, the blood pressure fell, and sometimes there was agonizing pain and the victim lay abed like a jackknife holding his stomach from bursting. Soon the patient's skin turned bluish, bluer, dark blue—and quickly the hearse came so this death wouldn't produce others.

Physicians were sent from Albany into Canada to learn what they could about how to combat the plague, but they returned as ignorant of method as when they went there: in Canada they were primarily praying, and it didn't stop the cholera; all that they could tell the people, on their return, was that the disease was spreading, boil water and burn all suspected filth and old garments. Yet the boiling of water didn't seem to help. The people cooked their food till it was tasteless, but still the number of cases rose: in July there were six hundred and thirty-two in Albany and two hundred and eight died; and in August, of five hundred and twenty-five victims, one hundred and ninety-three died.

So, the party of mystified men, moving as a posse in search of a terrible murderer, paced through the streets northbound, while the sympathetic townsmen looked at them through their windows. Prayers hadn't helped; in fact, people were keeping away from the churches. The physicians were as overwhelmed as any others, and the nurses in the hospitals could do no more than bathe and soothe their patients and carry away the great outpourings of excretion. Maybe, thought the Albany people, these brave men from "the Pasture" section of the city, with cudgels in their hands, would help. For strange ideas prevailed about the source of the contagion: they had some feeling that there was a real thing abroad; there were rumors among the people, seeped down from the medical world, that diseases were sometimes caused by small, unseen things; that these minute murderers often hid out in swamp country, in low-lying land, near water, near wells; fire might help, and if fire helped and that was a form of force, why then, maybe the offender could be stalked and spotted in its lair along the canal, and be stamped out by muscular force.

While this group moved resolutely toward the Champlain Canal, the disease itself went in other directions. It moved down the Hudson River on freighters, tugs and passenger boats, and it entered the big city. Swiftly the condition there became calamitous, with dozens of deaths daily, the people fearing to go into the streets, scared even to take food or to drink water, and mothers worried about nursing their children for fear they might give the sickness to their infants through the breast. The newspapers proclaimed an emergency, but the best thing they could do was to recommend praying, and staying out of crowded places. The disease went frontierwise along the Erie Canal, and it dropped off at each village along the Mohawk; it reached Auburn, and after that it spread west of the Cayuga Bridge. Frances, fearful of the toll being taken there, wrote to William Henry who was then in Albany: "The destroying angel continues to visit the dwellings of our neighbors, and why shall we escape?—After all, the lives of our boys are in the hands of Him who gave them—of Him who sees not as man sees."

William Henry was glad that Frances and the boys had returned to Auburn, where the disease wasn't nearly as widespread as it was in the capital. They had been with him in a suite at the Eagle for several months, when the Senate session opened in January, but there had been much illness among all three, and they went home.

In Albany the political life was paralyzed, the feuds of the day forgotten. The politicians, gathered at the Eagle, mentioned their regular affairs in a kind of subdued way. The question only was, who else in the Legislature has it? Did they bury So-and-so?

William Henry ventured alone down into the Pasture, which was the slums of Albany. Here the disease was at its worst. The land was low, the houses ancient and much lived in, the quarters confined, often airless, and the furniture and the kitchen utensils not always clean. The disease struck heavily in this neighborhood, the germs grazing with the greatest of lust on the poorest inhabitants. William Henry looked about: he saw the crapes on the doors, the funeral corteges; the buggies and rigs and carriages lumbering along behind the hearse wagons; the white coffins of the children, the black and brown coffins of the adults; and now the undertaker was carried away in his own hearse. William Henry was struck with the incapacity of man, he discerned the great untrod road of medicine, and he felt that there was a place here where Government must lend its hand. Musing so, he left the offensive district, where a stench of death and disease seemed to issue out of the houses into the open, and he made his way back into the upper streets of the capital.

A few days before the band of men went to slay the cholera monster with plain sticks, Weed hurried into William Henry's hotel room. "Seward, Seward—Maynard has the cholera!" William Maynard, the Senator from Utica, was the principal spokesman of the anti-Masons in the Senate, William Henry collaborating with him closely when measures went before that body. Maynard had been mentioned as a Presidential possibility. Weed, who guarded his political friends, nursed them, mothered them, and befriended them, said he must take a boat to New York at once.

Weed arrived in Manhattan and hastened to the hotel where Maynard was in the last stage of the disease and near to death. For a while, as Weed sat at his bedside, Maynard was delirious; he talked incessantly of politics, wildly, incoherently; and the journalist listened, studying the cyanotic tinge of the Senator's face, not quite understanding then that the anti-Masonic movement, which was already fading as a cause, would be given a new impetus toward its death by the passing of Maynard. Latterly it seemed that Maynard was improving, he was conscious and resting, and Weed said, "I hope you'll get your health back soon, now." Maynard answered, "My only concern now is for my supreme health."

The death of Maynard was one of the public sensations of the cholera rage, and it meant that the mantle of minority Senate leadership passed over to William Henry; but the rampage of the plague, which had thrown into shadow much of the political interest of the season, effectually lulled forever the anti-Masonic fervor that had lived this long. It was as if people felt, what was one disappearance, one death, Captain Morgan's, now that tragedy had befallen thousands?

Weed returned to Albany with the news that helped crush the anti-Masonic remnant at the capital. Somehow the handful of frontier leaders who had come up with the principle of anti-Masonry felt that Maynard's loss was irreparable, that the steadily doubtful question whether a political movement could survive on the basis of a single position was now in some large part resolved. They would take some new course soon.

Meanwhile, another party, the unique band of stalwarts who haled from the much afflicted Pasture section, they who had gone out like knights to slay with David-like weapons an unseen monster, returned through the burned and smelling and ash-covered lanes of Albany.

William Henry and Weed stood in front of the Eagle and they watched the parched procession of returning cholera warriors, 1832 version. They were weary from threshing the air with their clubs and sticks and axe handles, worn with striking wildly at shrubbery, the insects and the mosquitoes along the canal banks, wet and tired from delivering smashing blows at canal water, tired of facing a dread enemy that they couldn't see. Thorned and pricked and bleeding, they had opposed the air and the earth and the verdure and the running water for many desperate hours, and now, emptied of their hate, they trooped home to the gloomy and hurt community.

Afterward, the cholera departed, and since nobody knew why it came and why it went, they said in the Pasture that their men had, fortunately for everybody, stamped it out.

Chapter Eighteen

LADY IN WAITING

THIS time they boarded ship together, Dr. Samuel Seward and his son, and both were "errant." They were on a lark, the old judge having abandoned Mrs. Seward and the rest of his family in Florida, and William Henry had flown his Auburn coop and left Frances there with her boys and a new surge of the hypos. It was summer, and the father and son were traveling around Europe, arm in arm, seeing the sights of a half-dozen countries—and with the feud of a generation ended. The judge, who was now sixty-five, decided that William Henry, flourishing in the Senate, hadn't made a fool of himself at all: he was delighted, he was astonished, he was even proud of the littlest member of the family who was getting to be the biggest.

The Senator had been visiting his folks in Florida when the elderly jack-of-all-professions buzzed a hard-time story. "Henry, I'm sick. I'm almost an invalid. I got to have a change. Got to do something for my health, and if I don't do it now I never will. I've been held down here like I had tent stakes pinning me for the past half century, and I've worked myself to the bone. You've got to go to Europe with me."

What about Frances and his boys? William Henry remonstrated. He so rarely saw them as it was. But the old judge wouldn't hear of it and he faintly hinted at dark ingratitude. Why, dammit, he was footing the bill, and he didn't care what it ran to, and besides, this'd help in politics, couldn't he see that? That part was important, William Henry realized. A new party was coming up, the Whigs. The anti-Masons, the National Republicans and some dissenting Democrats were forming themselves into the enthusiastic and zooming Whig Party; and Weed, in the Albany *Journal,* masterminding the new political setup, was already talking of William Henry as a good candidate for governor of the newborning organization. Judge Seward was excited about that prospect; hearing his son spoken of as a possible governor elated him and triggered a load of rheumatics in his right leg, giving him a vigorous limp and practically invaliding him so that he only had strength enough left to make a trip

131

hole Continent, and only three months to do it in.
 over there to France and maybe even see General
ued. "We could have a deuce of a day of it. Now
me ideas of yours, Henry; you're a man of the
g real good, and you mark me, a trip to Europe'll
hty fine strategy, too. You wanted to go anyway
appened to you?"
ly did want it, more than anything in the world,
t well, she was angry at him for being away so
much, and this ... on top of the rest, whew ... what would she think of it?

That set the judge to whining and pleading, and he made out he was just about dying, he had to have this change. He pulled the meanest term he could out of his big vocabulary to describe just how seriously he was failing. "Henry, I'm a real valetudinarian. This trip is downright therapy for me, Henry, downright therapy!"

William Henry couldn't turn down his ailing father whose energies were so low that he could only plan an international junket. "Very well, I'll hustle home and tell Frances and spend a few days with her before we go."

The judge bristled. Definitely no! "By cracky, if you get up there you'll change your mind. Or Frances'll change it for you. Now we take the stage out of here tomorrow, we go down to New York, and we catch us the first packet to Liverpool."

Frances learned of it by letter. Her world-seeing, bounce-about husband was off on the biggest runaway yet. He was always running away, it seemed to her. She understood that there was some kind of rapprochement developing between the judge and his son, that it had been working up ever since Henry entered the Senate, that now the old doctor was proud of him; the judge was grappling Henry to his soul, she said to herself, and pulled a clause out of Hamlet, "with hoops of steel." The whole thing had an inception in the Legislature about two years earlier. The judge ran up to Albany and took a seat in the Senate gallery unbeknown to William Henry. He hid behind a pillar and looked down and watched the way his boy got up and talked about the need for a stronger state militia system, putting up such a holler for it that he even got the measure through. The judge didn't let himself be seen, but stayed on through one whole day of the Senate wrangle, virtually spying on the representative from the Seventh. When he heard his son rail against debtors' prisons the judge said to himself, "That does it. He's got the goods. My boy's got the goods." Convinced that William Henry wouldn't disgrace him in the Senate, and was a long way from making a fool of himself, he had rushed down onto the Senate floor, after the session was over, and embraced his son. William Henry was a little surprised to see his father in the Capitol. "Didn't know you were coming, Father."

"Well, I'm here."

And for two days afterward the State Senator was in a dither. He didn't quite know what was happening, for he saw a different man, almost a different father. Judge Seward seemed gay and exuberant in a way that William Henry had never known him to be before; he seemed full of cheer, with a new closeness to his son that was almost embarrassing— though it was what the son always wanted. He wasn't being accused of doing anything wrong, he wasn't being called errant, what had come over Father? That attitude had gone on, and it developed during the succeeding two-year period, so that this day arrived when Judge Seward, in a mood of celebration and love, swooped down on William Henry with this idea— and sure enough—they were gone—and sailing.

They got so chummy, in fact, that in his letters to Frances he referred to the judge as Samuel. He and Samuel arrived in Liverpool, got cleared by the customs, lodged at a place called the Adelphi, then it was evening, and they hustled to the theatre so as to begin enjoying themselves. There they met almost all of their fellow passengers, and were surprised to see their steward and his assistant, both colored men, in the box opposite. This was so different from the custom in America that they experienced a moment of shock, but William Henry recovered quickly. "I was pleased with the evidence that in England the caste of man is not determined by the color of the skin."

Back in Auburn, Frances spent more and more time in her upstairs room, keeping an eye on the children, with Fred scampering about close at hand most of the time, but she cloistered her thoughts to herself. The realization that William Henry might be gone for a long time produced in her a violent, a galling melancholy. When that happened she often got severe pain to go with it. Emotional upset seemed to affect her teeth. Her teeth ached, her jaws pained, a rheumatic horror of headache swept over her, and then she worked agonizingly at her mouth, literally trying to tear her teeth out. She was now missing several rear teeth; her wisdom teeth had been removed; and once she had pulled out a tooth by herself by fastening an iron to a string and tying the other end to her tooth, then dropping the iron and yanking out the molar. So that William Henry would have a letter from her when he arrived in Paris, she mailed one to him at once, and in it she let him know just how his absence had affected her. She described how her tooth hurt and how she nursed it along as much as she could, then:—by way of dividing my thoughts and feelings as though I should be insensible to bodily pain, I sent for Ball (the barber) and had the tooth extracted—you will allow that this is a singular and novel mode of driving away care— I found it of very little efficacy in this respect.

The fat letters from William Henry arrived every few days, all summer long. He poured out all the detail of the travel: *Liverpool: The English seem to be enamored of their aristocracy. The shopkeeper is most happy if permitted to display over his door the words, "By special letters licensed to make razors for the Duke of Cumberland."* Eighteen days they had gone on the sailing packet, *Europe,* and now he was by stages in Ireland, England, Holland, Germany, Switzerland and France. Yet the wonderful things happening to him only reminded her that his "ups" were her "downs." His triumphs and travels spelled out her denials. *Montereau, France: You should see the hunting that goes on in the forest of Fontainebleau, near here. The deer are tame and they can't even get them to run. The dogs can hardly be driven to the chase, they act as if they'd rather sit around at court, like their masters.*—The things that made him happy and high, sounding like a conquistador, only signified to her that she was in bondage to self-living, to husbandlessness. She steeped in introspection while the letters poured in from towns in Ireland, Scotland, and then from London, letters that scintillated with his comparative observations, the Old World and the New. He was being pleasant and entertaining, yet it was like following an account by someone else who wasn't quite her husband. It only made her more aware of her own personal world on South Street. Having two little boys to take care of at home, wanting to be with her husband and wanting to be the best mother, was trying: she was caught between the devil and the deep, she told herself, for want of what to do and how best to do it.

Dublin: Descending a hill on our return to town, we saw a whole family by the roadside taking food under the shade of a tree. We went into the circle and asked for water, which was immediately given us. The lady, well dressed and of respectable appearance, pressed us to take some hard liquor. It was difficult to make her understand that it wasn't from mere politeness that we declined it. She poured out a cup for herself, and said she didn't think it was good to drink water alone, it was so cold. I fear from all I've seen that the temperance society has but an indifferent prospect in Ireland.

She couldn't reconcile their hasty departure with the news that had been sent from Florida only a few days earlier. Mary Seward was desperately ill, deathly ill, they wrote. William Henry and Judge Seward were at her bedside constantly. They closed the front gate, and nobody was allowed to see her but her husband, the children and the physician. They had put up a billet of wood, like an obstruction, on their side of the street, the west side, to make people pass around and away from the house, so as not to upset her. In fact the neighbors thought that was carrying it a bit too far. Who did the Sewards think they were anyway? After a month's illness, Mrs. Seward felt better; and one day she sat up, she asked for food; and the next day she got out of bed; she was smiling again and ready to resume with her household chores—and a few days after that, maybe less than a few days—the rascals skipped out. Just as soon as Mary got on her feet, Frances said to herself. Maybe the son takes after the father, she thought; maybe there's a streak of the old gentleman in the son; maybe the judge is the original erratic one. Then she had a satisfying but perfectly preposterous thought: Why, if they had machines that flew in the air these miscreant souls would be the first to hop into them. *Dublin: We asked to see Newgate Prison where the leaders Emmet and Fitzgerald were kept, and the keeper showed us the place of public execution where they had capital punishment for ordinary crimes. On the second story there is a little chapel with a door opening to the street. Here the convicts are attended by the clergymen. At the appointed hour the condemned men are required to walk out, with ropes upon their necks, upon a narrow iron platform, the floor of which, on the mere turning of a crank, drops, and leaves the wretches suspended over the heads of the populace. Four are often executed this way at the same instant.*

She read, but with a certain abstraction, he abroad on his latest tangent, she wondering whether she'd ever have an understanding with the little man. *London: Saw the king and queen of Great Britain in the chapel at Windsor Palace. His Majesty has a benevolent but not particularly intelligent face.* She could be reading a brilliant description of a performance in a theatre, or his vivid picturing of a session of the House of Lords, and even while she scanned his words, within she was remembering days she had spent with him. *London: The immensity of the city has given me a sense of solitude and despondency. Samuel and I went to Covent Garden where we heard an opera, an invention and substitute for the classic drama. Lacking as I am in musical talent and taste, the opera doesn't appeal to me. I tolerate it only as being better than the vulgar shows and dull dialogue that form so much of our American entertainment.* She was living on what she had shared with him in the months she passed at Albany during the last two Senate sessions. Even the painful time when she had first gone there in January of 1832, the sick days, these were preferable by far to his wordy absence. When she decided to go to Albany at the beginning of the 1832 legislative session, and when she did go, it was almost disastrous. There was just sickness upon sickness, hers and the children's. Travel by canal and stage with small Augustus and Baby Frederick was hard on them and tiring for her. They no sooner settled at the Eagle when their troubles began.

She had arrived wearily, and met the wives of the politicians: Mrs. Weed, Mrs. Tracy, Mrs. Trumbull Cary, and other women whose men were associated with William Henry. They were surprised to learn that she still nursed Frederick, then aged a year and a half. "You're killing yourself, Mrs. Seward," the kindly women told her, "break it off now or your children may lose a mother."

When she was sick nobody comforted her as Lazette did; these wives of the politicians, nice as they tried to be, didn't read to her for hours without weariness, as her sister did when she was ill; they didn't sit by her bedside day after day and smooth the pillow and kiss her and say kind cheering words, and so, feeling lonesome, she slipped into a spate of quiet crying by herself. She cried for her sister and said to herself, "I want to see Lazette," and she knew it was childish, and that the way she said it to herself was a little like a child saying, "I want to see my Ma," but that was how she felt, full of the hypo, and now that she was in Albany with Henry —she was lonesome for Lazette and the house on South Street, and her father and Aunt Clary. So, till her cough got better and she got her strength back, she lay abed experiencing life in the capital in a pretty poor way, but at least she was with Henry and he came rushing to her each day as soon as the session was finished.

Glasgow: Saw a monument in memory of James Watt, from whose grasp our countryman wrested the honor of the discovery of the application of steam to navigation. The figure is colossal ... Fulton, whose genius accomplished the great work, and brought honor upon his country, who completed a discovery destined to contribute so much to the power of the United States—sleeps in an unhonored grave, and his children suffer want in the midst of millions of wealth created by his genius! She was so high strung those days in the capital that most anything made her cry, and one morning when she got a letter from home saying that fire had burned down the little wooden church which she and the family attended, she wept about it. It was a beautiful little church; she had many pleasant hours there, on Sundays, listening to sermons that had soothed her, and, as she was sentimental and inclined to cling to everything connected with gone by days, and as she had been going to this church since girlhood, she was much moved, but Henry had dried her tears and told her they would certainly build a nice new big stone church in its place. That made her cry a little more; Henry didn't always know the right things to say. *Edinburgh: We were amused to see a group of little girls enjoying a game identical with an American pastime. We never dreamed it was of Scottish origin. They were dancing about in a ring reciting, "How oats peas beans and barley grows, nor you nor I nor anyone knows, how oats peas beans and barley grows" which I played as a child.*

Just about when she was getting around the hotel room herself, and was moving out of doors and seeing Albany and becoming social, sickness struck again. This time it was Augustus come down with the measles. *Glasgow: We paid a visit to the lunatic asylum, one of the most interesting institutions I have ever seen. But in several respects the science of treating this unfortunate class has been carried further in America than here.* When Gus got better Frances could entertain the wives of the politicians again, and go to the State Chamber and watch the men legislate, and move about the town and shop a bit. Then the days turned faster, faster, faster. She became closely acquainted with Mrs. Weed. She thought Mrs. Weed to be a homely woman, and looked ten years older than Weed, but she had a practical manner about her, she kept a nice clean house, she had no pretensions whatever, and she regarded the care of Thurlow Weed and her three children as her paramount duty and interest. She had invited Frances to come to their house on Green Street and take tea at any time, and she would always find her "just so," meaning plain and unvarnished and friendly. *Tadcaster: Saw a pair of stocks conspicuous by the roadside. I did not believe till I saw with my own eyes that corporal punishments were still going on in this enlightened country.*

When it seemed to her that she may have scanned a letter a little absently, seeing other things, other times, she put it aside, then returned to it later, for second and third readings. To get the feeling that he might be talking to her, to hear his voice, through the pen, she reread, and the picture of his travels became almost as clear to her as to him. *London: At Drury Lane Samuel and I attended a concert by Signor Paganini. He played upon the violin pieces of rare difficulty and beauty. He is the fashion and everybody acts as ridiculously here as some do in America when it becomes the mode to worship a new theatrical star. The fashionable world is agitated by the report that he is to be married to an English lady of great beauty and wealth. He is fifty, and as uninteresting a man in his appearance as you will find among a thousand. I can't believe even London contains any female so extravagant a devotee to fashion as to fall in love with so plain a being merely because he plays well on the violin.*

137

She chastised him, as if he were there in the room to hear: "No, Henry, you couldn't imagine a wealthy and beautiful woman falling in love with a homely little man like that—you just couldn't, but I could." No, he couldn't, he answered. "Just imagine the amount of feeling a man like that must have, if he can impart it to thousands, imagine the feeling in that man—you can't, can you, Henry?" No, he couldn't, Paganini was too damned ugly, couldn't imagine it. "Well, I can imagine it, I could love a man like that myself, Henry, what do you think of that?" Henry answered in a voice that made no echo on her walls; he thought Frances was in love with him. "I am, but that man means music and wonder and beauty, and there are some things you just don't understand, or you wouldn't be away from here so much. Sometimes I think you love yourself and your career a lot more than do you me." He was protesting to her: Aw now, Frances, a man's world was a man's world and it was different, what did she want him to be, just some little two-by-four lawyer around Auburn? "Never you mind, William Henry, those two-by-fours around Auburn make better husbands than you do. They stay by their hearths, they come home to their wives at night, and they're not to be sneezed at." He wasn't sneezing at anybody, but for goshsakes, let him have this trip to Europe in peace, he'd never been there before. "Very well, have your trip to Europe, see if I care. But if I just wither away from lovelessness, don't you let me hear you complain!" She could almost feel her lips moving, with the one-sided but victorious conversation, and she trembled at his absence. *Delft, Holland: My surprise was excited by the large numbers of storks throughout this country. They serve as scavengers and are preserved with great care by the officialdom and by the peasantry.*

The cities he was visiting swam visually before her eyes, vague masses of structure and street, quaintness and Old Worldliness; he'd made these places vivid, and she could fancy him and his father walking the cobbled streets of England, marveling at the cleanliness and the dikes of Holland, excited by the gaiety of the French streets, going from theatre to theatre; she could see the diverse costumes of the European countries, and there were Dutch girls smiling at William Henry. *Delft: The Dutch ladies take their seats at the windows with their sewing and knitting work, and by means of double mirrors fixed to the walls, and without obtruding their heads, they see what's going on in the streets. Pass these windows and you may see the lady's face in the mirror as she notices you.*

To deepen Frances' loneliness, her sister moved away: Lazette and Alvah, and their children; they had sold their house in the eastern part of Auburn, and removed to the hamlet of Aurora on Cayuga Lake. It wasn't far, but distant enough to bring to an end their customary every-other-day visits. Now they wouldn't be seeing each other for months, and Frances wouldn't be able to rush up to Lazette's to pour out her frettings. A few days after the move, Frances wrote to her sister that although Lazette had occupied her head and heart almost exclusively since she went away, there had been no time to write till now. Moreover, on the day Lazette went, Frances had spent the whole day reading, unwisely reading, until she almost blinded her eyes—went to bed late and woke the next morning feeling very much as if *I have not a friend in the world—so much for the business of one warm heart—I have not been out of the house since you went away and feel no disposition to do so—the village appears nearly deserted—I am inclined to think my visits to the eastern part of the town will be few and far between this summer—it always did seem like a degree of profanation to see anyone else living in a house that you have occupied.*

And so her soft young heart carried a double burden of abandonment. *Paris: Found your letters assuring us of yourselves. I am sorry you are so desolate, Frances dear. We shall be home soon.*

He was writing long letters to Weed and to others too. In the three months of European travel and nearly two months of ocean voyaging he wrote eighty letters, filling nine hundred handwritten pages with his impressions. As rapidly as his notes arrived in Albany, Weed published them in the *Journal.* The publication was anonymous, for Weed, with an eye to effect, intended revealing the authorship when the interest in the travel account was at its highest. This stunt might help elevate his protégé to the governorship. William Henry, unaware that his letters were printed immediately upon their arrival, poured out his impressions with all the ink he could find in the hotels and taverns, and his thousands of words carried the exuberance of a schoolboy. *Rhening, Holland: This town is no bigger than Auburn but it looks as if it has stood unaltered for six centuries ...Utrecht, Holland: The farmhouses and barns hereabouts look exactly like those along the Mohawk, where the Dutch settlers have located. The barns are precisely like those the Dutch have built in America ...*

Several letters from home waited for him in Paris, and he read with special interest his wife's reaction to Mrs. Frances M. Trollope's recent *Domestic Manners of the Americans,* a book critical of American character and society, then causing a national sensation. He had seen many signs of intellectual maturing in Frances since he had gone to the Senate, but her comments on this book's content, style and impact, seemed especially acute:

Thursday, June 3, 1833

MY DEAR HENRY:

...I have just finished reading Mrs. Trollope and think her description of American society much more correct than at first I was willing to allow—had she confined herself strict to the truth I should not be disposed to cavil at a picture for which there is so little which is flattering to our national pride and the woman herself, notwithstanding of her literary pretension is neither very amiable nor very refined—her images are many of them good—expressions and phrases low and coarse, still there are some parts very prettily written—had she met with a more kindly reception at Cincinnati and succeeded in settling her son to her mind I am inclined to think her impression of the country would not have been quite so unfavorable—she would not have been so bitter in the expression of her sentiments...Your own FRANCES

It turned out to be a long summer, a long absence; it was early in November when they made port after thirty-two days of rough, stormy sailing.

Then Frances had one of the most frenetic weekends of her life, for she hadn't seen him for six months. For two whole days they were alone together, most of the time in the upstairs room, while the Millers watched out for the children. He had returned on a Saturday, and by Monday, Frances was ready to get off a letter to her own Lazette telling of her own Henry and of his return—and you must not expect a very long or sprightly letter, she wrote—I have never felt sillier in my life—we have had so many things to talk over that for the last two nights slumber has not visited my eyelids until after 2 o'clock—my eyes are of course a sea of happiness— I feel exhausted and weary and now crawl into bed but I know you will expect this letter tomorrow and I cannot disappoint you."

For a week he stayed about Auburn, having a real reunion with Frances, and he talk-talk-talked of all he saw, repeating what he'd said in his letters, but enlarging on it all, with the boys at his side whenever Frances wasn't clinging to him; altogether a terribly popular fellow. Yet over it all there hung, for Frances, a sense, the same sense as always, of a fleetness and a sweetness about it, as if it would not be for long. She had him as much as she could in their room, and held him and talked with him, and then all of a sudden, like a pungent scent blown on the wind into the lungs and out, where was Henry? He was gone, on the way back to Albany. Court was in session. The New York State Senate functioned then, in part, as a court, somewhat like the House of Lords in England. He must be there, to resume his seat in the Court of Errors.

So much for courts, so much for courting.

Chapter Nineteen

FOR PROFESSIONAL SERVICES RENDERED
IN CONNECTION WITH.....

H IS term in the State Senate ended, he was back in Auburn, and once more in law practice. But this time he was in a new store and office building situated dead center on the main street; it was an elongated wooden affair, just constructed and given the name the Exchange Block. William Henry's savings were invested in this venture; and he and Nelson Beardsley shared one of the lighter offices on the ground floor. There the ex-Senator was lost in his briefs, his consultations, his circuit routine . . . and trying to stay interested. He wished he had the zeal of his colleague. Beardsley was fortunate: no ambition in him for anything other than the law, financial enrichment and domestic happiness. But with the ex-Senator, as he finished writing a bill: "For professional services rendered in connection with . . . conferences . . . disbursements . . . stage travel . . . total $43.50" the thought passed through his mind—what a petty business I am engaged in. This is commerce, this is fees, this is money-grubbing. How, in this work, are the larger ends of the community served? What can a man become, doing this?—

There was his torment.

For, about the profession of law, he was in a duality, constantly at war with himself, and the inner argument almost never ceased, the public man incessantly opposing the professional. The public man in him, the ex-Senator, asked of Counselor Seward, "Have you overcharged this client?"

The Counselor answered, "He was pesky to do business with."

The Senator advised, "You shouldn't be so displeased with your work. You make a living at it. You and Beardsley get more business than most, and the test of your ability is that clients come back."

Counselor Seward answered, "There's no certainty in this work, Senator. No satisfaction whatever of a human sort. I look and look for truth in the law books, but it's not there."

"Don't say that out loud, Counselor."

"Nonetheless it's true," the Counselor told the Senator. "You search forever, and instead of finding out the truth of a matter, you find out at the end of a long and tiresome litigation that you're all wrong. If you're not wrong, then the court and the jury are. In either case you and your client have lost out anyway."

"Counselor, isn't it correct that you make some of your best political connections through your legal practice?"

"Yes, Senator."

"Then don't complain. One leads to the other."

"Nonetheless, Senator, as soon as I can I want to get rid of these law books and take up others. I want philosophy books; they may have the answers. History books might have them, the Bible might; but these damned law books don't—they only have decisions."

"Do you know of a better way to make money?"

"No, I don't. I suppose I'd rather be a lawyer than have any other profession, but I'm haunted by what Shakespeare said of it, he must have had to go to the law frequently."

Senator: "You mean that barbarous thought—?"

Counselor: "Yes, 'The first thing we do, let's kill all the lawyers.' I happen to know that many people feel that way after they've dealt with us fellows once or twice."

Senator: "Forget it, it's just a poet's image. The world will always need lawyers and always have them—"

Counselor: "What you're saying is, it will always be a world of hell, strife, misery—which we're supposed to straighten out."

Senator: "That's right, you and the judges and the jury are supposed to straighten it out."

Counselor: "Yes, and what it comes down to is we're all fighting for our fees—nothing else. Even the jurors get paid for jury service after a fashion."

Senator: "How else can the wrongs of the world be righted? You might as well object to the need for physicians."

Counselor: "A bad analogy, Senator. Medicine can become a science. The law and justice, it seems, can only go on becoming a more intricate mess."

Senator: "I'm sorry you're so unhappy in a profession which you carry on so well. I don't know what's going to happen to you."

Counselor: "I know. I'll leave the bar some day, for good, as soon as I can. When the public recognizes I should be in government and keeps me there."

Senator: "Counselor, if you think you've got troubles now, wait till you get in government."

Counselor: "I can't help it, Senator. It burns in me to get out of what I'm doing, and to lead. This is a terrible daily round—calls, messages, errands, letters, interruptions, disappointments, envies; the vindictiveness, the wrangling. Do you know how foreign this is to my temperament? I want to be amiable to my fellow men. I want to be generous, to have friends. This kind of business will turn me dyspeptic if I stay with it long enough. You think I want 'lawyer's stomach'? You think I like to shout at debtors and at clients, as my colleagues do?"

Senator: "No work, no vocation, no occupation is easy. Public life, which you think you want so badly, carries terrible responsibilities, and men who go up high in politics are tumbled regularly from clifftops into pits of anonymity, with the completeness of an avalanche of rocks. Are you sure you want to get up on these mountainsides?"

Counselor: "I'm doomed in that direction. I have to take my chances. Anything but the constant slavery of this office. Senator, do you know how supremely dull it can be to become totally absorbed in a client's problem? Do you know how repellent another man's problem can be to you sometimes, and how necessary it is to know all about that problem if you are going to help him and collect your fee?"

He looked up, out of the window, at the line of trees that reared above the buildings in the business center; he stared beyond at the blue sky, and he grasped a notion of the great planet revolving on its wheel, and held a momentary sense of the incredibility of largeness that lay beyond even his wildest comprehension, and he said to himslf, "Here am I drawing a paper accusing the deacon of the Presbyterian church of having property that trespasses a foot and a half over onto Mr. Halsey's lawn—something is wrong."

It was as if one magnet held him to his desk while another tried to draw him away to something else bigger and better that might lie beyond, out there in the battleground of public measures and philosophic principles. Yet inwardly he knew the uncertainty that underlay all ambition; if he stopped to think about it, he knew he'd feel fear of failure and inevitable disappointment and rejection. These demons lay everywhere, seizing upon the ambitious, thwarting them at the last gates. He had seen politicians tumbled from their berths by a few votes; he had seen parties rise and fall; and he was still young ... what else might he not see?

Spring was coming on, heavy with daylight and the vanishing of snow. It would be good to get far far away from these burdensome tasks of chancery and take something deep and alive into his chest; good to get

143

away from courthouses, away from papers, away from judges and people in distress hanging around courthouses, away from the minor snappishness that prevailed on all sides over points of property and possession and law— this is mine, that's yours, I want this, you are only entitled to that: property and self-interest. There wasn't much largeness of spirit on most sides. People didn't "give" much, even if they went to church and heard much about giving and forgiving. It was getting, everywhere going out and getting.

...As Weed and he tried to do not many months later.

For the journalist proposed William Henry as the Whig candidate for Governor in the 1834 campaign.

Early in the campaign they were in New York, with a third Whig leader, Frederick Whittlesey, and they looked for a New York City man for the position, as they didn't believe that a Western New Yorker could carry the city and state. But no one of stature was available, and they were in a quandary, so they wandered about the city wondering what to do.

They sat talking and thinking on a park bench.

William Henry laughed. He said that the situation reminded him of something. "I believe that we're reduced to the dilemma of King James and the clown. When the clown learned that the king was hunting in the forest, he went out to look for him, and, meeting him alone on horseback, he mistook him for a courtier, and asked him where the king was. The king told him to mount behind him, and he would take him where he could see His Majesty. He told the clown that he would know the king by his being the only person who wore his hat. When they came to the crowd, the courtiers took off their hats, crying, 'Long live the king!' King James, turning to the clown, asked him if he know which the king was now. The clown, seeing the king kept on his hat, and feeling the cap on his own head, answered, 'Not exactly, but I am sure it must be one of us.'"

They decided that that about summed up the quandary they were in, and they must ballot for one of themselves as the candidate. Weed was unanimously nominated by both of the others, but he positively declined. Whittlesey then voted for Seward, and Seward voted for Whittlesey. But Weed cast the deciding vote for William Henry.

The lawyer, dreaming of being free of the legal routine forever, plunged into the campaign. He hardly saw Frances at all. He didn't write to her as regularly as he should, either.

Serves him right, she thought, in November, when William Henry was defeated for the Governorship by a fair margin. That will teach him to stay at home.

Chapter Twenty

WILLIAM HENRY MAKES A PROMISE
TO FRANCES

IN THE spring Lazette, in Aurora, became alarmed at the tone of her sister's letters, and the word she received from Judge Miller. Frances was seriously ill. Lazette hurried home to see what could be done.

She knew enough of Frances' problem to know that it lay in the power of William Henry to help her or to cure her by simply doing something for his wife. And Lazette was determined that William Henry should buckle down to the most important task he could ever possibly have.

They were talking it over in the parlor.

"She badly needs a change," Lazette argued.

"I agree," William Henry said, "but what kind of a change?"

William Henry saw a bit of fire in Lazette's eyes. He was used to having the Millers take a part in Frances' affairs, and this time Lazette seemed to be laying down the law to the lawyer. He was respectful because he knew he shared a measure of guilt for his wife's flagging spirit and health.

How about taking a trip to the Mediterranean? he proposed. Summer was coming on, the warmth of the tropics, a new scene. How did that sound?

"Now, Henry, stop thinking of yourself!"

"Lazette!"

"That's just what I said. Stop thinking of yourself, Mr. Seward."

"I'm thinking of Frances."

"No siree! You're thinking of what that phrenologist told you." A phrenologist had recently examined the contours of his head and said his skull was remarkably shaped for its conscientiousness and certain bumps showed that he had a love for foreign travel. Henry had bragged of it, and he thought the phrenologist clever.

"Really, Lazette, my sole concern is Frances. It's summer. A balmy sea voyage, the Levant, Italy, sandy beaches!"

"Nonsense, you want Rome, and the high spots, and a talk with the Pope! Don't kid me."

145

"Aaw now, Lazette."

"Don't Lazette me, Mr. Seward. I know to whom I am addressing my-self!" She sounded arch and angry.

"Well, what would you propose?"

"I'd suggest something quiet, a ride down through the Shenandoah and the Blue Ridge, stop where you please, travel as much as you like, show her the country, take it easy—"

He looked at Frances. Her face brightened. She liked that better too. She ventured, "If we do that perhaps we can take Fred...."

"Wonderful," said William Henry.

Lazette pictured the trip further. "Perhaps you could go into the South. Let Frances see Virginia, then you could spend a month or two coming back up via the coast, to Philadelphia and New York."

The South! Frances had always said she would never never look at the land of slavery; yet now she was fascinated with the idea.

William Henry's eyes flashed. If they were going that far, they'd see Washington too. There was much she could see in Washington, and maybe...

"That's it," William Henry said. "A trip down to see the 'peculiar in-stitution'!"

"Call Fred," Frances said.

Lazette went to the rear door and called the five-year-old, at play in the side yard.

When Fred entered the room, Frances asked, "Fred, would you like to go with Papa and me for a long wagon ride down through Pennsylvania, perhaps into Virginia?"

Fred's eyes rounded.

He ran out of the room. They couldn't imagine why he left them so hurriedly and they thought he didn't like the idea. Then he returned, run-ning in, carrying his coat, and he was putting on his hat. "Come on," he said, "I'm ready...."

It was a kind of Currier-and-Ives trip, seeing Rural America in a way that most citizens couldn't, because few could afford to spend months traveling, paying the taverns, feeding the horses, shopping en route, em-ploying a coachman; but William Henry had several months of money-making after he returned from the Senate; the cases came in steadily, and he and Nelson Beardsley had all they could do to handle their clientele—and so the Sewards were on their way.

For a long season, the three of them, driven by their coachman, went into a half-dozen states of the East, deep into Virginia, and William Henry made the greatest effort of his life to preserve Frances' health. Once, in Pennsylvania, he wrote to his law partner:

Shannon's Tavern
Pennsbrough, Pa.
Monday, June 1st, 1835

MY DEAR BEARDSLEY:

I have been concerned for you, in regard to the labors which must fall upon you, and would show my sympathy for you, if I knew what particular trouble is heaviest on your hands at this time. But it would be idle to conjecture, and I have learned this much philosophy, that both duty and interest dictate the undivided application of our powers to the immediate occupation. Mine is to save the health of one without whose society and affection the most successful results of all my most diligent exertions would be valueless; and you attend to the more profitable duties.

Sincerely,

W. H. SEWARD

One morning, in the Blue Ridge Mountains, William Henry sat outside an inn; he had just dined, and he wished to sit and look about awhile before going on. He heard Frances nearby talking gently with a slave woman: she was blind, ancient, and she turned a great wheel over a lawn.

"Isn't that very hard work?" Frances asked.

"Yes, mistress. But I must do something. This all I can do now, I so old."

"How old are you?"

"Don't know; past sixty, they says."

"Have you a husband?"

"Wouldn't know, mistress."

"Have you ever had a husband?"

"Yes, I been married."

"Where is he now?"

"Oh, I wouldn't know that. He been sold."

"Have you children?"

"Had plenty children. But they all been sold too."

"How many?"

"Six."

"And you have never heard from any of them since they were sold?"

"No, mistress."

"Don't you find it hard to bear up under burdens like these?"

"Yes, mistress. But God, He do what He think best for us."

A few minutes later they entered their coach and they went on. But at once, Frances drew a delicate flower-designed handkerchief from a sleeve and she dabbed it to her eyes. He knew that she was easily moved to tears, but usually it was about matters of the family, the church or the town, of her children, perhaps his absences; as often as not she wept when she felt good. He knew better this time.

"The old woman has touched you?"

"Yes."

"You knew that you would see these things."

"Of course. Promise me one thing, Henry."

"Yes?"

"Promise me that when you can, you will strike this thing—"

"I promised myself that long ago. You know I've spoken of it in a half-dozen speeches."

"Speech isn't enough, Henry. Strike it!"

"Frances, in politics you time your moves—"

"I said when you could, Henry."

"Precisely. When I can. When I can, I will. Over and over I have seen prominent men hurled down by taking a right stand at a wrong time. I tell you—"

"Henry, there is nothing to tell me except that you will make more of your abolitionism than a preachment on the Fourth of July—"

"Believe me, I want nothing more than to see this blight cut out of our national vitals. Weed and I talk of it often, but we bide our day. We have to make a sharp distinction between what we as conservative Whigs can advocate and what Abolitionists advocate."

"If you walk like a cat, you'll think like a cat and do as a cat."

"You astonish me with your vehemence, Frances."

"What you call my vehemence is my Christianity. I have to be a Christian or I cannot endure."

"I think I have more confidence in the power of the ballot and the strength of the parliament than in the part Christianity will play in the drama of this shame's passing."

"I don't care how it passes, but it is wrong, terribly wrong!"

"Believe me, Frances, I will act when I can. But it must be done cautiously. On this matter a man can fall and be as forgotten as dirt. No question arouses in me as this one does my awareness of the chasm that lies so deep between a right cause and the need for care in order to realize one's ambition."

"I know the size of the political problem."

"This question will mature, Frances. When it does I can do my part." Then he added, "For one who wanted no politics on this trip, I must say this is a reversal—"

"If the former Senator from the Seventh will permit a reply?"

"Yes?"

"I see now that this politics is imposed upon all of us."

Suddenly the talk ended. Young Fred relaxed; he had pricked up his ears sharply at the electric conversation; there was a sharpness to it that he hadn't heard on the whole trip. Then, as if there had been no such exchange, Frances saw a bush of yellow flowers and asked Henry if he could identify them.

When, in the autumn, they returned north and they reached Aurora, on the east side of Cayuga Lake, Frances' grandmother, now aged eighty-three, was there, at Lazette's house, waiting for their return, and the woman who had been mother to Frances was dying. A day or two afterward she died, and Paulina Miller was brought back to Auburn for burial.

The last thing that Grandma Miller said to William Henry was, "I feared you would not bring Frances home to me before I died. . . . Remember, you have my treasure in your keeping. Take care of it while Providence leaves it in your charge."

For five months William Henry had taken special care of Grandma Miller's "treasure." He had done much to restore his wife's health and spirit and to replenish her flagging emotional life.

What Frances wondered was, would William Henry remain so devoted to her in the days to come? Or would he, as he had always done in the past, fly to his Mistress? Was this just an interlude to be stored away, like a beautiful maple leaf in the pages of an enjoyable book?

Chapter Twenty-One

THEY HAVE PLANTED A VINEYARD
AND WOULD EAT OF IT

H E WAS, suddenly, in the heart of pioneer country, shooting trouble, the hottest in the state. The town was Westfield, in the southwest part of New York, on the shore of Lake Erie. There was an uprising of the settlers on the Holland Land Purchase, a huge tract of wilderness covering most of Western New York. And the spot was dangerous. So perilous that Frances hadn't wanted him to go; she had talked against it strenuously before he left, and he had to argue the right to the venture. In the privacy of their room upstairs she had asked if he must take this case. "Frances, this isn't a 'case,' " he answered. "The Holland Land Purchase has always been the biggest realty deal in the state."

Couldn't someone else handle it?

"Someone else?" he echoed, with exasperation. "How can you say that? It's the most important thing I've ever been offered; a plum, and it's in my lap; there's money to be made, and prestige in it too."

Still, she would like to have him around, she said; so they would do with a little less prestige.

"Now, really, Frances, if I bring off this deal who will be the beneficiaries but yourself and the boys?"

She appreciated that, she parried, but living on letters was unsatisfactory; couldn't he go on making money around here, and not get too far away?

"But this is a proposition in hundreds of thousands! It's a million-dollar deal!" He was angered at her blindness.

She had an answer for that. "Did you ever think you might possibly get into something over your head? It's a revolt out there. If the militia barely kept them from demolishing the land offices, how will you stop them?"

He wasn't moved; most lawyers would envy him a chunk of legal business like this. "Frances, this one is big with political meaning. If I can straighten out that situation it'll be a feather in my cap. No other matter in the state right now has such public implications."

She listened, but coldly, and he persevered: how the whole frontier was involved, the entire state was looking at the situation, the politicians talking of it, wondering where it would end. She wasn't impressed. "I know the size of the interest, but I usually get the short end of these things, the boys and myself; and that's what it is again."

"It's too bad that you look at it that way, Frances."

"How else?"

"You might, you know, be able to see it as part of my career. Our career, I may say."

"*Your* career, Henry!"

"*Our* career, Frances! Anything I do, anything I accomplish, is for all of us!"

She toned down; she didn't wish to quarrel with him; she was merely a lonesome wife; half of their marriage he had been away; it was a grievance with a supreme validity. He was sorry about that. "You know how I love the house and the village and you and the boys. Can I control my fortunes? Shall I turn down my opportunities?"

She was weary; she said she supposed not; gently she raised her hand. "Henry, I don't wish to quarrel." Then she cut him. "I know enough about you to know that you'll do whatever you want to do. You always do."

"Never, without consulting you."

"Yes? As you consulted me when you went to Europe?"

"Oh, you know very well I talked of that a dozen times. I'd always talked of going there and you always said you hoped I'd have the chance to go."

"We're fighting, Henry; that isn't what I want. I merely want you around the house and the town."

He was disappointed in her, and he said so; she usually saw clearly the moves he made that advanced them.

"Henry, I'll put up with it. I always do. I'll wait—while my sailor boy is off to the seas—as usual."

That deepened his chagrin. He saw how loath she was to let him get away again. "I'll get home often, it isn't far away." He was already gone as far as she was concerned; so she talked in a different tone; she wished she could love stagecoaching as much as he did; she never saw anyone so happy up on the box seat of a wagon. "Candidly, I do love the sight of the country, since I must travel over it. Why? Should I be miserable?" Of course not, she answered. He sensed a weakening, said he wouldn't be surprised if the deal turned their fortunes permanently upward; it could lead to anything; Thurlow Weed said it was boundless in its implication.

"It's wonderful how you never fear failure," she said. "I wish I had your confidence."

Why should it be difficult? He was a lawyer and this was a legal matter; he was a politician and this was a political matter; it was a matter of people, and he worked with people all the time. He couldn't see anything but a favorable conclusion.

"Only write to me regularly, Henry, don't make me wait for your letters. I don't care what you put in them, but don't ever let a mail stage go by without placing a note on it."

He had gotten leave—in that manner—and then he had gone, first to Batavia, then southward, and now he was ensconced in Westfield, handling infinitely complex affairs that had reached a crisis five months earlier, in February, 1836, in a nearby village called Mayville....

You couldn't clearly tell who was leading the uprising, from the way the men and women marched in loose column formation over the snowladen road into the tiny town. Up front four determined men moved side by side: Asa Spear, Thomas Clump, Daniel Cornwell and William Monman, old-timers of the region who had fought wolf and winter, soil and sickness. It might have seemed, from the fact that they headed the procession, that they inspired it: but just behind them came another band of men, land tenants like those in front, and they seemed just as forthright. They were from Township Six, Range Eleven, as the territory of the Holland Purchase was then subdivided and called. Among them (some pretty shabbily dressed, considering the cold time of year) were Ozias Hart, Justus Hinman, John Cass and Drew Stebbins. If you were looking for ringleaders, it might even have been these. Most of the others trailed in a procession that strung out a couple of hundred yards in extent. They were mainly young men, for primarily only the youth of the East had the fortitude, the health and the need to settle in this primitive country known as the Chautauqua region. Men outnumbered women ten to one, for the forest was tough on women, and rigorous enough for the men too; and yet, a handful of women marched with these 250 demonstrators. The wives of Asahel Beach, Ambrose Dean and Salah Seymour were right up there alongside their men, trudging the snow down, treading the narrow path that led northward into Mayville, to the lonely suboffice of the Holland Land Company. "We'll be warm for a while when we raise hell with that building," Mrs. Beach said. "Now, now," said Mrs. Seymour, "you don't have to swear about it, Annie. We ain't doin' nothin' wrong, we just got to teach 'em we ain't gettin' off this land so quick after all we gone through to make it halfway fit for humans."

The settlers from all parts of Chautauqua County came by sleigh, horse-back and on foot to an agreed-upon place of convergence two miles from Mayville. It wasn't easy, arriving there in the snow from points ten, fifteen and even thirty miles distant, but they went anyway, whole families, and they took a certain joy in what they intended: a comeuppance for the Holland Land Company and their agents. They marched from the meeting place to Mayville, wearing the rude garments that they themselves fashioned, clothing made of the sparse stocks of broadcloth that were brought tortuously into the region, or decked out in hide coats, muslins and coarse cotton things, buckskin pants, shoes with no left or right to them but composed of thick skins bound at the ankles: no "boughten clothes" among these people, but knitted scarves and fur hats, and knitted socks—for the spindle and shuttle went steadily inside the cabins, the women making most of the clothes that their men wore.

The fact was that there was no single leader, because everybody felt like moving against the land company. It was a long-standing feud. The states of New York and Massachusetts had disputed this region soon after the Revolution. Then Robert Morris, the Philadelphia financier, acquired from both states a tract consisting of four million acres. In 1782, he sold the largest portion of this to men living in Holland: that was how it became known as the Holland Land Company. The Dutchmen, through American agents, sold the area in small parcels to settlers, farmers, small landholders, but throughout the history of these arrangements, there had been disputes between the proprietors and the pioneers. As new settlers came in, they took the position that their occupancy of the soil and their cultivation of it gave the land its value, and that the continuing claims of the original owners, distant from them, living in Holland, were unreasonable and excessive. During the previous year, 1835, three Western New York men of wealth bought from the Holland Land Company, through its agent in Philadelphia, a large slice of Western New York territory, almost the whole of Chautauqua County, the million-dollar sale into which William Henry was entering as attorney and pacifier. The buyers put down $50,000 in cash and agreed to pay off the remainder in subsequent installments. This meant that there was now a divided ownership of the land.

One of the new purchasers was State Senator Trumbull Cary of Batavia, a close friend of William Henry and Thurlow Weed. Cary was an anti-Mason, and now he was a Whig, and William Henry knew him well enough to dub him "Uncle" Cary. Cary's partners were Albert Schermerhorn, a founder and financier of Rochester, and another Batavian with money, named George Lay. These men got off to a bad start with their tenants. At about the time they took over the contracts to lease land to the small settlers, a law was passed stipulating that the Holland Land Company should contribute something annually toward the state's upkeep; this was upsetting to the trio of Western New York operators because they felt that they had the big job of paying off nearly a million dollars to the original proprietors living in Holland. So they posted notices all over the Purchase, in the region they bought, upping the price per acre on new lands, moving to recover lapsed, reverted and wild lands, demanding interest on money owing to the Land Company, and topping off that with the announcement that anybody who didn't pay up inside of two months must forfeit his property.

Since most of the settlers were in debt to the Holland Land Company, this amounted virtually to a notice of dispossession. Panic spread among the small farmers on the great reserve owned jointly by the Hollanders and the Western New Yorkers. The pioneers, always penniless, having no market to sell their surplus to, relying on credit and mortgages while they made the land productive and valuable, felt forced to defend themselves. They decided to resort to a good legal trick: burn all the contracts...

For, if they didn't do something, they'd soon be homeless and they wouldn't even have a spot in the woods to share with the wolves, bears, panthers and the lesser creatures, for the region was almost as wild and uncultivated as it had been in the pre-Columbian time. Get off this land? the settlers asked one another. And they murmured of the years they'd been here and the resolve not to leave "without doin' a little burnin' or breakin' or somethin'." Soon the newspapers would refer to these protestants as a "mob," and now the mob moved ahead, another mile to go, through the powdered hills, trampling the snow into a hard mat of footprints. Cool wind from Lake Erie rolled their way and tinged the air with bitterness; but the sun was out, and the leafless trees, save the evergreen, bowered the route over which the men and the horses kicked up snow. There was a gaiety about them; men in revolt tend toward a festive air; and they brought provisions along. They drew draughts from cider jugs to warm themselves, they passed fresh cornbread to one another, they dined on venison. Dogs tagged alongside and they barked, sensing a strangeness in the air as they ran the length of the column and back.

The whole history and experience of the Holland Land Purchase was the freight in this marching and rolling contingent: the land they had cleared and tilled, the illness and the denial they shared, and the exhilarations of life lived in the raw, the unforgettable moments and the long memories. They talked of their time here and what they had seen and who they knew and what they recalled, and it was the story of America, repeated, as it had been lived earlier in New England, in Virginia, in the

Far South. They'd all lived with the rifle close by, against the wild animal, and somehow they ate and lived, and their little cabins often became, later, good-sized houses. But nobody had any wealth, and they managed to live on here because they paid interest only to the Holland Land Company, and little or nothing of the principal. And some couldn't pay interest after a season's war with the soil, and the battle with hungry birds, and rains that came too often and stayed too long, or didn't come at all.

So they had the land in common, and the privations that it offered as well as the promise that it held, and there was no mood to relinquish it to some men suddenly driving a hard bargain with their lives. To them, it was still what the Holland Land Company said it was back at the turn of the century when they advertised for Easterners to come in here and settle and take land on easy terms, and bring the region into civilization.

The notices posted along the trail said:

Timber in black oak and white, and wild cherry is here, as well as the poplar, the chestnut and butternut. Settle if you will by the dogwood or the sugar tree, the white ash, or the cucumber tree (so like the magnolia). Level land is thine if so thee wish, or the gradually ascending earths may be settled upon, and valleys for they who adapt well to this choice; and basswood and lynn are here, and the lands abound with limestone. Rich soil, folks; rich soil.

They had settled here and found it was true, a land of Biblical beauty, needing strong arms and strong men to work it, needing new tools and time; and now all these fragrances were covered with snow until they unfolded again in a few months, but who would be able to work the soil and smell the scents of the trees if they were thrown off the land?

They turned in the road, and the little village of Mayville lay ahead. They could see the spires.

Mayville was only six years old, an infant hamlet of the state, sixty-six miles below Buffalo—and a long long way, two weeks away, from Albany by stage. It was on high grades overloking Chautauqua Lake, and it commanded a rare view of the snow-covered water. The aggregation of militants straggled into the town, passing by all its little wealth:

One Baptist church
One Presbyterian
One Episcopal
One Methodist
An academy for learning
One select school
A brick courthouse (costing $9,000 to be built)
One small prison of brick

A fireproof clerk's office

Four taverns (in front of which villagers now stood silently watching the unexpected entrance of this murmuring body of farmers)

Eight stores (which emptied themselves at once of their customers)

Eighty dwellings (scattered up and down beautiful little hills, log cabins, brick houses, and stone houses swamped in green by summer, and now covered by white)

A suboffice of the Holland Land Company (soon to be demolished)

And 250 souls.

That was the town on February 6th, when there occurred the first of a series of upsurges on the Dutch-owned Western New York soil.

A huzzah kind of sound rose from the men and women as they saw the three-story land office in the center of the town—and inside the office they saw a frightened agent.

The agent ran outside, and yelled, "What is this?"

A few farmers quietly told him to just step aside and no harm would befall him; they hadn't come for him.

"Let's get the papers out first."

Two dozen men walked through the clanking doorway. There were wooden files all along one wall, under lock and key.

Someone came outside and said, "Get the keys to the files from that fellow."

He turned over the keys, swiftly, gladly.

Then, in relays, the men came out, bearing the records, the maps, the legal documents of a whole generation of land dealings.

The papers and books were loaded onto two large farm sleighs.

The agent of the suboffice protested. "You hadn't ought to do this. It ain't legal."

"No, we hadn't ought to set fire to your britches either, but if you say somethin' more, that's what's goin' to happen."

The whole party swarmed through the small building, rending it board from board until it was a shattered skeleton of the original structure. They tore it apart; they smashed the chairs and sofas; they broke the windows, they ripped out the clapboards; they tore up the front porch; they pulled up the two-by-fours, shattered the big beams; they threw the wood all around, into the snow; and all that within only fifteen or twenty minutes, so that the building was fit only for kindling.

They looked at their work and laughed heartily. But that was only part of the day's business.

Two sleighs loaded with the records moved in front eastward out of the town, a distance of two miles. The Chautauquans followed behind, gayer than before, seeing how easy it had all been, and feeling a sense of accomplishment. Soon the party arrived at an open spot in the woods. The tall bare trees, in brown and gray and black, made the wooden frame for the bonfire they now made of the deeds, the letters, the notes, the court records, the debts, the interest figures. The fire flamed up so good and so high that many moved in close to get warm, and this was the high point of their festival.

The news traveled quickly throughout the state. It became the new interest at Albany; and in New York they read of the doings of their country cousins, how an alleged injustice at the frontier had led to violence.

Thereafter, in each suboffice of the Holland Land Company, the agents were in terror, for the residents in each county found an unheard of way to contend with the matter of the new owners who were in a hurry to collect.

The wiseacres said, "The Land Company don't have no title to the lands now. These burnin's'll make the judgments of the courts null and void. If there bein't no record of the contracts and the conveyances, how they goin' to know what's what?"

He had the schedule of a man of action now, which was what he liked: none of the small litigation that life in Auburn directed his way, and his notes to Frances pictured his momentary hassle from the time he left her late in June until now when he was in the little vale of Westfield handling the settlers. Once he even muttered that in spite of his troubles, he liked what he was doing "better than the perplexed life I led at home." Frances, when she read that, wasn't surprised. She knew there was something about the stationary life that was foreign to his nature. Something in him, fundamental, demanded motion, unceasing activity, and it defied resting and rusting. Perhaps he was "too big" for Auburn now. He had, after all, run for Governor of New York State as a Whig only two years before, when he was thirty-three, and he was defeated by William L. Marcy, running as a follower of Andrew Jackson. Maybe the village of Auburn seemed small, the arena not challenging enough for one just emerged from such an important battle, defeated but by no means humiliated. She let him know how unsettled he had left her, in spite of her consent to this move. A few days after he arrived in Batavia, late in June, there was a note from her, written almost as soon as he had left: "...and have had two bad nights and my nerves are not in a very composed state," she wrote. "I will not trust myself to say anything about your leaving me all alone and hope in time to feel that it is all right— Custom reconciles us to doing things which at first seem unendurable."

157

The trip to Batavia had been rough. He went over wretched roads, narrowly escaping upset twice and taking the Erie Canal part of the way, spending twenty-four hours in traveling sixty miles. Yet he was in time to see seven hundred tenants march on the main office of the Holland Land Company. But a militia force defended the building and the people within it, and the hostile settlers were repulsed. William Henry, assaying the situation, wondered whether he could ever pacify this throng, right the wrongs, stabilize the region: all of which was now his responsibility. "The whole tract of the Holland Company's lands, comprising seven counties, is wild with excitement," he wrote to his wife. "Men have fearful thoughts and dangerous plans. The Chautauqua office had long since been burned and the agent of that office has come to Batavia a terrorized man. Today armed men are guarding the land office here, the place is full of arms, and I hear news that demonstrations are taking place in each county."

He stayed in Batavia a month. He drew new contracts, he hired help, he examined the history of the Holland Land Company's negotiations with settlers and agents and attorneys; he discovered duplicates of the documents destroyed at Mayville, he ordered copies to be made; and most of all, he worked out a clear understanding with Trumbull Cary, George Lay and Albert Schermerhorn that he would only work on a basis of a liberal approach to the settlers; that he would extort nothing from anyone, and that nobody would forfeit his land.

Then he left Batavia and moved into the southwest part of the state, into the heart of the hostile region. When he reached Mayville and saw the demolished land office, and sensed the turbulent mood of the people, he decided that that was no place to make his headquarters. He would settle a few miles away in the village of Westfield, the pretty town on the edge of Lake Erie. When the Mayville people heard that—which meant they would have to travel to another town to have their lands relegalized— they became threatening. They told William Henry he would be driven out of Westfield and out of this part of the country; they didn't want him hereabouts, leave while the leaving was good.

But he set up in Westfield and for a critical week or so he didn't know whether he was going to make it. The job was to restore peace and he hadn't realized until he estimated the ferment all about what an undertaking it was. Yet the threats of violence and burning and bodily harm subsided.

In September the unrest was about gone. Word got around that the little redhead seated on the leather chair in the new land office was pleasant to deal with and he kept telling everybody that none would lose their land. The news spread that long-term arrangements were being granted to all, that people only had to pay the interest on their property in order to stay. That was a different story; it wasn't at all like what the "Genesee men" had come up with a few months earlier.

A few weeks later he told Frances that the business was so much under control, the region was so quiet, and the business so orderly that, "My life is without an incident even of the dignity of a court appearance, and as destitute of romance as a merchant's inventory." Nothing could be worse for William Henry than unromantic living; for he had to be in the heat of the political day, in the center of the controversies of the hour.

Then, typical of his whole nature, the ambivalent pendulum that swung inside of him all the days of his life, he began to long for home. The one magnet had drawn him here, and the other gravitational force was urging him to rush back and see the family. There were hours and days when the work he was doing seemed merely languid and tiresome and endless; then he often had a special kind of headache, a stricture that swept over his forehead, like a heavy hand passing back and forth, and it would stay with him until at night he reached his room at the local tavern.

When he was quite a hero throughout the southwest of the state, when it was clear that he had the situation in hand, he decided to improve his living quarters. He would be here a long time, he realized; the business, as such, might go on for years, for he was now a partner in the whole transaction, partner and administrator, and he had bought into the property, with the other three men, by negotiating a huge loan from the American Life Insurance and Trust Company. Now he was agent, lawyer, investor and equal in the whole deal, with as much of an opportunity for making money from the land as any of his partners. He was in a fair way, he believed, to winning the financial independence that might make it possible for him permanently to devote himself to public life. So he found a pleasant place in Westfield, known as the McClurg Mansion, and having in mind that Frances and others might visit him the following summer, he rented the house.

It was a big place in the center of three acres, surrounded by trees and shrubbery, two stories high with a double piazza in front, a garden in the rear, five big bedrooms upstairs, with cellars, outhouses, a smokehouse, an orchard. The way William Henry liked to live. Almost as nice a place as the one on South Street.

He moved in, starting with a party of his friends, and because he was a busy man, and needed stimulation, he said to himself, "To hell with that temperance stuff"; he was going to be an independent on the liquor question.

He settled into the rustic life of the town, busy by day, Santa Cruz rum in the evening, and good books to take up his long evenings.

Late in October, he went alone in a little rig through the villages and he thought how the cost of property was rising hereabouts, and how new immigrants were entering the region daily. Pretty soon, he mused, this will no longer be frontier, but a place new and settled and urban, and full of villages and busy economic life.

The situation was controlled. Once or twice he made a brief visit to Auburn. He stayed long enough to see his newborn daughter, Cornelia, and to cheer Frances. Then he returned to Westfield.

He was an important financial man now, administering a million-dollar operation, making an excellent income; and where politics was concerned, anything could happen.

Chapter Twenty-Two

AND THEIR POWER SHALL BE MIGHTY— BUT NOT BY THEIR OWN POWER

THURLOW WEED watched with pride, from Albany, how his friend subdued and tamed the Western New York threat, how William Henry satisfied the settlers, his employers, and even started himself on the way toward becoming well-to-do. The journalist enjoyed the idea that Seward was making money. People respected a money-making man; he would be able to present William Henry to the voters again. By now, even the Democrats were impressed by how well he handled himself in court, in the Legislature, in finance, in his personal affairs, and in his political life. The little that Weed had done for Seward, in recommending him as the trouble shooter in the Chautauqua affairs, was only a friend's return for a favor Seward had done for him several years before.

Weed recalled a day in 1833, after the anti-Masonic movement had faded. They were taking one of their favorite stimulants: a walk through the residential streets of Albany. The journalist told his friend that he thought he'd be leaving Albany, and moving out West. A fortune was in the West, there the new political movements would find their greatest strength, he wanted to be in on this; and he'd go to Michigan.

"Don't do it," William Henry advised. "You can do your best here where you are."

"I need money, Seward. I've a big family."

"You can make it here in the East."

"I don't think so. You have a better flair for making money than I have, Seward. You can make money anywhere."

"A lawyer has an opportunity and an insight for money-making—if that is what he wants."

"Who doesn't want it?"

"It's not my main purpose, far from it. I want only enough to be able to take care of my family most properly and then be free to take part in public life. Public service is my ambition, not private wealth."

"I well know that about you, my friend. But as for me, I have a drive toward money as well as a fondness for party life. And I may say I wish I had your wizardry for estimating the value of property, and knowing how to buy land cheap now and sell it dear later. You've turned quite a few pennies that way."

"So I have, but I am exposed to money-making opportunities. Men of property come to me for legal aid. I hear of lands, houses, businesses that are for sale. You have to depend on the one source, your newspaper and your printing business; and a political paper is no way as yet to make a fortune."

"I wish I could afford to be as indifferent to making money as you are."

"I am not indifferent at all," William Henry clarified. "I say merely that I see it as a means and not as a main object."

"I consider it a highly desirable object."

"Well, perhaps you should. However, candidly, Weed, I don't feel overly flattered that you believe me so expert in money-making. I want expertness in areas other than finance and law. I wish I could bring a little more prosperity to others. That would be achievement...."

"It certainly would be, and I think you're the man—"

"Yes, but that's a matter of enlightened public measures—and you know the forces that stand in your way when you make propositions for the general good."

"I certainly do. That's what makes politicians out of statesmen."

"Precisely. Here I am, devoted to the 'right' and yet I am very clear about the fact that honesty does not necessarily have a true place or a high place in practical politics."

Weed was silent, listening.

"—A forthright expression of one's heart can place a man on the ash-heap of politics," William Henry went on. "I'm convinced that all political events are underlain with uncertainty, that the pleasures to be derived from practical politics are not substantial, that the competition is inexpressibly keen...yet I can't control my desire to succeed in this area."

"No man with the bite on him real hard can plug up that hole," Weed said. "Stick with it. Your ambition is your greatest asset."

"I don't know. I wish I could be certain. I'm propelled by this drive beyond my wisdom and my innersight, in dull knowledge of its perils and usually dissatisfying ends."

"We can't help what we are—may I offer that platitude?" Weed suggested.

"My fear is that my enthusiasm for the right, the just, the honest is the

162

factor that can defeat the other ingredient—my ambition to succeed. Yet I can't rid myself of either passion."

"Nobody in the history of world politics who got anywhere ever yet said it was easy."

"My everyday experience teaches me that compromise is everywhere. It rises in front of me white as a ghost that a passion to be right can defeat an ardor to succeed—there's my weakness, Weed."

"We all have our weaknesses. The trick is to see how far we can get, in spite of them."

That amused William Henry.

"Don't talk to me of weaknesses, Seward," the journalist went on. "With all my participation in politics, I can never forget that I want money, lots of it."

"More than you need?"

"Perhaps. I want enough to forget my boyhood days when I mined and farmed and worked on boats and lumbered and wore out my back making pennies and saw my father in debtors' prison. I have fears even now that some ill fate may return me to back-breaking labor to get a few dollars. I dream sometimes of taking coal out of mines; they are white mines from which I draw black coal. I had a devil of a time the first twenty or thirty years, and I still have it."

"I know that; but Weed, you have power. Men follow you. You can be a force for good. Somehow you'll make money, I believe. Your paper will yet earn it for you. We are all growing; everything is growing in this country. Besides, you're too generous; you give money away; you sign notes for unworthy people; your generosity is a fault, it could even defeat your purposes."

Weed refuted that. "It's been my experience that generosity comes back in good will and in friendship, and that the good feeling I get out of giving is itself worth something very much like what money can buy."

"That must be true, Weed. I just never have to buy a cigar when you're around."

Weed said he'd given away twenty thousand cigars so far, and he expected to give away quadruple that number by the time he was done. "A cigar is magic. It's like a wand I wave over men. When I hand them a cigar, or two or three cigars, or a handful of them, some men act as if I am giving them a place in the Senate or a fortune. I have had men accept a cigar and I've seen a light in their eyes strong enough to light the cigar."

Then Weed asked his friend for the recipe for making money.

"I can advise you, Thurlow, but I can't teach you. A man either makes money or he doesn't. I have a suspicion that when the opportunities present themselves you'll know how to convert them. I think you're wiser about such things than when I met you. Meantime, on legal matters, or matters of investment—of course, I can help."

So the partnership between the two had an integral depth. It was bound, like blood to veins, with a kindred interest in cigars, Santa Cruz rum, money-making, philosophy, law and politics; and one gave to the other what the other lacked. William Henry admired the masculine power that Weed exerted over other men. Weed had borrowed thousands from Seward; he admired the fact that Seward could make a fortune at any time he wanted to, but that instead he remained principled, devoted to the public idea, and that he had a disdain for wasting his time "in mere amassing of wealth."

"All right, what about Michigan? What shall I do?" Weed asked.

"Stay where you are. I am taking a friend's freedom when I tell you, 'Thurlow, stay where you are.' "

"I'm sure the opportunities lie West."

"Not for you. You might walk right into failure. Here you're succeeding, yet you don't see it. The *Journal* has so much influence with the people it's bound to support you—and make a surplus too. You've got capital when you own a paper. You can turn that to account in many ways. Hold on to what you have. Some day when the country is bigger, the opportunity riper, you'll be able to sell the little paper you have now for a fortune."

"But land is dirt cheap in Michigan. You can buy it for nothing. In a few years you have a profit." Weed had a little surplus at the time and he was anxious to invest it.

"It's all wrong, I tell you. Weed, you've got good friends among the merchants here in Albany. They'll tell you what to do with a few extra bucks when you have them, but they won't tell you to go West. I want to see the West settled too, and I think it'll be the capital of the country some day, but it's not for you. It's too late in life for you to change businesses and go out into a primal condition like Michigan and live in a savage state."

"You've no great confidence in me as a businessman."

"I wouldn't say that. But your abilities as a political leader stick out so sharply they can be seen all over the country by everyone except you. You'll never be better at anything than you are as an organizer. You've an instinct for the jugular—in politics. You can go anywhere, do anything, take the country with you."

"What's to prevent me from being in politics in Michigan?"

"I'll tell you what. Change in popular opinions is as likely to occur here first as there. Meantime you're the center of the Whigs, a party that's generous, patriotic, at the heart of American progress and decency. We have a program that could bring prosperity and good will to the country forever. Why abandon it?"

"It's just that I thought...."

"I'm not advising you any differently than I advise myself," William Henry interrupted. "I am investing in some stores in Auburn. I know these'll rent very well, and the property will increase in value as the town's size increases. If this investment makes out all right I won't have to bother with any of the usurer's procedures that my soul hates. I'll be finished with lending money, taking notes, buying, selling, and the like. Stay here, Thurlow, and when you can, invest here."

"You've deflated me, Seward, absolutely deflated me. I had been looking forward to a regular covered-wagon trip to Michigan—and now you're keeping me here in Albany!"

"You'll thank me for that advice!"

The lawyer's approach was good. He stayed on in Albany, and his newspaper's circulation increased. The Whig Party grew much in 1835, '36 and '37, and the *Journal* was its principal voice. Printing business came into the news office from the Albany merchants; and Weed's home became an Eastern center for visiting politicians as the journalist deepened his connection with New York Whigs. He was happy that he took William Henry's advice; and his wife, Catherine, was pleased that they hadn't left the capital to do any further pioneering.

Since then, Weed reflected, William Henry acquired a statewide reputation; the next election, that of 1838, might tell a different story. Something new was needed to put over his friend....

Late in December of 1837 there was a light snow over the lower part of Manhattan. In the area known as Printing House Square, later called Park Row, there were a few buildings, already well-worn, where newspapers, magazines and booklets were issued. In one of these structures, at No. 18 Ann Street, a small publication called *The New Yorker* was issued by a twenty-seven-year-old unknown named Horace Greeley. You went up a rickety wooden stairs two flights, turned into an atticlike room, and there was the whole establishment: printshop, a desk for the editor, and the cumbersome press itself.

A few days before Christmas, Thurlow Weed and a companion, Lewis Benedict, who was State Chairman of the Whig Party, decided, while they were in New York, to take care of a certain important detail. They trudged from Weed's room in the City Hotel to the office of *The New Yorker,* they climbed the stairs and walked in. There they noticed a tall, sandy-haired, spectacled young fellow in short sleeves, wearing an apron, and he was diligently setting type.

"I'm looking for the editor," Weed said. He glanced about, and beyond the boyish figure who held a stick of type in his hands.

"I'm the editor, sir."

"You? Is your name Greeley?"

"Horace Greeley."

"Expected to see someone a bit older," Weed said, and he introduced himself and Benedict.

"Here, take seats," Greeley said. He knew both men by reputation, and he was pleasantly surprised at their call.

"You write those Whig editorials?" Weed asked, as if still trying to assure himself he faced the right man.

"Yes, I write them. I'm a tariff man, just as you are. Sit down."

The Albany visitors sat on floppy straw-bottom chairs.

"Would you be interested in editing a Whig campaign paper in Albany, Mr. Greeley?"

Greeley put down the type; and he looked over his glasses at the big man sitting in the narrow chair.

"Well, if you want an offhand opinion, I should think so," the blond fellow answered, "but who recommended me?"

"You recommended yourself."

"What do you mean?"

"Benedict and I have been reading *The New Yorker* in Albany. It's the Whig line. You write well, darned well. That's all we're interested in."

"It's the sort of thing I'd like to think about a bit."

"Certainly. Supposing you have dinner with us this evening at the City Hotel. By then you can let us know whatever is on your mind."

Later Greeley strolled over to the four-story City Hotel, built back in the time when Washington was President. It was getting dark as he quit his office and entered the streets. The gaslighted street lamps were just flaring on; Broadway was quieter, the carriages much fewer; the dogs were indoors for their feeding. He was an elated young man as he headed for the hotel, and his heart leaped as high as the steeple on nearby Trinity Church.

At dinner in the hotel restaurant, the conversation resumed, with Weed amiably telling how he himself was an editor, exactly like Greeley; and before the Albany *Journal* was in its present flourishing conditon, he had been struggling, and he knew what it was to do all the typesetting as well as the writing. "I've treaded pelts a thousand times," he said, speaking of a process of early printing drudgery. Then he got around to Whig politics.

166

The Democrats had held office a long time, he said, they'd be hard to beat. He told Greeley something of the power of the Albany Regency which he and Seward and others had been fighting for years, and hadn't unseated.

Greeley modestly mentioned that he was recently offered a place on the Whig city Assembly ticket, but he had declined it.

Weed bypassed it; he was interested in Greeley as a highly articulate, truly gifted literary propagandist. There was nobody else writing the Whig position at the moment as this fellow did, with fire and honesty. He asked the young editor about his family. Greeley said his wife was a school-teacher; and she wouldn't stand in his way, she was a great help. Yet he didn't want to leave her altogether; and he would like to spend a few days each week in New York City, with her, and with his magazine, which he wanted to continue.

What money would he want? Was there anything to prevent him from going to Albany? How could they work it out?

They settled on a salary of a thousand dollars a year and expenses. Greeley would go to Albany next month; he would spend three days a week in the capital, and the rest of the time he could work in New York.

"Can you suggest a title for the paper?" Weed asked.

"How do you like *The Jeffersonian?*"

"Wonderful," Weed answered. "There are wonderful principles in Tom Jefferson."

"You understand," said Weed, "our job this year is to make William Henry Seward the Governor of New York State?"

"Certainly. I admire him very much. He should make a brilliant Chief Executive."

"I like your enthusiasm, Mr. Greeley."

"Anything I can do for the Whig cause ..."

"Just let's get Seward into the Executive Mansion!"

"Believe me, I'll do my best."

"You can write, Mr. Greeley, you can write like hell."

Greeley hot-legged it to his room in Graham's Hotel, on Greenwich Street, to tell his petite young blond wife, Mary. He was exhilarated beyond anything that ever happened to him. This offer had come just when the fortunes of *The New Yorker* were at the edge of catastrophe. The great panic of 1837 was on, affecting everybody, and very much endangering Greeley's publication. Yet, fortunately, in the recent period he had been forwarding the Whig principles that Weed advocated. He was for a program of extensive internal improvements, a centralized national government, the development of industries, a unified nation. He had the conservative-progressive outlook that characterized the Seward-Weed-Whig program, and now opportunity had walked up his stairway.

As he moved through the snow-white streets of Manhattan, he could still visualize opposite him at the restaurant table the big overmastering figure of Weed, with the husky voice, and the manner of a lumberjack turned intellectual and powerhouse. There was something awesome about the man's mastery, his sense of decision-making; he spoke calmly and what he said came out as an order and a finality; and he had selected him, Greeley, as an assistant. The knowledge that he had looked into the face of power, of a reputed political boss, and a real one, that Weed was intent on making a governor; his closeness to the political method—all this worked in him. He was a nervous, sensitive young fellow; moods rose and fell in him like drifts of snow when a varying wind drives them. What wonderful things might not now happen, he thought, as he hurried to tell his Mary.

Chapter Twenty-Three

"...A GREAT MAN NEVER LIVES AT HOME"

THE swivels in the soul of Judge Miller screeched on their hinges from time to time. He knew that his daughter had become an unhappy woman, and he just about knew the cause. That damned redhead was away all the time. Instead of staying around the town and poking around the garden and spending an evening or two at home with the wife and kids now and then, he was always messing around Albany with Thurlow Weed and big-shotting it around with politicians and moneyed brass. He knew too that Frances was wild about him, and that she sat entranced, listening to him, when he talked. In fact, most people sat around that way when William Henry opened up, the judge mused. William Henry had wit and language and laughter, and the minute he walked into a room everything else took a position round and about him. The judge knew that William Henry was somehow overwhelmed here at the house and that he had always felt that way, and he knew that the town closed in on him; he was a fellow who needed a big arena; the world wasn't too big for him to operate in. He supposed that his son-in-law probably would go even higher up than he was, and he marveled at his money-making abilities. William Henry knew how to buy and sell, he was a trader; he knew where and how to invest, he studied the stock market, he got good fees from clients, and he could scheme up money-making ideas, so that Judge Miller had no complaint there. He wasn't a son-in-law who needed to be supported. He sure had independence; he'd always had that. But he was a wanderer; he couldn't sit still or stay still. The Deep South, Europe, the Frontier: why, this young fellow had seen more of the world than many a sea captain. And Frances, who was a devoted wife, waited for his returns just as if he was out to sea, and as if she were a seaman's wife. They got so as they joked about it in a grim way, sometimes, and they called him Captain.

The judge supposed that it was in some part his fault. He had insisted

169

on Frances staying about as long as he lived; and he had her there. The best thing for her was to be right here in the house all of the time getting the benefit of good food, a good shelter, and plenty of servants and family to help her out with her young ones. She was weak, like her mother had been, as he and Lazette had always known, and he didn't want two in the family to be taken by tuberculosis. Frances herself had to be watched and nursed and tended. So he fathered her constantly, excepting when he sensed that she wanted to be alone so as to think about Henry. William Henry was keeping his part of the bargain, but he sure snuck away a lot; and his daughter wavered like a late lily sometimes. Half the time she was abed, ailing with one thing or another, and the judge, whenever he heard a knock at the front door, wondered what new doctor there was in town. And none of them did a damn thing for her. Her dresser was littered with pills and bottles of take this and take that; and she flitted around the house and out into the yard, and chased about with her sons, and smiled some of the time, and laughed, and usually wound up, back in her room, writing letters to Lazette. It was no way for a woman to live: but he'd be damned if he'd give Frances up. No sir, he wouldn't do that. Besides, they'd tried it, and all such as that was too late now. The house was enlarged; there was plenty of room; Frances loved the place, as she loved her two boys, and whatever was going to happen—well, it was going to happen with things staying just about as they were. So it seemed to the judge.

He spent a lot of time pottering around the yard, cutting the weeds away from the flowers that grew under the windows; squirting powder on plants that were loaded with insects; keeping the grass cut nice and short and even, and barging around the barn. He was a gentleman, along in his sixties now, retired, vitally interested in politics, ready to coach his son-in-law on what move to make next, any time his advice was sought, and the old judge thought things were just about all right. Frances? Oh, she'd come along all right. That spat between her and William Henry, that'd come out all right. They were both pretty sensible.

That was what the judge thought.

Actually the situation was much more grave. Frances was seriously ill. During the next two years she entered into the dark period of her life. Gray illness came over her, and stayed with her, and she wandered about 33 South Street like some forsaken ghost. Much of the time, week after week, she stayed in her room, somehow showing one face to her children, that of a mother filled with love; yet betraying to her mirror the pallid color, the sunken cheeks, the dim and swollen eyes of a creature lost in some desperate inescapable chasm. Along with Henry's absence, there were her own native feminine weaknesses: a sensitivity that resulted from the great sheltering she had received from her family when she was a child, the fear of bad weather, the way she drew into herself when it rained, and the steady coughing in cold weather; and most of all there was the constant frustration because her needs as a woman were simply not gratified, so that she was inclined, as a result, to chastise herself in slight ways.

How, she asked herself, could he leave me when I was pregnant, when I was only weeks away from having Cornelia? Over and over she asked this of herself. Soon after William Henry went to Westfield, desperately, more in love with him than ever, she rushed off lines to him assuring him of this, almost as if she must assure herself: "You will not think that I do not love you abundantly because I have not written before, yet I think of you most of the time. I waited until yesterday to hear from you that I might know where to direct a letter."

Childbearing was desperately difficult for her, though she went through this cheerfully for all the usual reasons of motherhood, but after Cornelia's birth in August she had to stay in bed for weeks, she was so weak. Thereafter her womanly intervals were difficult, desponding her, and in October she wrote to Henry that she had not ventured out of her room in some time, not since her last sickness—"The weather is so dim and unfavorable—and rain rain rain without ceasing— This morning the sun smiles upon us but the gathering clouds are preparing soon to obscure it—and I shall feel dreadful."

She had hurt her finger and she kept William Henry informed of it, saying that it was no worse than it was and she hoped it would be better in time. "I feel that often I have not that confidence and trust in the goodness of God which I ought to have or I would not yield to despondency over trifles like this." Yet the trifles were there all of the time, irritations that flowed from a partial domestic life, a half-married state.

All through that fall, in the bad weather, as the Great Lakes cold swept into the small-lake region, Frances wandered about the house in a more or less chronic dejection. The new child absorbed her, yet in a dull way; she heard the voices of her boys about the house, and she loved them when she looked at them, but her mind raced with harsh dialogues that she conducted with William Henry....Imaginary love moods, when they said harsh things to each other, and sometimes soft things. Now William Henry was being very hard, and her inner ear listened, and an inner tongue answered....

171

"You accuse me of leaving you alone so much; this isn't quite true," he was saying.

"What do you mean?" she asked.

"You have your father with you, haven't you?"

"Of course, but that's not the same as having my husband about."

"Still, you cannot accuse me of bad faith. Your father wished you with him as long as he lived and you are with him and I have accepted that, haven't I? Didn't I suggest you return to this house as soon as I realized I would be away, having a public life much of the time?"

"I thought you had forgotten all that."

"I have forgotten it, I think it's fine that we all have what we have; but my agreement with your father and with you never stipulated that I couldn't leave the house and the town as I wished, to conduct my affairs— now, did it?"

"No, it didn't."

"So we work out our joint course. I remain an adopted son. You remain with your father. He retains you. I have you. You have me. I have my career. It is all working very well, I'd say."

"I suppose that's the way it must be," she said resignedly.

After that passed through her mind a headache came on and it stayed all day.

She wouldn't write to Henry about the dire two-way monologues she was having, but she would let him know of the headaches, and of her love. All into December, while little Cornelia seemed barely to be growing, Frances went on dimly in a post-maternal despondency that was worse than anything she had ever experienced. "I dreamed all night about you some nights ago," she wrote early in December. "You were very sick—your life was despaired of. I awoke crying and I went to sleep only to renew the same impression— Do take care of your health."

Actually William Henry was doing fine. He had the situation of the settlers in hand, and he had an enjoyable Thanksgiving Day, and aside from loneliness for the family, which he was feeling heavily these days, he was in no danger. The dangers were all there at the house in Auburn. He knew that her illness was, in some large measure, related to his absence. He would never have used the word "responsible" in his own mind, to describe his degree of culpability for her chronic dejection of spirit. He preferred to think that it was primarily her rheumatics, her periodic feminine distresses, her sensitive physical construction. He preferred to think that she was weak and easily hurt, and that this was her true and essential nature. He told himself this, even while sometimes he doubted it.

A line from one of her letters cropped into his mind from time to time when he thought of her languishing away on South Street. "I awoke this morning with an aching head and burning and swollen feet—as the delights of dancing all night." She had written that to him when he was three years in the State Senate, on the morning after a New Year's Eve celebration. He was in Albany, preparing to do great deeds in the Legislature, and she had been out to some party, he knew not whose, nor where, but doubtless in their own circle, and the romantic side of Frances had ridden like a madwoman on a racehorse all one night. He couldn't dance for one thing, nor sing for another; he could play neither the violin nor the piano, nor entertain in any of the usual entertainer's ways; he was a limited man that way; he had to be a wallflower at a dance, and just to chat with the ladies in all brilliance, and watch taller men whirl the girls around, so Frances had to suppress in herself the vivacious singing and dancing girl.

Too often he had stared at the phrase in her letters, "You have gone away and left us all alone again." Over and over she put it just that way, bluntly, placing the responsibility for her loneliness upon his absence. He knew he had only to be around and pay attention to her and her spirit brightened and her way quickened like sun suddenly emerging from white banks of cloud. He had seen this scores of times. But how could he stay in Auburn and still become a great political contributor and public servant?—which was his supreme wish.

He had, in fact, already earned a reputation as a professional traveler. Apparently he was known and approved all over the state; everybody seemed to know him personally, no matter what part of the state they came from. Once, at public meeting, a Whig, commenting on the Auburnian's popularity and capacity for travel, said, "Gentlemen, I have learned one thing by going to this convention, and that is, that a great man never lives at home!"

One of the ways in which he countered the realization of her loneliness was to pour consolation into his letters. He knew she depended upon them and that she secured much from them. Frequently, even when he could visualize her sitting around the house with stooped head, mooning and miserable, he wrote congratulatorily of her and himself and of how fine their marriage was. He knew that she was steeping herself in religion, beyond the interest of other women; the Bible was on her lap often and she read it and remembered its tales and could quote from the Book; and he, less religious than she, was moved to cement a relationship by absence, through the religious cord. "I hope that the greater leisure that I enjoy in this occupation [at Westfield, when business settled down] will enable

173

me to cherish, still more, this growing interest in these important matters, and, most assuredly, it is a strong motive with me that I may enjoy with you that communion of sympathy in matters of religion that I do in every other way."

It wasn't true. The simple communion of his being around was lacking, and it had lacked ever since they were married. But he wrote incessantly, emphasizing all that they had in common.

It was working out perfectly for him. There was the home when he wanted that; and outside was the world when he wanted that. He took them both when he wanted either.

He hoped that this wasn't too cruel. This was his curse, and it became hers. This was his trap and his life. He was a dedicated man; something had to give somewhere: and it was Frances' heart. Had she been a woman of little feeling, or if she had had his tremendous resilience, she might not have been so wounded; but there was this deep love she had for him, and his virtual unattainability, and it worked on her like a gyroscope of hope and frustration, and she was being sundered.

The fact was that she had enough affection within her to overwhelm a man, and he didn't seem to require even a small portion of what she could lavish.

She was very probably one of that large army of faithful women, represented in each generation of man, who rarely or never know an ultimate sexual expression. Then, denied one of the most vital experiences of living, and not knowing what it is that they have been denied, but knowing that the denial is great, these unhappy wives usually proceed from one arid oasis to another on quests of realization: books, music, doctors, causes, religion, gambling, other recourses. They are usually the victims of non-malevolent husbands who are merely ignorant of the emotional and biological needs of their wives, and most of all, ignorant of the simple anatomy of the female genitalia. With these matters in darkness there is only a half-marriage, with the female groping in her neurasthenic morass, and for these women, the hypos (so-called in an earlier generation) and the blues or neurosis (in a later one) are inevitable; and faint vapory feelings come frequently, from want of fulfillment.

Frances, in her despair, wrote to him that she feared for the lives and the future of her children. Perhaps the infant Cornelia looked puny to her and didn't grow rapidly enough. Maybe she doubted her own strength and feared she couldn't give the newborn all the attentions it needed. Something worked in her, and William Henry wondered about it. He wrote to her a strangely premonitory line: "When the mysterious ways of Providence are considered, it seems almost presumptuous to hope that all will be

174

spared to us and we to them, during the period of their childhood and youth." But, he cautioned her, while being concerned about such things, "never indulge yourself in such thoughts so as to produce morbid apprehension of undefinable evil."

Something was going on, almost supernal in its symptoms and its indications.

In her own unhappiness she was more than usually aware of the innocence and the delight of her children. She wrote:

"Fred," said I this morning as he brought out an immense number of toys for the day's amusement, "Fred, what do you want most at this time? It seems to me you have almost everything." He replied, "I want Christmas." I answered, "Well, Christmas is almost here, now what can Ma do to make her little boy more happy?" "Why, Ma, I am happy as I can be," said the dear little fellow, throwing his arms around my neck— Childhood is indeed a happy season when children are not much restrained— How often when I look at the bright faces of my little ones and think of their confiding affection, their purity, singleness of heart are the words of our Saviour brought to my mind, "Unless ye become as little children—"

She envied, perhaps, the happiness of her boys. And then, suddenly, there was a swift maturing of the curious premonitions that had passed between them....

She decided that her little girl wasn't behaving right and wasn't looking well, nor growing as rapidly as she should. Cornelia was languid, she nursed with disinterest, and the mother watched this for days, then became concerned enough to call Dr. Emory Humphrey. He was a physician well known to the Sewards, for they attended the same church.

As it happened, that day, Dr. Humphrey attended a smallpox case just before he arrived at the Sewards. He examined the infant girl carefully for several minutes, then he asked about the mother's diet so as to determine whether her milk was good or sufficient, and he said that in his opinion the child would perk up in a day or two and there was nothing to worry about. It was winter, everybody ailed a bit.

But he had handled the little girl in the way an examining physician should. He placed his fingers beneath her eyes and looked at the pupils and the whites of her eyes; he held his thumb on the child's mouth while he peered inside so as to look at the mouth interior and the throat; he poked about her ears, tested her lungs, took her pulse, he breathed into the child's mouth, from closeness to her. He examined her thoroughly—and perhaps infected her thoroughly with smallpox.

As he prepared to leave, and gave simple directions for watching her

175

and asked to be kept informed, he chanced to mention that he had been busy in another part of the town seeing two smallpox cases. But he had hurried straight from these calls over to the Seward house, out of deference to his interest in Cornelia.

Frances quieted a cold alarm inside of her and said, "Doctor, you mean you have just come from a house with smallpox?"

"Why, yes!" The physician's face reddened. "Have no fear, Mrs. Seward. I have been in practice many years."

"I merely asked . . . I . . . I . . ."

He resumed, "There is not a thing I can find wrong with your baby. She is puny, but she is a little girl, delicate, and if you feed her enough she will be all right."

After the smallpox incubation period, Cornelia went into fever. Dr. Humphrey was called again. His face whitened as he recognized what the infant had. "I fear it is smallpox, Mrs. Seward."

"Dr. Humphrey!" She looked at him with accusation. "You came from a smallpox case before you visited here last time."

"Are you charging her illness to me?"

"This is a carelessness on your part!"

"Mrs. Seward, I am a physician. I answer all calls. That is my oath. . . ."

Frances, who had learned to be sharp with most doctors anyway, because none had ever been able to do anything for her hypos, nor to prevent her dizziness, nor her headaches, nor to help her yearnings, said, "Dr. Humphrey, I wish to have the services of another."

"As you choose."

"That is my choice."

Another doctor came. He looked at the child and he said, "Mrs. Seward, you had better call home your husband."

William Henry was notified, and he left Westfield as rapidly as he could get a stage. He traveled night and day, for three days, and he arrived in time to see his daughter as her life was snuffing out. He watched how the entire household tried desperately to keep the infant alive, plying her with medicine and love, all of them exposing themselves to the disease with fearlessness and affection. Cornelia's eyes were closed. They had been closed for four days; and the beauty of infancy had left her face, and her cheeks were soiled with the dread malady.

When she died, Frances, who had always wanted a girl, and now had the girl and then no longer had her, hastened to her room to hide the most uncontrollable grief.

All through the house there was sorrow—and now, too, the fear that the disease might lurk inside anyone in the household. Within each there was an anger toward the physician who, apparently, had brought the disease into the house. Nobody else in the neighborhood had it; there were only two or three cases in the village.

On the following day, in the bitter cold of January, in weather near zero, the burial of the little girl took place in a cemetery on the outskirts of the village. It was a small funeral. A white horse-drawn hearse on runners went first, and inside there was this small white coffin; and the Sewards, in two sleighs, followed.

That evening William Henry went to bed early. He was a desolate man and he felt ill. He lay abed for several hours, not quite asleep, thinking how misfortune had struck his house, how inconsolable Frances was, and wondering what this would do to her, wondering also how terrible God could be ...

Church bells clanged.

He heard first the bells of the Episcopal church, his own church, and he knew the sound very well. Then he heard the Methodist chimes, faster, sharper; he knew that ring; then the rolling, clanging sound of a nearby Baptist church.

Just as he realized they were fire bells, he beheld red light beaming into his window. He had been under some vague impression, optical, that a ruddy moon showed, but the noise cleared his vision; and he reached out and touched the half-somnolent and dejected Frances. "What is it, Henry?"

He leaped from the bed and looked out of the window. It seemed that all of Genesee Street was in flames. A great red roar stretched fifty yards across and lifted high, and the cracking sound of the flames reached their house only a hundred yards away.

"It is right across the street from the Exchange Block!"

That was William Henry's block; or almost his block. It had been built only the year before, a two-story wooden building about sixty yards long, stretching from William Street to South Street, and he had invested heavily in the structure. Whatever he owned was in that building.

"You mustn't go near there, Henry!"

"I have to see what it is, Frances."

"What can you do?"

"I don't know."

He dressed as they talked. The thought occurred to him that if any of the smallpox was upon him, and he went out into the bitter night, he might be courting a disaster.

The northwest wind, always the worst to enter this region, was driving in, and it fanned the flame and carried the blaze high up into the air in their direction. The windowpane of their room reflected red and the flame was so high and wild that the crimson image of the pane rested on Henry's clothes as he dressed. "May as well burn there as here," he said, and he asked Frances for heavy clothing. She saw that he would go, and now, in the excitement, the other grief was overwhelmed.

The household awakened. The judge was too old to go and fight a fire like this; the boys too small; the women too helpless.

He raced to Genesee Street, even in the frigid weather sensing the wave of heat that came toward him; and when he reached the main avenue he saw how the town fire apparatus worked futilely to play a frozen hose on the flames that already burned out the Hyde and Watrous Company store and Bennett's Dry Goods. Small fires raged in Pease's Furniture Store and Camp's Hardware. The red tongues, whipped by the wind, reached across the street to the Exchange building. William Henry saw the first small flame lick up from the rooftop of his own building, but he decided that there was a single fighting chance to save the property. A few young men known to him consented to go up on his roof and help him put out the flare-ups as rapidly as they started.

Across the street the blaze swept westward to Crashy and Polkbun's Dry Goods Store. Sharp explosions came from T. M. Hunt's Drug Store, and then there was a large double report from Crump's Gun Shop: gunpowder exploded: and at once the fire spread to Bemus and Leonard's Restaurant. By midnight twelve buildings, the entire block from State Street to North, were aflame.

Yet a few feet away, on the Exchange Block roof, William Henry directed a half-dozen assistants with buckets of water and wet blankets. This crew doused the burning spots and fresh falls of sparks as rapidly as the shingles caught them.

The regular fire volunteers gave up, and they simply fell back from the flames and watched the business section of their town turn into yellow and red. The water had frozen in their buckets and in their hoses before they could turn it against the buildings.

Strangely, and it was the kind of anomaly that William Henry was fond of referring to, the heat of the fire that swept away one whole side of the street warmed the water that was in use on top of the Exchange Block.

By half past three fourteen buildings were in ashes, and the Canadian wind blew the ash all over the snowdrifts; so that ash and snow piled up against the Exchange building.

It was still the dark of night when he got home. The bells no longer clanged and there was no red light imaged against the Seward windows.

His clothes were wet and stiff to his body as he entered the house and fell exhausted on a divan in the parlor.

He slept on and on, and when he vaguely awakened they told him that they had taken off his wet clothes only with difficulty, that he had been sleeping so for hours. He could hardly answer them; he moved into fever and within another day he was near coma.

The doctors said that he developed the varioloid, a disease similar to smallpox, but a lighter case of it.

A day or two later ten-year-old Augustus came down with the same malady.

Now the house on South Street was one big hospital of death that had been and disaster that might be.

Two weeks later William Henry was sitting up in bed, and a couple of days after that he was moving about the house. But Frances was inconsolable. She, moving about, might have been sicker than he, recovering from a serious disease. There was a droop to her head as she walked, as she sat, as she looked at him. A light had gone from her eyes; it was as if she could still see and feel Cornelia in her arms, and her hands were nervous as if they had been robbed of something they needed to keep them busy. It gave William Henry the shudders to see her looking so. He tried words of consolation, but she listened apathetically.

He saw that he could not easily revive her spirits. The only thing that could ever accomplish this miracle would be his permanent residence here, and that could never be. He fell silent. Inside he was hearing wagon wheels; they were rumbling over the ruts in the road; the horses were neighing, and their tails flapped like flags of the road against their flanks; he felt the huge iron wheels churning, and they sent a hard echo through him with each complete cycle. Now here was the house again, filled with people, all in mourning, he himself disconsolate, surprised that he was alive, moving about the house gingerly, testing his limbs, sending a letter to Weed to see if the disease had left him bereft of his mental powers—for that was the biggest pride of his existence.

A few more days turned like this, as the wheels of a stage, going somewhere, and he knew he must go somewhere.

A letter came for him from Westfield. His assistants said there was great unrest among the Chautauquans. There was a rumor that he had absconded with money; the settlers believed they wouldn't get the deeds to their lands, and the old spirit of uprising was showing itself again. Come back as soon as you can, his clerks said; they were afraid, and didn't know what to do without him.

179

William Henry had resilience; it was one of his principal resources; he had bounce and recovery; there was little that could floor him for long; nothing yet had ever done so; he knew the size of the tragedy in the house, and what it was doing to Frances, but he knew he had to rise above this; he must, he would, and he dropped hints to Frances of the situation out west; and she knew very well he'd be going soon.

When he returned to Westfield he wrote a judicious letter to her, saying that they were again separated, my dear Frances, she had their living and their dead with her, and the home with which they were associated, and it was he who was far away and all alone; yet she would be the mourner, for she was the stricken one, she was the woman, the mother.

His words took on a certain beauty then, and he intended them to, for he knew there was little he could do now but assuage her with words. "The lightness that was in all my heart when I thought of you and your sanctuary, and those who surrounded you there, was the main constituent of my cheerfulness, for I was always thinking of you; I am now always thinking of you, but I imagine you sitting alone, drooping, desponding, and unhappy; and, when I think of you in this condition, I cannot resist the sorrow that wells within me." If he could be with her to urge her to more active pursuits, to varied study, or more cheerful thoughts, he might save her for herself, her children and himself—but he couldn't be, so he had another suggestion.

She could go to the arms of Jesus.

"I must commend you, as all must do who would console you, to the offices and to the consolations of that religion you so highly appreciate; and it will be in my power to meet you, night and morn, before the Creator, in asking him to make us both sensible of the purpose of the affliction we have suffered. Let this, then, be understood between us; and it will perhaps enable us to bear with a more fitting submission the calamity which has befallen us."

Written somewhat like a state paper, somewhat like a legal brief, very much in a poetic prose, and with an underlay of sentiment and devotion that he really felt, he had proposed to her that he, in Westfield, pray each morning and night and think of her—while she did the same in Auburn.

In her grief, Frances moved deeper into a mysticism in which the word G-O-D loomed prominently, frequently, in her thoughts. If she couldn't have William Henry at home as much as she desired, she could have Someone Else. When she got this letter, and it suggested a form of communion between them, a moment of meeting early each day across barriers of green hills and secular responsibilities, she was deeply touched; and each morning thereafter, when she awoke, alone in her room, she knelt by the bedside, and there, in prayer, she spoke through the Lord to William Henry.

To reinforce this telepathic connection with Frances, for it apparently gratified her, he became baptized into the Episcopal Church at Westfield. Two months later he described the event. "I was alone at the font," he wrote. "I thought continually of you and my boys, and our child-angel, Cornelia, that left her errand with my heart and straight returned to heaven." The death of Cornelia had moved him into a deeper religious feeling; it had brought him and Frances closer—though miles and counties and months separated them—and Frances could derive the feeling from this that she had influenced him toward her Church.

Chapter Twenty-Four

WHAT! BROOMS FIFTY CENTS APIECE?

EARLY in the winter of 1837, at about the time William Henry was ill in Auburn, there was an unprecedented excitement in the lower part of New York. Five thousand harassed and hungry men, men who had families, gathered in the snow-decked green of Union Square, and listened to a half dozen speakers urge them on to act against the growing crisis of unemployment, high prices, and tight money.

There was a way to show that they meant business, said the leaders: we were free men who had fought for our rights against foreign invaders, now we would demand our due from the rich and powerful at home. Men in Washington and at Albany had brought on this condition, they charged; speculators had plunged our country into desperate straits, so—on to the flour warehouses! Show them!

The thousands, in an angry surge, moved on the sidewalks and in the street westerly along brownstoned Fourteenth Street, turned down Hudson Street, and headed for the waterfront area, to Washington Street, where the flour was stored in a huge wooden granary. There was a dull drumming music up front, an ominous beat, *duUm duUm—duUm DUM DUM.* Over and over a simple marching chord, as the laborers, dressed in their wrinkled and soiled workmen's clothes, trod through the avenues with the ancient rage of men denied.

They reached the warehouse, and they smashed open the broad front door. They busted the windows and plunged inside. A relay of demonstrators carried sacks of flour into the street. Outside the mob ripped up the bags, and scooped up the flour with their hands and spread it over the cobbled pavement.

On and on came the white refined wheat in great brown-and-white burlap bags, and in barrels, two and three men manning each bag or barrel, and this precious germ they scattered till the whiteness rose as a fog of powder in the neighborhood, and it settled like a snowfall a foot deep on the cobblestones, and the clothes of the demonstrators looked white.

The leaders leaped to the stairs on the store fronts once more and egged on their followers to the other side of the town, to another warehouse. Let the snow fall again, and let the councils and the legislatures of the city and nation know that Labor was alive! Let the lawmakers get busy and restore work and wages and food, or prepare for a big change—and the hint of revolt was in it all.

But the police arrived in large numbers, blue uniformed men on horseback, and, with clubs waving, they charged the rioters.

The demonstrators never got to the warehouse on the other side of town, but what they did became news and a sign heard all over the country: this was the virtual signal that hard times had come to America.

It was, perhaps, the first bread riot in our history. From then on contenders for public office knew that they must consider thereafter the rights of the workingmen—and the Whigs, like Thurlow Weed and William Henry, saw in this a meaning and an opportunity. Now was the time for a political upheaval. The Whigs must consider the "workies," as they called them, and take seriously the rights of the nation's laborers.

An extravagant period of speculation had been on for years; nearly everybody sought land, houses, and business enterprises, or bigger bank balances. All through the 1830s stock-market investment was heavy; shareholding companies of many types formed in the bigger communities, and they ventured into construction enterprises; workingmen, if they saved a few dollars, tried to become businessmen or landholders. William Henry bought into housing and land; while Weed, with a few hundreds of surplus, entered into realty adventures around Albany which weren't profitable. Meantime, banking and governmental circles were rocked by a question: whether banks should freely distribute paper money. Andrew Jackson, in his regime that would close at the beginning of 1837, had overthrown the national bank and established a policy known as the "hard money" doctrine. He left the White House in good repute, after proposing Martin Van Buren as his successor, but Van Buren, just taking office, would inherit the problems of the financial disaster.

In New York City, two hundred and fifty businesses stopped paying their creditors. Then came scarcity, increased prices and black market. Brooms which had, for a hundred years, cost twenty-five cents, now sold for a half-dollar. Shad, the principal fish of the poor, couldn't be bought under seventy-five cents or a dollar a fish. Corn was scarce, meat and poultry so costly as to be prohibitive to most families; and the well-to-do who had bought up rich furniture and imported rugs were forced to sell their possessions. At the banks the people were maddened, and women with some small savings pressed against the doors and screamed "Pay! Pay!"

In politics there is no disaster that is not someone else's opportunity. As the financial collapse settled over the nation and reached the Mississippi, the prestige of the Democratic party, which had ruled for many years, fell away. People, looking for a new political force to pilot them out of their troubles, believed that this body was in existence: it was the Whigs, led by Weed and Seward, Francis Granger, Millard Fillmore and others.

On the evening of October 6th a huge Whig meeting was held at the Masonic Hall in New York. It was an oddity of the gathering that many of those present, who would henceforth call themselves Whigs, were, not long before, anti-Masons. A few weeks later the Whigs were sent into office everywhere, in large numbers; and especially they swept into leadership in New York State.

William Henry, guarding his interests at Westfield, stayed in touch with Weed, and campaigned for Whigs running for the State Senate and the Assembly.

Already there was talk from the Hudson to Lake Erie that the next governor, come the 1838 elections, would probably be one of two men, either Francis Granger or William Henry Seward.

Chapter Twenty-Five

FRANCES GETS A FITTING FOR A NEW WINTER HAT

IN MID-JANUARY of 1838 William Henry walked into the newspaper office of Thurlow Weed over Grange Sard's clothing store on State Street, in Albany. The journalist had a provocative greeting, "Look who's here, the heartless speculator—"

William Henry returned a wry smile. Weed went on, "Heartless speculators always welcome at the *Journal* offices—"

But William Henry didn't respond in the way Weed expected him to. Instead, as the Auburnian sat, he said, "Weed, I'm disgusted."

"What about? You're going to be governor."

"Oh, the worthwhileness of things—the little sincerity that I meet with, and I see practically no successful accomplishment anywhere. There's so little security that I can hold it in my fist with my fingers closed around the little that there is."

Still, Weed's mood was delight, and William Henry remarked, "I see a hundred and one sparkles in your eyes—"

Weed laughed triumphantly. A hundred and one Whig candidates for the Assembly had been elected in the recent statewide elections, out of one hundred and twenty-eight seats.

William Henry said, "I damned near get heart failure thinking about all this distress." He reached into a pocket, and drew out a handful of small printed cards. He laid them on the journalist's desk. "Here's what they're using in Auburn for currency and credit...."

They were called "shinplasters" and they were issued by companies, stores, individuals, anybody who could afford to print them. They were promises to pay, I.O.U.'s, and they were passed about from person to person, where the currency-makers were known.

The lawyer asked, "How long shall we be living like this—bartering our credit and our labor like primitives?"

"Relax, it's only temporary. We Whigs'll straighten that out."

```
TONTINE COFFEE HOUSE
This is good for
25 CENTS
In Edibles
Caldwell and Kenyon
```

```
I promise on demand to pay the bearer
Four Shillings
Alexander Walsh
```

But William Henry poured out his troubles. "I'm in a thousand scrapes. I don't scarcely have enough money to plant my garden seeds, yet I find all my neighbors, Whigs and Conservatives, wanting my name and my help. I just got a call from two close political friends who asked me to help them, and I can't do a damned thing for them. What makes it rough is that they don't believe I'm broke. They don't know I'm four hundred thousand dollars in debt to the Holland Land Company. They only see my financial reputation, not my contracts."

Weed tried a light diversion. "Where's the family?" he asked. "I heard they were with you."

They were, said Seward; they were at the Eagle; they'd all stay overnight, and head for New York the following day.

"It's quite a trip for Frances, isn't it?"

"I couldn't say no to the girl. We see so little of each other. When she said she wanted to go with me this time and take the boys, I surrendered."

The journalist reached into his battered oak desk and pulled out a bottle of rye. "Look, if you don't cheer up, I'll have to find another governor—" and he haw-hawed uproariously. Then he said, "I know what's *really* bothering you—"

William Henry looked inquiringly.

"I think you're upset by the attack of the Regency. Now if that's it, I want you to cheer up and forget about it. We'll lick those bums—"

Weed was right. William Henry was under a slanderous attack throughout the state. Principally the Democrats circulated handbills throughout the

186

state accusing him of being a "wealthy and heartless speculator by trade who is out to rob the poor settlers of Western New York of millions of their earnings." They claimed that the bonds and mortgages of the settlers in Chautauqua County were now in Wall Street—and the term Wall Street had the connotation then among farm folk that it has today. "A trust company has a deed to all the land of the settlers, and Seward has raised money in Europe at an interest of five per cent while he demands seven per cent of you, the settlers. He and his associates pay interest annually while they extort interest from you semi-annually."

When that handbill was brought into his office at Westfield he got a sudden bigger taste than ever of the terrible competition for high office; he sensed how unclean his world, the political world, could be; it was a shame, he thought, that a man who wanted to work in behalf of the public interest had to march through so much mud to get into the spot where he could put enlightened philosophy into life.

"What are we going to do about the 'heartless speculator's charges?" the lawyer asked.

"Ignore them right now. Wait till October, when the fight is high. Then we answer them."

Weed stood, and asked William Henry into an adjoining room. "There's someone in here that's working hard for you, Governor. Better come meet him."

They walked into a small quiet office where William Henry saw a young man in his mid-twenties, very busily moving a quill over white paper. The writer was scholarly-looking, with bright blond hair and a pale face.

"Greeley," Weed called out, "meet the Governor."

The young man rose. There was a slight stoop to his shoulders, as if he had done much studying, and as if the mark of it remained. He stood, much taller than William Henry, and they shook hands.

William Henry remarked how he had been putting out effort recently around Auburn, to get subscribers for the new paper. He had political workers in the field, they signed several hundred subscribers, but they certainly needed to do better. "Perhaps after we get the first few issues out the circulation will grow."

Weed interrupted: the first one was due about the middle of February.

Greeley shyly explained what he was writing; he was putting forward moderate views, which he hoped expressed the Whig outlook; he was trying to capture Democratic voters, he said, and hoping to pull them into the Whig fold.

"Excellent," said William Henry.

187

"I like just about everything Greeley writes and he has a free hand," Weed said.

Greeley nodded gratefully. Gently he expressed admiration for William Henry, said he hoped that his efforts would be of real help in the developing campaign.

Weed, with his incessant eye for the right small detail, pointed to a coat that hung over the back of a nearby chair. "See that coat?" he said to William Henry. "That white coat—?"

"Yes."

"Young Greeley here wears that damned thing; it makes him look like a snowman. Says he got it off an Irish immigrant, bought it for twenty bucks. Now you know, Bill, anybody that goes around wearing a white overcoat while everybody else wears them dark has got something on the ball!"

William Henry remarked that in this country every man was entitled to his own trademark.

Greeley felt indulged and flattered by the attentions of the two big Whigs. He glowed inside at the thought that he was supremely well-connected now and on his way: fortune was favoring him.

So the first meeting of all three was of the essence of warmth.

The next day the weather warmed, and the water dripped from the trees, the sun was out and the temperature was up. The Hudson trembled with weakened ice. The Sewards headed for Greenbush, on the opposite side of the river from the capital. From that landing they'd go by stage to the village of Hudson, and there board a steamboat for New York.

But first they set out in a small rowboat managed by two guides. The rowers took them well out onto the cold green water until they reached a ledge of ice. They reached the ice where they expected to be able to walk for a distance to an ice sled. But the prow of the boat crumbled the thin ledge, and the ice kept yielding. To add to the hazard, the waiting sled was only big enough to carry them ashore two at a time.

All clambered out of the boat, and they moved tenderly over the ice. It gave beneath them, and no one could stand still without sinking. The guides abandoned them, and ran on ahead. William Henry told his family to spread out, not to stay in one spot, else the whole sheet would crack. The parents lagged behind their two boys. August was twelve now, a heavy-set boy, athletic, with a rude vigor about him, and he was unafraid. Fred was only eight; he was slender, more a version of his father, and the more mental of the boys. Each, in his own style, leaped along, picking what seemed to be the sturdier ice.

Somehow they got in, all reaching the shore safely, but shaken by the experience.

They went on, to New York, to stay at the Astor House: but Frances saw the fallacy of her desperation to be with her husband. She knew now that her husband's life was a different thing than hers must be, and she knew how wrong it was to risk her children in this way.

A month later Frances and her boys returned to Auburn. She knew, when she got home, that that trip with her husband might well be her main, her longest intimacy with him during the whole year: from now on, he'd be a cyclone over the state, campaigning, passing time at Westfield, and making fleet trips to Auburn.

That was just what happened.

In the hot political days of summer, 1838, when William Henry was abroad in the state, giving speeches in the town halls of the state, meeting with local Whigs, combating the charges made against him by the Democrats, there was, at one time in Auburn, a silence from him that lasted for weeks. Frances was variously dejected, angered and anxious. Had something happened to him on a stagecoach? There were always such mishaps. Had he been battered at a political rally? Often the meetings were near to violence. The Democrats were fighting back hard now against Whig accusations that the Jackson administration brought ruin to the country. Or had he just been downright irresponsible and forgetful?

Where was he? What was he doing?— "I try to think you can explain it all when we hear from you," she wrote— "I am sure you would not give us so much pain— Our children too are sadly mortified—and I know I never had the horrors so dark—do write one line of consolation— Your own Frances."

Right after that a letter came; it had crossed hers to him, and she got some picture of what he was up against. He had a special rival in Francis Granger; many of the Whigs wanted the prominent Granger to be the candidate, when the time should come to nominate someone later in the season, and that was a ticklish political situation because he and Granger were excellent friends, and both were close to Weed. Moreover, the assault continued on him all over the state, his enemies charging him with being the friend of the rich and the bankers, and an enemy of the public interest; and he must handle hecklers at public meetings; and he was accused of being all over the state at the same time, in order to get the nomination. The controversy was simply tremendous, he told her, and he went to bed night after night exhausted. He tried to do his traveling by night, when it was cooler, but the steady movement over the state, day or night, was fatiguing, and it left him too tired to write, or to know what to say, and so, please excuse him. "Yet I know full well that it is the mind that makes peace or war," he wrote, "that it is my temperament and constitution that attract the thousand cares."

When he put it that way, she found a quill pointed with understanding:— "I am very sorry you have so many sources of vexation—but it is the lot of all, particularly those who are in any way distinguished—the higher the eminence the more thorny the path—you are better calculated to bear all this than most men—you have an equanimity of temper which is better than all the philosophy in the world—and then the comfort of a good conscience."

So she soothed him, trying, when she didn't depress him with the details of her vapor attacks, to spur him with her support. And he was responsive to her cheer, too; her encouragement reinforced him doubly when it came, for so often he was used to her disconsolate outpourings.

She well understood that it should be part of her activity as a politician's wife to entertain certain people about the village, politicians who worked for her husband, and their wives; but she didn't like large gatherings, she disliked entertaining, and she didn't care to have people fawn over her because of her husband's achievements; she didn't wish any importance to attach to her unjustifiably, merely because her husband was a doer; she didn't like to sense sycophancy in people, directed toward her because of favors her husband might be able to bestow; she was used to meeting with this attitude among people, and she sent a letter of complaint about such affairs to her sister— "I am undoubtedly thought very unsocial and wish I did feel more disposition to visit but the little inclination I once had seems to have very much diminished—this is a penalty that everyone has to pay for living in a large house—people who make themselves believe that you think you are too good to call on them if they are not called upon—for my part it seems to me that I should feel as I do feel when I am away from home, quite satisfied with a limited number of acquaintances— I cannot now manage to call upon all with whom I am on visiting terms once a year and the remainder of the inhabitants undoubtedly think excessive pride the consequence of their being neglected—perhaps you will think I overrate the estimation in which I am held but I know that the small degree of importance with which I am invested does not arise from any intrinsic merit— I have been led to make these observations now from having recently met a number of people in whom these feelings were so obvious that they could hardly disguise their ill will—"

Being a politician's wife had its complexities; being semi-invalided added to the burden; being disposed to fill her eyes with her immediate family, her children, and the other kin further intensified her hearth-loving characteristics.

An attitude like that was bound to lead to something inevitably, and one night when Frances felt much obligated to entertain several politicians and their wives, especially as the campaign for William Henry was mounting everywhere, she rather suddenly decided to have a little informal gathering at the house.

But it seemed to get swiftly out of hand, and it became a large party, she said, writing to him a few days later, with crashers wanting to get into the important Seward house— "I sent for Mrs. Benedict, Mrs. Beach and six or seven other ladies with as many gentlemen. They all came late and seemed inclined to make a regular party of it very contrary to my design— Dr. Frank Hamilton said he was informed that the invitations were very general—he hesitated about coming on that ground but happened to meet Mrs. Yates who set him right— I told him he could not desire less to be in a large party than I did— I believe the evening passed away agreeably to all—for my own part I took some ether to allay a violent headache which somewhat exhilarated my spirits besides curing my head— I was just felicitating myself on having at last obtained so desirable an object when all my fine projects were put to flight by a consultation with Dr. Hamilton who informed me that ether not infrequently produced apoplexy—the little boys were much afraid that I had killed myself that night— I had no apprehension as the quantity I took was very small—now I doubt this expediency of resorting again to so dangerous a remedy— the effect of the ether lasted until about 11 o'clock—by that time the company had all dispersed and I retired to bed—then came on my headache with renewed violence— I obtained but little sleep that night."

William Henry was at Westfield, taking care of his realty and legal affairs at the time, and he was a badly shaken-up man when he received the strange letter.

Where would it all end? he wondered.

What was Frances trying to do? Wouldn't she let him have his career?

What, he asked himself, would ever disengage her of her now-dangerous melancholy?

As the autumn came on and William Henry's prospects for the gubernatorial nomination seemed clearer than ever, he realized that he owed a debt to the brilliant young Greeley.

The gangly editor had a pen of power and magnetism, for, during recent months, the circulation of *The Jeffersonian* grew to 11,000 weekly. The paper circulated over New York State and beyond, so that Weed and

William Henry and the other Whig leaders were jubilant; soon, they hoped, Greeley's smash-bang editorials would bring the paper to a circulation of 30,000; then they would move in on the Democrats for keeps; in November whip them to a frazzle.

Weed sent a copy of another newspaper, the Fredonia *Censor,* to William Henry. In the paper was an article ostensibly written by William Henry, actually ghost-written by Greeley. The lawyer jumped out of his seat when he read it. What a clever writer Greeley was! He had mimed William Henry's own style.

"I have never seen anything better timed, or in better temper, or more discreet," William Henry wrote to Weed. "I started from my chair as I read it, and said to myself, 'No man could believe that this was written by anybody but myself.' Its temper, manner, and the very facts used, seemed to be exclusively my own."

So they were on their way: Weed, Seward and Greeley: a company literally to be known as an inseparable trio, as a Company, for a long time to come.

One day in September, when William Henry was in Auburn, he received a wire from Utica where a Whig nominating convention was on, saying he had been unanimously proposed by their party for the governorship, and would he accept?

Would he?

He wired back that he would—"with a profound sense of the honor conferred upon me." Then, in succeeding days, he issued the telling letter that replied to the Democratic charges that he was a "heartless speculator." It was a long detailed letter which described fully his relationship to the Chautauqua settlers. Addressing himself to the farm folk themselves, he said, "You will recollect that, in all the settlement of the estate, no cent of compound interest or of costs has gone into my hands; no man has ever lost an acre of land which he deisred to retain, with or without money —no arrears have been prosecuted—no foreclosures instituted, and every forfeiture relinquished, upon an agreement to pay interest."

The Democrats met at the same time the Whigs did, and they re-nominated Governor Marcy; but Thurlow Weed sensed a groundswell for the man he named. . . .

On a Saturday afternoon early in November, a few days after the statewide elections were held, and when the returns were official, a Whig parade moved along Genesee Street, turned into South, and stopped in front of the Miller house. Drums rolled for a while as a few militiamen set up a cannon on the lawn. The cannon boomed on and on until a hundred shots were fired. So they honored their redhead, and many remarked how an enormous majority had rolled up for him in Chautauqua County where a critical issue of the campaign had centered.

Inside the Miller house there were varieties of emotion.

The judge was as excited as a schoolchild.

William Henry paraded up and down the parlor, exclaiming, "God bless Weed! I owe this result to him!"

He experienced the elation of a man who hopes there is a heaven; he dies, and then he wakes to discover that he is really in heaven.

Frances wasn't at all surprised at his election, nor unduly impressed. She had sensed this coming for years; she must have, or it wouldn't have been in her dreams. This was simply something that he was capable of. He was brilliant; he could make money; he was full of philosophy; he wrote like a poet; he was a dreamer; and he had ambition enough for several men.

She knew that he was bigger than his size.

Anything could happen with this man who was her husband.

Added to that, he had Thurlow Weed in back of him. Weed was a powerhouse. Put two such men together, you'd get what they got.

Everything that was important wasn't happening in Albany, or in politics. She was pregnant again, and very subjective about the condition, naturally; perhaps more concerned with that actually than with her husband's election. He had in his grasp something that he wanted, and it was great; but she knew that soon she'd be feeling life inside her. That was an experience no man could possibly conceive the magnitude of, self-centered as they might be, vain as they might be, ambitious as they might be. A little quickening in the center—and a woman made something far more intricate than a transient political measure.

So she took this occasion, the very day of his political triumph, to confront him with his latest creation in another area.

"That means, Henry," she said quietly, "we're both having interesting things happening to us."

"What's that?"

"Yes."

"Why didn't you say so—?"

"I just did!"

"I'm delighted. I hope it's a girl."

"Whichever, Henry—as the Lord sees it. If it's a boy I'll name him for you."

"This *is* a full day."

How would his election affect her? she wondered. She had a hunch that

193

in some kind of way it would bring him closer to her: all of his successes did bring him nearer, but in particular spiritual, philosophic and religious ways. Physically his triumphs seemed to carry him farther away. Yet if he were in the Executive Mansion, he'd be there for two years, and be held there. No traipsing around the state and the country for him then. If she went to the capital, would she, under the executive roof, see and have more of him than heretofore?

She was thinking these things when something recurred to her vaguely, out of the past.

That was it, a dream.

She had a dream once, a dream of entertaining the Governor and his Lady. In the dream she had put on a winter hat.

Now isn't that odd? she mused, the Governor and his Lady. I must write to Lazette of this at once.

Chapter Twenty-Six

"....THE YOUNG MAN BEARING THIS NOTE"

ABOUT ten days before the New Year, William Henry, with an inaugural address in his buffalo-hide briefcase, and Augustus, with a big red apple in a side pocket, set off for Albany.

Gus was no stranger to the capital; he was a big lad, already taller than his father. Frances said he reminded her of some of the peasantlike Millers that she was related to. He had a facial resemblance to his father, but with brown hair, and the rest of him was just built differently—like the Millers, taller and bigger and broader.

On the last lap into Albany father and son were alone inside a coach; it was cold and dark in there, and they clung close beneath huge blankets.

"I don't think we're going to live in the house that the state bought for the outgoing governor," Pa told Gus.

"Why not, Pa? It's our'n."

"*Ours,*" said William Henry, correcting him.

"Well, why not?"

"I got another idea—"

"Not the Eagle?"

"Oh, no. We're through putting up there."

"Well, gee, don't you *have* to live in the governor's house? Ain't it a law?"

"*Isn't* it a law—" That street language he was always picking up! They had to watch Gus closely for his associations about the village. He tended to be drawn toward boys with specially mischievous streaks: William Henry once told Frances not to worry about Gus' associates if he only got plenty of love and attention at home.

"Son, if I can get it, I'm going to rent the Kane Mansion—"

"That big place at Westerlo and Broad streets...?"

"That's the place. I need a lot of room and a lot of privacy; and I don't like to live off the public treasury. I'd rather spend till I'm broke than have the state maintain me and be indebted."

"But Pa, you get a big salary when you're governor?—"

"Being governor'll cost me four or five times what I get for salary before I'm through."

"I don't understand. Don't get it—"

"Don't try too hard, Gus. It's the way I like to do it. Like to have a big house of my own. It's more relaxed, and we can have more people around—"

Gus flashed a big smile of proud agreement. "Who'm I to tell the Governor of New York State what to do?"

The big sleigh scudded on the snow-packed streets that wound down into the Capitol area. They were silent; Gus peered out the window at the two-story houses; he'd be going to school here now; and as for the Governor, he seemed to be dozing, but really his mind was full. There is a qualitative moment in everyone's life; perhaps there are many such moments in most lives, thinking moments, when two or more things have been joined, and there is discovery or realization, and time or change has taken place.

The young Governor was thinking of a friend, an important New England friend whom he'd heard from a few weeks earlier when his election became known. It was John Quincy Adams, the elder statesman of American politics, the big man of New England.

It came back to William Henry how he'd first seen and met and talked with Adams only seven years earlier. . . .

It was autumn of 1831; the anti-Masonic surge was high in the state; he was bumptious with success in the Senate, all eagerness to travel with the high and mighty, and be of them. He had received a letter at Albany from a Boston anti-Mason saying that in that city there was much unpleasantness over whom the anti-Masons intended nominating for President. He showed the letter to Thurlow Weed. Weed and Albert Tracy decided that William Henry ought to go to Boston and learn what the situation was.

A few days later he reached the plain little house in Quincy, Massachusetts, where John Quincy Adams lived. It was just a two-story structure about sixty feet long, with a few ancient and gnarled trees in the sideyard, and he took an old-fashioned knocker into his hand.

He waited in the parlor for "Old Man Eloquent," as they called him, to appear. The house is plain, even old-fashioned, William Henry said to himself. There was no imported carpeting from Turkey or Persia, no pier tables and no venerable piano with legs like pillars and lionlike paws at the base. A plain carpeting of brown over the floor, a solid-colored wall papering, simple chairs of mahogany, and a few portraits of George

Washington and Martha Washington, and another of Thomas Jefferson, and one haunting portrait of John Adams, Revolutionary patriot and founder of the Adams dynasty.

Down a nearby staircase a small man descended....

Perhaps he was sixty or more years of age, bald, serious of face, with almost a sorrowing look in his set features. It was Adams, and his eyes seemed reddish, as from tears, or too much reading, or too much living; he was dressed in an olive coat, a tie flowed loosely about his throat, and he wore a light gray-colored vest and pants of the same grayish color.

The visitor walked forward, handed over a letter of introduction written by Albert Tracy; and Adams took it, and told William Henry to sit while he glanced through the note:

...the young man bearing this note is a figure of prominence in his State, and of great promise. He is an admirer of your leadership, knows your work and writings profoundly, would deem it a great distinction to know you; and you in your turn, Sir, will have an opportunity to talk with one on whom an aura of leadership has already fallen, in spite of his boyish manner and hardly more than a boy's years.

They talked for three hours, of anti-Masonry, of the American people, and of personalities of the day; of the distinction of Daniel Webster, of General Jackson and of the Seminole War; and they drifted into talk of Presidential possibilities for the 1832 elections. The conversation got around to the leading Southern exponent, and Adams said, "I have long hoped that Calhoun would adopt better principles for our country."

"I believe," William Henry answered, "that he is unmitigatedly committed to slavery principles."

"Then it will do our nation no good," the former President said. "It is a shame, though, for Calhoun has enormous powers." The elder statesman went on, "I think him insincere; I think he has the sin of a frustrated and unending ambition."

William Henry was there as a leader of the anti-Masons, and to help find a Presidential candidate. They had discussed Henry Clay, and Adams said he had not an overwhelming confidence in that man. Then, suddenly, William Henry thrust out as President-maker, "And how about yourself, sir? Would you care to be our candidate?"

"I shouldn't desire to be President again, even if it were a unanimous vote. I know its duties, its privations, its enjoyments, its perplexities, and its vexations. I have been President."

"That is definitive?"

"If your party thought that my nomination would be better than any

197

other I would accept it, for I don't have, as a citizen, a right to decline, and I would not decline ... but I hope it will not be mentioned."

"I thank you, sir, for the expression of your view."

The recollection of the meeting, symbolical and practical, returned to William Henry and jogged before his eyes as the sleigh carried him and Gus into Albany.

Now he would have the chance to put into execution some of the principles that had grown with him as he had grown with them.

There was a thread in his life, and a cloth; and, with this opportunity, he could weave a flag of his own design. He knew that he—or someone— had to carry on from John Quincy Adams, the highest product of that political hour in American life—and that statesmen stemming from this time on had to carry on upward from Adams—or sink downward from Adams. There was no reason to recede, that was unthinkable in a nation and territory rising and spreading and flowing as this one then was; yet the need to carry on, spiral-fashion, from what there was to what there might be, represented vision, and he either must have it, or someone must have it. Why not he? True, Daniel Webster and Henry Clay were alive, and they stemmed from the Constitution-makers; but they were older men. He was of a young new party, which would likely become something bigger and better and different a little later; he and other young public men like himself would grow into the national process, become the country itself, the history itself, the guide for the spread of a broadening way of life.

A young politician had to sense all of this, as a poet sensed the green truth in the summertime, as an artist saw the annular rings within a tree behind the bark that he painted, as a composer might behold musical notes in the shape of a wild rose.

He must run forward, bearing the torch into some mystic future—to whatever course, whatever end, only the fates of unfolding political events could ultimately know.

He knew that Adams would be watching.

Chapter Twenty-Seven

THE WHIG PROPOSES—AND
GOD DISPOSES

THE Governor, in the executive offices of the Kane Mansion, spent his evenings working on the message to the Legislature. He had set up quarters in two rooms on the ground floor, nearest the street, a library, business office and secretary's quarters. Mostly he was alone, as he worked, but sometimes Gus ran into the chambers to see how his father was doing. Now and then Weed came in to go over what William Henry had written.

The speech that lay on his desk had been read by Frances and Judge Miller in Auburn, but they hadn't contributed much. Weed had much to say: and yet, when the address would be read to the Legislature, it would be William Henry's language and philosophy and outlook.

He knew that when the press carried it, he and his program would be attacked as visionary and experimental and impossible. But they would know what the Whigs stood for: progress, internal reform, a sounder economy, a spreading of the community, an attitude of sympathy for the unprotected. They would say that many hands had made the speech, and they would say that a college sophomore was here at work, instead of a statesman. But he had a credo, and it would be uttered.

He contended that the United States possessed enormous concealed resources, and that perhaps the greatest asset of all was its people. The inrush of immigrants from Europe was bringing in a reservoir of extra labor power that America needed. It was the heart of wisdom to accept gladly this inpouring from the Old World. Welcome the European, rather than exclude him; let him have the freedoms that were now being enjoyed by those who were already here, the religious and political liberties; let there be schools for the immigrant's children, and let us take into our fabric the culture and the manners and the habits of the nationals of other lands, and let there be great diversity in this country: let its diversity become its strength. Let there be no barriers against race or creed or religion. If we did this, then the American people were ordained to reach on this continent a higher standard of social perfection than the world had ever yet attained, and out of this could proceed the spirit which could renovate the world. Educate these newcomers to our way of self-government and open to all the widest channels of education.

There was a practical program that must go hand in hand with such a philosophic credo, he suggested, and he told the Legislature that the work on the canals must be hastened: these throughways would carry the immigrant into the West and the state itself would benefit in trade and productivity. Steam railroads must be built; all internal improvements possible should prosper; charitable institutions must be furthered; in the prisons of the state male and female should be separated, and discipline should be studied and investigated, and the emphasis should be upon the reform of the inmate; the standard of education needed to be elevated in all schools, and school-district libraries should be set up in all counties; moreover, it was necessary to make provision for the education of the colored children of the state; and courts must be reformed so as to spread judicial processes; unnecessary offices of the administration of Government should be dispensed with; and the state needed a mixed currency of gold and silver and redeemable paper; banking must come under general laws; and the ballot box must be protected from fraudulence.

Actually William Henry initiated a statewide revolution. These were reform ideas, and they were far from those which the Regency, the Democratic power, offered to the people.

To make matters difficult for the redhead, he and his colleagues by no means controlled the State Government. They had this large majority in the Assembly, and Whig sympathizers outside of Government; but the Senate and many key state offices were still in the hands of the opposition.

Almost each day Thurlow Weed came to see him at his offices in the Executive Mansion, and they discussed a line to take with respect to the more important practical matters. Actually they saw eye to eye, and Weed didn't impose his will on William Henry. It was rather the collaboration of two like minds, even though, everywhere, Weed was already known as "the Dictator." That didn't trouble William Henry. Only recently, during the political campaign, he wrote to Weed, "I had no idea that dictators could be such amiable people."

For a few weeks he and Weed collaborated closely on the question of patronage dispensation. After that William Henry had to move in his own orbit of leadership. He had a huge stack of correspondence daily, and he made it a practice to answer all of it; he had to interview delegations, politicians, advocates, all day long.

While this avalanche of detail spilled over his desk, and was processed by his secretary, Samuel Blatchford, his domestic interests stayed close to him, like a buzzer in the back of his brain that pressed him to give attention to the question of family, no matter how full were his political hours. His letters to Frances went out nearly every day, and he watched how Gus went to school, and returned from school daily, and he noticed who Gus' companions were.

In mid-January, just when the Miller and Seward clans were celebrating his splendid triumph—his only sister died. Cornelia, who lived in New Jersey, had been taken by an attack of quinsy, then often a fatal malady. She had introduced Frances and William Henry nearly twenty years earlier; and the Governor was so shaken by his loss that for days he couldn't take up the quill. At last he wrote to Frances, "Ever since that dreadful bereavement I have been unable to write. I could not write on that subject and it was treason against nature and affection to write on any other."

So that the achievement of a high office wasn't necessarily an unmitigated joy. No one knew, he reasoned, how life dealt with a man's successes and emotions, nor from what direction a setback or a sorrow might come.

So he began his career in the Governor's chair chastened by a personal loss.

Chapter Twenty-Eight

WILLIAM HENRY TAKES A SHE-BULL BY THE HORNS

ALL through January, and into early February, Frances fought the pressures of winter, pregnancy and her husband's calls for her to come to the capital and preside over the Executive Mansion. A few days after the New Year opened she received a short note sent on January 1st from the Executive Chamber. "My dear Frances: We are here. The ceremony is over. A joyous people throng the Capitol. This is the first message." A day or two later he pleaded for her to come. "I have had some friends to dinner daily, and we go on but awkwardly, in some respects, for want of your presence and supervision."

She was having serious morning sickness. She was about three months pregnant and this was always a bad time for her. Visibly there was no sign, and if she went to the capital, her condition could be unknown, save to those women she might wish to acquaint with the fact. But the prospect of the journey eastward in the bitter cold horrified her.

One personal or domestic matter after another interfered. She intended on the first day of the year to write and wish William Henry a Happy New Year, because she felt unusually well in the morning, but on that very day she received a call from Dr. Humphrey. That upset her so badly that she was obliged to go to bed with a nervous headache. She couldn't understand why the doctor insisted on obtruding himself into a house where he was so unwelcome—"God knows I forgive him the misery and disappointment he has occasioned me—if I did not I could not kneel with him at the same altar, but his presence here disturbs me exceedingly, bringing as it does so vividly to my remembrance all the painful circumstances relating to the sickness and death of our dear little girl in which he acted so unfeeling and unprincipled a part."

She exerted all her strength to strike off those words, closed the letter and retired to her bed and fell into a suffering half-sleep.

For the next week she was miserable from other reasons: she was impressed, unfavorably, with the terrible dangers of a public life. Word reached Auburn that there had been an assault upon the Kane Mansion by a mob on New Year's Day. Political colleagues of her husband, back from Albany, told of a tremendous and unruly demonstration at the house immediately after William Henry was sworn in as Governor at the Senate Chamber. Whigs, and Democrats now called "Locos," had literally invaded the Executive Mansion.

Something of the sort had been expected, for it was a custom, on important occasions such as New Year's, or the inauguration of a new executive, to throw open the doors and feed whoever came to offer congratulations or to look at a spectacle.

The Kane House itself was a huge yellow-brick affair, with expansive wings. It was enveloped by a four-acre grove of hemlock, pine and horsechestnut trees. Through the center of the house there was a broad hall about fifty feet long and twenty feet wide: parlors ranged off one side and family rooms branched out on the other. In the entertainment wing there was a huge ballroom that was as big as the corridor that went down through the center of the house.

At noon on inauguration day, the crowds pounded up the front staircases. At once the crush was so complete that someone knocked down one of the several oil lamps that decorated the gateway and the porch. Inside, the oil-fueled chandeliers and the mantels were alight: and there were so many lamps glowing that the house interior was a brilliant yellow. Coal stoves warmed the center hall and in the parlors there were grates that burned coal that was imported from Liverpool. In the rear of the house was the kitchen, and in it a dozen cooks and helpers were busy preparing food to feed the crowd.

William Henry took a stand in the center of the main hall, and there, surrounded by his military staff, he began an endless handshaking ordeal with the Albany citizenry. After the visitors shook his hand, they went to the long, heavily stacked tables, and started eating. The carpets had been taken up, and the visitors, walking on the wooden floors, made a steady scuffling, tapping sound that became a sustained and unpleasant music: their voices rose, there was laughter, backslapping, crushing: and the tables had to be re-provisioned.

As the afternoon wore on the party developed a kind of wildness, but in general one that was friendly to the Governor. They behaved as though this celebration was their due; and the tables crashed, the liquids spilled, fallen foods made the uncarpeted floors slippery, fixtures were pushed in, the walls soiled, windows broken; a sofa fell in from too many people crowding on it. Meantime, as though there weren't enough noise, military

Canaille

parties arrived, each with their own band, and the *booma-da boom* kept pounding inside the place till it seemed to the Governor that he was entertaining inside of some huge drum. After the bands played, the musicians adjourned to an upstairs hall where they were served with turkey, ham, chicken, fine breads and sauces: and so the city of Albany, in shifts, squeezed into the big trembling house. Outside, other thousands who couldn't get in, had to be fed. Food was passed over the heads of those inside, it was brought out on the porches, and a steady relay of full plates was fed to the outside crowd. By the end of the day seven barrels of New Year's cakes had been passed out to those who couldn't get within.

At night, after William Henry shook hands with no less than three thousand people, and the crowd filed out, the doors were closed. The Governor had a momentary consultation with his head housekeeper. They looked about. How long, he asked, did the housekeeper think it would take to make repairs and put the place in order?

About a week, he was told.

"I suppose it was all in good will," the Governor mused.

It didn't seem like an act of good will to Frances. As the news reached her, it appeared to her to be an unfriendly, or at least an unpleasant demonstration. They exchanged notes about the incident, Henry saying that he was all right, so was Augustus, so was the house, but she was prompted to get off a whole variety of middle-class reflections:— "Though your house and furniture were not entirely demolished by the Locos I should judge by the information of those who were there that your Whig friends behaved badly enough—they abused your house and stole your provisions— Upon the whole the canaille at Albany and the canaille at Auburn do not materially differ— I insist still that a private house is not a suitable place to entertain such company— Am I glad I was not there!— No woman ought to be willing to see her home so desecrated— I felt grieved, vexed and insulted last New Year's by the abuse of our home and furniture— the defacement and destruction of articles peculiarly mine seemed like a personal affront— Independent of all this the custom of feeding the rabble in this way is in my estimation decidedly wrong—demoralizing in its influence— I would that one so good as you are would not encourage it by your example—but I have said enough on this subject, perhaps already more than you will think kind...."

Throughout the month the pressure continued on William Henry: Where is your wife? When is she coming? The big Executive Mansion needed a charming woman for a hostess, and his Whig friends kept prodding. Thurlow Weed asked, and William Henry mentioned that Frances was pregnant and had her problems, but she'd be along soon. "I might have to go west and help her make the trip," he hold his friend. "I hate like the devil to leave the Capitol so quickly, after just being elected, but it might be the only way."

By mid-January she seemed no nearer to making the trip than at the first of the year; she had only time to write a few lines, she said, as her head ached violently— "I think if you still consider it advisable for me to come to Albany that I shall be able to go as soon as the 1st of February—about a fortnight from now— I do not know how many maidservants you have— will it be necessary for me to bring Nana [one of her house staff] to wait upon me— In haste, Your own Frances."

Her notes continued every two or three days, toned with fear and procrastination: the weather was exceedingly cold, so cold the past few days that she hadn't ventured out of her room— "We have some trouble to keep warm with our green wood"— And still later, late in January, it snowed without any cessation, she told him, the roads were impassable; still, she was making ready to go. She spent the past week with her dressmaker, and had the usual vexations getting several dresses fitted; used all of her strength assisting the housegirl in putting wood on the fire— "In the present state of my health trifles appear formidable— I have no doubt that it will be inconvenient for you to leave Albany, perhaps not possible— but you promised me a visit this winter if I were not able to accompany you."

The handwriting was tortured, minute, the lines, written with an ink made of blackberry juice, waved uncertainly.

That settled it.

When he got that letter hinting that she might not leave the house and might not see the Executive Mansion this year, he decided that enough was enough.

She was sick, he knew, a genuine invalid, but she nursed herself too damned much; she coddled herself and she made herself sicker than she was; it was in some considerable part a matter of mind, with her, and the time came when he had to do something about it. He couldn't and wouldn't let her whims and moods, her feminine negatives, upset his political equilibrium. Take the bull by the horns!

He ordered the coachman to hitch up and take him to the Albany stage depot.

She was in her room getting off another letter to him when he came in the front door. She was writing that Fred was slightly indisposed:— "The

205

effect of a cold— I think he will be as well as usual with proper care in a day or two."

It was a last attempt at postponement, a final try at avoiding functioning as First Lady.

William Henry quietly stole into the carpeted room and looked over her reluctant shoulder as she signed the letter *Your own Frances.*

Chapter Twenty-Nine

LIFE AMONG THE BIG WHIGS

LAZETTE and her husband, Alvah, lived in a pleasant two-story house in Canandaigua, near the business center of the village. Alvah, as a lawyer, active in Whig politics, made a good living, and he was politically ambitious, but he just didn't have the gifts of his distinguished brother-in-law, who was now Governor. Yet some of the prestige of the Sewards brushed off on him in Western New York politics, and he was busy building his fences. Lazette, nearing her middle years, had two growing children; she was buxom, and physically and psychologically healthier than Frances. She had always been maternal as well as sisterly toward her sensitive sister, and one of the vital experiences of her life was the close, the near-telepathic relationship which she had with Frances, daily, wherever Frances was, wherever Lazette was. The letters flew between them two or three times a week, and each preserved the correspondence of the other.

A month or two after Frances was in Albany, and her letters, descriptive of life in the Executive Mansion, reached Canandaigua, Lazette thought she noticed some slight change in her sister's handwriting. She examined a few letters written by Frances two or three years earlier, when she was nursing Cornelia, and she compared the hand. The early letters showed a nerve-wracked, verbose writing, small, waving, but now it seemed that Frances' writing style was larger, less words to the line, the letters seemed more vertical; and the notes were a little shorter, as if Frances was busier, more occupied, somewhat more outside of herself than she had been.

Perhaps, Lazette thought, her sister was taking some satisfaction out of her newfound situation of social distinction; possibly William Henry's present distinguished relationship gave heart to her. She was glad to feel this of Frances, and she hoped that her instinct was right. God help her out of her complicated emotions, Lazette breathed, maybe she is freeing herself of herself.

From some hesitancy at first, then with a gradually ascending confidence, Frances eased into the role of hostess at the Executive Mansion. Acting with modesty and her natural charm, invariably polite, and keeping to herself or to her letters to Lazette her real thoughts about people and politics, she discovered that the change wasn't as terrifying as it had seemed to her to be back in Auburn where she had led, if not a monastic life, still a comparatively quiet one. She told herself, Other women are governor's wives in other states right now, others have graced these quarters, I shall probably do it as well as the next.

Then the possibilities of the new life began to intrigue her. Henry was sure he sensed in her the beginnings of a kind of glow; perhaps a little of the excitement and high romance that she had always favored and dreamed of, but never had, might somehow be provided for. So the Governor decided that the time had come for her to preside over a full-scale Executive Mansion affair, and he proposed it. As a result, on an evening late in March, they staged one of the large entertainments of the season, with about forty guests.

They gathered in the long main hall in the center of the house, as lamps and candles almost everywhere gave off a brilliant yellow illumination. John Cook's Band, of fifteen players, played the light airs of the day as the company arrived, and set the tone for a gay evening.

Frances had long since acquired the air of a semi-invalided woman. She sat while others stood; she stayed home while others went visiting; she retired to her room when others poured new oil in the lamps; and all who knew her were used to hearing her say that she had a bitter headache, and that she must leave, or lie down, or call her physician; and it was in this defensive spirit that she sat, as one who is somehow lame or only half capacitated, in a rather ornate chair at the interior end of the large reception room.

Catherine Weed, in a similarly upholstered chair, was close by. She, looking middle-aged now, was dressed carefully in the fashionable, flounced, flowy silkens of the period. She and Frances were quite close, nearly as friendly as were their husbands to one another; and Catherine visited her at the Executive Mansion frequently. Now Catherine remarked to Frances that no one could possibly tell that she was so many months pregnant; for it was one of the beauties of the large, outflared dress style that it concealed so much. Yet Frances murmured regrets at not being able to dance, for there seemed to be many good dancers whirling about to the music. So she sat, observing the enjoyment of the guests, and receiving them, without rising, as, one at a time, or by couples, they were brought into the depth of the room by William Henry, or Weed, or by the Governor's secretary, Samuel Blatchford, and presented to her.

Principally the callers were State Senators and their wives, Whigs from New York City, a few judges of prominence, some high state officials, several literary notables, a painter or two. Lieutenant Governor Luther Bradish and his bride entered, and so did the distinguished jurist and Secretary of New York State, John Spencer, and Mrs. Spencer; and many of these were already known to Frances. Two other men walked in, both fated to become governors of the state later on, John A. King and General John Dix: each escorting a bejeweled or well-begowned wife. Besides these, there were others, not quite so famous, perhaps, yet politically vital personages, and soon, many of them were dancing about the center of the warm reception hall, or hanging about the long linen-decked buffet table, sipping cocktails and talking of everything from new drinks to new political fortunes.

At about the time all of the invited notables arrived, a writer, well-known in that time and in that company, halted before Frances. This was John Stevens, a world traveler, a frequent visitor to Albany and a friend of the Governor. Not suspecting that the Governor's lady was indisposed, the handsome globetrotter asked her if she cared to dance.

"It chances," she replied, "that I am very partial to writers, but tonight I am not even dancing with the literati. Not even with him—" and she nodded pointedly toward a far corner where the distinguished and controversial James Fenimore Cooper stood alone, leaning against a square wooden pillar.

"He's a dour-looking fellow, if you ask me," Stevens remarked, "and I'm rather astonished to find him in Whig company." Cooper was very conservative, and normally this crowd wouldn't be his dessert, but by the special invitation of Frances he was here this evening.

"Mr. Cooper is a lion," the Governor's lady said, "and it is his right, I suppose, to look or act like one."

"If you don't mind, Mrs. Seward, I think my contemporary over there is a much more likable person—" Stevens pointed to a middle-sized man with a roundish face, a double chin, and a general look of comfort.

"Oh, we all know that Mr. Irving is the most lovable man in the party."

After a time Washington Irving strolled around to talk with Frances, and at once he inquired, in a mock whisper, "May I ask the Governor's madame a most personal question?" His eyes twinkled.

"Certainly."

"Is my wig on straight?"

"It's absolutely topsy-turvy," she replied mischievously, because the wig was on precisely.

"I think I have my answer," he said, wisely. Then, "I see one of my rivals is here tonight."

"Mr. Cooper? Is he one of your rivals? I thought you had no rivals."

"Well, thank *you*, Mrs. Seward. But I fear Mr. Cooper is a challenging competitor. They seem to feel he strikes a more popular chord and that he is more of a storyteller than I."

"I was under the impression that these were your virtues."

"Mrs. Seward, I have a better idea than literary talk—I know of something far more entrancing to occupy the attentions—"

"Is there some lady you would like to meet?" she asked, intuitively.

"Precisely. The woman who has scented up this place so marvelously."

"Now whom can you possibly mean?"

"Why, the lady who runs the kitchen, of course! Take me to her, will you?"

Frances, with a burst of airy laughter, arose and led the way. "I didn't know you were such a gourmet—"

"Everybody else knows."

They moved into the kitchen where the usual staff of several was at work on a meal to be served in an hour or so. A stately woman of color, immaculately dressed in white, was in charge; she seemed rather elderly, and as Frances and her escort entered, they heard her voice and observed her bustling about, so that Irving remarked, "I think I am setting eyes on the most important figure in your party tonight."

"Possibly. This is Mrs. Johnson—" and Frances introduced Irving as one of our great writers, and she told the cook that he had asked, of all the notables present, to meet only her. As the chief cook and the writer shook hands, Irving drew in a deep and ecstatic breath of the kitchen flavors.

Mrs. Johnson beamed. "I invite you-all to take a sniff out of each precious kettle."

And the short-story writer, essayist, biographer of Columbus and soon-to-be Ambassador to Spain did exactly that. He stood in front of each copper pot, by turns, and inhaled a fume, to the amusement of the kitchen workers and the enchantment of Frances. He passed from one collation to another, took that deliberate stand each time, and a deliberate, eye-rolling sniff. Yet he performed with the solemnity of one who signs an important state paper.

"I presume," said Irving gravely, after completing the tour of the pots, "that you were elected to this office?"

That set the kitchen staff into a howl of gaiety.

Oddly, Mrs. Johnson took the remark a little more seriously. "Well, I been out of office ever since Governor Clinton die. When the canal Governor been alive there wasn't nobody else in this here cookroom but me, and whoever I take to be with me. Then he go and pass away and I had to leave out, they done fired me out. But Mrs. Seward's husband, by him knowing where at to find me when he came here to run the country, I be's back in office again."

Irving seemed charmed by her, and hinted for a word or two of her recollections of former governors for whom she had cooked. "Well, now," said Mrs. Johnson, "you bein' a writer, I believes you should be interested in one-two things about this place that I ain't even told Mrs. Seward —not wanting to worry her none."

"Oh?" said Frances.

"Now let me take you over here to this stairway." Mrs. Johnson led them a dozen steps to a door that opened off the kitchen. She turned a knob, and said, "Now look down there..."

It was dark, as the door opened, and there was nothing to see but the vague outline of steps when went down into complete blackness. "More things done happen down there than happen over at the Legislature—"

"Well!" said Irving, with a look in his features that said I-want-to-know.

"Yessir, down that very staircase Governor DeWitt Clinton fell and he broke his kneepan, went right down those stairs—"

"What's down there to make them hurry so?"

"Wine. Just wine. That's the wine cellar. That's where Governor Tompkins stored his old Madeira—and I seen him come down through my kitchen, and carry a candle down them stairs into that cellar many a time when he went lookin' for somethin' special—"

Several of the other employees gathered around the party at the head of the cellar entrance.

They explained that the basement was enormous, that it was spangled by passageways that led to rooms that weren't in any use, and one was darker than another, and you could get lost; and the only thing below were the walking remains of old dead folks who'd had something to do with Capitol life.

Washington Irving seemed beguiled, and Frances remarked, "Please, Mr. Irving, spare us any effusion to be called, 'The Legend of the Kane Mansion.'"

The fun in the kitchen was over. The author piloted Frances back to her place, and he drifted on. Frances mentioned to Catherine the amusement in the kitchen. By now the band had full control of the entertainment; the guests talked louder so as to be heard, and the scene was relaxed and less discriminate. Pairs, groups, gathered along the side walls, some danced, and the big business of cocktailing and political talk-talk-talk was on.

Frances asked of Catherine, "Who is that approaching with your husband? Would it be Greeley?"

"That's right."

Weed strolled toward the women. "Catherine, here is your favorite New Yorker." Greeley shook hands with Mrs. Weed, with whom he was well acquainted; for on his trips to Albany, he often stayed, often dined at the Weeds. Then Catherine and Weed jointly introduced him to Frances.

Frances at once asked about Mrs. Greeley.

"She couldn't come. She's still very ill."

"I heard of that," Frances said, "but I'm surprised she is still sick."

"Yes, it's eight months since all that." Last August, on one of Greeley's returns to New York, after working in the Capitol, he arrived in time to find Mary seriously ill from a surgical childbirth, and the boy she had borne was dead.

Frances, who knew much of childbirth and child rearing, sympathized, then drew him into other conversation. She understood literary people, and at once she remarked that he was certainly the most youthful person present, and this wasn't his only claim to validity. But it all seemed to embarrass the New Yorker.

He simply wasn't at ease in this environment; he couldn't afford to dress as well as the other men; he hadn't been experienced in social gatherings of such ostentation and political importance; he was more at home with books, at a desk with a quill dipped in blackberry juice. His work as a Whig propagandist ended in February of this year, *The Jeffersonian* then closing down, and he was staying in New York to edit his own *New Yorker*. But he was here for this event at the invitation of the Governor and Weed.

He wished he weren't here; he had problems, real financial pressures, and they preyed on him. He didn't feel right about leaving Mary in New York and running up here to fraternize with notables who, he felt, were somehow beyond and apart from him. He wasn't impressed that the Governor and Weed invited him to socialize. They knew he needed work and money and financing—or should know it—and they were in some position to do something about it, perhaps to help him launch another Whig publication; but they were inactive about it, and he, down in New York, was fighting what seemed a losing battle against creditors; and his publication, *The New Yorker*, wasn't doing well. He was heavy of heart over all of this, and now, the brilliant lamplight and startling women and important men and the bigtime atmosphere of the Capitol Mansion seemed unhelpful, and a harsh and hurtful contrast to his pressing concerns.

Frances and Catherine watched William Henry and Thurlow as they strolled down the side of the long room, inseparable as Siamese twins: Weed looking his usual, long-limbed, powerful self, a ruler; while the Governor moved at his side gracefully, short, but always an estimable presence.

Taking strength from the Executive Mansion scene, Frances wondered momentarily how and why she had been so weak all these years. In a way she had possibly let down William Henry, she was thinking. Catherine Weed wasn't like that: a simple woman, Catherine; she had so much work to do in her early years, and no servants to help her, and so much poverty, and yet she had shown so much faith in her husband that she was beside him, like a stalwart tree.

She, Frances, was a tree too, but a waving and wavering one that whipped in the breeze, that needed the sheltering strength of some larger tree close by, to ward off some of the winds—and she hadn't exactly had that. And yet, now, there was this...a famous husband, who was still young, with the world before him...and before her.

After the party dined on the sumptuous menu prepared by Mrs. Johnson, a dozen of the men drifted off to a well-lighted sideroom. For a while their talk had the character of a political soirée, but then, of a sudden, one bored Senator remarked, "To hell with all this rubbish, here comes Professor Cribbin of the seminary. He knows all about clairvoyance, and works in the field. Let's put him to work."

The young professor, a mild-mannered chap looking somewhat like Greeley, raised his right hand gently in protest. This was an affair for politicians, he said, and the scientists had best lie low.

That was all he needed to say. It was like an invitation to bulls to charge. They goaded and egged him on to give a performance in mesmerism. A few knew that he was purported to be rather expert in that area, for Professor Cribbin had placed an article or two on the subject in the medical journals of the state.

"Gentlemen, gentlemen, let me explain—" He was trying to say that mesmerism required a mood, a tone, a proper subject.

"Well," said the aging General Paul B. Porter, who fought at Chippewa in 1812, "I'm perfectly willing. If you can put me to sleep and make me do the things that your crowd says can be done, I'm willing, I'm perfectly willing."

That seemed fair enough to Professor Cribbin—if he must do this—a willing subject; so the professor made a few suggestions. First they must all be quiet; the lights on the side of the room must be doused; the candles in the chandelier had to be put out; and would everybody kindly move their chairs back toward the wall? While the preparations were made, and the chairs were scuffled off to the side, and the lights dimmed out, word got out among the dancers and the talkers in the main room that an exhibition in mesmerism was to take place.

There was a rush into the smaller parlor, so that all forty-three guests came in. Most of the chairs were taken; a few men rose and gave their seats to the ladies, and afterward gallantly stood behind the chairs. In the center of the room, Professor Cribbin sat on a straw-covered chair a few feet opposite General Porter.

The professor gave a last look around the room. "Are we all quiet?"

There were murmurs of assent and a genuine silence followed. The professor placed a lamp on a table that was set between himself and the general. General Porter had a slight tremor in his hands, it was there constantly, probably some product of age, but otherwise he was alert, physical, a man of great energy, a big fellow, and a Whig policy maker. He delighted in being the subject.

"Now then," said Professor Cribbin, "is everybody in the room ready for a trip through the White House?"

Through the White House! There was an echoing response all over the assemblage, the silence was off for an instant. The professor went on, "I shall put the general asleep and he will then transport us to Washington where he will give us a detailed description of the interior of the White House. Is this all right with you, General?"

"Fine with me. I always wanted to see the White House. Ain't done it yet."

"Very well."

And now the silence was on again, as Professor Cribbin spoke softly to the general. "You will fall asleep soon, Mr. Porter, soon you will fall asleep."

The general made no motion of his head, neither yes nor no.

"You will note that this lamp casts a shadow across your face as I pass my hand between the lamp and yourself?—Don't speak—" the professor went on. "This shadow will fall over your eyes ..."

The professor was off his chair and moving about softly, making no noise as he went, for he had taken off his shoes so as to be sure of quietness, and now his fingers and his hands went sleight-fashion between the lamplight and the general, and the shadows fell over the man who had fought at Chippewa.

The audience was entranced. A mood came over them; they were willing to be shown.

But the general refused to fall asleep.

It went on for a half hour and the general who fought at Chippewa was still fighting, only now he was fighting the professor from the Albany Seminary, and inwardly he was saying he'd be damned if he'd let this young fellow make a fool of him.

He just stayed awake, till Professor Cribbin, tired of moving about like a prizefighter, a little full from the banquet he had eaten, and doubting now that he'd succeed, sat in the chair opposite the general, and his voice drifted away and away and away...

"What do you know!" someone murmured. "General Porter is putting the professor to sleep."

The mesmerist was wearied, and the audience was wearied. Only the general was alert, like a man challenged. His eyes popped with wakefulness.

"Ain't nobody going to catch me napping," he suddenly announced.

That broke the mood of the room, and the burst of laughter that it produced brought the seance to an end.

The seance and the party.

Chapter Thirty

THE PART OF THE GOOSE
IN GOVERNMENT

THERE were two big green sofas in the hall just outside the Governor's office. Ordinarily, by daytime, visitors, delegations, petitioners sat on them and on the nearby chairs, but late at night, after the Governor was finished with the evening's entertainment or being with his family, or through caucusing with his political colleagues, that hall served its real function. At eleven or twelve o'clock the Governor himself put these sofas together, side by side; and there he went to sleep. But at three o'clock or so he was awakened, a servant taking care of that: then he went to work.

While it was quiet, as the Capitol slept, when Thurlow Weed and Secretary of State Spencer dreamed on of greater political triumphs, the redhead plunged into his most energetic work. Then he wrote the replies to the sheriffs who were always in touch with him about one criminal case or another; and he answered the governors of other states who had questions for him. People wrote to him for money, and he handled the requests variously, depending on the nature of the appeal; he declined invitations to speak, for these came every day; and he tried to oblige autograph collectors. Authors wrote to him for a kind word about their latest book, and he did what he could, if he had the time to do anything; and in the early morning hours, he looked over the endless requests of convicts in the state prisons for parole, or commutation of sentence if the crime was murder. There were troubles at the Canadian frontier, and much correspondence was involved with the Canadian Government, and he'd be working at it around the time a cock's crow came to his ears, or a gleam of morning light entered the hall window.

There had been hell to pay and a rampage of fun in the press, after the demonstration of animal magnetism at the Executive Mansion, and he had to get off notes of explanation to Whigs in other parts of the state who wrote and asked what it all meant. Was it true, as the Democrats charged, that "the state is being run by animal magnetism"?

In the West, his brother, Jennings, was conducting his Chautauqua interests, and he heard from him frequently, and often he had to write and give his advice. He must remember his mother and father in Orange County and send them a note every few days; and Judge Miller, in Auburn, expected to hear from his son-in-law personally. So William Henry's right hand went all night long, every night, the goose quill dipping incessantly in the inkpot, a hundred gestures an hour.

Each day he had to go to the State Legislature until it closed on May 7th. Then there were things to do in New York, and he went there for new rounds of public talks and private political meetings, and some fun and drinks with his friend Philip Hone, the former mayor of the city, who had given the Whig party its name. Then back to Albany.

"Frances," he suggested, "how about staying on here at the Mansion and having the child here?"

No, she answered, she wanted to go home and have the latest in the same room where the others were born. So, in the middle of May, he and Frances and the two boys took a line boat on the Erie Canal and glided westward.

Back in Auburn, William Henry had a certain amount of rest forced upon him because it rained every day.

When the rain let up, he had the perfectly preposterous and wonderful experience of casually going about the village, just as if he were one of the fellows, a town lawyer routinely meeting his friends at the post office, in the street, in the local newspaper office, or the lobby of some hotel where he'd stop in at the bar for a friendly nip. "Hiya, Bill," the folks said to him, as though he wasn't Governor and they saw him every day, and he hiya'ed them back as if he was still about the place making collections for Judge Miller.

The third son, William Henry Seward II, arrived on June 18th, weight seven and one-half pounds. Lazette, in town for the event, stayed by Frances' side. She comforted her sister, petting her as she would some little girl, and murmuring soothing thoughts, telling her, "The boy is just grand, the boy is just beautiful, Frances; he is just wonderful."

The invalided mother, with the streak of weakness waiting always to assert itself, slipped into a period of sheer ennui, and a worse illness than any that had yet succeeded a birth; she could hardly take nourishment, she could barely speak, she had all she could do to nurse the infant. The doctor came daily, and Lazette, weary with her day and night vigil, herself became ill.

But the State of New York had to go on, and the Governor felt that he

217

had to, too; so he told Frances he would return to the capital, but he would be back again, very soon.

"When, Henry?"

"Very soon, as soon as I can."

"Promise me?"

"I promise."

Chapter Thirty-One

THE LEGACY OF ZENO

EARLY in July of 1839 a schooner lay at anchor in the port of Norfolk, Virginia. While the captain waited for the boat to be loaded with oak timber, tobacco, bales of cotton and other regional produce, a ship's carpenter who worked about the port was sent aboard to make some repairs. The carpenter was a slave called Isaac.

Three of the seamen were men of color. They were free Negroes named Peter Johnson, Edward Smith and Isaac Gansey. They made their home in New York City, and they fell into conversation with Isaac.

"You a fool to stay here and live like you doin'," Johnson said.

The slave was at work in the hold and he put down his hammer; he looked into the faces of the free Negroes.

"I a slave. You thinks I wants to be?"

"Slave no more," one of the others said, "if you wants out."

"What you-all mean?"

"You get good wages North, man."

"Cain't swim that far."

"You won't have to swim—we seein' to that."

"Stay 'board ship?"

"You fix what you doin', then you stay down in the oak timber. We shows you where, we feeds you and take care."

They placed Isaac where he would be well hidden, in a great pile of live-oak timber that the schooner was to carry to New York.

As soon as the boat quit the port, Isaac's absence was discovered. His master immediately hired two agents to head for New York and be at the port when the boat landed.

That is what happened. The agents, going by horseback and by train, beat the schooner north, then accosted the ship's captain as soon as the gangplank reached the dock, and told him that they believed a slave had made his escape and was on board. The captain said he knew nothing of it; he'd let a search be made, and take part in it himself.

They went through the cargo carefully and they found Isaac: swiftly the slave was manacled.

Then the agents turned to the captain and accused the three colored seamen of having aided Isaac in making his getaway. They demanded that in simple justice to Virginia all three be arrested, and brought to court along with Isaac.

The case appeared in the Recorder's Court, and the judge had no alternative with the slave other than to order him returned to Virginia. But he was not so certain that there was any reason to return the three men who helped Isaac. He felt that they had violated no Virginia law, and the most that he would do, for the time being, was to lock them in the Tombs.

Isaac was returned to his owner; but the State of Virginia, hoping to establish a precedent which would prevent free Negroes or others from aiding slaves to escape, prepared papers demanding the surrender to the State of Virginia of the three seamen. They were charged with having "feloniously stolen" the property of a Virginian.

One morning, late in July, Governor Seward was in his office as a man named Charles Caphart called, bearing papers signed by Lieutenant Governor Hopkins of Virginia. William Henry read the requisition, and asked the Virginia agent: "Where are the men charged with the theft?"

"They are in prison in New York."

"The New York court is holding them?"

"Yes, they are awaiting your decision on the requisition."

"I see few details of the case on this affidavit," the Governor said. "These papers do not look to be prepared in full, as such a case requires." Then he asked, "Where is the slave?"

"Oh, he was caught, and he's back with his master. The requisition for the others has been made since."

"They got their slave back. What more do they want?"

"Virginia wants the three men who stole him."

This is novel indeed, William Henry reflected, Virginia wants to punish three black men for helping a fourth to escape—and us to have a part in the punishment.

"I shall have to think about this, sir."

The Governor called his secretary. "Mr. Blatchford," he said, "I don't want this man to go back to Virginia empty-handed. Prepare a written memorandum in effect that the papers are not satisfactory, they are defective; say in this memorandum that I feel that these men should be heard before I make any decision, and that I will give this subject further consideration."

Charles Caphart returned to Virginia. A copy of the memorandum, prepared by the Governor and his aide, went to the Sheriff of New York, with instruction that it be shown to the accused, so that they would know that their Governor was not hastening to turn them over to their traditional enslavers.

But by the time the memorandum reached New York, the Recorder ordered the three seamen to be freed: Virginia had no right to them.

So began the Virginia Controversy, a dispute destined to stir the North and the South.

As to the Governor, there was little or no question in his mind, from the minute he read the requisition, as to where he stood and what his course would be. All of the current of his life had prepared him for this moment, this challenge: his own views, his wife's, the Whig enlightenment, and certain scenes of his childhood....

Zeno, the slave boy neighbor, chased William Henry across the back meadow of the doctor's property in Florida. "I goin' get you, Mas'r William," Zeno hollered at the wispy red-haired boy. They were playmates and excellent friends; they were the same size; and they had about the same luck in wrestling.

They grappled for a minute or so, and then William Henry slipped down, to the earth.

"Say 'down', Mas'r, else I won't let you up!"

"Won't!"

"Down, Mas'r!"

Zeno tightened his grips, he pressed his arm into the redhead's neck and it hurt, till, of a sudden, the "Mas'r" eeked out, "Down, Zeno."

At that instant Zeno loosed his grasp—but all was fair, as in war, and instantly William Henry forgot that he had said "down," and he scrambled again to get Zeno beneath, because the colored boy had been foolish enough to weaken and believe him.

The wrestle raged for a few minutes more, till they were both tired, and the word "surrender" replaced the word "down" and surrender meant business, and no betrayal to it.

So they played, in their offhours, when the slave boy wasn't busy doing a slave child's chores for his master, who lived on the next farm, and when William Henry wasn't busy with household and farm duties. They thought up the hundred pastimes that boys think up when they have trees and hills and rocks and sheds and pets as their means, and they were friends from the age of five.

William Henry had other, even more vital relationships to slaves. He

221

prowled around the kitchen where Dr. Seward's slaves, Chloe Coe and Margarita, did the cooking; in fact, he stayed around that part of the house most of the time, especially in winter, if it was too cold to be out, and if he weren't in school. Chloe and Margarita fascinated him, and he found his own family dull by contrast.

On winter days, when it was too cold for any work to be done at the barns, and the labor of the boys wasn't needed anywhere, the judge's son and Zeno crouched by the warm jambs at the big fireplace in the Seward kitchen. A grown man could stand next to the mantel, it was that high. The hearth and the erect brickworks just about stretched across the rear of the kitchen; it was full of blazing logs and coals, and the room was warm and smelly with the cooking: the long arms of iron swung out from the fireplace, while copper kettles, filled with steaming food, swung from the bars. Sometimes eight or nine kettles pivoted around the snarling fire; and chicken, soup, stewed apples, Indian corn, succotash and boiled pumpkin and sirloin were getting done at the same time. William Henry savored the smells into his nostrils, and he watched the husky, aproned, big-stomached Chloe as she moved through the kitchen like a general, commanding the irons, the kettles, the coals, the logs and Margarita; how she whisked over to the fireside, pared potatoes, shucked corn or washed yams, while she babbled incessantly of herself, the neighbors, her life in Africa, yet often hinting darkly about the heavy burden she had and wondering why it was expected of her.

She grabbed hold of William Henry. "I know whats you waitin' for!" and she pulled a roasted corn from the coals and slipped it to him. She gave an ear of corn that was just as big to Zeno, who pressed next to William Henry in the warm corner that was their gallery. William Henry ate, and kept his eyes on the colored participants in the kitchen drama, and he waited for Chloe's stories.

Chloe knew that her talk fascinated the white child, so she didn't spare him any of her thoughts, none of her mother wit, and none of the lore she had brought from Africa.

She buzzed to Margarita, "Don't you-all turn that loaf of bread upside down—"

"Yeah, I know—" said Margarita.

"—'Cause you know it goin' to drown a ship somewhere out at sea!"

"I sure knows that," Margarita echoed; and she and Chloe looked into the corner where the boys munched the kernels.

Then, of a sudden, Margarita turned the loaf of bread upside down anyway, and with an excited little shriek said, "Just what I'm goin' to do!

Maybe I could drown me one o' them slavey galleys; them folks be better off down the bottom—"

"Oh, don't do that!" Chloe yelled.

"No, no!" shouted William Henry.

Zeno shrieked, "Don't turn that bread upside down. Now look what you gone and done!"

The two women laughed and tossed a look at the crouching boys and asked them if they wanted more corn.

It was much different here in the pit of the house than up front, where Father waited on the town trade and all was so sober, and the jingling of coins so important.

"When I dies," said Chloe, "I goin' back to Guinea."

"How do you know that?" asked William Henry.

"I know that 'cause they ain't no other place *to* go."

"Maybe you'll go to heaven."

"Guinea—that goin' to be heaven, that's right, and that where I'm goin' mighty soon now."

"When are you going, Chloe?"

"Just soon as I reach me a hundred, that be a few more year, then I goin' back to Guinea."

"Where you came from, Chloe?"

"When I was a little girl, yes, and brought here 'board that slavey ship. When I die the Lord puttin' me right back where he branged me out of."

"But that's not heaven—"

"Yessir, young mas'r, that be heaven and I know bettern you!"

"When you go back to Africa, how you going?"

"That not my affair. I know I just goin' then. All us black, when we die, we goin' back to where we borned at in Guinea and thereabouts."

He sat, thought, waited. There'd be more strange talk, he had only to wait. It always came. This singular knowledge poured all day, different from what he heard in the front part of the house. The slaves imparted a uniqueness which magnetized him and which must have some central meaning that he didn't know about yet. Of course, it was right that they should be doing what they were doing; working, performing the hard tasks; and behaving. And it was right that they should not run away, as some did.

The hot fires from the logs brightened the room; the black faces of the slave women looked at him with affection, and toward them he felt the same warmth. He looked upward sometimes at the ceiling; above was a garret where the slaves stayed at night. And so this part of the house held the most interest; and it was forming him; and within him there developed a faith in some vast anomaly which he did not grasp; some great falsity, a tremendous wrong. He absorbed this realization by intuition, by listening to the slaves, by studying Zeno, by watching how the blacks kept running the engine of the house, feeding all, tired always, yet seemingly tireless, with a murmur of protest in their doing; and yet, often, a song of grudging, religious compliance leaped from their throats. Then there were the long strange conversations between Chloe and Margarita, or between one of the women and Zeno, which seemed to be over his head, as if they spoke to each other with telepathic meanings in addition to the words, or in spite of the words, things that sailed over a white intelligence and belonged only to them.

The white boy wondered why they were black, and why so different. His parents had never disapproved of slavery, and if there was anything wrong about slavery he hadn't been told what it was. Yet Dr. Seward and Mary Seward never said anything to make him believe that he was superior to the slaves. It was just a way of life, a great perplexity that one lived with.

A day came when Zeno whimpered up to the back door looking for William Henry. The white boy asked, "What's the matter, Zeno?"

"I been whupped on bad, and I ain't like it."

William Henry examined the marks on the other boy's back and arms, and on the back of his neck. He wondered what Zeno had done to warrant the threshing.

"I ain't done nothin', I just got befo' the mas'r when he didn't like to see me get befo' him, and he took after me."

Zeno gave William Henry a real meaningful look, but didn't say what he had in mind.

The next day, Zeno, aged ten, ran off.

The slave hunters of Southwestern New York went in search of him and they found him and brought him back. For a while Zeno wore an iron yoke around his neck. Everywhere Zeno went the white boys tantalized him.

Zeno wandered about for weeks in iron and disgrace; then he broke the collar, and he went away more carefully this time, never returning.

In the small intelligence of William Henry at that time Zeno had done something wrong, and Zeno was immoral and had been bad; Zeno had been wicked and therefore he was punished. Zeno had not been grateful to his masters, and Zeno had been wrong, and to add to it all, he had flown. It seemed so to William Henry, but it also seemed to him that there was something untold and unanswered in the whole slave presence, in the fact of black and the fact of white.

He thought about all of this more than he did of any other one thing. As he became a bit older he began to think differently about slavery than his father or anyone else in his family. He heard the word "abolitionist." He heard his parents speak of a band of men, still very few, who called themselves that. He learned that Quakers didn't like the institution.

Often, after Zeno ran away, William Henry dreamed of his black friend: they were flying a kite, or wrestling, or chasing after a dog, or leaping a hill. For the memory of little Zeno sank, like a scar, indelibly, far far down into the pit of his soul.

The years matured his concern and his viewpoint; and at last he had position in the land, and opportunity. Now a conflict was at hand as an escaped slave named Isaac was returned to Virginia.

Chapter Thirty-Two

THE REVOLT OF THE INVALID

WEEKS went by. Frances was still in bed; sicker than she'd ever been, so ill that she could only sit up occasionally and, in shifts, write a few words each hour; and she was trying to find the right things to say to that delinquent husband: "I am writing in bed feeling that no one else can easily communicate what I wish to say to you— We have been looking for you home the last two days—your letter disappoints us— I am able to sit up sometimes two hours at a time but cannot walk without much pain—while in bed I am very comfortable—though I gain strength slowly. Dr. Mosin left last week, and Dr. Thompson has taken his place in the village—he has been here twice to see Lazette—she was very unwell while here— Dr. Mosin bled her once in the arm which undoubtedly increased her indisposition— Dr. Thompson has since taken some blood from her head—but she went home in a way relieved— I am sorry you cannot see the garden in this season of its beauty—everyone speaks of its looking charmingly—roses and lilacs are very abundant and various— I hope you will be able to read this illegible scrawl— I have written it with difficulty—at intervals— Your own Frances."

A week or more later, when he still hadn't come home, and he was instead, as she said it to herself, "traipsing over the state on his politics,"— he was actually on a pretty important political tour of Northern New York, enjoying the respect and attention and hospitality that a governor usually gets—she decided to give him holy hell.

The idea, not getting back to see his new son, named after him, too! instead wanting, like a vain child, to be showered with the attentions of those hacks in all those little counties to the north, fiddling his time at watering places like Saratoga, when his wife was at home ill after a terrible ordeal; unfeeling ... !

She decided not to write that.

She tore it up, as she had torn many an angered note, and decided to try to be the judicious politician with him: he understood polite political talk, beneath which lay torrents of feeling, so she'd give it to him good, his way: "I received your letter from Saratoga yesterday morning—I immediately wrote an answer explaining why I had not written before, but on reflection concluded not to send it, fearing you might think I had said some things which were unkind—the truth is your unwonted negligence about writing me grieves and disturbs me more than you can well imagine— I have some difficulty in persuading myself at all times that you are not somewhat indifferent to one to whom you cannot afford to devote ten or fifteen minutes in as many days— I am not a believer in the entire supremacy of your official duties—which perhaps you may be. . . ."

The silence continued. Henry didn't come home.

Very well, she'd show him!

She'd get out of bed if it killed her!

She wasn't going to let him have all the fun in the world while she languished in her upstairs room.

Not any more!

She'd had a heck of a taste of high life herself last spring, and she was going to go back there for more. It had its compensations.

This time she'd stay, keep her eyes on him, and have herself a time! As for little William Henry II, he'd go too, and have plenty of attention at the Executive Mansion from her and from everybody.

She got up and she moved around the house. Her eyes were on the things she'd pack. But she was weak, so very weak, and it wasn't easy to pack up, manage the boys herself, make the arrangements to go by stage or canal.

She dragged through July, into August, still resolved to go east: "Henry Clay made us a considerable visit— Pa insisted on him here— Mr. Clay seems most seriously to want your support for the Presidency— I was quite ill when Mr. Clay left, having made no small exertion to see him— I am better now and notwithstanding the extreme heat, continue to gain strength— I take a meal or two with the family every day—this morning walked far enough in the garden to see two beautiful dahlias which are in flower— I saw Mr. Clay a few minutes in the evening and the next morning at breakfast—he seemed to talk with some difficulty, being exceedingly hoarse from speaking so much in the open air—probably talked much less here than he would have done had you been at home— I was pleased with his appearance but it was altogether different from all I had fancied—"

All through the month she tried to find the strength to make the move eastward. It was torture:—*August 28th:* My head aches so violently, I hardly know what I write— As ever— Your own Frances.

He still wasn't asking her to come east. Perhaps he thought she was too ill to leave her father's house.

Two weeks later ... *September 15th:* My dear Henry— I have been more unwell for a few days past—for the first time nursing seems to disagree with me— I am much troubled with loss of appetite and pain in my heart— have not sufficient nourishment for my babe—hope to feel better when I regain my appetite— I shall feel much solicitude about you until I hear from you or see you—

She was thrusting, perhaps cautiously, waiting for an invitation from him to come to the capital. This time *she* wanted to be there; *he* wasn't anxious to invite her.

Friday, September 20th:— I have had the whole care of our dear little boy—yesterday I was sick all day with nervous headache— Pa has grieved me exceedingly by cutting down and mutilating our beautiful trees—it seems to be rather discouraging to attempt to ornament a place which does not belong to yourself— No one who has not experienced the same feelings, can know how fondly I am attached to every tree and shrub about the place, which has been a loved place and home so many years— I am very busily engaged in making preparations to go to Albany— Tomorrow is the eighth day since Willie was vaccinated— Will hasten my departure as much as possible—

September 29th: Your brother Jennings has probably informed you either by letter or personally that I propose coming to Albany some time next week— I have been looking all the week for a line from you to approve or disapprove my arrangement—it does not come—

Very well, she was going anyway, family, kit, kaboodle, the goods to go on separately by canal, the servants to come with her, the whole retinue....

The Miller barouche took them to the depot of the Auburn and Syracuse Railroad: she, the babe in her arms, tall Augustus, lively Frederick, helpful Peter Miller, a new hired man, Nana, the maid, Nicholas and Harriet Bogart, the cooks at the Miller house (to help out Mrs. Johnson at the Executive Mansion)—all these for the Governor's Lady—and they headed for Syracuse, and from there they canaled slowly eastward toward the Capitol and Governor Pa.

Chapter Thirty-Three

EXCITEMENT IN AN UPSTAIRS BEDROOM

AUGUSTUS and Fred shared a large bedroom in an upper part of the Kane Mansion. Each had a big square bed to himself, and still the room was so big that they had plenty of space to move around in. At night, when they were shipped off to bed, they had, practically always, an exciting talk of the exciting life of being Governor's sons. The big news of the hour usually trickled to them at the dinner table, when they listened respectfully, and for the rest, being the Chief Executive's children, each put forward an effort to be exemplary in school. Gus figured he was going to go on to West Point, and have a military career.

Both attended the Pearl Street Academy; that was a long walk from the Executive Mansion, it was near Patroon Street, yet neither of the boys minded the walk. Anything to be out of doors and out of the stuffy atmosphere presided over by L. Sprague Parsons, the principal. Gus was way along, doing advanced work, and Fred was plowed under in elementary Latin and Greek and fractions. When Fred finished with his classroom recitations he stared out of the window across the street at the two-steepled Dutch Church and the town clock. He couldn't wait to get back to the Executive Mansion, where he could tear around on the big property, and then go inside to his father's office and hang around, and look into books, and listen in on all the state business going on.

He understood more than they thought, and he picked up plenty of information about the Virginia Controversy. Ever since Pa wrote that Virginia governor that he wasn't going to send these three fellows back South, there had been plenty of hob all over the country. The Virginians sent insulting legal letters to the Governor, and Pa sent restrained little notes back to them saying they were out of line, didn't know the Constitution, and they couldn't force him to do anything he wasn't required to do.

Gus sometimes said he thought Pa was getting the state too far into debt on the canal question, but Fred argued that internal improvements couldn't really be a mistake, and he quoted his own father, who had said, in effect, that no nation ever lost power or declined because of a policy of spending money on internal improvements. Gus fell quiet when Fred pulled a quote out of Pa's hat, just like that.

Actually, young Fred, pushing ten, was twice as political as his older brother, now a big fourteen. Gus did his studying in his room, but Fred prepared his lessons in the shadow of his father, in the Governor's office, with William Henry being well aware that Fred was at a small desk in a far corner of the room, his head bent down in his multiplication and division tables. Besides that, Fred liked to read generally, and the office had books by Shakespeare, Irving, Dickens, and the latest magazines.

One evening, as the lads prepared to retire, Fred asked Gus, "What do you think of the revolution? What's going to happen?"

"Oh, it's no revolution. Pa'll handle it with one hand tied behind his back."

"It *is* a revolution, Gus. They won't pay their rent. That means they want to take the land away from the folks that own it—"

"Well, it ain't a revolution quite. Just watch the way Pa takes over on that ..."

"Oh, I know Pa means business, else he wouldn't have sent out all the soldiers in the state; but that's what makes it a revolution—just about the whole State Militia is in on it."

"That still don't make it a revolution, Fred. It's an uprising, it's a kind of a riot sort of thing ..."

"Well, Gus, Pa says this is dangerous, it's a bad example ..."

"Now, Fred, take that thing out in Chautauqua a couple years ago. Didn't Pa quieten that all down—just like that ... ?" and he snapped his finger.

"This is different, Gus, it's a revolution ..."

"Aw, Fred, go to sleep. Pa'll take care of it."

Fred had overdrawn the danger of the uprising, then being called the Helderberg Revolt. But he had imagination and, after all, this insurrection was about the biggest thing that had happened since Pa took office nearly a year ago ... it might even be hotter than the Virginia Controversy....

Because, among those not exactly liberated by the break with the mother country, and still pinched by a harsh overlordship, were at least sixty thousand tenant farmers who lived along the northern part of the Hudson River. They were still under the thousand-year-old system of feudalism, and they were owned by a famous American family, the Van Rensselaers. It was a pretty big stick of territory on both sides of the river to be owned by one family, but so it had been since 1629 when the first Van Rensselaer received a grant of the region from the Dutch Government, and proceeded to bring in settlers. The individual Van Rensselaers who, from one generation to the next, held lordship over the tenants became known as patroons, and the way they ran their estate called for the farmers to have perpetual leases with whatever Rensselaers happened to be alive and to reign, to pay rent with poultry and wheat, and occasionally to put in a little free worktime for the patroon. In return for this they had a house of sorts to live in, and they could work and eat and stay alive.

With this new spirit of landowning that was abirth in the country in the thirties, the Rensselaers began to encounter difficulties. Early in 1839 General Stephen Van Rensselaer III died; he was known as the Good Patroon, because he was a little easier on the renters, but his three sons took over early in that year and tried at once to collect back rents which their father had allowed to pile up. At once the tenants opened a campaign of resistance. By now they felt that their working of the soil over the generations gave them part title to it. They wanted a new deal, new contracts that made them less serfs, no payment of back rents, and more ownership rights in this soil than they now had.

The Van Rensselaers sent Sheriff Michael Archer to a few farms to begin the collections, but the officer found groups of tenants quickly gathered to say no, and to scare him away.

East and west of the Hudson, in the mountain areas, in the valleys, wherever the lands were tenanted, the officers from the Capitol met with a kind of "Deputy, Go Home" type of remonstrance. Some writs were burned, and they almost gave one sheriff's aide a tar treatment.

The Van Rensselaers demanded Government action against the still muted uprising.

On December 2nd, seven hundred deputies were sought by public notice in the city of Albany, so as to put down the rebellion in the area where it was hottest, the Helderberg region, which was a rock cliff country that reared from the west side of the Hudson and rolled inland. The land wasn't too good hereabouts, it was mostly hard, stony country, and the farmers had a tough time getting a few potatoes out of the ground. Late that afternoon a band of five hundred deputies actually marched to the village of Clarksville; but the Helderbergers were out in larger numbers. Battle-line formations developed, in which the deputized throng was overwhelmingly surrounded by determined serfs armed with pitchforks and clubs. There were a couple of rushes against the peasant people, but the deputized army was driven back, with nobody getting very hurt. One of the deputized leaders was former governor William Marcy—and word went through both battle lines that he suffered a bad case of torn britches: the only casualty of the long day.

That night Sheriff Archer hustled to the Executive Mansion and whispered into the calm ear of Governor Seward that there was the clearest insurrection in the Helderberg, and what about sending out the State Militia?

William Henry disliked the antiquated economic rites that bound so many residents of the state, and he was willing to see a big change in the situation. His experience at Chautauqua taught him that people who till the soil need to get something for their work and fidelity far beyond mere subsistence; but the law was the law, and the anti-renters were going about this the wrong way: this was a bad example, and it must be handled summarily.

At midnight he and Weed and Secretary of State Spencer and others in his "Cabinet" conferred. It was an all-night session, for they were loath to call out the State Militia, and yet that was the group decision. William Henry got busy, with his usual facile quill, and he worked out a proclamation authorizing the sheriff and all other military forces involved to put down the revolt, "being careful to avoid destruction of life." In return for ceasing resistance to the law, the tenants would get every break possible in the courts and in the Legislature, for their claims.

It was breakfast time when this paper was finished. Fred was up, and he came running into the executive offices when he heard there had been an all-night hassle over the events along the Hudson. He arrived in time for his father to say, "Fred, I have an important job for you."

The Governor handed him the Seal of the State. "Here, press this seal on our proclamation...."

Fred put his fist around the handle of the seal and stamped it on the stiff white paper.

He ran back to the breakfast table. "Gus, Gus, guess what I did...!" And he told his brother how he stamped the proclamation demanding a cease-resistance.

"You really stamped it, Fred?"

"Sure, sure. Got some of the ink on my hand too. Look..."

The State Militia, out of Albany, and from nearby Troy, and troops from New York City, fully armed, including small artillery, moved into the Helderberg country, and the authorities carried with them certain writs of arrest for specific anti-rent leaders. The troops never did find the leaders for whom they had the warrants, but for a few days the entire Helderberg area looked as it had once before in the Revolutionary War—occupied by the military, but minus the smoke and flame.

During the week, representatives of the anti-renters, acting on the liberal terms of the proclamation, sent word to the Governor that they would not offer resistance to the troops, nor to the sheriff.

The militia returned to Albany on a Sunday morning, at the last having to walk through a dozen miles of snowdrifts. They brought three prisoners, and as they reached the outskirts of the capital, and their drums boomed loudly enough to be heard in the Executive Mansion, William Henry got into a sleigh, Fred and Gus with him, and, with the Governor himself snapping the whip at a pair of horses, all three Sewards sped up State Street to the Schenectady Railroad Depot.

After the troops, looking cold and snow-bedecked, walked into the stationhouse, the Governor thanked them for their good behavior and their patriotic work. The soldiers gave three cheers for the redhead, and then marched to their armories.

That was the end of the first battle of Helderberg. It was a dispute destined to go on for a generation, but for the time being, William Henry took the anti-renters easily, with no one injured. The claims of the farmers were, at last, clearly to be aired before the Legislature.

That night, Gus and Fred, in their usual last-minute sum-up of the day's social and political events, discussed their part of the Helderberg campaign.

"You see," Gus said to his younger brother, "it's like I told you. It could have been the dickens to pay, but Pa did it up right, just called out the troops with no hemming or hawing about it—"

"But Gus, they hemmed and hawed all night."

"Well, maybe so."

Chapter Thirty-Four

THE PENDULUM SWINGS HOMEWARD

FROM the time when Frances went to Albany without urging by William Henry, and through the next nine months—the longest period she was ever away from Auburn—she prevailed at the Executive Mansion. Although she wasn't vain for public favors, as was her husband, something of his reputation brushed off on her, and gathered her up, and perhaps—even if ever so slightly—it quieted some of the need within her. William Henry was sure that he sensed in her an upsurge of spirit; she was taking an interest in his political affairs that seemed genuine and in excess of what she had ever shown before.

The glow of Capitol life was still with her when she returned to Auburn early in June. And somehow the season of bright joy appeared to enhance everything in the village. Now she was anxious for Henry's return, for a summer visit, and she was busy, and so were others, making the house ready for him: "Auburn is a charming place," she hastened to tell him, after she was settled a few days. "My local attachments are so much stronger than yours that you can hardly imagine how happy it makes me to find myself once more at my own home, a place endeared to me by a thousand pleasant and paining associations— The place is in better state than I expected to find it— Peter has exerted himself to put the ground in order preparatory to your arrival...the house is no less convenient or more ill arranged than it was formerly, but the odd things about it are much more striking, after an absence of nine months—the south room entry and appurtenances continue to greet the eye as you open the street door."

She babbled on of the household life, how Fred was happy to be with his pet skunk and his kittens: he didn't like the idea of returning to school here, he had got to like it in Albany. Augustus was grown astonishingly, she told the Governor. Apparently the change, and the boy's own physical resources, all had been good for him and he'd flourished. "His voice has become harsh or hoarse and he is in many respects wonderfully like the young Millers around Romulus—but he is still a good dutiful affectionate boy— I must not quarrel about his entire deficiency in grace or manners

234

and conversational powers—which though not unimportant are of much less moment than a good heart and good principles— I trust he will improve with proper instruction so as not to be very singular as are some of his relatives on both sides of the house ... the weather is delightful ... the roses are all in bloom ... do come home and look at them ... Your own Frances."

When the Governor read that he knew it was a siren song; she never let him rest, he was thinking, she must have him at any cost; he could be President of the World, and she'd want him to come flying home to her in the country, and let the world go hang; so he disposed of that recurring nonsense swiftly this time: "You must make no calculations upon me. I am overloaded with cares and labors, besides the duty of perpetual audience and attention." He did say that he wished the boys were in the capital with him; a handsome rifle company had come in from New York, and they had pitched their tents on the lawn of the Executive Mansion: they'd turned the lawn into a regular martial scene of war, and the boys would certainly be delighted with all the excitement.

He had replied hard, she realized, when she read that answer to her latest come-on-home urging, but she managed to take it lightly. "Oh, my God, there's his awful taste in music!" she said aloud at her dressing table, as she noted William Henry's remark on the rifle company: "They have a fine brass band, and the music is very cheering to one fatigued and careworn as I am." Well, well, she mused, he is getting to appreciate music, even if it is a military brass brand.

Overwhelmed he was, his gubernatorial career deep along, his problems multiplied, and his cares, as he told Frances, mounted like the hill on which the Capitol buildings were situated. He was opposed everywhere in his concern for roadbuilding and canal building; it seemed that there was always an army worried about debt, preferring a strait-laced budget and opposing change of any kind. They charged that he was too enthusiastic about such things, and he had to answer that nobody who had a canal running through his town, or one of the new steam railways, was willing to relinquish either. He pressed continually for an improved and a strengthened military. The fight with the State of Virginia over its demand for the return of three colored citizens of New York went on in an exchange of legal papers aired to the public, and he told the Virginia governor, "I need not inform you, Sir, that there is no law of this State which recognizes slavery—no statute which admits that one man can be the property of another, or that one man can be stolen from another." And yet, in New England, John Quincy Adams, watching the career and public performance of William Henry, expressed the opinion that the Governor was altogether too mild, too legal, too gentle with the Virginians.

Another view was destined to have repercussions throughout his career: he spoke of the need for education for all children of all classes, and he remarked that many boys and girls were being deprived of the advantages of the public school system by reason of differences of language and religion. "I do not hesitate, therefore, to recommend the establishment of schools in which they may be instructed by teachers speaking the same language with themselves, and professing the same faith." He had advocated as a means of answering the needs of these children the parochial school, and he won the good will of the Catholic group, but aroused the wrath of Protestantism and many of his own Whig friends.

It was the beginning of an issue in national life destined to unending controversy, and for that stand William Henry was attacked in the press, reviled in the Protestant Church. Primarily it was a Democratic party assault, and he was accused of being in league with the Pope, he was a Jesuit, he was ruining the state. All over the nation, the politicians took careful note of this policy and they stored it away into their memories and their books for any decisive day when they might, with advantage, need to point to this.

His approach of encouraging the integration of the foreign-born and of all minorities into the national character wasn't understood. It led to criticism even from members of his own party, and once, in the course of making reply, he put forward a concept, the higher law idea, which would develop and have its real impact later on. He answered one Whig's objections in a private letter to him: "For myself, so far from hating any of my fellow citizens, I should shrink from myself if I did not recognize them all as worthy of my constant solicitude, to promote their welfare, and entitled of right, by the Constitution and laws, *and by the higher laws of God Himself* to equal rights, equal privileges and equal political favor, as citizens of the State, with myself."

In the autumn of 1840, William Henry was re-elected Governor, and William Harrison, a Whig, was elected President of the United States. The Governor, through his own campaign, shared heavily in the President's election. He had long been a supporter of Harrison. Oddly, this was the last time that William Henry would ever run for public office, the final time his name ever appeared on a ballot—in spite of all that he was fated for in a governmental way.

Again, as two years earlier, William Henry and Weed had the help of Greeley. The slender young litterateur and journalist had begun a new publication, *The Log Cabin,* and the force of its rather considerable circulation helped William Henry a second time; and Greeley shared in the wordage and clamor that helped elect Harrison.

Later when Weed called to see the Governor, William Henry remarked, "I've a letter here from the adjutant."

The adjutant was Greeley.

The Governor went on, "I don't always understand our younger friend. I asked him to come to dinner here and he says no."

Weed glanced at the letter. Greeley wrote that for dining as an art he had a due respect, but he wasn't good at that type of thing—"I lack education—I have no taste—no time." Could he be excused?

Greeley had wanted something more than mere approval from his associates for an even bigger Whig newspaper he hoped to launch in New York. But no real offer of backing came from them, and he was piqued.

The New York *Tribune* was launched by their enterprising colleague; yet Greeley began his paper without their help. Perhaps the editor had in mind securing some patronage, perhaps some printing work or other income from the big Whigs, in return for his journalistic services; but if so, it wasn't forthcoming. The new paper evangelized against alcoholism, slavery, gambling, prostitution, smoking. It purported to be for the people and against anyone who bilked the people. And it was. But William Henry and Weed stayed aloof of it; they found Greeley hard to handle, and the *Tribune* may have been too radical for them: even so all three continued to be close friends, and the *Tribune* supported the Whig Administration at Albany.

Throughout 1841 and 1842, the measures that reached prominence in the early days of the Whig regime rose to higher expressions of controversy. The Governor was shocked to discover the extent of opposition to his suggestions about public education. "If there was one policy in which I supposed all Republican and Christian citizens would concur it was this; I found, to my surprise, that the proposition encountered unkind representation." He complained that a press which should have seconded his suggestion perverted it, and attacked his motives; yet he was determined to educate a lagging public and remiss political leadership on this very matter.

The anti-rent dispute deepened, and no solution of it seemed to be at hand. By now the proposal had been made that the tenants have the right to purchase the land from the Van Rensselaers upon the death of the owners. A part of the community was surprised to notice the vehemence of the illustrious James Fenimore Cooper, who defended the right of the

237

manorial proprietors to retain title to their holdings forever, on grounds that they were gifted and successful and therefore they naturally had such right. If, reasoned Cooper, the plebeians came into possession of the land by their own numbers and by political means, this would be morally and historically wrong—and so the Helderberg war raged on.

The argument with Virginia continued even after a new gubernatorial regime took over in the Southern state: so that the nation, for three years, followed the obdurate exchanges of philosophy and law that pictured the Northern and Southern positions.

All the days of his office, William Henry dealt with appeals for pardon and commutation of sentence of the accused and the truly criminal. These cases took hours and days of study, for final determination of life and death so often rested with him, and this phase of gubernatorial responsibility plagued and challenged him more than most other problems.

Once, there was a great protest at his door over the conviction and sentencing of a famous citizen of Buffalo, Benjamin B. Rathbun. William Henry had met the man far back, in 1824, when he and several Sewards and Millers took a trip to Niagara Falls. Since then, Rathbun had grown rich and propertied, but he had overextended himself in business, and finally he engaged in forgeries amounting to two or three millions of dollars. Rathbun was imprisoned at Auburn, but thereafter, a portion of the Western New York public, recalling how he had helped to build Buffalo, sought to get him released. This was the kind of instance that crawled unpleasantly inside Governor Seward: he didn't like to yield to the pressure and the influence of the mighty, including people in his own party, when class took care of class: he was supposed to be just, impartial, so he turned down the appeals of an important leadership in the Buffalo area. Rathbun served out his term, and neither the influence that he had worked up, nor the strength that mobilized about him after he was imprisoned, swayed the Governor who tried to rule impartially and without class feeling for all of the people.

When the World's Antislavery Convention was being held in London, and Americans like William Lloyd Garrison, Wendell Phillips, Gerrit Smith and others were over there, the Governor got a message from the convention descriptive of its proceedings, and he answered:

I concur entirely with the convention, and with enlightened and benevolent men, in all civilized countries, in regarding slavery as a great moral evil ... inconsistent with the spirit of the Christian religion ... at no time shall I fail to do whatever is in the scope of my lawful power and rightful influence to promote the great and philanthropic work of universal emancipation.

So he went on record internationally as an Abolitionist, then a unique and forthright stand for a state governor.

An eloquent Onondaga chieftain came to him with a problem, how white pressure was being put upon his tribesmen to sell their property, how his people had taken peaceably to farming, and how he wished their treaty rights to be sustained. William Henry was much moved by his appeal: "Father, you are young in years, we hope you are old in counsel; so our white brethren tell us, and we believe it. Your red children desire to know your mind..," and he replied that while he was Governor they and their lands would be protected. "Say to your people that if white men seek to obtain their land by force or fraud, I will set my face against them."

He moved to complete the reform of the abolition of debt; he helped establish the first state hospital for the mentally ill, then called a "lunatic asylum"; he initiated moves to develop a state banking system; so that all day and into the night, his pen moved with his proposals, his decisions, his advices.

Late in his gubernatorial course, he had a special house guest. This was Edward Stanley, a prominent Whig member of the House of Representatives, of North Carolina. William Henry had long been urged to meet Stanley. "You must see him, he is your double, he looks like you, talks like you, acts like you." He had been told this by many politicians who saw Stanley on the Congressional floor in Washington.

Finally they had corresponded, each curious to meet the other—and now the two were together in the Executive Mansion.

For two days William Henry stared into the face and features of the human mirror before him. He beheld an ambitious and an eager face; he saw a physical form and frame that, though slim and slight, was a magnet of energy, alacrity and plainness: here was no physical beauty, no athletic look, but a much electrified body that possibly worked faster, thought faster, moved faster than other bodies.

He observed a face that women could not love for its own defeaturings: such a head must have other claims for attention.

They sat opposite at mealtimes, each glancing into the calm-water reflection of the other.

"Whose hair is redder, yours or mine?" the Governor wondered.

"I think they've the same tinge."

"So that's what my nose looks like...." William Henry mused.

"I fear it does," the congressman answered with a smile. "We are both stuck."

"I can't get over the fact that we're exactly the same height," the Governor murmured.

"...and the same weight—you say yours is a hundred and thirty?" the Southerner echoed.

"Yes, we're both in the featherweight division."

The Governor remarked that he often heard himself described as having a head slightly too large for his body.

"They have told me that too—"

"You look more like me, I believe, than any of my brothers."

"You don't suppose we're in any way related?" the North Carolinian asked.

"Well, only historically. We seem to come from the same British Isles stock."

The congressman said he was pleased that they were both Whigs.

"That's almost too much," William Henry sighed, "that we even think alike!"

Peering into Congressman Stanley's face, he saw now what the caricaturists saw, what the political cartoonists lampooned. He gazed at an intellectual, oversize head, and he discerned the political ambition in the Southerner. Here was a man capable of moving and calculating just as he had done, only the congressman had no Thurlow Weed to back him up.

Nothing can ever change my features or form, he told himself. I am a faceless fellow. I have to win the world with my thoughts, my work, what I do for people and the country. They can never be endeared to me for what I look like.

Can I really be like that? he asked himself, as he contemplated the cerebral look of the other, a face and head from which there peered, almost as if spelled out: p-u-b-l-i-c m-a-n.

He was dismayed.

From then on William Henry wasn't anxious to be painted, nor to have daguerreotypes made of him, and he was forgiving of all those who slapped at him for his slightness, for the flame of his hair, for his nose that jutted like a hunk of property. They told the truth.

When he wrote to Frances of it, he was ashamed to put down on paper what he felt about what he beheld in his double's appearance. He wanted to see Stanley, "since my unfortunate person had brought me so many ungrateful attentions. But I believe I will not tell you now what was the conviction of the truth of these disparaging reflections..."

As his administration moved toward its finish in 1842, he was wearying. He had his taste of high office, his feeling of power, and he felt oppressively the weight of public and party and press, so that he began to look forward to retirement. He had long ago announced he would not be a candidate for a third term. He believed that he had made friends among the people, that politicians and public in the main approved him, that he had escaped the perils of high official service with the least amount of damage to himself...and in the midst of such self-consolation, the unforeseen occurred.

Chapter Thirty-Five

THE MAN IN THE LOCKPORT JAIL

ONE DAY, early in November of 1842, the new secretary, George Underwood, walked into his office with a sheaf of petitions asking for commutation of sentence or pardon for an admitted murderer named John C. Colt.

William Henry glanced at the top papers, and scanned the appeal. "Colt... Colt," he murmured, "a familiar name."

"It should be, Governor," said the aide. "John Colt is the brother of Samuel Colt, the inventor of the Colt revolver."

That was the beginning of a tremendous assault on him and his office. Partisans of Colt demanded his freedom, and those who wanted the murderer executed opposed pardon. The campaign mounted during the next two weeks, and it eclipsed all other state business. As the protest worked up, the Governor's desk became a mass of legal papers, petitions, printed and handwritten matter, and over these documents there spread a disarrayed pattern of notes in various hands... death threats, anonymous letters, denunciations. He picked up the latest, a note written on a fine grade of paper in a careful, literate way. Obviously from some well-read man, perhaps a churchman, an upperclassman. No crank's note, but an impassioned warning.

You have time to grant a pardon to him whom your prejudices are about to deprive of a life as dear to him as yours is to you. You have full time, Sir, but not the disposition. But by the Almighty God, should he suffer an ignominious death, his corpse shall not be interred before *yours* pays the forfeit!

You may disbelieve me now, but too soon, perhaps, you will be dead and past regretting. As for Judge Kent, him who consigned Colt to the hangman, his fate is sealed if Colt hangs! Governor Seward, you will either pardon Colt, or *Die!*

JOHN COLT'S FRIEND

More than a year earlier in New York City, the handsome young businessman, John C. Colt, was at work in his publishing office on the second floor of the Granite Building at Chambers Street and Broadway. He was a "well-born American," for he claimed descent from Sir John Coult, and he traced his ancestry back to a Colt who had arrived here in 1658. Colt had a broad education, he could write; he was a slender, good-looking six-footer; he had light-brown richly curled hair, nice dark-brown eyes; he was courteous, a man with, ordinarily, a gentle voice; and he was a churchman. He had just written and published a successful technical book called *Book-keeping*. He was reading quietly at his desk when a knock came at his door.

Samuel Adams, a job printer, entered, rather brusquely walked to Colt's side and said he was glad to find Colt was in. Adams was about thirty, he was known in the business community, but he was not at all well-to-do, and he didn't have the polished background of the other. Colt owed him some money for a printing job recently done, and Adams' efforts to collect, in the regular way, hadn't succeeded.

"I'm rather hard pressed," the printer said. "I need the money."

"Why, Adams, I do intend paying you but you're wrong about the figure being $71.15."

"What's wrong with it? That's the sum we agreed on."

"We agreed to nothing of the sort." Colt, still seated at his desk, drew a portfolio from a drawer, and, pointing to some figures, he argued that the sum due was fifteen dollars less; that there had been a certain item conceded by Adams earlier.

"I don't remember any such concession. I only remember talking about it. It seems to me you just don't want to pay off."

"I hardly like being called a cheat, Mr. Adams!"

They resumed hassling over the figure. Finally the dispute narrowed down to a difference over $1.35. Still Colt was unwilling to pay. Adams was angered. "Trouble with you is, Colt, you're just pulling some sharp practice on me!"

"That's a lie!"

"Sure, sure, I'm a liar. But you're the famous bookkeeper. Write books about bookkeeping. When it comes to paying your own debts you got two sets of books!"

"That's damned rotten of you, Adams!"

"...But it's all right for you not to pay your debts—when you can afford to!"

"...Besides," Colt parried, "you're late delivering that print stock to me. What about that?"

"You mean I should keep giving you credit—send you sheets—when I haven't been paid?"

"I didn't know you'd be so difficult to deal with, Adams—or I'd have got another printer."

There was an enraged pause. *"Colt, you're a deadbeat!"*

They grappled.

At first they fought with clenched fists, each aiming at the chin of the other for a swift decision. They tumbled about the room. But, as the anger of each went higher, the fight grew fouler. The printer seized hold of a neckcloth which Colt wore, and started to turn it and squeeze it, strangling Colt, at the same time pressing Colt down on a table. The printer struck the other man in the chest three or four times with his free right hand, and then he grabbed hold of Colt's genitals. He twisted the sensitive instrument so that Colt groaned with pain.

Colt saw black.

He worked to press Adams away with his free left hand, and he tried with his right to raise himself from the table.

Nearby was a hatchet; and out of the corner of his pained eyes Colt saw it, and he reached for it. He gripped the hatchet, swung it. Adams fell backward, probably dead at the first blow.

Colt struck again. Then a third lethal blow. A fourth furious chop down in the center of the skull, at the cranium. More blows around the ears, the side of the head, all over the head of the dead body lying on the floor.

For a while the publisher was dazed, and he stood over Adams' body wondering what had happened and how he had done what he'd done. He looked out of the window below into Broadway where people moved. The large drays clattered over the cobbled way. The office walls were thin and this building was occupied by many people; still nobody had rushed in to learn what went on. Perhaps nobody had heard. All was silent. The murderer was alone in the room with quiet Adams, and he was undiscovered....

Guilt worked inside Colt momentarily, and he reflected whether he should turn himself in, go to a certain judge friend and make a clean admission of what happened. No. He put that aside. Keep the secret, only dispose of the body somehow.

First he made sure that the door to his apartment was shut; he drew the curtain, then, frenetically, went to work.

He stripped the clothing off of Adams so that nobody would be able to identify the murdered man by his clothes. He bound the body with rope, condensing the figure as compactly as possible, for he must stuff the man into a rude, thin-slatted box only three and a half feet long. But Colt first covered the body with canvas, so that no blood would seep out. He worked for some time, jamming Adams into the small box. Adams didn't go in easily, and once Colt had to get up on the trussed body and stand on the printer's protruding knees to push him down in. That dislocated the dead man's limbs, but Colt did manage to pack him in.

He nailed the box down, ludicrously trying to tap the nails in as quietly as possible, for people worked in the adjoining loft, and Colt wondered why they hadn't come to his door.

It was by now nearly nightfall.

The room a mess, Colt busied himself washing the floor. He rubbed it down with oil and ink and tobacco so as to conceal the blood. Adams' clothes lay in a pile on the floor, and Colt picked them up, temporarily tossed them into the sink. There was a watch belonging to the printer and Colt put that in his pocket until he should find a better way to dispose of it.

He looked around. That was all he could do for the time being.

He opened the door, went out into the hallway, locked up, and hurried a few blocks away, in the darkness of evening, to a bathhouse to wash the stains out of his own clothing. He had an appointment with Caroline Henshaw, and he was already late. Her lodgings were a few blocks away; he hurried there, and he stayed there all night.

Early in the morning, earlier than he usually arose, he left Caroline; he returned to his office and began again to remove the evidence of the bad business transaction of the previous afternoon.

He put plenty of strong brown paper around the quiet trunk, plenty of cord around the paper. Then he labeled the box with an imaginary name and address in St. Louis. He pushed the burden out into the hallway.

He went out of doors to find a truckman. He located one and returned with him to the Granite Building. He went with the drayman and the package to the port a few blocks away.

At the ship's offices he took a receipt from a clerk for the dispatch of the merchandise (books) to St. Louis. It would go by ship express down the east coast to New Orleans, thence up the Mississippi. Soon, Colt believed, the package would be on the high seas.

He was in the clear ... so he thought.

The murder had occurred on the afternoon of Friday, September 17, 1841. On the following Wednesday news notices of the disappearance of the printer were published in several New York newspapers.

During that period Colt himself made several calls at the office of Samuel Adams to learn whether there was any news of the absent man.

But on Sunday, the 26th, just before the ship to New Orleans was about to leave, seamen could no longer stand the stench in the hold of their boat. They made a search, found the package—and the body of Samuel Adams.

It was known that Colt was the last man to see Adams alive, and he was promptly arrested.

Newspaper competition in those days was beginning to be keen, and headlines were livelier, so for the first time in our history there appeared the news blazon:

TRUNK MURDER

The arrest of John Colt was a New York sensation. A man of prominence and culture, he had friends; he was in politics in a small way, he knew people, men liked him, he was a sportsman and hung out with the swankier set in Manhattan. They were sorry for the plight he was in, and his story of murder in self-defense received support at least from the class he traveled with.

When the trial occurred in the summer of 1842, the dead man could not speak for himself. Only Colt's story was told in court. Yet he hadn't a single mark to show for his fight with Adams, nor had any such marks been found on him when he was arrested. A witness from the quarters adjoining Colt could testify only to a confused sound and a heavy fall, but not to any prolonged struggle such as Colt said had occurred. Adams was unknown to have ever hurt another person, he had come there unarmed, his strength was probably about the same as Colt's. Moreover, Adams' watch had been found in a trunk in Colt's apartment.

The case became complicated; the trial prolonged; the public interest enormous: they produced Samuel Adams' head in court. They had exhumed it, and there it was, a skull severed from the rest of the body, stationed on a desk next to the judge, on the exhibit table, and it was studied by lawyers and doctors, and it stared Colt in the face for days.

The jury was cold about the status of the defendant in the social and literary life of Manhattan, and indifferent to his early American pedigree. They judged the facts, didn't think much of the plea of self-defense because Adams had gone there unarmed. They found Colt guilty of murder, and he was sentenced to be hanged on November 18th, 1842.

In the period between the time of Colt's sentence and the date of execution momentous things happened in New York in consequence of the case. The newspapers rolled out extras on the subject; public meetings were held; petitions drawn. Sentiment was divided between partisanship for Colt and sympathy for the dead Adams.

Imprisoned in the Tombs, in the lower part of Manhattan, the literate John C. Colt wrote his "authentic true story" of how he had defended himself, and it sold two printings. He denounced the law, the courts, the times. "Give me wealth and I could put my foot on the neck of the universe," he said. Clearly he tended to strong measures. Reporters camped on the jail steps. Journalism itself learned new techniques in circulation-getting as a result of the sensational and word-coining "trunk murder." Colt's partisans developed in influential quarters, among politicians, moneyed men, judges, the powerful newspapers. His story became known across America, and people in small hamlets everywhere were taking sides: Hang Colt! No, pardon him!

Colt's lawyers went from the circuit court where the defendant had been found guilty to the Supreme Court. But the high court said no, they saw no grounds for another trial, or for any course other than the death sentence. The lawyers went to the chancellor, and the chancellor, at that time an influential juridical position, turned them down. The courts uniformly regarded the incident as one of the most cold-blooded murders; Colt must die.

There was only one other chance for the partisans and lawyers of John Colt. Take the case to the Governor. Appeal to Seward. Seward'll commute the sentence, or pardon Colt, they said. Seward is a Whig, a liberal, a sympathetic man, he'll save Colt! The Governor is enlightened on penology, he's pardoned a few criminals; put the pressure on him!

The Governor, mulling the latest threat, pushed it aside, glanced wearily at the voluminous legal papers, the petitions; so much of it that it excluded all other matters then before the state. He chewed disinterestedly on his cigar. His forehead wrinkled with the size and the strangeness of the problem. He wanted to do the honest thing, and it wasn't easy being a Solomon. Yet any way that he looked at the case, he saw, as the courts had decided, only a cold-blooded murder; and Adams wasn't alive to confirm or deny Colt's story.

He moved across the room to the window. He looked out, saw distantly the waters of the Hudson River. Below, in the street, the many-styled coaches, the varicolored carriages, the big drab dray trucks, made a clatter that swept upward. It sounded better to him than the protests by letter and delegation. Politicians and prominent lawyers came to Albany to urge him to pardon Colt. Each docking of a steamboat from New York brought the influential. His own political supporters, big Whigs, arrived hourly, and breathed the words, "Pardon Colt." He felt like a trapped man, for he wondered whether he'd live to finish out the gubernatorial term only a month away from completion. He moved about his office in an excitable way, chewing up one cigar after another. For four years he had directed the state, and had done a good job, he believed; and so did his party; but now, with only days of office remaining, this developed, the sharpest controversy of his career. He was losing friends all over by the instant. "Thank God," he murmured to the walls, "I'm closing out here in a few weeks— if I live. I never want to see office again. Nobody will ever get me back in the public seat!"

He was chagrined that his good friend Horace Greeley, who ran the *Tribune,* was involved. Colt's lawyers tried to intimidate the sheriff of New York County against the execution, and they had managed to get their protest published in the *Tribune.* A public howl against this effort to overawe the sheriff forced Greeley to suppress the edition soon after the first papers hit the streets.

It was now the sixteenth of the month; Colt's hanging was only two days away; and still the statewide appeal mounted.

Underwood gently opened the door to learn whether the executive would see the latest petitioner. "It's the phrenologist," the secretary said.

"Show him in."

Phrenology was the psychological game of that period. The "science" of reading physiological markings of the skull and cranium by which character and habits were interpreted and behavior predicted—so the phrenologist claimed—was something that interested William Henry, but didn't entirely convince him. He regarded phrenology as an approach to a science, as an area of experiment possessing some sensibility. But phrenology was a madness in the country, had been so for ten years since it was imported from Vienna. Every physician studied phrenology, most attempted to practice it, and bump-reading was the great national pastime, in parlors, stagecoaches and hotel lobbies.

This doctor had visited Colt in the Tombs and placed the caliphers to Colt's head and measured the extent of his ambitions, his will, spirit, amativeness, religiosity, and the rest.

"I have examined Colt," he began. "Colt's measurements reveal a man of great gifts, much discernment and ambition, and some vividness of temperament."

William Henry nodded. "I understand he is a man of specialties and gifts of mind."

"Yes, I found his bump of ambition highly developed. It would be a shame to see him cut off in the prime of his life."

"Colt seems to have cut off the prospect of some of his ambitious leaning by the temperament you say he is also in possession of."

"If you wish to put it that way ... I admit I found in his contours, especially at the temples, indications of remarkable volatility. Yet there were other signs in him of self-control."

"The opinions of the court," William Henry said, "have been that his opportunities for self-control have been slighted."

The physician adopted his most authoritative manner. "I candidly do not believe he murdered Adams in anything other than a spirit of self-defense." He added tightly, "The measurements prove it."

The Governor searched for words with which to cope with the phrase-juggling phrenologist. He remarked that the killing was unusually brutal, violent.

"So he was, truly violent. I must say the way he trussed up Adams in that trunk has been as unpleasant to my imagination as to the jury that convicted him."

"What do you expect of me?"

"I expect you to pardon him."

"Pardon him? Let him resume in everyday society? What do you take me for, Doctor? I am here as a protector of the people, not as the perpetrator upon them of a hatchet man."

"He has mean bumps on his head, that I acknowledge, Governor Seward. But I must insist that society has cultivated these bumps."

"How?"

"The nature of our world, its greeds and competitions, its graces and disgraces have fostered in him his native aptitudes and tendencies and given exaggeration to his natural propensities."

"Interesting."

"It is society which should be hanged, not Colt!"

"You expect me to hang society?"

"If you could, I would expect it!"

William Henry stood. He was a man of composure, but this time his face crimsoned over gently, in a way to match his famous carrot hair. He meant to hold his tongue but to end the interview. "I will give your views the same consideration as I have given to those of others who have appealed to me. Thank you."

Bewildered by the statewide demonstration, certain that he must proceed with Colt's execution, he resorted more than customarily to letter writing to Frances. In a way what he wrote was a continuation of his lifelong love letter to her—a single unbroken letter, continuous all the days of their lives, a letter that was one long living apology for not being with her as much as she wished; and yet, through these notes, Frances was always half at hand, though miles, states and counties separated them.

She had written to him wondering whether there might not be merit in commuting Colt's sentence. Perhaps she was, in part, fearful that her husband might lose all popularity by appearing immovable and hard of heart, and she'd asked why he didn't yield to the pressure. "It is a bright and lovely morning, my darling," his answer began. "The snow is high outside and it sparkles, and above the Capitol the blue is almighty blue. I wish you and the boys were here, or I once more at ease with you in Auburn..." Then he talked of the Colt case.

His work distracted him, he said; he was sick and tired and hurt. It seemed to him that all of the mystery of political life had rolled up into the single knot of this experience. "I am disgusted with politics," he confided. How strange, he said, that they were making *him* the manslayer, not Colt. Not the man who had hacked up a fellow businessman and jammed him mutilated into a package for shipping off to eternity by express, but he, the Governor, was now the greatest culprit-in-process in the state—to listen to the protests. Life, he remarked, contained such a peculiar gyroscopic action that ultimately everything walked on its head. It dawned on him, he told Frances, that he probably wasn't the first governor to be in a position of being regarded as the real killer in such a manslaying. There was a reason for not pardoning Colt, he told her, which he could not, with any good effect, give to the public.

He couldn't conscientiously pardon a well-to-do man convicted of murder, while another, poor, unknown, had to be hanged by the state for the same offense:

"In the jail at Lockport there is lying a condemned man waiting his death, yet incapable of distinguishing day from night, and so counting the hours as they carry him along toward an inevitable doom, and no one thinks of *him*. He is poor, a stranger, and an outcast. Colt has connections, relations and associations with the educated class...."

That was it. That was what tore at his conscience as governor and as a man trying to rule honestly—the vagrant in the Lockport jail. It was a question of class; and he wanted not to rule in favor of the well-to-do. A governor ought to be impartial. And this thought, written in all his gloom, "It is a wild and fearful tragedy calculated to disgust us with humanity."

That wasn't the kind of comment he'd ever make to the public in a speech or a published writing, but the truth could be told to his wife.

To the end the Colt case inflated into a thing of terror and tragedy. A few hours before the execution was scheduled, Colt was married to Caroline Henshaw, so that their child would have a name. The news fanned interest in the multitude that gathered around the Tombs, where the prisoner was lodged.

On that last day Colt's brother visited him in the cell; so did counsel, so did a minister. Someone gave the condemned man a knife. He carefully cut a hole in his clothes over his heart, and a few minutes before he was due to be taken from his cell, he plunged a dirk between his ribs and his heart. At the same moment the cupola of the Tombs went on fire. Flames rose high in a roaring yellow, and the thousands in the streets surged and hollered. At four o'clock, just as if all was going as planned, the City Hall bell clanged for the execution to take place.

Rumors passed through the crowd that Colt might escape in the confusion, that he already had escaped, dressed as a woman, and when the word went out that the businessman was inside, dead by his own hand, it wasn't believed. They said a dead convict had been substituted for him. While hundreds rushed out of the flaming prison, other hundreds ran inside, perhaps to recover Colt; and a regiment of police swept into the neighborhood, surrounded the prison, and seized control.

The fire was put out; the body was examined at another inquest; and there was a cry abroad to find out where responsibility and culpability were now.

There had been neither clarity nor decency nor meaning in the whole bitterness, from its inception to its end: only the human tragedy raged on, all the way from Manhattan to Albany, mankind, politics and class inextricably involved.

Chapter Thirty-Six

THE PENDULUM SWINGS HOMEWARD

AND SO William Henry rediscovered the role of the unexpected in
human affairs. He learned a great humility from this, and he saw
that no pride could surmount circumstance, that expectation must
always be tempered with a readiness for adjustment. The injustice of it
all: that he who strove to aid his state could be so vilified. He had a faint
suspicion that the human beast lacked something that dogs possessed in a
large degree—gratitude. He suspected that truth and error might be brother
and sister, that no matter how complex the world was, it was even more
complicated than it seemed.

He rested his hands on his desk; he slumped his shoulders slightly;
and he thought of Frances. He knew he hadn't been the best husband to
her. Here he was, in office, which was what he wanted supremely, and
she, back in Auburn, wanted him: there had been this lifetime clash with
her, how to satisfy his own ambition, and how to please her; and he hadn't
exactly succeeded. But now he was almost through. Soon he'd put it all
behind him, as if it were some big strange dream, not all bad, not all good:
the realization of a man's desire, and he'd had it. Yes, he'd had it. Four
years of rocky going, running this big New York State, the biggest in the
Union, facing a thousand problems, contending with every human difficulty that society could conceive and put before a governor. Will I be glad
to get out of here, he thought, will I? Something tells me that this time
I'll be able to plank down next to Frances and stay with her for a long
time. The bug is dead, long live the bug. He believed he was finished with
political life forever.

He was that tired.

He was worried too about having to return home broke, with a big family to support; and he feared that being forty years old wasn't young any
more, and not a money-making season; but he wrote to Frances that he
was studying retrenchment in every form, and preparing to try to settle
his affairs when he should return. "You will help me all you can in this

matter, I know. If I had only had your prudence years ago, I should now have less to accomplish."

The process that worked in him now was a torment: the big torment of his life. Inside him a pendulum swung, as from a cord in his soul; it was heavy, made of all the taut fiber of a man's human and emotional problem. It worked sometimes as a lifeline that gave him freedom, and at other times as a chain that bound him to earth. It swung between two destinies, his life as a husband, father and domestic man, and his other life that turned on his public course, his ambition, his patriotic zeal, his want to serve his country, and to be remembered for his service.

The two drives clashed inside him and became the twisted rope and the pendulum at the center of him, and gave him the joy of life and its bitterness. It had been that way ever since shortly after marriage, and it was still like that.

Now the pendulum swung homeward, where the pull was heavy with love and the hope of peace ... and he couldn't wait.

He was going back—to a private debt of $400,000, which he would have to meet or mitigate somehow, and to law practice, to the quiet of small-town life and the savor of domesticity. The idea of resuming a legal practice in the village wasn't pleasant to him. He might, he thought, write a book on American government, politics and law. That would lift him out of the grime of the professional routine. But he wasn't sure. He'd wait ... get back home ... then see.

There was a small thing he would definitely do after he got there. He would finish reading Dickens' tale, *Nicholas Nickleby*. He had put down the Englishman's book when he was halfway through it, on the eve of taking the governorship in 1839; then, in all the time until now, in the haste and uproar of State Capitol politics, he hadn't had time to read a single history, novel, or other literary work. He wrote to Frances to please set aside a room that he could use as a library: no clerks to be admitted there, no clients, no business transactions whatever in that room, just give him a place where he could study again, be by himself, have quiet and think. His state papers, books, maps, documents, letters, were freighted westward; for he wanted those things, composing a stack of material big as a half-cord of wood, to be placed in that library as a memento of his embattled days as Governor.

Frances' last letter arrived, and she told him that of course she would have a room set aside for him as a library, and she talked to him about his diet as she did from time to time, how the indispositions he had been suffering of late might be remedied by a little home cooking. She had always urged him to avoid having a great variety of dishes, to be careful not to have too many meats and desserts: "Your liberal spirit has led you into this error more than once—too many varying foods besides indicates a want of taste and is now decidedly *mauvaise*—though there should be no deficiency in quantity or quality of such as you have— I suppose we can remedy all this when you are home again— I need hardly tell you that the whole house is on tenterhooks—it might be judicious if you vacationed a bit and stayed about the house a few days before resuming practice—but I shall leave such decisions to your discretion— Fred's yellow cat is ailing— Gus' turtles are all dead— I believe he is now finished with this hobby— Pa will probably ply you with plenty of political talk— I told him to let you rest, unless you feel like engaging in such talk but then I never knew you, tired or not, to object to politics— I think that I shall try to suppress my feelings of excitement at your return by simply making this letter short and say nothing further till I see you— Your Own Frances."

At the end there were pleasant repercussions of the forthright stand that he took with the State of Virginia.

The colored citizens of Albany met one night in the vestry of the Hamilton Street Church. It was not a large gathering, only about fifty men, women and children, but they met for a single reason: to express their gratitude to the departing chief for refusing to send to Virginia the three men who helped a slave to escape.

The Negro leaders, Primus Robinson and Stephen Myers of Albany, and the notable Dr. James McCune Smith of New York, spokesmen for the slave population, addressed a resolution to the Governor: "... We do this not for vain ostentation, but because we believe it our duty to thank our benefactor in behalf of those who cannot speak for themselves, and who have so few advocates to speak for them."

In the remaining days letters of similar sentiment came to him from slaves in Virginia who scrawled their thanks, and from black Abolitionists in New England. He was heartened by all this and it helped to displace some of the disillusion with human nature that he experienced after the Colt case. People did remember, an effort might be worth while, perhaps there would be a realization in the future....

So he sat down to do his last letters as Governor of New York and these were his acknowledgments to the resolution and the letters sent to him by the watchful free Negroes and the handful of articulate slaves.

To the distinguished James McCune Smith, who was nationally known for his journalism and his oratory directed against the slave power, he wrote his profounder and his final thoughts:

254

nascence

Only time can determine between those who have upheld and those who have opposed the measures to which you have adverted.

But I feel encouraged to await that decision, since in the moment when, if ever, reproaches for injustice should come, the exile does not reproach me, the prisoner does not exult in my departure, and the disfranchised and the slave greet me with their salutations.

One day, after the new year opened, and a new noise was heard over the Capitol, the noise of a new administration, William Henry prepared to take leave of Albany. He and Weed stood under the shelter of the roof of the Schenectady Railroad Depot, waiting for the stage to start.

William Henry told the Whig party boss that he felt as if he had survived a thousand perils. He had made friends, but a thousand enemies too. He had offended people unavoidably or imprudently, and he could see these, like a regiment, in the back of his brain, rising up before him, still threatening him, like those who hated him for not pardoning John Colt.

"Sometimes, Weed, I'm surprised to find myself alive and kicking, after four years of trying my best, and pleasing almost nobody."

"You took the positions you had to take, Governor."

"I did. And yet, with every stand I took I found that somebody, the Democrats, or the public, or my own party, didn't like it."

"People aren't always ready for a principled position."

"I'm afraid I've lost friends, and all I wanted to do was to make them."

"You made friends, Governor. Except you don't always hear from them so quickly. It's your enemies that let you know they're around."

"And my personal friends, my Whig colleagues?" William Henry asked. "Now that I'm out of power, will they desert me?"

"If they do, they were never very much."

William Henry murmured that he believed he was through with public life forever. He felt he was lucky to have emerged honorably, and because of that he somehow felt safe: he was still young, he might even be able to repair his private fortunes.

Weed merely listened; for he retained an inner set of reflections about all that. William Henry was tired out, he needed a rest and a change, but he could be called upon again, and he probably would be. He had groomed the redhead for the governorship, and in that position he had grown to national stature; he had made no grievous error that alienated him from the public; he had been parlayed along to a considerable height for a young man, and inwardly Weed was loath to think that such a product as this was destined for nascence. There was the Senate, there were ever higher offices. He's wait, he'd see ... he knew William Henry very well.

The passengers boarded the stage. William Henry and Weed shook hands. Then the Governor nimbly climbed to the driver's seat, high up at the front of the carriage. His customary place.

The wagon rolled as he faced westward. The horses galloped and the snow designed downward and it speckled white the Governor's gray traveling clothes. Stagecoaches had played a great part in his life, riding to local destinies, changing his professional courses, ending his philosophic periods. Stagecoaches had played a major part in the nation's life too, the stages going westward, always westward, politics in its most powerful forms moving ever toward the Mississippi, William Henry's thoughts westerly ones.

He felt better now; the Capitol was receding, and the cares of office were in the hands of a new governor named Bouck. So William Henry could settle into the warm buffalo hide on the driver's seat and watch the white winter as the horse railway rushed on, smell the raw air driven in from the Adirondacks, study the leafless designs of naked trees along the route, spot the likeliest vales where not long before Indian campfires had burned; draw America into his system, the real physical-geographical-natural America.

Once, as a small boy in Florida, the little place surrounded by hills, which he must get beyond somehow, he had acquired an inward figure or sense that sometimes operated within him, as if he experienced a climbing, an image of getting beyond a hill, or of being beyond one; it was an urge that worked in him, part of his life force. It ticked inside him at critical moments, at changes of seasons, this sense of the hill that needed crossing; and now, finished as Governor, he had this feeling of a hill in his life being crossed.

He folded the buffalo robe up around his back, put his fingers deep into his woolen-lined leather gloves, and he settled into quiet observation of the salt-colored Mohawk Valley. Long thoughts rode with him across the bright fields, and the people and places of the last twenty years—the years of James Monroe, John Quincy Adams, Andrew Jackson and Martin Van Buren—sifted pictorially before his eyes, like the snowflakes that flurried groundward. . . . A man doesn't make a transition from high office to private life in an easy stage ride, in a day or a week. The steady whirr and grind beneath the wheels, the relaxation, a nostalgic snowfall . . . these carried him into long remembrance.

The scenes, the journeyings, the contentions of twenty packed years, of seven thousand days, filmed down through his vision, somewhat like the snowflakes that dropped downward, toward him, then slipped past him, and he remembered . . . and he remembered . . . and he remembered.

Chapter Thirty-Seven

THE BEGINNING

I T WAS a Saturday night when he arrived.

Now it was as Frances liked it: he was home, he'd be a husband and a father again, and a village lawyer, as she had always wished, a man around, the house being taken care of, and a family life being lived. He'd squire her to church again, and take the children out for an occasional sleighride; in the spring he'd get busy in the big yard and plant and cultivate, and townsmen would come to the house for casual evenings of talk and coffee.

Her husband had completed his governorship in honor and distinction; and she was the wife of a distinguished man. She had a certain good feeling about this, there was a compensation for her as well as for him. The seasons at the Capitol had lightened her spirit somewhat, and perhaps she partially forgave the errant wandering that he had done; for, at the Executive Mansion, she learned how truly important politics was in the everyday life of the millions, and a woman had to abide the imperfections of a man who could be of so much use to so many people. Reluctantly she faced up to the fact that perhaps his long absences that amounted to desertions were inevitable in order for him to become the Governor that he became.

Not that there was any definable physical or physiological alteration about her because of this realization; nothing happened to reduce or eliminate her generally subjective and invalided nature; that was jelled in her, for it had become the pattern of her life; it was too late for any fundamental change to take place in her torn and erupted nature, her split loves, her feeling of not ever fully attaining William Henry—that might never change.

But she was adjusted to his uniqueness—even if she would never never enjoy his absences....

Now he was back home, and that meant ever so much. Who knows, she thought, he may even stay close to the hearth. Yet even as she hoped, a cloying doubt would not be stilled.

On the following Monday morning he strolled to his law office in the Exchange Building. It was early in the morning, blistery cold when he arrived, and he pottered around a stove to get the fire started. Then he scouted about the office in search of something...he found it...an old tin sign.

WM. H. SEWARD, ATTY.

He went outside, in front of his office, and he tacked the shingle on the door. He was in business again, this time without a partner.

He walked a little distance to the office of the Auburn *Journal*. There he chatted briefly with the clerks, and he left a little announcement to be printed that day, and he paid for it:

NOTICE

The subscriber will attend to any business which may be confided to him in the courts of law and Court of Chancery.

WILLIAM H. SEWARD, Exchange Block.

He returned to his office; it was warm inside now, and he sat down to wait for the first client.

Late in the morning a farmer strolled by in search of a lawyer, and he saw the tin sign. He looked inside and there was the Governor.

"By golly, I'll see if he takes my case."

The farmer edged in. "Be ye open for business?"

"Yes sir, come in and warm yourself."

"Now let me tell you what happened. Jack Hollister's damned breachy oxen busted down my fence, and I want to make him pay, I want him to build me a new fence. Can you help me out?"

William Henry said that this would have to go into the peace justice's court. The client wanted to know how much the fee would be, and the Governor asked, "Will five dollars be too much?"

"No siree, that's just right."

When the first client walked out, William Henry trailed behind him for a breath of the cold air and a glance at the main street. He looked upward into the gray sky and he tried to figure out how many cases a day of "damned breachy oxen" he might have to handle to pay off the $400,000 that he owed to the Holland Land Company proprietors.

The computation he reached made him laugh.

He peered down the street, into the future, into all of the uncertainty that all men look into from day to day.

258

Five dollars. Like when he came here long ago, and began as a new attorney in the stripling settlement.

It didn't seem credible that he could have just retired from the governorship of this great state, and yet be starting out all over as he had once before—in the same place.

Even so, a moment of sentiment settled upon him, a springlike mood. It was good to be away from the state burden. The Oliver Goldsmith line went through his thoughts as he glanced up and down Genesee Street, *Sweet Auburn, loveliest village of the plain....*

It was cold, the snow was deep underfoot, only a few people were out, the sun was white and distant, it might be the deserted village all over again.

And yet he knew that in each house there was warmth and life. New smoke swirled from the housetops. New flakes lowered over the town. Newness and beginnings everywhere.

Everything has a beginning, he mused, as he re-entered his office. Everything.

Part Three

THE GOVERNOR AND HIS MISTRESS

Chapter Thirty-Eight

WEED PLANS TO NAME A CERTAIN
MAN PRESIDENT

JAMES FENIMORE COOPER, when he reached middle age, was a man of well-fed, Anglican look. He was an early-day American of British origins, and enough of the traditional royalty worship remained with him so that it was natural for him to fall in with the conservative views of his own time: save chattel slavery, which he came to feel was foreign to the American milieu.

When he returned from Europe, in the mid-1830s, after being lionized there as the American Sir Walter Scott, he returned to the family home at Cooperstown, New York, in the Mohawk Valley. There, he and his wife took up residence in the great brick family home called Otsego Hall. This was a Gothic-style place that had been closed during Cooper's travels in Europe. While the master of the house was abroad, the villagers of Cooperstown formed the habit of crossing the grounds, as a short cut, because the property severed one of the streets. When Cooper resumed provincial living he straightened that out right away: nobody could walk over the grounds of Otsego Hall and hereafter they must go around the block. The townsmen murmured unpleasantly about that, but they disliked even more the fact that Cooper forbade the community to use as a swimming spot an area known as Three Mile Point, on Otsego Lake.

This was owned by Cooper's late father, and as not much had ever been done with this property, it fell into general use as a picnic resort and as a lovers' lane. In fact the people believed that this was now public property.

One day the townsmen read in the local paper, *The Freeman's Journal,* a notice saying that the Point was not public property but it belonged to the Coopers, and the public should not injure the trees on it. James Fenimore warned against trespassing, said he would rigidly enforce the law, and the public had no right to the Point, beyond its use as conceded by the liberality of the owners.

Sixty townsmen got together at once, they resolved to oppose this warning notice, to hold him and his threat and his conduct in perfect contempt, and furthermore they urged the town library, called the Franklin Library, to remove Cooper's books.

The newspapers had some meat: a leading novelist in trouble is always hot news, and a novelist who takes an unpopular position is follow-up copy for some time. The Chenango *Telegraph* was the first to report what happened, a news story unsympathetic to Cooper; and then Thurlow Weed, at his desk at the *Journal* in Albany, picked up the Chenango paper. Thereafter, the news of Cooper's latest tiff with society spread around the country; and Cooper began the first of a series of libel suits against a variety of newspapers.

Weed lost a suit to Cooper in 1840, a verdict of $400; and by 1842 he lost three more suits to Cooper. At one of these trials, in May of 1842, Weed had a wonderful time in the courtroom reading Cooper's newest novel, *The Two Admirals,* while the lawyers for Cooper were giving Weed's attorneys a drubbing. In that way the scrappy Cooper went on until 1845, winning and losing lawsuits for libel (chiefly losing) and fighting with words and courts his one-man battle against American society, while belaboring that society, while also proving his own independence as a writer, and pursuing his espousal of unpopular causes such as the manorial side in the Helderberg war.

But he was having a wonderful time, in a way, taking on all comers, and the biggest were not too big for him, not Weed and certainly not that noisy but clever journalist, Horace Greeley.

In 1842 he sued Greeley. Greeley defended himself in court, didn't do a good job, and a verdict of $200 damages was returned against him. This wasn't enough of a fine to discourage litterateurs like Greeley from continuing their field day with such readable copy as Cooper.

The matter finally reached a state where the question of libel law itself became an issue. The defeated journalists began contending that libel law wasn't clearly defined, the courts needed new definitions of what was libelous. The press was taking wing and wanted more opportunity for wider dealing with personalities, and they didn't want to have to pay every time they went after someone. Where, asked Greeley, in all of this, is freedom of the press?

Cooper believed that the public itself was becoming despotic, that too much power was in the hands of the people generally, that a spirit of "anything goes" was rising in the country, and that this was bad. If it went on, nobody would be free from what the press could and would do to them.

It was a very legitimate thought.

Moreover, Cooper backed up his ideas by hinting that commerce, profit, money were becoming a new morality in the land; that the newspapers were proving this, trying to build circulation at the expense of human personality, by attacking anyone for anything, in this case Cooper: the theme of a moneyed nation with a money-moraled outlook came to dominate his writings and his thinking.

It was, actually, one of his most farsighted observations.

Finally, his dispute with Greeley reached a point where, Greeley realized, he couldn't fight in court as well as a lawyer might. The journalist knew a certain attorney who, he felt, had some obligation to defend him.

So that only a few weeks after William Henry returned to Auburn, he was on his way east again, this time to Albany and New York. Before leaving he spent several days preparing special pleas for Greeley in two libel cases brought by the novelist. He had the feeling that libel laws were too harsh, that a definition of libel was needed that fitted the accelerating American scene and the rise of flourishing journalism, and he looked upon the Greeley-Cooper feud as a test of the issue of freedom of the press.

It was one thing to defend Greeley as an editor, and another to try to understand him as a man who "monkeyed with politics," as William Henry viewed it. In Albany, stopping to see Weed before going on to New York and into the Supreme Court, he and Weed talked about the problem they had with the man they called the adjutant. Greeley talked Whig politics in the *Tribune* daily, he took political stands without consulting with others, he put forward policies that other Whigs regarded as dubious. They couldn't control him; he had a forum of his own: a real "tribune," and he used it.

"I have to candidly confess and confide to you that I don't grasp Greeley. I don't know what he thinks he is." That was Weed, in his newspaper office.

William Henry answered, "Now that the matter is in the open, I must say I share your uncertainties."

263

"He thinks he is a practical politician. Can you imagine anything more absurd?" Weed asked.

"No, I can't. But he is something more than that to me...."

"Yes?"

"He's a special person, Weed. There's a ruggedness about him and an independence that amounts to querulousness. I almost think he's a new breed, peculiar to our soil. The independence flows out of him like lava from a volcano...it's his principal product."

"And the source of his best thinking too, I'd say...but Seward, he disappoints me sometimes as an adjutant. I tell him I'd like certain things to be done, and he balks like a mule...."

"Maybe the image of the balky mule isn't right. Maybe we've got a tiger by the tail."

"Oh, no, no, no. I think he can be relied on in the usual situation. He's a Whig. He thinks like we do, he's one of us."

"Not entirely. He recently told me, 'I have to make my own Political Economy as I go along.' That's the statement of a man who can wind up anywhere. He senses that he's an adjutant and not really a partner. I think he senses the real relationship is yours and mine and that he feels he can never share bonds with us as equally as we do with each other. I think he has the feeling of being an extra wheel when he's with us."

"We've done a lot for him, Seward. We picked him when he was tottering in a piddling printer's way down in New York; he came by his reputation through us, and I am inclined to feel that we're entitled to his loyalties."

"He's built the *Tribune* by himself. With the sense of power that he has from that, his independent streak has run off with him, and you and I can't expect to influence him in any way that he doesn't want to be."

"Well, just so long as he stays in line..."

"That's his specialty, that he won't stay in anyone's line. He likes to offer opposition."

"I don't mind opposition. I just have the feeling that he never speaks fully to us. I get the feeling there's something left unsaid after he's spoken and shared views with us."

"You know what it is, Weed. He thinks he's a politician when you and I know he's an editor, and first-rate as such."

"I get that sense from him too...that he prowls in politics, without quite being all in the open over it."

"Well, I'll see if I can get him out of this jam with Cooper."

The Greeley case met with a snag in the court, and the first of a series of delays resulted.

William Henry returned to Auburn, and he resumed with his Central and Western New York practice. During the succeeding months he found the time to dip into philosophy. Nights, weekends, sometimes at home, and sometimes at his office, and even when he was away from the village and alone in a hotel room, he read deeply, and he compared what he studied with what he experienced as a governor and what he felt about the new nation rising about him. When he traveled, on those interminable stage-coaches and looked outward at the towns, and saw the people at work, the busy community life everywhere, he sensed the breadth of the country, and he contrasted what he was looking at with what the early colonists might have beheld, and he tried to imagine what the national picture would look like to later generations. His thoughts came in broad strokes of political imagining, and a whole philosophy of the nation's growth. Actually, for years, a special and personal view had been germinating, and he began to articulate it.

Here was a young social revolutionary America to which the whole world gave obeisance for its daring experiment, its readiness to fight and to defend itself, its welcome to the spirit en masse, its hailing of democracy, its open ports saying to all immigrants and political exiles, "Come, give us your strength, join with us if you are elsewhere oppressed..." and he saw the country as a well that took in streams of strength from distant hills.

He was invited to address the Phi Beta Kappa Society of Union College. It was to be a commencement address in July, and he wondered what he would say. Could he express his new views?

He wrote a speech, and when he finished with it, he wasn't sure of its merit. If it was a good address, he told Frances, it wasn't half long enough. If it wasn't good, then it was twice too long. Would she, he asked her at the dinner table one night, find time to listen to him and to make any suggestions that she might?

Later, when the children were out of the way, and they were alone in the library, he told her that he regarded this speech as an effort to express something that had been long forming within him.

"Try to speak clearly, Henry—and if you could only improve your tone."

"As well try to change the shape of my nose."

"Then at least make your pauses effective...."

She sat attentively in a tall-backed mahogany chair. He moved energetically in the center of the soft-carpeted room. There were papers in his hands.

"Shall you be reading this one?"

"I think so. I may want to use this paper later or develop the idea further."

"What have you called it?"

"The True Greatness of Our Country."

"Sounds just right for college students."

"I have a feeling this goes beyond student interest. . . ."

"A virtuous citizen," he began in his throaty tone, "is not satisfied with knowing that his country is great and free and happy; he wants to understand why this is so, what are the elements of its empire, how long will they endure. . . ."

He took on confidence, looked about the room, on either side of his wife, as if there sat the audience.

She interrupted. "You are daddling with the index finger of your free hand in a way to detract from what you're saying. . . ."

"Just listen for content first, and not for delivery," he answered. Because it was impossible for him to stop doddling the air. He resumed:

"I have the authority of Lord Bacon . . ."

"Henry?"

He stopped, lowered the paper.

"Shouldn't you more modestly say, 'We have the authority of . . .'"

He crossed out the I, changed it to we, and quoted the English philosopher as saying that the greatness of kingdoms and estates and the means by which they became great was argument fit for mighty princes to have in their hands; they might then not overmeasure their forces, nor lose themselves in stupid mismoves on the one hand, nor undervalue themselves and stoop to fearful and weak counsels on the other.

She interrupted. "Does this speech take its departure from Bacon in its entirety?"

"I suppose, yes. He's talked of the greatness of kingdoms, and that's my theme—"

For an instant he floundered; he felt unduly interrupted; he placed his free hand in the handkerchief pocket of his coat, searched for a cigar, and when it wasn't there, he plucked one from a bowl on a table.

"Not now, Henry," she said. "Don't smoke when you're rehearsing a speech—"

But he lit up, he puffed away, and went on, how Bacon had remarked that there were some states great in territory and yet they were not apt to command, and others bore a small dimension and yet these were the foundation of great monarchies.

William Henry intended that his Union College audience visualize

266

broad and powerful Russia and China as examples of great estates yielding as yet a cultural lag, and they would see Bacon's small England risen to a monarchial sway. Then they'd be ready for the American example....

Here he flowed into a kind of poetry, which most of his speeches contained, a language rich in a simple imagery of sun, moon, stars, mountains, deserts, elementary natural figures: and he pictured how the United States was a belt across the continent, a continuous, a compact and an inseparable dominion; he described the rock formations, the trees infinite in their variety, land and waters rich for cultivation, for viewing, for living upon: the woods ready for conversion into farm, home and temple, wharf and ship and school; he limned the long-branching rivers with their lifegiving uses, the great-chested lakes to the west, the bays large and ample as the muscles of giants, and upon all these, he said, were men's strenuous additions: the roads, canals, steamboats, the hissing engines bringing comfort and life to the citizenry; and so, these two, nature and the utilitarian, were coming together in a wedding of power and growth.

She let him read now, and he went on, saying how all this spelled manufacture and markets, and how there impended great trades with Africa and Asia; there'd be new and unknown means of communication with these distant lands, and we should soon be reaching populous India and China, and there'd be communication with the islands of the South Pacific, "mysterious regions to which we now send out bonds of appeal and whose need for us we are aware of—"

Here was the prospect, and we, in a destiny that embraced our national fortune with that of the rest of the world, should know this too: "An intellectual and active people, holding a position favorable and possessing resources so boundless, could not fail to secure freedom of the seas, without which no nation in modern times can be great; while they would furnish a political alembic which, receiving the exhausted civilization of Asia and the ripening civilization of Western Europe, and commingling them together after their long separation, would disclose the secret of the ultimate regeneration and reunion of human society throughout the world.

So, there was a "one-world" advocacy in the land, back in 1844, and the idea was ventured forth this night to a lone woman listener, who nodded her head, and made still another gesture to him to put down his cigar.

He went on, of the American people, "...I dwell on their martial ability, not because they are or ought to be a warlike people but because courage and fortitude are equally elements of greatness, whether pacific or belligerent, and because no inert or effeminate nation can enjoy peace or security."

The population, by 1950, he predicted, would be 150,000,000—and he hit that right on the nose. He swept along now, of the tendency of the nation to increase strength with its increase in numbers and with its capacity for assimilation of the world's human variety. "All exotic elements are rapidly absorbed and completely assimilated." He was overly optimistic about that, but he pressed on to a more intrepid thought: that mere numbers without moral elements meant nothing; and so we must have what we already showed we had: the discipline, the energy and the resolution of free men.

His voice lowered. . . .

From time to time war was necessary, and he spoke of preventive war and of Burke who said that war was occasionally necessary and sometimes inevitable. There were times when war was "a danger to avert a danger, a present inconvenience and suffering to prevent a foreseen future and a worse calamity."

He quit smoking now; he held the paper in both hands, interested, as if he challenged Frances to dare interrupt him.

He denounced arbitrary power, even if it came from God: "Arbitrary power procures the performance of duty only by terror by penalties. Laws relying on that motive alone will be ineffectual, whether written in the statute book in blood, or engraved in the rock by even the Almighty hand."

No, there was something better than arbitrary power—a republic. For sixty years, the working wonder of the republican form had been observed by the entire world, and in spite of hostilities and factions, the nation had doubled in territory, and there were twice as many states as at first, and seven times the original population, and there had been no armed and organized sedition, and in forty years no one had been accused of treason.

Of course, he said, there is the danger of secession. "Yet disunion is no longer a real terror, but is sinking into an antiquated superstition, haunting only minds which morbidly court the enervating spell."

"Are you sure of this, Henry?"

"I have to say this, Frances, and I have to believe it. We must propagate faith and belief in the integrity of the Union. It must be inculcated. I am addressing students."

"Even if secession came," he read on, "we Americans would do it without violence, we would show the rest of the nations of the world how a separation would occur, we would show them that our long habits of mutual affection and discipline would result in an amicable parting and reconstruction without the loss of liberty."

That was the way it seemed to him in 1844.

Finally, he warned, we must be careful about the possibilities of decay. There were the seeds and the signs of degeneration already; there was much in the land to seduce men from their decency and virtue; power and wealth were temptations; and our own virtue and moderation must be renewed and fortified under circumstances new and peculiar.

He was nearing the end of his reading. And where could we go to inculcate the right motives and passions? Only to the domestic fireside and the humble school, where the American citizen was trained.... "Go then, laborers in a noble cause, gather the young Catholic and the young Protestant alike unto the nursery of freedom; and teach them there that, although religion has many and different shrines, yet that this country has appointed only one altar and one sacrifice for all her sons, and that ambition and avarice must be slain on that altar, for it is consecrated to Humanity."

Thurlow Weed had nothing to do with such excursions into the realm of philosophy and public policy. He may not even have been capable of this, for few men of that hour were capable of it: if they had been, they would have given the "elements of empire" address, not William Henry: they would have foreseen a day of territorial extension and national survival on a high plane and an America spreading a liberal democratic faith across the oceans.

A spirit of "manifest destiny" circulated these days, John Quincy Adams hinted of it, and the term made its appearance in print occasionally, but William Henry tried to make the idea graphic and particular and geographical and real. Each time he uttered these sentiments, he believed them from his heart; he made his predictions, the right ones and the wrong ones, and on each occasion he told the young to keep their eyes on stardust, and not the spoils, if they wanted for themselves and their country any true greatness.

At such times as these Weed only read in the papers what William Henry had to say; he studied what his confidant uttered, and he felt confirmed in the reliance he placed upon the Auburn lawyer. He knew that the Governor, as he continued to be called by everybody, had in him the elements of greatness and leadership, even as the country itself. And the Governor had to be worked with and groomed, parlayed along, and permitted to make no grievous error that would alienate the public, if that could be prevented; for Weed had in mind another objective for his friend, protégé and comrade in public arms: the Presidency of the United States.

Chapter Thirty-Nine

WILLIAM HENRY TAKES A SPILL
ON THE GRASS ROOTS

HIS mother was gone. From her he had received much, perhaps her amiable manner, for she had been cheerful, affectionate and temperate, and much of his physiology may have been from Mary Jennings Seward and the Irish line from which she issued. In December of 1844, William Henry was on his way to Orange Country to see her when she passed away.

After the funeral, he boarded a stagecoach and moved northward again, quietly, sadly, the cold time of year seeming apposite to his mood. Atop the stagecoach, in the driver's seat, he gazed at the fields, hard but snowless; the trees, he knew them a hundred yards away, alder and spruce, maple and horse chestnut, and they were masses of light pen strokes, the branches bared and waiting for the fall of snow. The weather was stark, changeable, as they moved over the rutted highways, everywhere the strain of threatening snowfall, but he smoked his incessant cigars, listened to the driver crack his whip, and he thought of politics and the world. His beloved state unrolled on either side of the wagon as he speculated on his law cases. Inwardly he prepared briefs, munched over the Greeley-Cooper action, wrote letters to his friends, worked up his Whig ideas.

His coach headed for Stockport, a small spot along the Hudson River, and the wheels made time, ten miles an hour or more, four horses galloping and pulling the big wooden box. But the stage was worn; it had made too many trips without repair, and the road was rough, so that suddenly William Henry and the driver heard a crunch beneath the coach as the axletree broke.

The wagon went down on its right side, and it heaved William Henry far out into a gulley. The stake clattered to a stop a few feet beyond, turning over, the horses neighing, passengers screaming, and the driver somehow fallen clear of the wreckage unhurt.

As William Henry lay in the ditch he felt pain, and a numbness, and the shock somehow unleased a spring of nascent absorptions, a bubbling up from his unconscious of the early law cases, and with each jab of hurt a title came to him exactly as recorded, just as it had imbedded itself in his consciousness, *Jackson ex dem Hardenburgh v. McLallen, Covenant in Lease to Build a Shed and Keep it in Repair.* His leg felt twisted and an ache nerved out from his ankle up to his brain, and the title continued— *Action on Covenant Lies for Breach.* And another, *Lee v. Glover,* the Indian litigation, *Conveyance by Indian Void—Whether He Reside with His Tribe Immaterial....* Kaghnatshou, the red man, leaping to the top of his skull in a jab of agony. A few feet away the coach lay topside, askew, its four wheels spinning ferociously as if they were still running on schedule, due north along the road...*Cumpston v. Field and Bracket* (*1829*) *a second fieri fascias cannot issue until after the return of the previous execution*...and then he heard voices.

None of the other half-dozen passengers were injured and they gathered about the Governor.

"Better get me to some house," he said.

"What seems to be wrong?" the driver asked.

"The arm. It doesn't move. My hip too, I think..."

He tried to get to his feet, but he couldn't budge.

A farmer approached. "I'm Zeke Butler, live right here," he said, pointing to a farmhouse. "Bring this little man to my place."

"This little man's the Governor of your state, sir," someone told the farmer.

Butler looked hard. "Why, Mr. Seward—by gods—I'm the beneficiary of this!"

Frances, at Auburn, received the details in a letter from a Stockport Quaker who wrote for the injured attorney:

DEAR MRS. SEWARD:

By request of thy husband I write to inform thee that thy man has been thrown from a coach, but thee must not fret thyself as he is in good hands, and Friends of the Lord have him in their care, and thee shall have him home before long and though he have a slipped shoulder and a hurt hip to burden him, still he shall prosper and thee must consider thyself fortunate that he is among the living. He desires me to say that thou wilt not think of coming, for he will be enabled to journey to thee ere long, as everything necessary is done for him.

Very respectfully,

JOHN STANTON GOULD

271

Two weeks later he was still in Stockport, seeing through a window the barren village; outside the same scattered little array of one-story and two-story houses, and the farmlands stretching to the Hudson; but he wasn't yet moving about. His arm was slinged, his shoulder was hurt and immobile, and new hurts developed in his right leg. He couldn't even get out of bed; and he couldn't lift himself into a sitting posture.

He was lonesome for home and for a sight of the new baby girl, named Frances after her mother. The infant was born in November and at once they began calling her Fanny, so as to distinguish her from her mother.

On a snowy January day, William Henry was helped aboard a stagecoach; better to be in bed at home, he decided; and, after several days of wearying travel, a coach sleigh took him into the Finger Lakes village. The vehicle turned up and down the Genesee hills, into South Street, and reached the last loop at the curbside into the driveway and alongside the house. There a cluster of villagers were gathered to help him out and to get him inside by the blazing fireplace.

In April he still couldn't lift his hand, but he could write with it and he could attend court.

In May he went to New York to appear before the Supreme Court in defense of Greeley. But the city was never attractive to him, nor lucky for him; he sensed something abnormal growing here, an unnatural speed and materialism, and the racket of horses and carriages on Broadway rattled his country nerves. He passed the time with Greeley and other Whigs. Greeley astonished him by his expression of socialist views; the journalist wanted to see the complex civilization of the city converted to the simplicity of the Fourier system; and the Auburnian once again secured an uneasy feeling about his unpredictable political colleague.

Greeley was in everything, but not in a straight line.

The day came when William Henry told the Supreme Court what he believed were the issues between his client and James Fenimore Cooper. He said that the rules of libel that obtained in England were no longer appropriate in a democracy such as ours. In England, it was presumed without proof that if a publication reflected on a man's character, he was entitled to damages. He contended that here it would be wiser to open the doors wider to defense in such cases. If the courts didn't pursue a different course, he said, libel actions might fall into the hands of litigious and corrupt men and become a means of extortion and oppression.

Finally the court split over the question, handing down a judgment half for Cooper and half for Greeley. Yet the decision had the effect of altering libel actions thereafter so that plaintiffs must be better able to prove their charges than was the practice until now.

Back in Auburn, still ailing, thinner, his walking pace slowed and his arm recovering slowly, William Henry decided that he needed to take the summer off. He must stay away from law, do something to rebuild himself: and he hatched the idea to take a kind of exploration trip westward into the Great Lakes region, into Canada, his Whig friends, Jim Bowen and Seth Hawley, to go with him.

Once more he was on the road, this time with two sturdy outdoor men, Bowen, a fisherman and a businessman, and Hawley, a colonel with a military flair and a love of the outdoors and a way with axes and knives in the forest; two good companions for a too-civilized and secularized politician, and he'd leave to them much of the rough work of pitching tents and cutting their way through woods.

They reached Buffalo by train and coach, the Governor having no fear of the highway in spite of his accident...Maple leaf and pine needle, black fly and bee, the buttercup, and the bluejay dipping for a beetle, the thin tree trunk of the young birch that was white as a wrist and as delicate, the gray sky behind which the blue laughed quietly and inevitably, and the endless floor of green and brown trod by rodent, insect, snake, stretching endlessly from coast to coast waiting to be churned to some man's use, or simply to be seen and admired: all of it revived him as he bounced along on the coach tops westward, chewing his cigar, scouring his lungs with the clean air of the new nation.

Perhaps the reason why he was so taken with nature, the out-of-doors, and the fascination of wilderness, stream and field, sunlight and snow, was because he privately believed that the only true virtue in the world was in absolute nature: the honesty of a tall tree, standing for a century in the clear light of day and the dark of the moonlight for all to see, plainly and clearly for what it was, a tree; the sincerity of a wild sky, bent on its own directions independent of all other phenomena and concern, the gray billows deepening down in the sky, upon their own course, true, unswerving; and finally, the simple but universal accomplishment of the sun, burning, toiling, heating, doing all, occupying its allotted place in the universe in full fruition.

These sights and senses gave him a feeling for the incongruity of life: "How often have I reflected that, whatever care and diligence we exercise, our fortunes in life are beyond our own control!"

Only man's affairs were clouded with such paradox and irony that prophecy was doomed, expectation so often bound to be cut off before realization, and anomaly only to rule and reign. This fundamental understanding gave him a focus through which he could see the scheme of the

273

undependable nature of the social and political world, and it led him into pragmatic philosophizings: so that aphorisms, swift judgments, keen observations came from his lips and his pen with a sad regularity: "Defeats are bad for the end of a political life, but not bad in the beginning." He uttered these comments with a kind of cheerful gloom, taking the disappointment and chagrin of human experience with a dose of high laughter. Generally he rated as a very optimistic man, a being who radiated the finest positiveness, but inwardly he had a private misgiving about the course of life, and he confided it often to his wife, also to Thurlow Weed and to his own inner ear. "How painful the reflection is, that the way of patriotic duty is uncertain, like the navigator's path on the ocean—exposed just as much to winds and tempests, or unseen or misunderstood currents."

Steamer Wisconsin, on Lake Huron, Saturday morning, July 12th— We have reeled off seven hundred miles, and still our course is onward ... We have now followed six hundred miles the line which separates our country from the sister republic that is content to remain a dependency on a European State ... Our hospitable steward spread for us last night a supper of woodcock, oysters and lobster ... We are now following the shore as it winds to the northwest, and soon we'll be at the straits of Machilimackinac. It is a hundred and seventy years since white men reached these straits.

Always he had this sense of history, and it was his knowledge of history which gave him his intellectual grasp, which turned keys for him into the future. Canada troubled him. It ought properly to be part of the States, he felt: and he couldn't understand why people wanted absentee rule and control. Not this for Americans.

He saw a vision of the American future and it was a nation of nations he beheld, and it needed the pure air of good thought and decent works to be built into something that was en masse, and he was one, working in politics as Whitman in poetry, and Melville in prose. There were painters painting the valleys and the prairies, and Indians stalking game while themselves being stalked; there were high canyons and the white-hatted mountains, the little divides of counties and the Great Divide farther west, all territory, territory—what a word, *territory,* that spelled power and hope and wealth and a place for people to live: all this had to be put into political programs and brought to the people and by them voted into life and by the workingmen built into cities and structures and libraries, hospitals and homes and museums: all just at dawn now, and it took a league of orators and classic politicals to guide the thing along to what they were everywhere calling "manifest destiny," the high hope of man, and the leadership of the world: set the example for the feudal areas of the planet to follow: take this Stone Age America of the red men and fire it forward fifty thousand years into a new philosophic force, and carry forward the highest hopes of the human thing that called itself man. He knew that they were alive, these Americans, all over now, especially in Boston: Thoreau and Emerson, the new suffragists, the temperance people; reform was the grand democratic thing. His own inner springs, his emotional drive came from this picture of America unfolding beside the horse carriages, alongside the canals, just beyond the train lines: and in this way, moving through it all, and across the boundaries, the town and the country and the world had become part of him.

For days William Henry and his friends, on board a privately hired barge, with steam and sails, steeped themselves in the Canadian woods, going up remote river passes into Indian country. The air was rich, and the trip heavy and hard for a recuperating politician. Once, as they walked among tall trees that blinded the light, William Henry felt ill, too much enriched by this element, and he slipped to the ground wondering what he, a small man with a cultured outlook and city-type constitution and a civilized frame, was doing here in this defiant terrain. Jim Bowen asked, "All right, Governor?" He'd be all right, he answered, just let him rest awhile. Seth Hawley remarked, "You look kind o' green, Governor." The lawyer laughed; the green was real, a little of it had come into his face; and he lay for a while resting, absorbing, recouping, and he fell asleep, sound sound asleep, so that his friends pitched camp here for a day where the Governor had found a spot that he made his own.

For two days the white men and their Indian guides moved down Lake Superior, their craft going day and night. They reached the rapids, the Indians alive to it, easy and fast with the oars, taking the boiling current, the spray clouding their boat. Then the taste of the fast spring in dangerous rapids, yet they moved across them, and were suddenly in calm water . . . and now soon, they'd take steamer on to Chicago.

In Chicago he found a letter from Frances. She was feeling better than she had during the winter, she wrote: "The warm days are helpful— When the house gets too heated Willie and I go to the grape arbor and he plays there in its coolness and I find the writing chair the best resort— When your letter arrived from Buffalo yesterday, and as I read it, my head began to ache—it ached till I finished reading—I was enabled to feel the enjoyment you took in the prospect of your trip into the wilderness and some of its excitement must have taken with me in this peculiar way— However, Dr. Perkins has left with me some headache powders that are mysterious and good and helpful— Please do not concern yourself with these attacks of mine— They pass, so does time, you will be back with Fanny and Willie

275

and me soon, and do not return till your health is good and only bear in mind that here we all watch out for one another in utmost love— Delight me with your letters as often as you can and I shall try to breathe the Canadian pine through your fingertips— Your Own Frances."

When he returned to Auburn he told her, "I'm strong enough now to take on the world."

It was well that he felt that empowered, for at the outset of 1846, and for most of that whole year, he did take on and he did oppose just about the whole world....

Chapter Forty

THE MYSTIC CHORDS OF MEMORY

ONE DAY in the middle of March, 1846, when Frances moved about her house busy with her baby girl and the six-year-old William Henry, Jr., immersed in her own thoughts, living the particular brand of peace and the domesticity of her days, she was abruptly lifted from her occupations and reveries by a din in the street. It was the sound of enraged voices, and she hurried to the front window and looked out. The street was gray and cold, and a sheet of hammered down snow lay on the road, and over this wintry way there came a loose procession of sleighs, men on horseback, several hundred pedestrians running, and a strange and abnormal hollering rose out of the whole scene.

In one of the sleighs she saw the reason for it all: they had captured William Freeman, the young black man who had murdered most of the family of John G. Van Nest, at their home on Owasco Lake. For two days they had hunted Freeman in the surrounding counties, they had found him, and now he was trussed in the vehicle and being carried to the scene of his crime to be identified by a fifth victim who had survived his wounds, and as the parade moved along South Street, Frances heard over and over, the cries: "Lynch him!" "Kill him now!" "Don't let him live, burn him, burn him at the stake!" But William Freeman was guarded by a whole sleighful of armed deputies, who stood about their prisoner and prevented the possibility of a lynching right there in front of the Seward house. Swiftly the procession went on, and Frances continued to hear, in recollection, the calls for vengeance.

She knew John G. Van Nest and his family. Henry even represented the Van Nests at law. The two families were well known to each other; and now Mrs. Van Nest was dead, so was her husband, so was Mrs. Van Nest's mother, a woman named Phoebe Wyckoff, and an infant son, George Washington Van Nest. Four dead and a fifth, Harry Van Arsdale, badly injured. And why did William Freeman do this?

Nobody knew. He didn't know the Van Nests; they had done nothing to injure him, so far as anyone knew; why had he gone miles and miles

Empathy

out of the village to start in with the Van Nests, and, as he intended, to go on from there, killing all white folks?

Whatever motivated William Freeman nobody knew, and most Auburnians didn't care. Only Frances, and perhaps one or two others in the village, might then have suspected that the man was mad, and the whole thing a tragic misunderstanding, and only she perhaps at this moment felt that the murderer was entitled, by American law, to a defense and trial, even if he was the most savage killer in the history of the region.

She was tempted to write a calm letter to her husband, who was then in Albany, and she did, saying: "There is still something incomprehensible about it to my mind— I cannot conceive it possible for a human being to commit a crime so awful without a strong motive, either real or imaginary for the act— In this case no such motive has been discovered— Bill Freeman is a miserable, half-witted Negro but recently emancipated from the State Prison and did not know by sight the members of the family he has murdered— He says he should have murdered others, had he not been disabled and also that it was his intention to set fire to the house— He has been out of prison six months and has had the same opportunity every night, and then, when he first left the prison would have been the time that any other man, believing himself the object of an aggravated justice, would have chosen to wreak his vengeance upon an enemy—then, while smarting with the severity of prison discipline— No, I believe he must have been impelled by some motive not yet revealed— There was a terrible commotion in the village as he was carried through— It is a matter of wonder to me now that in the excited state of popular feeling, the creature was not murdered on the spot— Fortunately the law triumphed, and he is in prison awaiting his trial, condemnation and execution—which so many feel unwilling to defer even for an hour."

It was a reasoned letter; almost a legally restrained letter, as if her husband had influenced her to look without passion on matters that would enter the courts. Perhaps Frances, who groped so much on the dark side of her own moon, felt an empathy for the violence and the contradiction of the situation, for the tragedy of the community, for the unaccountable action of William Freeman. Perhaps some ray of understanding of the idea of provocation and suffering, of the human condition, was in her possession; perhaps it was her natural Quaker-bred liberalism; or maybe it was the touch of science that marked her now, the wand of William Henry's influence. Possibly it was that she, like her husband, had learned to think and stand individually, and to try to stop to think clearly when others were lost, dismayed, hysterical, moving as a mob. Doubtless a whole complex of factors, motives and influences were at work in her when she wrote the faintly provocative letter to her husband; but she had told herself once, in the South, when she saw slavery, "This is wrong," and when once this has happened to an American, deep inside, he goes on thereafter differently than before.

When William Henry returned to Auburn he heard the views of Frances and of Judge Miller that Freeman sounded insane. He strolled over to the jailhouse and he tried to talk with Freeman, but he too decided that the man was in some condition of advanced disease, that his brain was disordered. The demented man asked for no defense; he didn't know what a defense was; and the name Governor Seward meant nothing to him. He simply said he had set out to "kill 'round awhile," they hadn't treated him right, he hadn't stolen the horse he was accused of stealing, the alleged theft that got him a five-year sentence to Auburn Prison; and William Freeman seemed quite content with what he had done.

As to the sanity of Freeman, William Henry was of no doubt the black man was insane; as to the motive for the murder, he knew of no motive, neither did anyone else; as to the propriety of defending Freeman, it was certainly unwise to do so, politically as a Whig, and communitywise, for his own relationship to the townspeople. They'd hate him for it, and he had a family that had to go on living here. Yet he knew that if he didn't defend Freeman, nobody would. And he sensed that Frances had a special interest in the case. She was faintly prodding him to be man about the matter, it seemed to him. He liked that: he liked it that she interested herself so deeply in a matter of morality, scientific principle and law. But one of the spoils of his having been Governor was that Frances had grown political. It was a change in her from the Frances he once knew, who had no interest in politics. He liked the fact that she was so deeply interested in something so far outside of herself, and so deeply lodged in the life of the community. He liked it that she lost her usual sense of caution about this case, and that she seemed motivated by the press of principle, and while no word passed between them, he saying he would defend Freeman, and she never urging him: still, they waited for the day to come when William Freeman would stand before the bar and be asked to plead. And what would happen then? Who would defend Bill Freeman?

It was generally believed that any man who killed another should himself be put to death. Few had any sympathy for or understanding of the question of insanity as a motive in a slaying. The law so far had made little headway with such an approach; lawyers tried this defense from time to time, few had succeeded; the intricacies of the human mind and the possibility of a diseased brain did not yet have status in the sphere known as "medical jurisprudence."

It chanced that William Henry was interested in the question of the defense of murder by reason of insanity, and only a couple of months earlier he defended locally, with partial success, a convict of Auburn Prison, Henry Wyatt, who slew a fellow inmate. It was rumored that Freeman had attended the trial of Wyatt; if so, it was whispered, he may have got the idea from that trial that he could go out and commit murder and get Seward or someone else to defend him on grounds of insanity—and get away with murder. It was one of many rumors, and when William Henry returned to Auburn a few days after Freeman was jailed, he heard ugly reports on all sides: "The Governor better stay out of this, we want to hang Freeman."

The day arrived when William Freeman, in manacles, was brought into the county courthouse to plead to four indictments for murder. William Henry was in the dock, along with many other local attorneys; the court itself was packed; Frances had a seat in an early row; the judge was a local figure named Bowen Whiting, much prejudiced against the defendant, for he had already made the remark, "No Seward will defend Freeman."

But the judge didn't really know. He couldn't know that William Henry only a few days earlier wrote an intimation to Weed that he might possibly get in on the case: "Freeman is deaf, deserted, ignorant, and his conduct is unexplainable on any principle of sanity. It is natural that he should turn to me to defend him. If he does, I shall do so. This will raise a storm of prejudice and passion, which will try the fortitude of my friends. But I shall do my duty and care not whether I am ever to be forgiven for it or not . . ." In fact, Thurlow Weed himself was worried. What would happen to Whig Party influence all over the state if one of the leading Whigs got in on so troublesome and unpopular a cause? But this was one of those initiatives of the Auburn attorney that Weed had no control over and didn't try to determine.

The sheriff brought the prisoner before the judge. Freeman was slight, with a heaviness about the shoulder; he was part-Indian, part-Negro in his origins and in his look, and because of his disordered brain he had a vapid stare.

The district attorney read the first indictment, and asked Freeman how he pleaded. *Ha?* was the answer. The judge repeated, and the accused answered, *Don't know.* Was he able to employ counsel? *No.* Was he ready for trial? *Don't know.* Had he any counsel? *Don't know.*

Watching all of this, William Henry couldn't quite bring himself to stand and to intercede. None of it seemed credible to him. It seemed, not like a courtroom, but a fantasy out of some imagined play, possibly a scene from another world; this couldn't be going on in the state of which he had been governor, could it?

William Henry couldn't take his eyes off of the shackled and maddened black man. He imagined the disease in Freeman's brain, it must be diseased; he saw a scourged soul, driven by some mysterious motive, some unusual hate, all of it the result certainly of great provocation. This realization surged in the lawyer in an eruptive way, as if from the deepest well of his feelings. He feared that he was about to break into tears. That would be awful, it had never happened to him in public or in a court: but his lips tremored and he felt a rush of tears to his eyes, and all unexpected he leaped up, so as to get out of the room, and he thrust a couple of attorneys out of the way as he headed for an anteroom that adjoined the judge's chambers.

The local Universalist minister, the Rev. John Austin, had been watching William Henry; he saw the Governor suddenly rise, wheel about, and hurry from the court.

Something was wrong. Why didn't the Governor speak up when it was time for him to rise, if he or anyone else were to defend the black man? He rose from his seat and followed William Henry out of the court.

The minister walked in on William Henry and watched the man who was always so self-controlled sobbing like a small boy, absolutely unable to halt his shaking frame.

"Get hold of yourself, Governor! Stop this!"

The door opened silently. It was Frances and she looked inside: she saw how her husband moved a white handkerchief over his wet face, and she observed his shaking shoulders.

She and the minister exchanged a swift glance, and she decided that this was a moment he must have to himself. She couldn't and wouldn't influence him. She reopened the door to the court and returned to her seat.

"What's happened to you, Governor?" the minister asked. "This isn't like you at all. How is this going to help?"

William Henry said that he would be all right soon ... broken, spluttered words.

Then, bit by bit, the torrent of tears exhausted itself. A kind of rigidity came back to him; he was steeling himself; his face was entirely wet, and the minister removed his own handkerchief and gave it to William Henry.

In a hushed way he apologized to the clergyman. He said it was the first time since the death of his mother two years earlier that he had wept.

"We mustn't weep now, Mr. Seward," the minister said, "now we have the biggest fight of our lives."

William Henry re-entered the courtroom, not exactly the most composed attorney in the world, but there were no more tears in him. He stood before the judge, and he remarked, "May it please the court, I am the counsel for the defendant."

Thereafter William Henry entered upon one of the great fights of his life, a war that lasted all summer; for what resulted was the first acknowledged case of the defense of murder on grounds of insanity in our history. It was the first time that a thorough examination of the human mind was ever made in a court in this or any other country.

Frances kept her sister informed by frequent letter. "I love Henry," she wrote, "but when I see him battle for principle and a human life and his convictions in the way he is doing here, then my adoration for him is beyond my capacity for description— Until the Freeman trial began, Henry was of course advised to cease all efforts in the murderer's behalf— He will do what is right—he will not close his eyes and know that a great wrong is perpetrated, without offering any remonstrance—and yet this is the course advised by many who call themselves his friends— I can conceive of no spectacle more sublime than to see a good man thus striving to win to deeds of mercy and benevolence the perverse generation among whom his lot has fallen— The trial itself hurries on, all conceding this to be the most unique cause since the nation's founding—Freeman himself is rapidly sinking into a state of idiocy, although it seems certain that he will be a victim to satisfy the popular vengeance—on the Fourth of July our village experienced the most disgraceful episode since John Hardenbergh established the settlement—a multitude of townsmen gathered in front of the courthouse and clamored for violence against both Freeman and my husband and had it not been for the care of the sheriff and his deputies the rioters might have burst into the court and attempted their object— On that day the preliminary trial of Freeman, to determine whether or not he was sane, came to a close and the jury delivered an unheard of verdict, that the defendant was 'sufficiently sane, in mind and memory, to distinguish between right and wrong,' and he must face trial as a man who was at least partially sane— The trial has been going on these weeks—scores of townsmen have been brought to the witness stand, the examinations and the counter examinations have been endless and detailed—and it has been wonderful to see how a segment of the town, small but powerful, has rallied to Henry's cause, and how staunchly certain townsmen, and so many of the medical men, have sustained the belief that Freeman is insane—"

The two trials of Freeman wore on, through June, into the late days of July, and the witnesses on either side attested to the strange talk of William Freeman when they interviewed him in jail and asked him why he had slain four people whom he did not know. All that emerged with any clarity was a profound but unclear motive of revenge. He'd been wronged —wasn't guilty of stealing the horse—imprisoned falsely for five years— nearly deafened by guards' blows—so, kill 'round awhile—make the state pay—make everybody pay—made up my mind ought to kill somebody.

"A great question of Henry's political fortunes and the fortunes of the Whig party has obtruded itself in the trial," Frances wrote to Lazette. "The clamor throughout the State against Henry for defending the wretched Freeman threatens the Whig force with a defeat in the autumn elections and it is freely predicted Henry will not survive this act of his, that he is lost to political life forever— I hope not, I believe not, I cannot think that a man engaged in so dear a course, the exploration of the profound questions pertaining to sanity and insanity, can be punished by political extinction as the reward for his effort— Only hours remain now, and the cause will close, and the verdict will be in—and though Henry has summed up, warning the court that a prejudiced jury hating Freeman, and hating him for defending the Negro, must beware lest it bring in a false verdict, for he will fight on—still we are not sanguine of any just decision— The case has been deeply complicated by the fact that John Van Buren, the State's Attorney General, has prosecuted Freeman with a diabolical cleverness— as you know, there is no love between Henry and Van Buren—they are politically opposed— Henry has always opposed John's father, Martin—and so the trial is streaked through with a political vengeance as well as its other issues— John Van Buren wishes to destroy Henry as a political force, and Henry is fighting for his own life as well as for Freeman's."

Issues of the will, the memory, moral responsibility, sensory responses, social mores, and scores of other facets of the human equation were thrashed out, analyzed, attacked and defended. Doctors, alienists, men who had spent years as physicians in mental institutions, gave testimony, submitted to cross-examination, recited their experience, gave opinion.

Yes, there was a time in American life when a man so demented as to sit idiotically all through the court proceedings and smile and laugh... was tried as a sane man, and finally, despite the brilliance of his defender, found guilty, and a day of sentencing set, and the grinning Freeman was brought into the courtroom and ordered to stand.

He was quite deaf and the judge ordered him brought close by, and said to the man who couldn't hear and didn't care, that the jury said he was guilty. Did he understand? *No.* Did he know which the jury were? *No.* He killed Van Nest, did he understand that? *Yes.* Sentence was going to be passed, did he understand? *No.* He was going to be sentenced to be hanged. Did he understand that? *No.*

And the judge, knowing that the prisoner couldn't understand him, simply addressed the crowded court, spoke of Freeman in the third person, informed all that Freeman would be executed on Friday, September 18th, 1846, hanged by the neck until dead.

William Henry appealed the verdict to the State Supreme Court, and he got a stay of execution. Once, Frances visited Freeman in the county jail, and she told her sister: "I was affected to tears by his helpless condition— I pray God that he may be insensible to the inhumanity of his relentless keepers— He stood upon the cold stone floor with bare feet, a cot bedstead with nothing but the sacking underneath, and a small filthy blanket to cover him—"

A few months later the Supreme Court reversed the judgment on the whole case, gave William Henry one of his greatest legal victories, and set a precedent for American jurisprudence. A new trial was ordered.

But the tragic Freeman never lived to go to trial a second time. He remained in chains in the county jail, where his mind and body steadily deteriorated, and he died in his cell. An autopsy by the leading medical men of the state disclosed a diseased brain, a shattered mind, even though it took death to bring about a degree of vindication for the victim and for his defender.

And now Frances wrote to her sister: "It is done, Lazette, and well done. Henry has secured a curious kind of triumph and a half-legal victory— Freeman died in jail of tuberculosis and the physicians said that insanity was a frequent result of his disease— But we have not recovered the faith of the community— The townsmen are ashamed that they were so precipitate, so hate-filled, and somehow we sense a continuing resentment toward Henry as a result— It is as if they do not care to be instructed and despise one who will teach them a truth— Perhaps it is what the Bard called the operation of human nature— Henry has not met with gratitude about the town, but respect he has resecured—and Weed writes us that the Whig fortunes are no longer impaired by his effort— I have a curious feeling that I somehow had a part in this, Lazette, an unstated part, that William Henry looked into my thoughts, and went ahead, to what results we are now experiencing— Your Own Sister Frances."

In Albany Thurlow Weed grasped to his heart once more the distinguished little man in Western New York who single-handedly fought society and introduced into law the faint scatterings of the new science, not yet called psychiatry, then just having its beginnings.

Little was understood in 1846 of what is known today as the unconscious area of the mind. At that time there were only faint gropings into phrenology and the slight beginnings of neurological tracings of connection between the brain and the rest of the body. And little is known today about whether there may be a similar area in the experience of human society itself, an unconscious in history itself, as it were, where the experiences of man are stored, and as a result of which happenings occur, under the influence of ancient and historical or special stimuli.

The great question in the case of William Freeman was: What was his motive for killing a family unknown to him? Why, when the village of Auburn contained many people who had victimized him, did he select the Van Nests several miles from Auburn in the Dutch settlement of Owasco? He had been scorned, jailed, hounded, harassed by many throughout his childhood; he had been underpaid, whipped in prison by guards who were living free about the community at the time Freeman struck his avenging knives. Why did he bypass all of the people he knew, whose death might have given him satisfaction, to select the innocent Van Nests?

An incident that occurred ninety-five years before the Auburn events was unknown to William Henry, and perhaps it was unknown to most others at the time of the Freeman trial. Even if a few villagers, the colored, might have heard of this occurrence, they would, in all likelihood, have established no connection between William Freeman's murders and an earlier tragedy that occurred back in 1752.

In December of that year another man named Van Nest, this one called Peter Van Nest, was also killed, and also by a young colored man in Somerset County, in Northern New Jersey. According to the records, Peter Van Nest, a landowner, took a leaf of tobacco out of the pouch belonging to his slave, and he didn't pay for it or refused to return it. Whatever other history of relationship there was between this master and this slave is unknown, but the slave, it was alleged, struck his master with an axe and killed him.

The white folks of the region decided to make an example of him, and this slave was burned at the stake.

As the murderer flamed up in the courtyard of the Somerset County Court, at Millstone, a ring of blacks, the slaves of the neighborhood, were forced to stand around and to watch. A second ring of armed white citizens circled around the blacks to prevent them from running away and to force them to watch the slave burn. It was intended that this punishment should remain in their memory; the slaves should tell this story to one another, from one generation to the next, so as to teach Negroes not to avenge themselves and not to strike back.

But sometimes such acts as these have not burned compliance into their victims, or the community, but have bred revolt. The slave, Abram, according to the records, "stood the fire with the greatest intrepidity and shouted, 'You taken the Bough, but you not taken the Root!' "

The white folks of this neighborhood were primarily Dutch. After the Revolutionary War many of them in the villages of Somerville and Millstone, where the slave was burned, migrated to Central New York. The Dutchman, John Hardenbergh, who settled Auburn, brought his own slaves with him, and they may have known all about the incident of 1752: for it was intended that the slaves remember.

William Freeman was the grandson of the slaves of John Hardenbergh; and it is possible, even plausible, that the story of the 1752 murder and the burning at the stake went on in the memory of the Negroes, in their folklore, in their travels two hundred miles northward into Central New York, and that when William Freeman was a boy he may have been told, and probably was told, many times, of the burning at the stake of a black kinsman. He may also have been told that the descendants, white and black, who figured in that tragedy, had moved north, and they lived in the vicinity of Auburn, along Owasco Lake.

So that, in the darkness of crazed William Freeman's mind, when he could have moved against anyone in the village, something out of the unhappy past of the colored group sprang up in his thinking, and he moved instinctually, unconscious of its historic meaning and impetus, out of the town of Auburn several miles away to the quiet house on Owasco Lake where another Van Nest family lived.

The loose line of coincidence between the two Van Nest murders encompasses many anomalies pointing to a mystic connection between the events nearly a century apart.

So although William Freeman may have had no motive for killing the Van Nests, it is possible that history and time and human experience, and the American kind of experience in particular, the strange close relationship that has always existed between black and white in all ways and in all parts of our land—it is possible that this reservoir of the unconscious of our national experience yielded up its own relationship and its own motive.

Frances' original intuition that there was some strange imponderable in the whole affair may have been well founded, beyond her wildest imagining, beyond the dream and suspicion of anyone; a mystic connection of generations, an impossible expression of the peculiar American heritage of master and slave; perhaps a groping, psychical explosion of the unremembered, out of the very substance of our history.

Chapter Forty-One

HENRY IS AT WORK AND EVERYTHING IS WORKING FOR HENRY

ENRY was back in politics in full force. His own party suspected that he would soon return to Government. It was generally understood that his resumption of public life stemmed from his success in the Freeman case. He had opposed nearly the whole community, he had refused tradition, and pioneered in medical jurisprudence, and, from having been widely hated at the time of the trial, he was now restored to the community's grace on a higher level than ever. He increased his law practice and he intensified his public appearances.

Weed urged him on. "You know what your position is now, don't you?" he asked, and then gave answer: "You're regarded as one of the very first men of our country. The next step for you is the United States Senate, if I can swing it."

So, throughout the next year, William Henry combined his law work with making speeches at one political scene after another: Albany, Boston, Washington.

By now his apologies for not being home with Frances were penned off in an almost perfunctory way. "How unfortunate it is, that for such a large portion of our lives we have been robbed of each other's company." Such remarks came from him frequently, but she knew they were garlands without scent.

She knew he was making a thrust for some new status in the national community and she must not grudge him his prolonged absences. Rather, turn inward, homeward. So she settled into a kind of steadied invalidism, never quite able to do as much as she wanted to, doctors playing a part in her life and she always in quest of a physician who would quell her disquiet, and never quite finding him. She made more and more of a retreat out of the house, till each design in each carpet was familiar to her— while William Henry moved over the land, headed, she suspected, for some imminent political elevation.

On a night in September of 1848, William Henry addressed a Whig gathering at the Tremont Temple in Boston. Three thousand turned out to hear him and a few other Whigs from various sections. He talked extensively about abolition of slavery, and the Whig position that slavery should not be extended into any territory that was now free, and he hoped that these were only the preliminary views of this party and that later on the Whigs should drive further and harder against the institution.

One of the others seated on the platform with him was a Whig member of Congress from Illinois, a tall, abnormally lean man with an aquiline-shaped face, a large, poetic chin, an ardent and direct look.

Afterward William Henry and the smooth-shaven gentleman from Illinois met at the same hotel. The man from the West sounded very reflective. "Governor Seward, I have been thinking about what you said in your speech. I reckon you are right. We have got to deal with this slavery question, and got to give much more attention to it hereafter than we have been doing."

It was the first meeting of William Henry and Abe Lincoln.

Occasionally William Henry attended Congressional sessions in Washington simply to see his friend Greeley perform. Perform is what he did: for when he stood to speak, all in the House turned to watch him, to see and listen for whatever new crusade he'd come up with. He was spectacular, electrical. Greeley had been elected to fill out an unexpired nine months term of a New York representative: and now he was in heaven, for there was nothing he wanted more than public office.

William Henry was astounded at Greeley's behavior on the House floor. Certainly, he thought, Greeley belongs back in New York editing his newspaper. What is he doing, trying to reform Congress all at once?

Many of the journalist's objectives were good; but they were extreme for a Congress that always moved slowly: he'd abolish slavery in the District of Columbia; he opposed serving liquor to sailors and marines (voted down swiftly); he tried to change the name of the country from America to "Columbia," ("Give Columbus his due!"). And he wanted to cut the pay of congressmen. He was about as popular in the House as a shark in a pond of goldfish: and just as conspicuous. He wouldn't let the representatives adjourn until much later than their usual hour of dismissal, and several times he stood up long enough to vote against the whole House.

William Henry couldn't reason with Greeley, and when he tried to, the editor fussed with him. Greeley seemed not to understand such important ingredients of political action as caution, strategy: and he confounded his colleagues and even the public with alternating touches of conservatism, wildness of radical objective, and unexpected bursts of reformism and special morality.

William Henry conceived of the editor as neither radical nor revolutionary, but simply downright eccentric, congenitally heretical and therefore unpredictable.

Yet any time that William Henry said anything important the *Tribune* played it up big; Greeley was a straight Whig then, and a colleague; and the New Yorker did more to popularize William Henry than any other journalist of that time.

So their friendship ticked on like a clock with an inner uncertain mechanism, with its own springs, its own wheels within wheels and its capacity to go on or to stop. But there was psychological clash and political difference here, and there were varying moral levels, and the springs of the relationship were taut and strained.

No one knew, not even Greeley, that out of his egocentricity and his political ambition, he had in him the power, one way or the other, to influence and to rework the nation's course.

William Henry campaigned for General Zachary Taylor as the Whig candidate in the 1848 elections; and in November Taylor was elected, with Millard Fillmore as his Vice President.

It was a period of Whig tide, and as the new year opened, with a new White House Administration, the big talk in Albany was the vacancy in the United States Senate.

Weed, the engineer of Taylor's election, now moved among the Whig legislators to obtain the Senate seat for his lifelong friend. He knew what that would mean: it would, for one thing, project the antislavery outlook to a higher plane than ever; moreover, there was a chance that William Henry might be able to influence the new President on a liberal course.

In February of 1849 the Whig legislative caucus elected William Henry to the United States Senate. He wasn't yet forty-eight; his red-brown hair still had its colorful vitality, and only in the Senate would the russet crop start turning.

Chapter Forty-Two

WILLIAM HENRY LEADS THE ANTISLAVERY CAUSE

EVEN when Frances arrived in Washington to be with Henry at the outset of his senatorial career, her family was the most important thing, and the care of Willie Jr. and Fanny was paramount. She knew that the capital was full of politicians' wives, like herself, left alone much of their lives, during the long absences of their traveling and ambitious husbands. She didn't intend to see too many of them; and she'd try to keep their house on F Street as quiet as Washington life would allow. They took an unpretentious red-brick place, an ordinary city structure just twenty-five feet wide. It was near the Post Office, a shopping area was close by, and the Capitol was a few blocks away. William Henry had a study in the basement; there was a large parlor on the first floor, and bedrooms were on the second and third stories. Fred was with them, for he was just out of college, and he was here to act as his father's secretary.

On the first day that William Henry entered the Senate Chamber as a senator, everything about the room had a magnified character. He had seen it many times before, but now, as a participant in the fortunes of the august hall, sight and meaning were deepened.

He who had studied intensively the Greek civilization felt at ease in the Greek-modeled semicircular place, with its decorated and domed ceiling, its even-spaced twenty-six treelike columns of marble. Potomac marble, he said to himself.

Not many seats seemed available, but the new senator found one on the Whig side, and he settled into it with a pleasurable feeling of its comfort and a sense of how natural it seemed to be in such a chair.

But an old man with a cadaverous look walked toward him. It was "the Great Pacificator," Henry Clay, now in his seventy-second year, who said, "Sir, I am sure you can grace that seat as well as I have been doing for some years, but it chances I am used to sitting there."

William Henry sprang up, looking about helplessly.

"I believe," said Clay, with a voice deep from a cavern of ill-health and time, "that that one is unoccupied."

It was a seat to the right of Clay, at the extreme end of the back row of chairs. Nearby was a private door through which William Henry might easily exit if he wished, and it was a quieter part of the chamber. He could hear the figures about the Speaker's dais with ease, and it occurred to him, "This is inconspicuous too, I shall likely stay here."

He fingered the goose quills, the inkwells and the sandpots on the desk. He looked toward the Speaker's desk ornamented with candelabras on either side, then upward at the famous hundred-light chandelier that hung from the center of the ceiling and dipped low into the center of the room. Candles were no longer burned in it, and it gave off a bluish gaslight. The effect made the red draperies at the edges of the chamber seem purplish and rich; and his eyes roved over the scene that would be his home now for the next twelve years.

Outside in the streets of Washington the weather was cold, there had been rain, and the streets were muddy. In these shabby unformed avenues, about forty thousand people moved, most of them somehow connected with Government business, serving or supplying the lawmakers. Houses weren't numbered yet; streets were amorphous, with large spaces and sudden dead ends, and there were shrubby and muddy patches in most unscheduled spots. The avenues were unpaved; slaves walked freely in the streets, it was a South town.

That about set the tone for the city—and for what everyone knew was going to happen at this, the Thirty-First Congress. The country seethed with fear of disunion; nothing was talked anywhere but the slave question; what was the possibility of civil war? What would they do down here in Washington?

Any question that rose anywhere seemed to veer over onto the roadway of the slave principle. California, running with prospectors and gold, and made rich and powerful overnight, asked for statehood, and the big question was: Whose state, the slave power's or the North's? The war with Mexico had resulted in the snatch of a large portion of Mexico, and Free-soil representatives in Washington were howling that the new region must not become slave territory, keep slavery out. Also, how did it look for this very city, Washington, and this district, the District of Columbia, to have slave pens and auction blocks only a few blocks away from the White House? How about abolishing slavery at least in the capital? Southern congressmen were screaming about their rights, too: What about the North returning escaped slaves the way the Fugitive Slave Act of 1793 specified?

The new President, General Taylor, was known to lean toward Freesoil ideas and now William Henry was bending the ear of the President and exerting God knows how much influence upon him. For, soon after he reached Washington, he found the "backstairs way" to the man in the White House. And from the outset, William Henry was, very possibly, the most influential man in the country, after President Taylor himself. It was in this period, for the first time, that the term "Premier" came to be applied to him.

The situation was serious, the slavery advocates feared; the Whigs and antislavers suddenly gaining all kinds of power; and in the galleries of the House and the Senate, Abolitionists were showering a confetti of printed petitions below into the ranks of the lawmakers.

This had been a united country for a long time; compromise held it together in a pretty workable way; but now, with this new Congressional setup, where Democrats and Whigs were evenly matched and a handful of Freesoilers held the balance of power, the Southern blood riled.

In the House, Congressmen Richard Meade of Virginia, roused over the idea of abolishing slavery in the capital and in the territories, stood up and shouted that if ideas like that became law, then by God, he hoped he'd never set eyes on another Speaker of the House, and the South would defend itself and maintain its honor!

The New York Whig, William Duer, leaped to his feet shouting at the Virginian, "You're a disunionist!"

"You're a liar, sir!" Meade answered, and they rushed at each other with fists poised.

The whole House rose, there was an excited roar, congressmen rushed toward the embattled men to pull them apart or cheer them on.

The Sergeant of Arms stepped in. He carried a mace, an instrument practically never used in the House, but he was prepared to slap it around now. It was a long rod, with a flat wooden head at the end of it, and it was intended to help iron out any undue departure from straight statesmanship.

A congressman yelled, "Keep that mace out of this. It's got no authority here!" And the Sergeant of Arms, his moment swiftly ended, was pushed back.

When that ruckus was over other collisions threatened; it went on like that for three weeks while they tried to agree on a Speaker.

A stalwart from Georgia, Representative Robert Toombs, howled, "If these antislavery petitions are accepted, I'm ready to pull out of the Union, ready to fight physically, and I'll devote my all to that end!"

Finally, they did get a Speaker, another Georgian, and Congress settled down a bit.

But in the more austere Senate a rumble began late in January, and early in February it shaped up as a political battle of the century: it was the Great Compromise Debate, and this was where William Henry assumed leadership of the nation's antislavery force.

The four Sewards, Frances, Frederick, William Henry, Jr. and little Fanny, who was now six years old, sat in the section of the Senate gallery that was reserved for senators' families. Frances and Frederick, well knowing their father's speech today might cause a sensation in Washington and beyond, watched and waited for him to get the Speaker's attention.

Frances looked upward at the cast-iron ceiling of the Senate, and the paneled stained-glass dome seemed close by. She could see the arms of the various states on the panes, the bronzed moldings that held the glass together. The gallery, on a day when it was filled, might hold a thousand persons; but today there were only a few dozen in the hall. Neither Clay nor Calhoun nor Webster was scheduled to speak. Even if it had been bruited around that William Henry would take the floor, that wouldn't mean there would be any turnout of Washington politicos to hear him. He had no public magnetism, as the famous giants had; and his intonations weren't always clear; they didn't know that he had a bad case of catarrh, as it was called, when he was small, and it had left him with a rasp in his throat. He didn't have the largeness of Sam Houston, nor Houston's spectacular robed cowboy look. He didn't have Clay's height, nor the powerful rotund appearance of "Little Giant" Douglas. Physically there was so little to him, only his brevity, and his incessant cigar beneath his large nose; but one thing, though, he had plenty of hair, and no need to wear a wig.

Frances had been in the Senate gallery a half-dozen times in recent weeks: first on January 29th, when ancient Henry Clay rose wearily on the floor to dangle a paper over his head, and declaim, "I hold in my hand a series of resolutions for the consideration of this body." She studied him, the man with the reputation of having an eye for the ladies, even at seventy-two, another frustrated aspirant for the Presidency, the father of the Great Compromise of 1820, which had held the North and South together until this day. Now, when disunion threatened, Clay was trying once more to play the original role of patriot and Union man, holder-together of the nation. On that day late in January Clay came up with an eight-point package deal to save the nation: admit California as a free state, he told the Senate, but in return for that, the North had certain concessions it must make, including the return of escaped slaves from the North; and the North should not interfere with the domestic slave trade.

A few days later Frances returned to the Senate to look down again on the second phase of the unfolding conflict. This time she saw the second old man of the Senate, the Southerner John Calhoun, barely this side of the grave, and he just about made his way forward to the forum; then, unable to find strength to read his last great speech, he asked another senator to do it for him. Senator Mason read off the gloomy words that the South was being given no alternative other than to submit or resist; the South could not compromise, there was no surrender to make; and his part of the land had no alternative but to propose that the United States split into two, let each part have its own government, each go its own way.

Three days later she saw the other member of "the great triumvirate," Daniel Webster, rise bull-like in a height of oratory, and support Clay's compromise solution. He spoke not as a party man, but as an American: he talked for more than three hours, saying that peaceable secession was impossible; that the way for the nation to survive was the way of compromise, Clay's way; and he was willing to enforce the law that called for the return of escaped slaves to their masters. Sick and dying Calhoun came back into the Senate chamber to hear Webster; everyone in the gallery saw him enter the hall, and heard him call out, "The Senator from South Carolina is in his seat." After Webster finished, Calhoun rose to utter one more protest against compromise and to make a final assertion that the Union could be dissolved.

These weeks of debate rocked Washington, and the Senate gallery was filled with all the dignitaries of this country and the embassies of foreign countries. The families of the senators crowded the Senate Chamber on the days when Clay, Webster and Calhoun spoke, for these three scholars and statesmen most reminded the nation of the Founding Fathers.

Now, on the 11th of February, a younger member of the Senate, a recent arrival, rose to express a position opposed to Calhoun's—Calhoun, for the extreme South, and now William Henry for the Northern extremists, he too against compromise, he too unwilling to surrender, but opposed to separation. There was a moral recourse still left in this total and tragic picture, and he would put this forward as a last attempt to shame the South away from its secessionist position.

He answered the objections of those who said that California should not be admitted because it was too large, or because it had taken boundaries to itself without their having been authorized by Congress, that California was violently barging into the Union and might get to be too powerful because of its size and its sudden wealth. These were not the true points at issue, he declared, it was only slavery that was the real matter.

Frances, looking over the assemblage, sensed that the compromise senators were the most worried as her husband talked. For William Henry denounced compromise anywhere at any time.

"But," he said, "if I could overcome my repugnance to compromise in general, I should object to this one on the ground of the inequality and the incongruity of the interests to be compromised."

Then, speaking of California's right to come into the Union, he chanced to say he was so much in favor of that right that he would have voted for her admission even if she had come in as a slave state.

Senator Foote of Mississippi, quick to guard the slave power's interests, and swift to want to trap an antislaver like this New Yorker, leaped to his feet—"Will the honorable Senator allow me to ask him if the Senate is to understand him as saying that he would vote for the admission of California if she came here seeking admission as a slave state?"

Frances listened tensely. I warned him about that phraseology, she said to herself, and here he had been trapped by it, but William Henry tried to recover. "I reply as I said before, that even if California had come in as a slave state, yet coming under the extraordinary circumstances I have described, and in view of the consequences of a dismemberment of the empire consequent upon her rejection, I should have voted for her admission, even though she had come as a slave state."

It was legal sleight of hand.

He leaned against a marble column; an unlighted cigar was clenched between the index and middle fingers of his left hand, while his right held up the paper from which he read. His clothes began to take on that worn and loose look, as if all suits were a little oversize for him.

Frances' gaze roved over the Upper Chamber and she noticed how Webster eyed her husband in a startled way. Webster was beholding in her husband the consistent antislavery advocate. Webster himself had already experienced the wrathful reaction of the North for his support of the Clay compromise; now he knew that the New Yorker expressed the opposite side of the Calhoun argument. Calhoun leaned his head on his hand and sat immobile, listening, perceiving the widening possibility of disunion.

She knew many of the senators and she looked from one to the other as her husband disposed of the whole compromise idea fought over since January, and moved into a moral attack on the slave institution. Senator John P. Hale, the Whig, had been a lawyer, and he knew an important brief when he heard it in court, and an important message when he heard it in the Senate. Smiles lit his face, and he glanced into the gallery at Frances. Thomas Corwin, the Ohio Whig, was utterly absorbed by William Henry, and he was wondering how a man who had such ordinary delivery could be such an influence on his state and upon President Taylor. Thomas

Hart Benton, of Missouri, had been in the Senate since 1821, and he had seen senators come and go, become Presidents, go home disappointed; he had seen everything that can happen to a man in the Senate; he was a Southerner, but a patriot opposed to disunion, and he was a spokesman of President Taylor. He had heard much about Seward, and the Bentons had been at the Seward home on F Street. Benton had an eye for the men who might go far and high in national life, and he picked Seward for some such destiny. He knew that in the lawyer leaning against the pillar speaking in a gravelly voice words intended to go out to the nation, something new had hit Washington. He recalled that Seward had spoken already briefly once or twice since he had arrived in the Senate, but this was the speech where he staked out a claim as leader and statesman alongside the old triumvirate who had just battled around the question of compromise. Seward represented the year 1850, and Webster, Clay and Calhoun were still talking in terms of 1820. Frances watched the intent way that the old-timer, Benton, leaned over his desk and listened.

She saw Senator Henry Foote, a compromise man, short, bald, nervous, whispering from time to time with Senator Douglas.

The Southerners sat immobile, hard, ready to secede.

William Henry disposed of the whole compromise idea fought over since January: arguments clever and subtle, he said, bold and earnest oratory and gentle persuasion had been used in this Chamber, all of it winning as the voice of the turtle dove when it is heard in the land, but it had failed to convince him of the soundness of the principle of the proposed compromise. He persisted with his moral attack on the enchaining of men. "The right to have a slave implies the right to make the slave; that right would be and must be equal and mutual, and this would resolve society in a state of perpetual war."

He moved into the constitutional area, and he denied that that document recognized property in man, and then he passed quietly into a realm above and beyond the Constitution, and beyond all legal debate over its meaning and all of its tradition. That document governed the whole public domain, the American soil, its land and water and the air we breathed, and this domain had been acquired by valor and with the wealth of the whole nation:

But there is a higher law than the Constitution, which regulates our authority over the domain, and devotes it to the same noble purposes. The territory is a part, no inconsiderable part, of the common heritage of mankind, bestowed upon them by the Creator of the Universe. We are his stewards, and must so discharge our trust as to secure in the highest attainable degree their happiness. . . .

He had struck out for the slave in the name of God!

There was a shifting at the tables. Every senator squirmed at his desk. A lawyer and a famous lawyer had departed from legal practice, from taking apart the laws of the land or the laws of history, and he had gone beyond Burke and Bacon.

He said quietly that the bold and awful question which presented itself was simply: Shall we establish human bondage, or permit it by our sufferance to be established?

The constitutional authorities in the Senate stared hard at him, wondering how he dared to depart from this traditional keystone instrument.

Webster, and even his close friend Senator John M. Berrien, asked themselves how a lawyer like Seward, who was famous for the briefs he wrote, the causes he argued before the high court, the celebrated cases he had taken without fee—how could he violate the protocol of this august body by giving them God and moral causes to contend with, instead of the accepted bounds of the document on which American society was held together?

Yet he continued on that course, leaning against the pillar, his rusty hair straggled over his forehead, caricaturing his beaked nose.

"I confess," he said, with an appropriate pause and a glance around at his colleagues, "that the most alarming evidence of our degeneracy which has yet been given is found in the fact that we even debate such a question."

In the galleries there was no applause, only that same intent look which the senators gave him. Now he sounded like an out-and-out Abolitionist. Shades of Garrison and Phillips and Frederick Douglass! How did this man get into the Senate?

Word reached the House of Representatives that Seward was in the other Chamber saying something new, daring and offbeat; and one by one the congressmen filed into the Senate Chamber. They came in from the doors behind the big columns, and they stood at the exits or nudged inward a few steps to listen. Even those who entered late, toward the end, heard him say things not usually said in the Senate, and they didn't notice his weak voice or his slovenly manner of leaning against the marble.

He wouldn't stop to debate with those who said slavery was economical or humane. He hinted that there were axioms of American foundation, in effect, that all men were created equal, had inalienable rights of life, liberty, and the choice of pursuits of happiness. "A question, a moral question, has risen," he contended, "transcending the too-narrow creeds of parties."

He doubted that dissolution was near at hand. He saw passion and partisanship on all sides, yet most of it was here in the Senate where it had begun a year before. He doubted whether the South and its leaders would be in a hurry to revolt from the North.

He pictured, like a dramatist, what would happen in this country if secession were to take place. He graphed fratricidal war, the way in which transportation and communication would be altered, torn up, dislocated; the people denied the use of lakes, railroads, and canals; travel and trade stopped, slave revolts, border warfare, the breakup of the army and navy, some of it to go to the North, some of it to be shared by the South; how the nation might be broken, not only North and South, but by East and West; there would be new taxes, repressions of liberty, drafts, all the horrors of war. Why? What for? Would the secessionists do all this to preserve African slavery? "We are now arrived at that stage of our national progress when that crisis can be foreseen, when we must foresee it. It is directly before us. Its shadow is upon us.... We hear of nothing but slavery, and we can talk of nothing but slavery."

There were ways out of this dilemma. The slaveholders could be paid some enormous sum in return for removing the free colored population from the slave states; but he could not see the Southern position of demanding from the North the surrender of the fugitives from slavery: "This guarantee you cannot have, as I have already shown, because you cannot roll back the tide of social progress. You must be content with what you have...."

As to the attitude of the territory of California, as to what its future inhabitants might say, could say, would say, what all of its future generations would say if they could speak of this hour in the nation's life, he was certain they would say this:

Waste your treaties and your armies, if you will; raze your fortifications to the ground; sink your navies into the sea; transmit to us even a dishonored name, if you must; but the soil you hold in trust for us—give it to us free.

You found it free, and conquered it to extend a better and surer freedom over it. Whatever choice you have made for yourselves, let *us* have no partial freedom; let us *all* be free; let the reversion of your broad domain descend to us unencumbered, and free from the calamities and from the sorrows of human bondage.

William Henry took a few steps back to his desk, and slid into his seat. He placed the long, written message on his desk, and he breathed heavily.

There was a murmuring all over the Senate Chamber. The Speaker said, "It is late in the day. I entertain a move for adjournment."

Nobody heard the move or its second, for the crowded Chamber emptied out.

From behind the network of wire surrounding the reporters' gallery there was a hasty scramble outward. The newspapermen sped along the inner corridors, they headed for the press room to busy the telegraph wires.

Along in the dark night, in Delaware, on the day the papers reported William Henry's speech, squat, powerful Harriet Tubman, the Underground Railroad operator, made one of her stops at the home of Quaker Thomas Garrett.

When the slaves were hidden out in the dark of Garrett's cellar, Harriet and the Quaker chatted in the parlor, and Garrett told his friend what Seward had done in the Senate. "He has done thy cause and my cause a great good deed," said the Quaker.

"He ain't afraid, Mist' Seward ain't afraid."

"Thee are proud thee know Mr. Seward, Harriet?"

"When I goes through Auburn that where I stop, on South Street, and leave my folks there in his cellar. I done sleep in it many time, me and my parties. He send us on to Fred Douglass in Rochester." Then Harriet asked, "Mr. Garrett, you say Mr. Seward say there a higher law than the Constitution."

"Thee understands it, Harriet. A higher law."

"God's law, Mr. Garrett?"

"God's law."

"God's law higher than the law of this land?"

"That is what he said."

"He right. He standin' in the way of the slavemaster, Mr. Seward, and the light of the Lord shinin' on him. He the North Star as much as the one up there..." She pointed out the window at the little lights in the dark sky outside.

But these were the antislavers and the Abolitionists. And it was perhaps right, or understandable, that they greet William Henry's speech as they did. In New England the Abolitionists exulted. At Boston the ardent Wendell Phillips hurried to the home of William Lloyd Garrison and proposed a large antislavery meeting to commend Seward for defining the core national issue.

Yet others, more moderate, and the Southerners, received the higher law address differently, some as an expression of a more serious moment in the nation's life, others as a challenge for secession and the war to begin.

No one ever knew for certain just how President Zachary Taylor took the higher law speech, but it was said he didn't like it, that he believed William Henry had got the Administration into a mess. A Southern Whig,

Magnum, stormed up to Taylor and said he'd turn Democrat if Seward was to be the spokesman for the White House in the Senate. Conservative Whigs everywhere opposed the speech.

But the Washington *Republic,* understood to be the personal mouthpiece of the President, declared that when a Senator said that he held a commission to legislate as the representative of Almighty God, it was time anything could be believed. Other Whig papers picked up that criticism, and rehandled it variously. What did Seward think he was, a Lazarus sent down from heaven to preach meekness to the well-to-do? The speech was called heterodox and dangerous, Seward would lose his influence at the White House, it would lead to disunion. Yet here and there a religious paper supported William Henry's reference to higher law.

The debate went into the streets; and the question of higher law, and whether or not it was higher than the Constitution, was argued in every town in the nation—North and South. The crackerbarrel talks, the saloon talks, the gossip in lumber camps, the talk below ground in the mines, on all the farms: it went on by twos and threes, the people gathering all over to raise the question of slavery one notch higher, to a moral level, a sky level, a star level it had not had before, and everywhere people had to make up their minds what they believed: whether Constitutional law was the last court, or whether "God's law" should help decide the fate of the nation.

Chapter Forty-Three

ROBIN HOOD AT THE BAR

IN a later day a drama known as the Western would make its appearance in literature and motion pictures. William Henry, through the controversies he was connected with, the celebrated law cases, the private and public wars, was living and making for himself and for others a kind of early-day Eastern-style Western. Now he was at the ridge again, where farmers fought the railroads.

All through the summer of 1851, for four hot months, he waged another of his court wars, this one in the roused city of Detroit, in what came to be known as The Great Railroad Conspiracy. The cause was so complicated and it represented such a wide interest in the State of Michigan that no ordinary courthouse could hold the mass of witnesses, and it was destined to become the longest trial until that time in the nation's history.

"At last we are at the beginning of the end," William Henry wrote to Frances early in September. "We are in a vast room, with a vast audience gathering. Public sympathy is doing its work. Public meetings are gathering in the country. The city is moved and the prosecution is alarmed. Greeley's reporter is here; and we are preparing ourselves as well as we can. If I can seem forgetful of you, remember that I am doing my professional service in the cause of humanity."

Though he viewed himself as a good legal Samaritan, he wasn't looked on that way in the Michigan city. The Detroit papers didn't spare him. He was no hero here; and one newspaperman depicted him as a kind of villain, a pet fox made vain by too much public and private adulation; he sat pursing his mouth like a toothless old lady, his twinkling gray eyes saw everything in the room, and when he spoke to a witness he rubbed his hands exultantly, then tossed his head prettily, dipped into his snuffbox, and went doggedly ahead with his examination and his argument.

It was true that he had lost the sartorial elegance that concerned him so in his early days. He tried to dress conservatively, and have a press in his clothes where a press should be, and a nicely knotted neckcloth, not too elaborately colored, but made of costly cloth. But he was scrupulously afraid of looking like a dandy or too much a gentleman. Not for him the aristocratic look, nor for him the Tory manner; but rather, a democratic plainness, for he was constantly with people in taverns, courtrooms, parlors, and he needed to look acceptably casual. It led him sometimes into becoming careless, and even a little sloppy. In this hot courtroom now, he looked shapeless and unimpressive. Yet he preferred that to looking rich and exotic, as some men tried to deck themselves out. Especially—when he made money and he traveled among so many who did not—be careful, he told himself, not to wear the size of your bankroll on your back. No, he'd never take a prize for being the best-dressed man in a particular group. But nobody ever took him for a workingman either; there was too much of a flair about his face, and he had the clothes of a secular man, the unmuscular figure, the smooth face of one who didn't push plows, or mine coal, or hammer out the shape of a horseshoe: but he may have looked like a rural lawyer, small-townish, a seed or two about him. Except when he opened up and talked. Then people gaped, for there was the language he commanded, the sense he seemed to make, and the political and philosophical nature of the man.

William Henry, in his examination and counterexamination of witnesses, and the attorneys for the people in the course of their prosecution, drew a story out of the community, and out of all those involved, that went backward several years....

The crack locomotive, Dexter, going thirty miles an hour, sped west on the Michigan Central road westerly late one day in 1849. As the train, bearing a load of timber, entered the eastern part of Jackson County and approached a little settlement called Michigan Centre, the conductor, Harmon Spaulding, who was riding in the engine with the engineer and the fireman, spotted a piece of timber stretched across the track. He called out the danger, and the engineer swiftly reversed the engine.

Spaulding stayed on the train while the engineer and the fireman leaped off. The wheels crushed the log, and the train went gliding along for a distance and stopped near a crossing, at the hamlet of Michigan Centre.

A gang of townsmen walked up to the locomotive and saw that the man in the engine looked troubled. The conductor recognized two of the men, Abel F. Fitch, the village's leading businessman and political personality, and the other was Ammi Filley, who ran the local tavern.

"What's wrong?" someone asked the trainman.

"What's wrong? What's wrong? Some damned hyenas went and put a timber on the track, trying to run us off, that's what wrong!"

Another in the crowd yelled, "I wish you'd been run off."

"Why?" asked Spaulding. "What you got against me? I ain't even been running on this road for some time."

The tavern proprietor snapped, "Well, we don't give a damn who gets killed. We'd as lief get you as anyone else!"

"What for, for God's sakes?" Spaulding asked.

In an agitated voice Abel Fitch answered, "Ever since this new stretch of train been put through the county by the Michigan Central Railroad, the farmers' cattle been getting killed and ain't nobody been paid for it. And by gods, that company won't never run their trains safe through here till they come out and pay us our price for killing cattle and doing other damage to property hereabouts."

Spaulding remarked, "You folks musta thought this was the passenger train coming through here, and you was out to kill, because you couldn't a known this timber train was going through."

A voice in the crowd answered, "We know our business, Mr. Spaulding."

The conductor was irate and out of sympathy with the farmers. "Now if it comes to pass where the company can't do business on this road, I for one am ready to defend the company with arms if I got to."

"O-ho," said Fitch, "so that's how you feel! Well, let me tell you, sir, I got two double-barreled guns and some loaded pistols and am ready to do business at any time, and we got the men to use 'em."

The trainman decided to hold his tongue: the crowd looked ugly, and he might get hurt. In the meantime the engineer and the fireman came up to the train. They and Spaulding boarded, and went on. But all along the way they found obstructions, and the train had to go slow. Spaulding got out from time to time and he removed from the tracks bars of strap rail, the skin of a dead cow, and a log laid across the rails.

That incident was actually only one of scores similar to it that had occurred for several months in guerrilla warfare along the line of the Michigan Central Railroad, from Ann Arbor, on the east side of the Michigan peninsula, to New Buffalo on the west. For three years this line had been constructed across the state; it was already operating at a profit, but throughout the development of the enterprise the farmers of the counties all along the train route developed an animosity. In the spring of 1849 there was a flare-up of small violences across the state, for everywhere there was the same complaint: the trains were killing cattle, hogs, goats, sheep. The right of way over which the trains ran wasn't fenced—the railroad was out to save every dime it could—and they were already doing so well that they earned $200,000 a year and were paying eight per cent dividends on earnings. Finance like that was objectionable to the farmers, too; they worked hard and didn't understand people who clipped coupons, and they had a natural distaste for corporations and big power, and the word "monopoly" rolled from their tongues with a harsh taste. The big hardhearted railroaders weren't paying fairly for the killed cattle, and it meant that the farmers were paying, in part, for the new big train service that carried people westward.

The railroad company charged that the farmers who owned the cattle were the trespassers; the cows moved up onto the tracks when they ought to know better. As the farmers were only being paid half the value of a killed cow, going to law over the expense wasn't worth while.

In one little stretch of the road twelve miles long Michigan Central trains had killed 160 livestock in a short period of time; and there the farmers derailed an engine. At other places they greased the tracks with lard and fat salvaged from the dead carcasses of cows killed by the trains; at one point, Marshall, villagers shot at the trains when they went by; and it got so that leading citizens in each town spoke up for their less vocal neighbors, and the newspapers were filled with letters of protest. Even a prominent minister condoned the violence along the railway because, he said, there was no other way to handle the matter. The cry was raised high that the railroad should fence its line and pay full value for the destroyed animals.

As the excitement developed, it began to center around one man, the very likable Abel F. Fitch, who perhaps never should have got himself so deep into all of this.

Fitch was a Michigan man for the past twenty years, having come from Connecticut. He began as a tavern proprietor, switched to real estate, got tangled in a bad banking operation, survived that, and went on to become one of the leading businessmen and politicians of Jackson County. A Democrat and an organizer of militia, he knew how to make friends, and within a few years he had a big house worth seven or eight thousand dollars, and five hundred acres of land on which there was a private lake and a private deer park. His wife Amanda and his two adopted children filled out his household, and though he had the rude talk of a man who wasn't exposed to much education in his early days, he set out, after fortune settled with him, to acquire a taste in music and art and writing. Perhaps, then, it was natural that when his townsmen were threatened by the railroad ogre, he stepped forward as their spokesman. He hadn't actually lost much in the way of struck-down cattle, but his friends were irritated, and at forty-three a man like Fitch is in his prime.

The things he said about the railroad reached the ears of Superintendent

John W. Brooks, one of the builders of the Michigan Central and the man being held responsible for not fencing in the road and only half paying for killed cattle. Fitch and a couple of other townsmen went to see Brooks at Detroit, and were told that if they and the farmers living along the road had any complaint, why then, to take it to the Supreme Court and get a ruling on it.

"Sure, the courts," said Fitch. "You got the lawyers and the money and you like to have lawyers handle things like this."

"Well, legally," said Brooks, "the company ain't liable. Just ain't, that's all, and we're willing to test it out in the courts. What's more, there's any more work you fellows do to try to coerce us, we'll hold you morally responsible for what happens."

Back in the town of Jackson, addressing a crowd of local farmers, Abel Fitch repeated what Brooks had said. "He just gave us the bunk," Fitch said, "and there's no other way to get back at 'em but makin' it dear for 'em every time they kill a cow."

"How about goin' to court, like they say?" someone in the crowd asked.

Fitch said they'd waste their time. "Everybody has got their price and so have the judges. And I'm personally tellin' you that I don't have no more stock in them on the Supreme Court than them down below. Them railroads is a big monopoly, I say, even a aristocracy, and they're mighty enough to influence a court and buy a court."

Someone else called out, "Hurtin' innocent people on the trains ain't no way to get even, it seems to me."

In the weeks that followed, along the stretch of road where Fitch lived, there was more violence against passing trains. Shots were fired at the cars, and the whole region was tense. Every evening there were dozens of farmers out, at various points, making it rough for the trains, and the big cars crawled along at half pace, sometimes at just three or four miles an hour, while conductors got out and went up front and removed obstructions. The contagion grew, and the ideas grew: how to harass the big Michigan Central, and show them despits, aristycrats and monopylists how little folks could fight back. Company lumber was stationed along the road at various points, and around Michigan Center the lumber piles went up in fire.

Early one morning, about a mile from Michigan Centre, Abel Fitch and two townsmen watched a train crew try to put out a lumber fire.

"How about helpin' us put out these fires?" the conductors and engineers asked.

"Hell no," said Fitch. "You fellows ought to be burned up with your damned lumber. You know what'd happen then—why, the company you're workin' for'd turn around and pay your wives half price for your ashes."

"Still, you ought to help put out this fire and save property when it's being destroyed."

"I never put nothin' on no tracks and I wouldn't take nothin' off even if I saw Brooks and the whole Michigan Railroad Company was in a car comin' along, and wouldn't care if it knocked 'em all to hell."

Superintendent Brooks decided to force the conflict into the courts. They had a good case against the farmers now: they were destroying property; the courts wouldn't sustain that, no matter what the grievance. He hired company police to stand guard in the most troubled area, Fitch's town of Michigan Centre.

Months passed; still the representatives of the Michigan Railroad weren't ready to move yet. They didn't think they had a strong enough case. They waited. The town of Michigan Centre was honeycombed with spies; and there was a new mood in the villages along the road, a hatred of the company for sending strangers into their midst on such an evil purpose. All that the railroad had to do to settle matters was pay full price for a killed cow and fence the railroad line: and instead, they were spending all kinds of money on stool pigeons.

Early one morning, November 19, 1850, the one-year-old Michigan Central freight house, in Detroit, burned to the ground. Inside, as it burned, there were about $40,000 worth of wheat, corn and flour, for which an insurance company had to make good. On the day after the fire one of the local newspapers said that the cause of the fire was unknown but it might have been spontaneous combustion from the friction of elevators. Could the cause be an incendiary? some asked. That possibility was bypassed at the time even by the Michigan Central Railroad.

Late one afternoon in April of 1851, on the nineteenth, two trains moved slowly into Detroit from the central and western parts of the state, with a haul that wasn't passengers and wasn't timber. It was prisoners, one of the biggest roundups of accused men ever to be brought in at one time—until that time—forty-four arrested men of the two hamlets of Michigan Centre and Jackson; and among them was the biggest catch of all, Abel Fitch himself.

The night before they were routed from their beds by more than a hundred deputies. Two trains moved into the trouble zone, one going east from Detroit, and another starting out from the other end of the peninsula, at Niles. Loaded with armed men, authorized to make arrests, they reached

Jackson County early in the morning, and then, as the trains halted in the disaffected zone, small groups of officers moved from one house to another picking up everybody who had ever been known to be seriously critical of the Michigan Central or suspected of damaging their property. On board, the arrested men wondered what the charge was, and once or twice they got an inkling from the more verbose deputies, "Huh, this'll teach you fellows not to burn down depots." The word went up and down the trains that there was talk of their having burned down the Detroit depot, and as the party arrived in the city they were bewildered and frightened.

They were marched in a column from the depot to the jailhouse. It was a long procession, two by two, with a guard for each captive. Up front was Fitch, slightly amused by it all and already, in his mind, composing a note to his wife, Amanda, telling her how the people of Detroit who happened to be out at that time had a good view of the up-country folks.

From that time, the city of Detroit and the county of Wayne and the State of Michigan moved, with one illegality after another, to literally railroad the Jackson County rebels. They were all charged with having burned down the Detroit storage depot, counterfeiting, and planning to burn down other depots. The bail for each was $50,000, and in addition to that the company slapped a civil suit of $150,000 damages against the whole group. The newspapers howled for their conviction; they were accused of being part of an interstate crime syndicate dedicated to blowing up trains, and in general were treated as outlaws.

Detroit was alarmed; the public was excited by the press; and there was a mood everywhere for conviction. The news spread so far and became so distorted that a claim was made—as far away as New York by someone who had traveled through Michigan—that his drinking water was poisoned. And now, the "lawless gang of monsters in human shape," as one paper described them, needed a defender. The local talent didn't feel equipped to handle the big array of experienced corporation and criminal lawyers that the Michigan Central had in its stable, and one of the defending counsel turned east for help.

William Henry couldn't turn down the appeal of the Michigan attorney who asked him to take the case to defend Fitch and the others. It wasn't the money, only a $2,000 fee; the fee was small for United States Senator Seward, but by now he had this reputation as a defender of unpopular causes; he had his intrinsic beliefs in the underdog's need of principled defenders; he had the influence of his senatorial position to help them with —and his forensic gifts. He also had his independence; and when prominent Eastern politicians, friends of the Michigan Central, said, "Seward, don't fight the railroads," he answered that he had to do what he had to do.

He didn't arrive in Detroit until June 5th, and by that time the court and the Michigan Railroad had moved far against the indicted men. Nobody could get out on bail because nobody could meet it; the imprisoned men were packed in a close jail in the hot Michigan weather, and they suffered by day in court and at night in their cells.

Cooped up in jail, Fitch and the others could do nothing about their defense; everybody who could possibly be a witness for him and the others were imprisoned: in fact, that was why they had arrested so many, so that nobody who might in any way defend the accused could do so: all possible witnesses were accused of conspiracy.

Fitch, from an original mood of optimism, began to feel his imprisonment and to take sick. Though he was pleased that William Henry was his defender, the Senator was a big gun, as he put it, his dyspepsia troubled him, he was gloomy, and he wrote letters tinged with a sense of farewell to his wife.

The prosecution declared that the burning of the Detroit depot was in no way accidental; a special kind of "match," a contraption, had been used to burn the place, and the fire had been set by a man named George W. Gay. A half-dozen spies planted in the two little towns of Jackson County attested to all statements of hostility uttered by the townsmen.

Still, all of these assertions by scores of witnesses for the prosecution and the counterassertions of hundreds of witnesses for the defense, didn't have half the effect of something that was happening fast in the County Jail.

Early in August, Fitch's dysentery became serious; he could no longer appear in court, and in a series of rather eloquent letters to his wife he portrayed himself as a martyr to the rural fight against the railroads, and in a very real way, of course, he was.

He wrote a final note from jail, on the day when they took him to the Sisters of Charity Hospital, telling her: "How long I am to be kept here I know not, but if nothing but the pound of flesh nearest my heart will satisfy my enemies, and they seem to be determined not to be satisfied with anything less, I don't know but with their power and influence they will compel me to yield it to them. I fear that many of us will be obliged to sacrifice our lives to appease the wrath of this soulless corporation."

On August 14th, his wife was at his bedside at the hospital for the last time; the doctors and prosecuting attorney were present too. It was a time for deathbed statements, and Fitch told the prosecutor that he was innocent of the crimes charged to him; he had simply expressed his opinions, he supposed he had a right to do that, and it wasn't just that he be punished for this.

The death of Fitch produced a new set of reactions, doubts and sympathies, in Detroit and throughout Michigan. It was a stronger argument for the defense, perhaps, than any William Henry was able to work up. Even so, as he summed up the case, he attacked the credibility of the spies hired by the company to frame Fitch and his neighbors. This wasn't easy in the hostile Detroit air, before a judge sympathetic to the railroad, and addressing a jury composed of the most substantial businessmen of Detroit, men who believed that a secure railroad system was bound up with their own prosperity.

William Henry finally reached his main point: There was a conspiracy all right, but it was a plot of the Michigan Railroad to destroy Fitch and others, and to this end they had hired a whole stable of convicted felons. For weeks, he and his defense colleagues attacked the credibility of the prosecution's witnesses, revealed their prison records, tried to tear holes in their stories.

When the case was done there were over four hundred witnesses for both sides. The jury was out only nine hours; it returned, finding twelve of the defendants guilty, it exonerated twenty of the accused, it threw two of the principals on the mercy of the court. Two men received sentences of ten years in prison, six received eight-year sentences each, four were sentenced to serve five years apiece. All twelve were sent at once to Jackson Prison.

In this case, as in most of the celebrated causes argued by William Henry, his clients largely sustained legal defeats, but won moral victories. This action was a partial triumph because of the large number who were acquitted, but the moral force of his defense paid off in other ways. Later, one of the chief witnesses admitted that he was forced to testify for the prosecution. Still later, there was another fire at the Michigan Central property in Detroit, and nobody ever said it was incendiary, and this could have meant that the first fire was also accidental. So much conflicting evidence made its appearance in the trial that other observers, as time passed, doubted that Fitch and the others had anything to do with the burning of the depot, even though many of the defendants admitted harassing the railroad line in other and lesser ways.

More than a century has passed since "the great railroad conspiracy," and Fitch is remembered as a local martyr to the cause of the plain people.

And in the town of Jackson and at other points across the Michigan peninsula they remember William Henry, in their annals, their plaques, their street names, and their statues.

Chapter Forty-Four

A HORSE OF A DIFFERENT HENRY

JUDGE MILLER was dead. But he was victoriously dead. He had won the old wager with his son-in-law, and Frances had, as he said she must, lived with him all of his days, till he died in that house.

William Henry no sooner finished the trial at Detroit and reached Westfield, on his way home, when her letter arrived urging him faster—"Father is declining rapidly—I wish you would be here for I fear the bitter end is at hand—he is prepared to go—he has no regrets—his fine repose makes it harder for me—the children are quiet and they understand."

Death was coming faster now, it seemed to him: it came that way in families as their members got on. William Henry had lost his own father a year or so earlier, but the old judge of Orange County lived to see his son enter the United States Senate, and he passed away believing that his son would surely become President. Henry hurried to Auburn and he arrived in time to see his father-in-law before he went.

Hundreds of townsmen attended the judge's funeral, and William Henry was prompted to write Weed: "Judge Miller's death was sublime. The homage paid to his memory was touching and soothing."

But it went deeper than that with Frances. She had been too long in the same house with the same man not to experience his passing with something like the burning out of a candle in her life's light. Not that her father's death would in any way alter her relationship to her husband: he wouldn't get home any oftener; the pattern of their life had been set long ago.

In the days that she privately mourned, she recalled a moment long ago, soon after she and Lazette had begun to live in this house that Elijah built. She was young, only seven or eight, and Lazette was only eleven or twelve, and the two had romped in the singing backyard where it was literally forest. At the time she called her sister Zetty and Zetty called the younger one Fanny.

"Zetty, I am hurt."

"What is it, darling?" The older girl ran to her little sister who held out a hand and a bleeding finger.

"I cut it on the fence."

"Oh, here, let me put my handkerchief to it."

Fanny cried.

"Does it hurt, Fanny?"

"Yes, it hurts, Zetty, fix it, Zetty."

"Here, I'll do what Mommy would do if she was alive."

Zetty kissed the bruised finger and said that would make it well.

But Fanny kept sobbing, and she said it hurt.

"Here, I know what let's," said Zetty. "Let me hold the finger and look at your palm, and I'll tell you a gypsy fortune."

Fanny's sobs slowed.

Zetty said, "I see a handsome Prince Charming you will meet when you get to be a grown girl. He will be oh so tall, he will have very black hair, and black eyes, and he will ride a white horse and he will come here to this very house and pick you up and take you away on his horse and you will be happy ever after."

"Do you see that, Zetty? Do you really see that?"

"You will travel all over the world with your handsome husband and he will never leave your side. You will never never be alone."

"Never?"

"Not ever alone, Fanny."

"Oh, I don't care, Zetty, as long as you stay with me."

It hadn't turned out quite that way, Frances thought; she hadn't married a tall handsome mustached romancer, and she hadn't traveled all over the world as Lazette said she would; it was the other way around: she stayed at home, and her husband did the wandering.

Still she loved the peripatetic Henry, more than she ever thought she could care for anyone so unlike the pictured hero of their childhood fantasy. It was a satisfaction to her to know that he was, as one of their important Whig friends, Seth Hawley, put it, "grown enormously popular in the West. He is allowed to be the great man of Congress and the great power at Washington, second only to the power of slavery."

It was true. Within a year of the Compromise debate, the big guns of the old school died: Webster, Clay, Calhoun. And it left on the field of the Senate primarily William Henry as the dominant voice, the carrier-on of the great tradition of the Senate statesmen. Through him, she knew, once again the spirit of John Quincy Adams breathed at the Capitol: and he assumed easily and swiftly and held the mantle of primary antislavery advocate.

311

Perhaps he was a very big man on a very huge white horse. Perhaps he was.

Chronically invalided now, never easily able to move far beyond the confines of the South Street acreage, severed in heart by the special distentions that had been made upon it by her father and her husband, Frances settled down into the quiet behind-the-scenes role of gentle counselor, sympathetic adviser, patient waiter, constant lover of the man who, all knew now, might soon be President.

Chapter Forty-Five

GREELEY RATTLES A LETTER

HORACE GREELEY arrived at his offices in the *Tribune* building at Nassau and Spruce streets at his usual time, at noon this day. He hustled up three flights of stairs to the editorial rooms and he entered the big city room. His reporters and rewrite men were busy at their desks, scratching with the new steel-point pens the day's copy. It was a proud room to enter, in a way, because so many literary notables were on his staff, and as he passed down a center paper-strewn aisle, to his own private office in the rear, he nodded curtly to one or two of the more important figures who caught his eye. "Morning Bayard," he called to Bayard Taylor, the novelist and poet. He walked on, nodded, "Fry," to William H. Fry, the famous music critic; "Hi Rip," to George Ripley, the naturalist writer whose columns were much beloved by the nature-loving reading public. He was peppery as he stepped in, refreshed from a night's sleep; and as he reached the political desk that was close to his own offices, Stebbins called out, " 'Morning, Mr. Greeley, 'nother dispatch here from Karl Marx." He brisked by and said, "Send it in to me."

And then he went through his regular day, seated at his tall pine desk in a gaslighted little office, busy with pen and papers, scissors and pastepot. The scissors kept getting away from him, as they always seemed to, and once more he tied a cord to them and the tool dangled at the side of his desk. Occasionally he dashed into the city room and raised hell with a rewrite man, or demanded to know why someone let certain typographical errors get into print. Clumsy fools, he cussed, don't know that when some readers see that they figure the reporters don't know how to spell.

He worked through a harsh day, till he heard, on the ground floor, the sounds of the presses operating, and he was tired. A nervous wreck, he told himself; for he was a man with inestimable personal problems.

His wife was losing one child after another. (Of nine children born to her, seven died.) He never quite got over the death of his favorite child, called Pickie, a victim of cholera. And the hard time that Molly had bearing children and having also several miscarriages, had made a hypochondriac of her. She was a far sicker woman than Frances Seward, but she and Frances were only two women in an army of troubled politicians' wives at that time. His home life was stormy, and the years had made Molly into an argumentative creature.

But beyond his private misfortunes, which always included money troubles, he had recently gone to Thurlow Weed and asked to be put up for Governor of New York. Weed, who had no confidence in Greeley as a Government man, ducked around that; and when Greeley asked to be run as a lieutenant governor, Weed moved away from that. Greeley was in favor of forming a new party, the Whig party was dying, he said, and he believed that Weed and Seward lagged behind him. A little irritably, Weed told Greeley that he was directing his politics at all times with the object of returning William Henry to the United States Senate. Greeley's requests wouldn't help in that objective. That burned Greeley, and he had the feeling he was certainly a neglected and a truly junior partner in the Whig leadership.

This night, November 11, 1854, he stayed a little later. He could no longer contain his feeelings about William Henry, and the letter that had been bursting within him, to be written and sent to the Auburnian, he must now write. It was quiet and he could think. Slattery was on the dogwatch in the city room; outside, the New York night was clear and cold and quiet, and his pen moved, as from a compulsion. All his feelings poured into a letter that had been urging within him for weeks. The words flowed, and he enjoyed what he did with a particular joy. His brain was actually feverish—it often was—and his overtaxed energies needed renovation, still certain things had to be uttered....

Like a man who has become very successful and looks back with nostalgia on his salad days, he looked backward, but not with nostalgia: "I was a poor young printer and editor of a literary journal," he wrote, when he joined up with Weed and William Henry. "I did the work required to the best of my ability ... when it was done, you were Governor, dispensing offices worth $3,000 to $20,000 per year to your friends and compatriots, and I returned to my garret and my crust, and my desperate battle with pecuniary obligations heaped upon me..."

He said that it ought to have occurred to Governor Seward to offer one of those places to him, but nobody at Albany ever inquired of him how he was doing financially. He had performed in the same loyal way, he went on, in the Harrison campaign, and at the close of that campaign he was still in poverty. And then, as if these neglects and insults were not enough, he had gone on to wage a campaign for General Harrison for President, and nobody did more than he did in that cause. "I asked nothing, expected

314

nothing; but you, Governor Seward, ought to have asked that I be Post-master of New York. Your asking would have been in vain, but it would have been an act of grace neither wasted nor undeserved."

Then he had founded the *Tribune,* and money and aid had been promised, but nothing had ever been done for him, and he had to float that ship by himself. He pouted over the fact that Weed and Seward had moved much of their allegiance to another New York newspaper, the *Times,* edited by H. J. Raymond, and he had helped Seward again in 1848 when he was sent to the United States Senate. He detailed other slights, real and fancied; he recalled how Weed made a special trip to New York to say he could not support the *Tribune* chief for governor; and all of this he wrote in an injured tone; the hurt crept from each clause, and a new hurt began after each comma. Weed had humiliated him; he had nomi-nated for Lieutenant Governor Greeley's worst rival, Raymond of the *Times;* and all that was left to Greeley was to make the fight for the Whig election, which he did.

He moved toward the close of his long letter, bitterly, predictively: "Governor Seward, I know that some of your most cherished friends think me a great obstacle to your advancement; that John Schoolcraft, for one, insists that you and Weed should not be identified with me. I trust, after a time, you will not be; I trust I shall never be found in opposition to you; I have no further wish than to glide out of the newspaper world as quietly and as speedily as possible, join my family in Europe, and if possible stay there quite a time—long enough to cool my fevered brain and renovate my overtasked energies."

He drew near the close: beginning with the morning after the coming election he would pursue his own course without reference to any ties that he and William Henry ever held in the past.

He ended with a line of appreciation for the legal services William Henry had tendered him.

Then he thought about the letter, and he thought more of it, whether to mail it or not—and he mailed it.

No man ever warned another any more fairly than this that he hated him and would fight him and would some day do him injury.

Chapter Forty-Six

THE GREAT PARTNERS FALL OUT

THEY had risen to the surface of the northern political force, William Henry, Weed and Greeley: and all through the mid-fifties none but these three and their wives knew of their shaken alliance. Greeley went on in his public journalist's way, while privately dreaming of the Presidency, and with his jealousy of the influential William Henry ever intensifying. As to Weed, there were signs that he was taking a special course of his own, and shifting his allegiance away from William Henry. He worked cleverly in the New York State Legislature in the spring of 1855, so as to make it possible for William Henry to return to the United States Senate for a second term. And yet, immediately afterward, he moved away from his lifetime friend. The new Republican party was forming, and Weed wasn't sure he could elect William Henry to the Presidency. He sponsored another, a less controversial candidate....

And William Henry was stunned with rejection.

Disconsolate, puzzled by Weed's maneuvers, angered by the rejection of the Whig-Republican force at the very time when he was the acknowledged leader of the antislavery power in Washington, William Henry turned homeward to Frances, for sympathy and support and understanding.

One day, in their library, after Colonel John Frémont had been nominated for the Presidency by the new Republican party, they discussed their old-time associate. Frances said she had always felt that Weed was politically unstable.

"I fail to understand how he puts by all the years you have been together, by any term other than opportunism," she said.

"He conceives the political situation differently than I."

"What are you trying to do?" she asked, "become a master of understatement? Have you lost your power of forthrightness?"

"He can't wholly be blamed. He has to stay afloat in the wild surface of politics."

"I disagree. He should have put you up for the Presidency. How could he ignore your leadership in the Senate?" It was true. The nation wondered at his bypassing in favor of Frémont.

"In politics," William Henry went on, weakly defending his friend, "you have to measure cup by cup, a cup of this, a cup of that. He is afraid of the Know Nothings. They have become powerful and they hate me for my policy, and their opposition could be fatal to the new party."

"There is such a thing as obligation, Henry."

"Frances, obligation is weak in practical politics, apparently."

Afterward William Henry wrote a blisteringly polite letter to Weed, saying that he hoped he might some day find out that this was a necessary course on the part of political friends, but still he didn't think it was kind or generous toward him, and besides, he was thinking of giving up public life altogether as soon as his Senate career ended.

The coolness between the pair might have blown in from the unknown regions of Alaska.

Yet there were deeper reasons for their quarrel. The pressure on William Henry to break from his traditional friend was strong; and perhaps Weed sensed it, and possibly Weed was yielding to William Henry the chance to break, if he desired to do so.

For Weed, they said, was growing a tail, a long tail, long as a railroad, and it bulged behind him so that the whole political community could see it. He had come to have a wonderful Mephistophelian manner: he smiled and beamed like a master mind, and he was a master mind. He had become white-haired, a big flowing mane of white hair domed him, and he had bushy white eyebrows, his jaw stuck out masterfully, and he fired cigars at people as if they were magic bullets: he had completed the conquest of his own style of controlling men and situations so that powerful figures were moved by him and did his bidding. He invested heavily in railroad stock, he was making money, he used his influence in the Legislature of New York to help his moneyed friends, and they, in turn, did favors for him. Weed had closed the link between politics, Government and big business. Not that he was motivated by evil, or that he was evil. He simply believed that business was good for the country and good for him; businessmen were builders; he admired their accomplishment; it was a world where money was respected, and he meant to have respect. But he had earned the name "the Lucifer of the Lobby," and they could see his tail wagging wherever he went.

For months William Henry and Weed quarreled bitterly by letter; the mails were afire, for they were at variance over one policy after another.

William Henry, acting independently on the Senate floor, and from motives of patriotism, supported a Democratic Party measure to suppress a Mormon revolt in the West, and Weed attacked him for siding with their traditional enemy. . . .

Weed to William Henry: What is the idea of proposing an army of suppression of the Mormons? How can you countenance such a view? These are religionists and a minority; and our interest, it seems to me, would be to let the Democrats handle this and to steer clear.

William Henry to Weed: Because it is bad policy, that is why. I am thinking of the general good, and in a situation like this, where the Government's dignity is involved and the supremacy of law and order is involved, it is incumbent upon a nonpartisan interest to restore the rule of safety.

Weed to William Henry: How can you, with such aplomb, abandon party interest and declare that you never cared for party and never would? What can have happened to you? Where is your sagacity in the face of a powerful political force such as that of the Democratic power now determining Government?

William Henry to Weed: Patriotism demands the closing of ranks in many situations, and the unity of parties in the face of impending threat. This is a lesson of all political societies, of all history, and from where I stand, in the Senate, the duty simply seems clear.

Weed to William Henry: And what can you possibly mean that the battle for freedom is already won? Who has won it? Where is it won? Is slavery abolished? Is the political pattern so convincing to you that you can be certain of victory, of inevitability in politics? I venture to suggest that not fifty men in the North know what you mean by this or understand any sense in which it is true.

William Henry to Weed: Weed, I profoundly regret, it seems to me we no longer understand each other. Instead of sympathy and understanding, it appears that all that I can expect from you now is harsh judgment and the reprimand.

Weed to William Henry: It has not seemed so to me. I believed we were political allies. I believed that our motivating relationship was one where "him whom he loveth he chasteneth." If it were possible to reverse our positions you would see with my eyes, and I feel with your keen sensibilities. But I have added to a former folly by writing again—a folly all the more to be regretted if it begets a reply. It is not worth one.

Weed's last letter begot no reply.

The feud was dying.

They simply couldn't break with each other, not wholly, not completely nor permanently. Somehow, somewhere, out of this correspondence, they discovered that Weed was Seward and Seward was Weed.

William Henry decided to let the matter drift.

And so the great moment passed in William Henry's life when he might have broken with the other man and not endangered himself by riding on or alongside Weed's Luciferian tail.

Chapter Forty-Seven

WILLIAM HENRY GOES UP
ON THE MOUNT

ONE NIGHT in the autumn of 1858 William Henry made a routine campaign address to a gathering of citizens in a small hall in Rochester. It was raining that evening and not everybody who wanted to hear him could get there. There was trouble with the gaslights too; they flickered and went out, dimming the picture of him up on the platform, till they lighted new gas wicks.

After the speech he boarded a coach and drove back to Auburn. During the next few days he was astonished at the results of that particular rally. For the thoughts he uttered, sentiments he had expressed for years, views that he had been uttering for several weeks at rallies all over the state, chanced to catch fire. Apparently there is a moment of ripeness in politics; for that night his words touched whatever exposed nerve had developed in the national body, and the flame that was lighted produced that kind of excitement which resulted from his "higher law" observations eight years earlier.

Describing the imminence of collision between the free-labor system of the North and the slave-labor system of the South, he asked:

Shall I tell you what this collision means? They who think it is accidental, unnecessary, the work of interested, or fanatical agitators, and therefore ephemeral, mistake the case altogether.

It is an irrepressible conflict between opposing and enduring forces; and it means that the United States must and will, sooner or later, become either entirely a slaveholding nation, or entirely a free-labor nation.

It is the failure to apprehend this truth that induces so many unsuccessful attempts at final compromise between the slave and free states; and it is the existence of this great fact, that renders all such pretended compromises, when made, vain and ephemeral.

From the time he used the expression "irrepressible conflict" there was no peace left in the United States, and apparently no peace possible thereafter. The phrase arrived during a new political climate; the seriousness of the national crisis was evidently everywhere realized, and now all was ripeness.

The newspapers went to work North and South, and they either denounced William Henry as an incendiary and as a radical or they defended him for his correctness and his moral force.

Horace Greeley rallied to William Henry eloquently in the *Tribune*. The Senator was pleased by the brilliance and flattery of his defender, and proud of his long association with the journalist, who, he said to himself, always came through in an emergency.

Not long after that a Greeley editorial said that if there were half a dozen true democrats in the whole world one of them was certainly the proud product of New York State, William Henry Seward. That editorial delighted Weed and he republished it in his own paper in Albany.

Weed and William Henry corresponded about the fine way in which their friend was showing up. And yet, to Weed, this was as it ought to be. Weed, mother hen of present political life in the North, must warm many chicks these days, and he must believe his chicks were his own.

Early in May of 1859, William Henry said good-by again to Frances.

"Believe me, Frances, this is a trip I am not really anxious to make."

"Then why make it? You've been to Europe twice before."

"Because the next period is crucial for us. It is a time when I must make no mistake. It is best that I am not at my Senate seat, to leap up and say something some day that may upset our life plans—"

"Isn't absence at this time a course of timidity?"

"Not at all. Only a course of the highest strategic value. Weed thinks so, I think so—it is a time for me to be silent while my friends whip up my cause. Frances, believe me, in Europe I will meet the men whom I will have to work with when I am President, and this period of traveling among them will help me enormously in the 1860 campaign. What an argument it will be when I can return and list the roll of the mighty with whom I'll confer! Who else in America will be able to do this? Don't you see, Frances?"

"I suppose so, Henry."

He went to New York preparatory to the long removal to Europe. He'd meet the big ones of the Continent, and he'd send letters back home that would find their way into print so that the public could see him royally received over there, where it was always important; he'd broaden himself, and make new and valuable connections with the Old World monarchs, which he'd need when he became President.

His prestige was enormous all over the nation.

It was so great that even Horace Greeley acceded to it, and came before Weed and William Henry as their traditional admirer and friend, so that William Henry, before his boat left, wrote to Frances, "Weed reports to me that Greeley has become all right at last, politically, and goes off to California, seeking to be useful there. Greeley is going by the Overland route. He has been with me today at dinner."

Two or three hundred Republican friends went to the steamship dock to see him off on the steamer *Ariel*. There was music, the firing of salutes from the shore, newspapermen covered the event; Greeley's reporters were there to describe the departure of the great man.

On the upper deck of the *Ariel,* just before his friends must get off the ship, he made a parting speech, perhaps the most self-conscious of his life; for, during the past year or so, the adulation he secured wherever he went affected him much.

At this moment he believed himself to hold literally the destiny of the country in his hands; he felt that he was immortal; and he knew that, however egotistic his feelings, they were perhaps the natural emotions of one as adored as he now was by the Republican North.

He knew that he was going to be President of the United States at the close of the following year; Weed knew it; everybody in the North suspected the strong possibility; the South feared it; Frances hoped and believed it; and he as much as told this to his friends in his farewell remarks.

Sounding a little like a Moses who was to ascend some Mt. Sinai to return with the Commandments, he said, as the ship rocked at the wharf, that he was going across the sea to get the knowledge derived from the sufferings and strivings of the European peoples over the ages so as to teach him how to improve and elevate the condition of his own countrymen.

What might happen during his absence, Providence only knew.

Whatever, he was sure that at last the great questions of justice and humanity before the American people were destined to be decided, "and they may be safely left to your own hands" he told the Republican gathering melodramatically, "even if the instructor never returns."

He was gone for a long time, into early 1860, and during his absence John Brown and his band of twenty-one men struck at Harper's Ferry: and the nation moved swiftly toward the edge of disunion.

A cry rose all over the land that the "irrepressible conflict" incitement of William Henry Seward had driven John Brown to undertake the overthrow of chattel slavery.

Chapter Forty-Eight

THE REVENGE OF HORACE GREELEY

*Yea, mine own familiar friend, in whom I trusted, which did eat
of my bread, hath lifted up his heel against me.*

Psalm 41

ONE DAY early in March of 1860 Thurlow Weed sat at his desk
in Room No. 11 at the Astor House. It was one flight up, a large
room with many chairs, two sofas, a picture of Benjamin Franklin on one of the walls, for Franklin was the patron saint of Weed. Mostly,
when Weed was there, the room choked with smoke; he kept a box or two
of snuff at hand for anybody who took snuff and might chance to run out
of it while with him; he had one whole drawer for cigars, and in another
he kept liquors for the special occasions when his colleagues might just
need a nip or two to celebrate an appointment, an election, or the fun of
having whipped hell out of somebody they thought deserved it. It was the
most famous room in New York for a whole generation. Here Presidents
were made and unmade, and political campaigns planned.

Weed talked this day with a political crony, Julius Wood, from Columbus, Ohio. Wood was in town to report on the outlook in his state for the
approaching nominations for the Republican candidate for the Presidency.

"I'm expecting Seward any minute," Weed said. "I'd like to have him
hear your report." William Henry had recently returned from Europe.
He had been accorded a regular triumphal-march procession all the way
from New York to Auburn. Huge throngs of loving citizens gathered at
each train stop to cheer the man they wanted for President in 1860. His
personal favor was never higher than at this hour of return: and now
Weed was working out the details of the next and final last stage of the
mutual advance to national leadership of his friend and himself.

Weed passed the Ohioan a drink and they talked of family awhile.
When William Henry arrived, Julius Wood got to business immediately
after the handshaking. "I want to tell you gentlemen that we are going
to have trouble from Illinois. I have information that they are going to
try to gather candidates out there in a way so as to block the Governor."

"I don't think there's any danger of that," Weed said.

"The Blairs, Mr. Bryant and Mr. Greeley and many others are hard at work," Wood insisted.

"Yes," said Weed, "we know that, but something more than their opposition will be necessary to beat the man upon whom the people have set their hearts." He looked at William Henry.

A few days earlier Abraham Lincoln had given an address at Cooper Union Institute in New York. Wood interpreted the meaning. "Mr. Lincoln was brought to New York to divide your strength, Mr. Seward."

William Henry answered, "I shouldn't worry about that if I were you, Friend Wood. I don't think it means anything."

But Wood wasn't finished. "You know I've been in town a few days—"

They waited.

"On Sunday while I was just hanging around the hotel here, who walks into the lobby but Greeley—"

"Yes?"

"Well, he don't make any bones about it—he told me straight and clear, 'We shan't nominate Seward, we'll take some more conservative man like Pitt Fessenden or Bates.'"

Weed and William Henry stared at each other: it was second nature with both to expect to bandy talk about the perplexing journalist.

William Henry said, "I saw Greeley only a few days ago. Weed brought him to me right in this hotel. He is all right."

"I believe he is all right," Weed said.

"Now I am not wrong about this, gentlemen! Greeley will go to Chicago and he will work against you!"

William Henry didn't seem alarmed. "My dear Wood, your zeal sometimes gets a little better of your judgment."

Weed passed around cigars.

A few days before the trains started west bearing delegates to the Republican Convention, Horace Greeley went to Albany to see his longtime friend Weed.

He spent a day and a half at Weed's house, assuring him that he was going to Chicago to support William Henry for the Presidency.

Then, a little earlier than Weed was ready to go, Greeley boarded a train headed for the convention city.

At Auburn:

"Shall you be going to the convention, Henry?"

"I think not, Frances."

"Why not? Is there some protocol about this?"

"Not especially. But there is more dignity in staying at home."

"Is dignity the consideration at this moment?"

"I think it is all in the hands of Weed. There's nothing left to do or say. The campaign is done."

"Then I shall have you about for a time—?"

"I'll need to rest, and write my acceptance speech."

Horace Greeley arrived in Chicago on Saturday night, May 12th.

He went from the depot by horse and buggy taxi to the Tremont Hotel. He checked into his room; he tossed his baggage on the bed, and took a quick look at himself in a mirror to see whether he looked Greeley enough to start canvassing the delegates. He combed his flock of sandy-whitening hair, fussed with his sidewhiskers, wiped dirt strains from his glasses, put his glasses back on his nose, gulped a drink of water that he poured from a pitcher on a small white table, gathered a deep breath, and went to work.

In the same hotel there were delegates from certain doubtful states, primarily Indiana and Pennsylvania, and he must reach them right away. Balloting for the Presidency might be only four and a half days away, for the convention was to open on Wednesday. (It chanced that that day was the fifty-ninth birthday of William Henry, and the New York State entry for the nomination intended celebrating the event quietly at Auburn. There he expected to receive the good news by wire from Weed. It was understood that any telegrams would be signed simply T. W.) Greeley went down to the lobby and made inquiry where certain delegates were quartered.

When he talked with the Pennsylvanians and the Indianans, and told them that he didn't go with Weed and Seward, it became instantly the biggest development of the convention's opening.

The politicans at the Tremont thought this to be so significant that they sent messengers to each of the city's forty-two hotels, with brief hand-written announcements scrawled on long thin strips of paper:

GREELEY AT THE TREMONT: WEED AT THE RICHMOND HOUSE.

The rumor spread that there was a break in the New York delegation. From that instant, there was much that Greeley had to work with. In Indiana where Henry S. Lane was out for the governorship and in Pennsylvania where Andrew Curtin was the candidate of the People's party for governor, there were strong Know-Nothing and native-American

325

movements. These were conservative nationalists, opposed to the foreign-born, luke-warm about suffrage of all kinds, for Negroes, for women, for immigrants, and opposed to much that William Henry advocated. They didn't like slavery, but they feared too much liberalism; the New York Stater wasn't popular with these voters; and by many, on the inside, at the convention, his early-day advocacy of anti-Masonry was well-known. As a result, Lane and Curtin believed that they must oppose his nomination: and men who want to be governor can't be expected to step aside because another man, whose career is not their career, wants to be President. There was anti-Seward sentiment of this sort in Illinois and New Jersey, where delegates also felt that he was too radical on the slave question: and Greeley, as he moved about, and as small groups were brought to him, used these arguments to tear support away from the man who had never elevated him politically, but only irritated him by telling him that he was primarily a gifted editor, but never a good practical politician.

Greeley was out to show his old rival that he knew something of the art of maneuver and organization. As he buzzed into the ears of the doubtful or movable delegates, he didn't hesitate to mention that Thurlow Weed was tied in with the franchise legislation in Albany so as to benefit the Street Railway crowd in New York. Seward was integral to the Weed money machine, Greeley whispered: and the word spread that this kind of money backed the Auburnian. The delegates from the interior states, far removed from big-money operations, fearing the ogre of monopoly, absorbed the mood that Greeley and his growing phalanx of dissidents dispensed. Greeley had great prestige: he had managed to wangle a position at the convention as chairman of the delegation from Oregon: here was the pure West, and a pure editor making out a noble case against big money. All of which was being converted to the killing political term called "unavailability."

Other factors worked for the New York editor. This was the first big Republican convention in Chicago; it was the home state of another candidate, and this candidate's friends were busy generating enthusiasm for him. He too was not in town; he was at his home site in Springfield, Illinois, where he maintained close contact with the local telegraph office.

Beyond all of this, Thurlow Weed, if he was a dictator, was a limited dictator, limited by the newness of the Republican force itself. No tight machine, well oiled, under his control from coast to coast, was yet organized. Too many new elements were fusing. Weed simply didn't control them all. Ambitious men in the various states, and a half dozen governors and senators who wanted to be President, were prepared to make deals—and when the exuberant Greeley, dressed in his perennial long white coat, with his eager bewhiskered face, came among them with his arguments based on his inside knowledge of the team of Weed and Seward, with his journalist's knowhow, his show of moral feeling and indignation (and shielding to himself his personal history with his quondam partners) he split the potential unfused force of the convention into separate bargaining and dealing and double-dealing camps.

On the night that Greeley arrived, the big new Wigwam to house the convention, built by the Republicans of Chicago, formally opened.

It was the largest audience room in America, two stories high, constructed of wood; it ran a hundred and eighty feet along Market Street and a hundred feet on Lake Street. The structure, thrown up hurriedly, cost five or six thousand dollars to build; the inside was fixed up with a main hall, spectators' galleries, a speaker's platform, committee rooms, a press area, a big space for musicians; and altogether it was vast enough to hold a crowd of about ten thousand. The place wasn't completed until the eve of the convention: in the last two or three days a crowd of volunteers, mostly women, prettied up the huge rough hall. They wreathed and festooned the interior, placed evergreen throughout, and hung red-white-and-blue drapes from pillar to support to pillar. Big paintings of Liberty, Plenty and Justice decorated a brick wall at the rear (the wall was part of an adjoining building), streamers and flowers were plentiful, and to make it all up to the minute, gaslight was installed.

That evening, while Greeley was busy in the hotel rooms, the Wigwam was noisy with celebrants. Bands boomed, there was singing, and orators told themselves and the others how wonderful they all were, "for the ball begins to roll and the signal guns of the approaching contest between Freedom and Slavery will be fired tonight. Let every man be at his post."

So the new rallying place was dedicated, the big wooden tent jammed, the money raised then and there to pay for the Wigwam, the flags flying ... and when old Mr. Johns, a delegate at large from Iowa, told how he walked a hundred and fifty miles to reach a train to get here, he set the crowd into uproar.

The next day they had religious services in the Wigwam, Presbyterian and Baptist pastors conducting ... and by Sunday evening all Chicago was alive with a huge street throng. At the hotels a man was glad to have a chance to sleep on top of a billiard table—and pay for it, too. By Monday and Tuesday the crowds poured into Chicago in the heaviest stream of all, and the town's population was doubled; but mostly they were Illinois people. They hoped to get inside the convention hall and do a little shouting.

327

Actually the arrivals from the various states, bringing banners that put forward favorite sons, were by no means committed spiritually or practically to any one figure—even though it was everywhere agreed, even in the camp of uprising which Greeley churned, that William Henry Seward of Auburn would be nominated.

Why not? In the streets of Chicago, the broad central avenues where business boomed and the decorations were gay and the air salubrious and patriotic, huge processions of Seward supporters paraded the streets all day and each evening. They flew Seward banners, and they sang in great joined choruses the popular air of the day, "Oh, Isn't He a Darling!"

The Seward boosters, in from New York, acquired at once the reputation of being real hellraisers; and they were headed up by the famous prizefighter, Tom Hyer. Whole contingents of Sewardmen were in and out of the saloons with the regularity and rhythm of the swinging doors themselves; they howled slogans in the streets, they sang in choruses that could be heard blocks away, and if anyone asked them why they were so darned tootin' noisy they answered, "We're opposed to bein' too damned virtuous," and besides it was a lie that their man couldn't sweep all the Northern states.

The momentum mounted through Wednesday. On board the last trains coming in to Chicago they had taken straw votes, and William Henry won handily in all, except on one train. On board the new Albany and Salem, an Indiana train, a straw vote gave the Illinois man, Abe Lincoln, fifty-one votes, Seward forty-three, and one hundred thirty-one votes were divided among other candidates.

Whatever this convention was to be, it was no well-oiled machine clearly controlled by any one man or group anywhere in the nation.

The big Republican force, committed to opposition to the extension of slavery, grew in a lopsided way, like quick flowing grass that reached up everywhere, came up in patches—and it was ripe ground for the unexpected.

On Wednesday and Thursday the convention was organized and a platform adopted. All Thursday afternoon the delegates wrangled whether a line from the Declaration of Independence should go into the platform, and finally it went in: but it was late then. Even so, someone moved that they ought to start balloting for the Presidency; and at that moment, the probability is that the Seward enthusiasm was so high William Henry might have been nominated then and there . . . that evening.

But someone up on the platform, after a moment's delay, called out . . . "Just a minute, folks . . . No, they're not here."

Then he made an announcement that the official papers on which they intended tallying votes didn't seem to be at hand, but someone would bring them in a few minutes.... The crowd waited and buzzed, ready to go on with the work ... but here suddenly, some unknown, a new voice in the crowd, loudly moved for an adjournment till the following day, and the huge crowd filed out of the Wigwam. They went into the streets to enjoy the spectacle of seeing people from all over, the big circus look of it all....

That was probably the instant of the final change in the tide of fortune for William Henry. There are those who say he would have been nominated that evening if the tally sheets had been quickly available on the speakers' platform.

Early that evening and all through the night, Greeley flitted from room to room, from hotel to hotel. Wherever he went he had with him a band of Lane and Curtin men, and they buttonholed the movable delegates, and gave them the arguments about William Henry's career, the anti-Masonry, the sponsorship of the idea of financing parochial schools, the linkup with the Weed money power, his too-ardent Abolitionism; all the contradictions of William Henry's career.

Though two-thirds of the conventioneers believed that they were for William Henry, a powerful seed of vacillation had been placed in the Chicago earth.

The politicians everywhere, that night, rigged and devised and circulated, and re-thought their positions; and considered alternatives in the event something unpredictable might happen the next day.

On nomination day William Henry was, of course, in Auburn. His fifty-ninth birthday had passed, not too quietly, in that community, two days earlier. The whole town observed that incident as if they had in mind shortly celebrating a larger event.

William Henry, trusting to the organizing powers of Weed, trusting the mark he had made on American society, trusting human nature as it might possibly reside in an old friend such as Greeley, calmly moved about in his own back yard.

There were certain details that needed attention at home. There had just been a fire that swept away barns in their back yard; and he was needed there to give attention to how these should be rebuilt; no need for him to be in Chicago; and of course Frances always liked having him around anyway.

And so, William Henry fiddled with his barns while another kind of music played at the Chicago Wigwam.

On Friday, the day of the nominations, the Cayuga County Republicans came into town by horse and buggy, whole families driving in, to be around South Street and Genesee Street when William Henry should receive the nomination. They would like to see his smiling face, and applaud him, and also laud themselves: "Our home town man the President!" Pride and an ineffable joy filled the townsmen, thousands, as they came out, dressed in their best, and made of this a holiday. The servants could take it easy; the stores were relaxed, and would close altogether during the day. Some of the main shops simply let their help go home because nobody felt like working.

Sweet Auburn, loveliest village. The scents of spring, fresh and earthy, were over the town. The tall barked maples along the sidewalks, those trees which stand to this day, a hundred years later, a hundred years wiser, acted as a canopy beneath which the villagers walked. Down the various hills to the town center they came, and turned south on William Street or South Street to be near the "Governor" and his wife.

In front of the Seward house two loaded cannon were set up. They would be fired, with huge, resounding blank cannonades, aimed upward, to greet the nomination when the word should be received. Flowers strewed the pathway from the sidewalk up to the front door of the Governor's house. Two stone lions, sculptured and beautiful, crouched impassively on each side of the staircase, these also waiting for the news, their shaggy necks adorned with garlands of polyanthus and dahlia.

The people crowded onto the grassed lawn of the Sewards, pushed through the gateway of the lattice fence, and then simply walked all over the yards, and on this exceptional day the Sewards allowed this freedom. There was no keeping the Auburnians from crushing about the house, looking in the windows, and moving up on the side porch to shake hands with the beaming and genial William Henry.

He was more affable than ever, the very essence of democratic neighborliness. Always famous for amiability, humor, a casual word, a simple joke, he was more that way today than ever. He greeted all his lifelong friends by their first names, Nick and Steve and George and Norbert and Mark and Harold, and they called him Bill, simply Bill. They grasped his hand and said, "Bill, we'll be calling you Mister President after today."

They crowded in close to see invalided Mrs. Seward seated in the living room, with her flock about her. From here on in, if she were invalided, it would be in the White House, and she would be an ailing First Lady of the Land. Her smile was gentler than ever, her heart warmer, her day never more beautiful—albeit a bit tense because one could never be certain about what a political convention was going to do.

330

The first draft of his acceptance speech troubled him a bit. He decided to rewrite. "There," he said, after he read it aloud, "that sounds better, the country will like that much better."

"It does sound better," Frances agreed.

At last William Henry was on the front porch as a crush of villagers crowded close. Beside him stood a former law partner, Christopher Morgan, with such an air of pride and proprietary interest that it almost flowed over his vest and paunch. If William Henry became President, Morgan would be part of the inner circle. In fact if he reached the White House, something of the influence and the wonder of it all would brush off on the whole village. That is why the citizenry was on hand, sensing a historic moment, and to be able to tell their grandchildren, "I was there when Seward got the news he was the Republican choice."

There was a rustle of excitement that spread from the sidewalk through the gates and up to the porch ... a message. A fast man on horseback came from the center of the town, on a gallop, and the throng pushed aside and made a lane for him to come into the gates on horse and stomp right up to the doorstep with a clackety clutter of hooves. He handed a telegram to William Henry:

FIRST BALLOT:

For Seward 173½   Lincoln 102

Morgan read it to the sprawling convention of townsmen, and they applauded.

He did not expect to secure the nomination on the first ballot, William Henry told them: more likely the second.

A little later the same scene repeated along the slate sidewalk that led to the Seward staircase, the rider on horseback returning with his second wire.

Once more Christopher Morgan read the balloting report from Thurlow Weed:

Seward 184½   Lincoln 181

"I shall be nominated on the third ballot," William Henry said. His voice was rich, hoarse, confident. The multitude applauded his confidence, cheered. He was neatly dressed today; Frances had insisted on his looking well for the occasion.

The spring warmth was a green sweet thing over the village, the flowers saturating the Seward property, the lilac odor sweeping down the main street. The bees buzzed at the eaves of every house. The sparrows chirped

331

from each tree, their sound a little less apparent than usual because there was so much excitement in front of the Governor's house and out beyond the walks in the macadamized South Street. The robins streaked overhead with their broad wings and their orange bellies. The maples soared over the Seward house, the monarchs seventy and a hundred years old shielding the house, the man, the community. The branches, like great hands, spread over the old Miller mansion—branches that were wands, wings, hopes.

But deeper in the village, at the railway station opposite Auburn Prison, where the telegraph office was located, a young freckle-faced telegrapher was the first to get the news. It came in this fashion:

dash/ dot dot/ dash dot/ dot dot/ dot/dot/ dot dash/ dash dot/—spelling out *L-I-N-C-O-L-N*.

Then this telegraphy:

dash dot/ dot dot/ dot/ dash dash/ dash dot/ dot dash/ dash/ dot/ dash dot dot—

N-O-M-I-N-A-T-E-D

Signed: *dash/ dot dash dash—*

T-W

The telegrapher bounced from his desk with the message scrawled on the sheet; he hurried outside to where his horse was hitched to an iron post, he leaped to his saddle, he galloped a quarter mile away to the center of activities.

He gave the message to William Henry personally.

It is a fatal thing for Presidential aspirants to hang about their homes on nominating convention days in wait for the word to come that they shall be candidates for the Presidency. They should be at the convention whooping it up for themselves, embarrassing their weaker friends, nailing their foes, clawing with each sharpened fang.

They saw his face silent and whitening, transforming. They watched him turn on the porch and walk uncertainly inside. The voice of Christopher Morgan went suddenly hoarse repeating the two words:

Lincoln nominated.

On all sides there was, swiftly as a torrent that might have turned into their yard after a rainfall—a torrent of simple weeping. The townsmen could not stand it. They cried. You could hear them gently sobbing to one another all over the Governor's lawn. Simply crying, en masse, a democratic and a loving crying.

They saw their great man, the little fellow with the condensed force, and the years written into his lined face and into his whitening hair, as he turned into his own house, into the privacy of his own despair.

They straggled away, they drifted down South Street and into the main street, unblushingly showing their tears, their handkerchiefs and their regrets. They vanished into the side streets. The farmers unhitched their horses from the wagon posts, and they started away from the center of the town, and the *clop-clop* of the horses' hooves was outward bound, the sound dimming away *clop-clop* like the faded hopes.

A few stayed on, the close friends, to console the President who-might-have-been—but even these suspected they weren't wanted right now, and they drifted off.

Silently, swiftly, three or four young men moved the cannon away from in front of the porch. They picked up the garlands of flowers and carried them off. They picked up every last flower, and the walk was clean again, clean and lost of its flowers. They rolled up scores of flags (the same kind of flags that were then unfurling, at that very moment, in Springfield, Illinois).

For the next few hours there was a quiet over the town that was like the quiet over Fort Hill Cemetery up behind the Seward house. There was just this deathly quiet, and the people were in their homes or they were in little clusters on the main street—mourning.

But late in the afternoon, Cheever, the editor of the Auburn *Daily Advertiser,* came to the door, hat in hand, and he told Frances that he had to ask the Governor something if he could.

William Henry was called to the door.

"Governor, they won't nobody write the story of the convention."

"Why not?"

"They can't. Can't anybody pick up his pen."

"Why don't you?"

"I can't. I *won't.* None of us will. If we never print it, we can't."

He was impressed with the love of his fellow villagers and he said, "Come in, Cheever."

The Governor sat at his desk and he worked with his goose quill.

Cheever heard the scrawl of lines, a half-dozen, ten, wonderful lines of a man's resilience and resignation. . . . "No truer exposition of the Republican creed could be given than the platform adopted by the Convention contains. No truer, firmer defenders of the Republican faith could have been found in the Union than the distinguished and esteemed citizens on whom the honors of the nomination have fallen. Their election. . . ."

And so on, for Union and Liberty.

There was, after all, someone in the village who could write something powerful and supporting about Abraham Lincoln's nomination.

Chapter Forty-Nine

LINCOLN'S RUNT IN THE
1860 CAMPAIGN

D URING the succeeding days William Henry heard the story of the convention: how Greeley had moved in the hotel rooms till he was nearly exhausted, meeting with the delegates, mustering all the latent enmities and doubts that they felt about the Auburnian. He was told how, after the last ballot was taken, Greeley sat at his seat in the Wigwam, wreathed in a smile of victory. His own choice, Bates, hadn't been named, but William Henry was whipped. "At last I got even with Seward," he said to those around him.

And while Greeley exulted, Weed openly wept on the convention floor. The story reached William Henry: and momentarily he felt murderous. Yes, he would like to see Greeley dead. But he couldn't sneak up on Greeley at point blank and just shoot him. He could only wish him dead, dead, dead.

It came back to him how thirty years before in a small hotel room, the Merchants' Exchange, in Albany, he had taken into his young hand the withered paw of Aaron Burr, slayer of Hamilton. But Burr had destroyed himself along with Hamilton. There was a great lesson in that. A great lesson in what not to do.

Yet his situation paralleled Burr's remarkably. Hamilton had thrown his weight to Jefferson, and Burr was licked for the Presidency. Greeley had thrown his weight against him, and Lincoln somehow, out of several candidates, was in.

But he was no Burr. He had as much ambition, but more sense, more restraint, perhaps more love of country. He'd kill Greeley in a different way; just forget about him, to hell with him, they'd be dead to each other forever.

The whole thing reminded him of another occasion, early, when he began life. The upperclassmen at Union College had heralded him on their shoulders, crossed the campus, deposited him in the ignominy of the campus lavatory.

Now something very like that happened again.

There were always two William Henrys: the inner one, who was this time shocked and dismayed, and the public man who said and wrote things for the record which expressed his higher and most civilized sentiments. He now wrote gracefully to Weed that the "dictator" had done all in his power that he could do and that he knew of nothing that could have been done that might have changed the result.

He also said that no man had the right to expect his country to repay good services with the Presidency or any other position: the nation owed no man that high office.

He had always been conscious of the role of the unexpected in human affairs, the vanity of making prediction, the senselessness of the prophecy in which politicians engage. As he got along in his career and as abrupt things happened to him, the victories he didn't count on, and the defeats he didn't want, the sense of the unexpected became an ironic undertone in his thinking. To himself he said, often, What next? Will it be this, or shall it be that? I am expecting this, therefore I better prepare for its opposite.

Now he thought he should prepare for "the opposite."

For a while he wanted only to retire from it all, to stay at home with Frances, and to cultivate his garden.

And yet, from this time on, there were greater things in the land than the feud between three big Whigs. A great booming was on, the threat of secession everywhere, the prospect of Lincoln's election exciting the inner core of the country, the hatred of the South moving as a wind, the heart of the Union dividing: there was a country that was in tears and anger, and it was a bigger thing than Weed, Seward, Greeley or Lincoln, bigger than all individual men, all the politics, enmities, jealousies, backbiting of rivals; and the services of experienced men were needed.

In New York the Seward Republicans were loath to get into Lincoln's campaign and most of them didn't. But like the true sportsman and politician that he was, William Henry threw himself into the campaign for Lincoln's election: and no one in the nation traveled farther or campaigned more furiously than he.

In fact, throughout the land, the election crowds came out to see the valiant, but now secondary Republican, and to hear him who, they supposed, would probably run the country if Lincoln were elected.

In the East, the Russian minister to the United States, Baron Edouard

335

de Stoeckl, studied carefully the campaign speech of William Henry, given at St. Paul, Minnesota, on September 18. The Republican said: "Standing here and looking far off into the Northwest, I see the Russian as he busily occupies himself in establishing seaports and towns and fortifications, on the verge of this continent, as the outposts of St. Petersburg, and I can say, 'Go on, and build up your outposts all along the coast up even to the Arctic Ocean—they will yet become the outposts of my own country—monuments of the civilization of the United States in the Northwest.'"

The baron, who had adopted that title, sent a copy of the speech back to Czar Nicholas, with the comment, "This man has a long eye, Your Majesty. He is looking at you."

The Civil War has its thousands of aspects. The story of Lincoln has its hundreds of focuses; but one of the fascinating facets of that time, and itself a great secondary drama of the larger conflict, is the unique and important relationship of these two, of tall Lincoln himself, and of, as a Southerner once called William Henry, "Lincoln's runt."

Chapter Fifty

THE TONGUES OF MEN AND
OF ANGELS

THE reliance and trust which Frances so generally placed in William Henry's political judgment she suspended late in November of 1860—and it was perhaps never fully restored to him throughout the Civil War. Her own position was severely critical and antislavery; it was Republican, like the position that was developing among the militants throughout the North who opposed compromise with the secessionists.

The break came with an incident late that month when Thurlow Weed in his Albany *Journal,* fearful of secession, and believing, like William Henry, supremely in the importance of Union preservation, proposed that a concession be made to the South: restore the Missouri Compromise line; this would assure the South all of the territory it needed in terms of soil and climate for the perpetuation of slavery. Weed called for a convention of delegates from the North and South to meet and discuss means of averting secession and civil war. His article created a wrath among Republicans, who said it would do no good. Many felt that this was an hour to "brandish the lance and shout for war."

This was a retreat from the Republican Party position on which Lincoln was elected, and at once it produced a restive feeling in the North. Did Seward, who was to be in the Cabinet, and perhaps be "Premier," believe this? people wondered, for he always went with Weed, and Weed with him. In fact it was believed that the policy was William Henry's and he had fed it to his associate.

The wave slid over William Henry, and it came to the door of his house on South Street. Frances was deluged by letters attacking her husband and Weed, the correspondents demanding to know whether compromise was afoot and would it not weaken the Northern cause and all that had been striven for?

She was disturbed.

Citizens were trying to reach her husband through her. It wasn't the first time. Besides, there were reports abroad that Frances, in a quiet way, exerted as much influence on William Henry as Weed—that there were only two real influences in his life, his wife and his Weed.

The excitement became national and William Henry, in several newspaper statements, disclaimed responsibility for the idea. Weed announced, "We speak only for ourself," and William Henry, in the succeeding weeks, fell silent.

But Frances wasn't.

"My dear Henry," she wrote. "There is much commotion in the community about the proposal of Weed to restore the Missouri Compromise— It is said here that you are the initiator of the idea and that Weed is spokesman of it— I myself do not know but doubt much that this is your view— I hope my remarks do not seem too intrusive upon your convictions— Nonetheless I have been so troubled by unremitting letter writers in recent days that I thought to speak— The air is filled with such strange tales of compromise and concession that I myself do not know what to believe— Weed's paper has of course openly espoused a view that is regarded by almost all as a retreat in the face of the Southern threat—this has brought embarrassment virtually to our own door, for people conceive that your attitudes will of course be similar to those of Weed— There is the feeling here that this is the time to speak bluntly to the South and not to make concessions— You will of course do as you please, as you must, but I thought it my duty to tell you of the atmosphere here and the way I have been besieged by letter writers who think they can influence you through influencing me— Your Own Frances."

William Henry, who wanted agreement from Frances, answered in a few days: "Mr. Weed's articles have brought perplexities about me which he, with all his astuteness, did not foresee. But you need not expect, or rather fear, that I will act unwise or wrong ... The madcaps of the South want to be inflamed, so as to make their secession irretrievable. Good men there want moderation, on the part of the Government, so that they may in time produce a counter movement. Our Senators agree with me to practice reticence and kindness ... I am very sorry that the mischievous reports of the letter writers have disturbed you so deeply. But I am disposed to be satisfied, after all, since the circumstance has drawn out from you such a beautiful, noble, and touching letter. You need have no fears. I am, thus far, silent, not because I am thinking to propose compromises, but because I wish to avoid, myself, and restrain other Republicans, from intermeddling, just now—when concession, or solicitation, or solicitude, would encourage, and demonstrations of firmness of purpose would exasperate. I have faith that my good angel won't desert me, as long as you and I keep together."

But William Henry's "good angel" was deserting him. So was the angel on South Street, who may have been his best angel. For, from then on, they saw the war differently—and she frequently thereafter chastised him for his moderation. She had sheltered slaves at her house; she had seen and talked with them in the South, and she was committed uncompromisingly to the abolition of the institution.

She continued to press her views upon him, her fears, her wonder at the moves he was making toward Union preservation, and, as it seemed to her, preservation of slavery.

Weed and William Henry felt a profound fear. They had worked for a generation to build the antislavery sentiment of the North; now that sentiment was an accomplished fact; the nation teetered on the edge of war. Was it a sense of responsibility that motivated Weed and produced the same hesitation in William Henry? The Senator had once pictured on the House floor the terrors of civil war. Now the possibility of it was imminent, and he and Weed alone might have it in their power to prevent this. Would war solve the problem? Would it only make possible the collapse of the country, perhaps the intervention of European nations? These were profound considerations, and it was actually the responsibility of Weed and William Henry, above all others, to look to the possibility of other alternatives, if they existed.

When Weed received a letter from Senator Preston King denouncing him for his course of moderation, saying, "It will prove distasteful to the majority of those whom you have hitherto led," Weed answered, "The normal proclivities of the American people are democratic, and we, the party in power, need to have our wits about us, and a stronger issue than that which has just given us success, and one which will absorb all others."

What new issue could absorb all others? What issue was larger than the one where the millions of the North opposed the millions of the South? What issue could transcend a condition where states were seceding, and a new nation even threatening to form in the South?

Weed may have had something in mind then, that he could have suggested to William Henry when they met a few days later. Or perhaps they both had the same thing in mind—an issue larger than the issue of civil war at home.

For it was about this time that Weed alone, or Weed and William Henry together, fashioned the idea of a foreign war which would have the effect of reuniting the North and South in the face of a common, a foreign foe.

339

William Henry was in a unique and trying position. His party had not favored him with the Presidential nomination, yet his situation of leadership among the Republicans was such that, in the interim period, while the outgoing Buchanan Administration weltered in secessionist activity, and the new party was not yet in power, the Republican force in the Capitol was under the Auburn senator's aegis. Buchanan had two more months in office, after the first of the year 1861; Lincoln was not yet in Washington; secession wasn't yet real and complete; the nation was in limbo, and William Henry somehow headed up this limbo.

On the third day of the new year he wrote to Frances that the Southern rebellion was gathering pace; it had its friends in the White House and the Cabinet, and the Republicans were powerless to forestall this current. Buchanan was paralyzed, caught between the two forces; and he, William Henry, was high up, catapulted to some high point over some undefined bridge in time, and he could look down and around; so he wrote to Frances: "I have assumed a sort of dictatorship for defense; and am laboring night and day, with the cities and the States. My hope, rather my confidence, is unabated. My letters must be short, and I fear less frequent. But I shall not forget you all."

From then on there was quickening in the lives of all who were connected with public events. Ideas came faster, letters moved more often and they were shorter; decisions came swiftly, and men's actions had sterner consequences than ever before....

Frances didn't like the conciliatory tone in his speech before the Senate on January 12th. He struck out as peacemaker; he was poet enough to be able to imagine a carnage that might not make the country better; he was so deeply involved himself in having helped prepare the mood that made men ready to go to war that now he stopped, and looked at himself, and asked himself: Did I help build these people up to this strength of purpose where now they are ready to lay down their own and other lives? Do they know what they are in for? Isn't there another way out? Am I responsible for the pass to which this country has come? Did my words "irrepressible conflict" help bring this about? If men die, is it upon my conscience? What will the gains be? Is it possible that the Union will be destroyed? Can all who are in hysteria be right? Is it wrong to be reflective, dispassionate, at a time like this?

Here was retreat, torment, doubt, patriotism and compromise, all in one, and he poured it out to the Senate, in a speech that altered nobody, and changed nothing, for the mood of separation was complete, the course of it perhaps inevitable.

Frances pursued him, as everyone in Washington, with another don't-compromise note: "I have read your speech and I must say that I do not like the concessions you make to the slave power—they are insatiable and cannot be placated— Henry, I cannot imagine what possesses you to reverse the position I know you to have held all of your life— You are like Canute who would turn back the tide—a tide in this instance which you yourself in such great measure helped to generate, and it is no wonder that all fall upon your views and rend them—perhaps it is the position you are in that makes it difficult for you to see what is so clear to others—whatever, I love you— Your Own Frances."

That struck. Everyone in the world against him, even his own wife. Here he was, trying to forestall what might be one of the greatest holocausts in the history of man, and few understood him—he and Weed and a handful of others against the world.

He answered that he was not surprised that she did not like the "concessions" in his speech, but she would soon enough see that these were not compromises, but explanations, to disarm the enemies of Truth, Freedom and Union of their most effective weapons ... he was trying to get home, he said, but as yet he saw no change— "It seems to me that if I am absent only three days this Administration, the Congress, and District would fall into consternation and despair. I am the only hopeful, calm, conciliatory person here ... There is no courage, or courtesy, and not one word is said to disarm prejudice and passion, and encourage loyalty. They invoke arms; but arms ought to be the last resort ...

Her letters pressing him to a more militant statesmanship continued ... But William Henry insisted he wasn't compromising. "Mad men North and mad men South are working hard to produce a dissolution of the Union, by civil war. The present Administration, and the incoming one, unite in devolving on me the responsibility of averting those disasters. My own party trusts me, but not without reservations. What I say and do is said and done, not in view of personal objects, but of such fearful responsibilities, and in this case, above all others, I am looking, or rather leaving, to posterity to decide upon my action and my conduct ... Once for all I must gain time for the new Administration to organize and for the frenzy of passion to subside. I am doing this without making any compromise whatever, by forbearance, conciliation, magnanimity."

But the revolution had begun.

Chapter Fifty-One

SOME THOUGHTS FOR THE PRESIDENT'S CONSIDERATION

AFTER the inaugural, William Henry sat at a new desk in a different building. It was the brick State Department, two stories high, with about thirty-five rooms, with awnings over each window to keep out the strong capital sun on hot summer days; and around the place, which was erected long before this Administration, there were large trees that had been planted when the country was young.

He occupied two rooms in the northeast corner of the second floor; in one he studied and wrote and worked privately, and in the other he received a procession of visitors during certain hours of the day. Frederick, who was about thirty-one now, and married, occupied an adjoining room: he had been named Assistant Secretary of State by the Senate, at William Henry's request; and Fred had the intricate duty of protecting his father from the political rush.

As Secretary of State, William Henry stood in a new relation to Government and Society; and he was in trouble with himself trying to determine what that relation was. He had been a much-flattered man for the past twelve years. He was supremely important during the last few months, since he returned to Washington as senator and presided informally over the destinies of the country prior to assuming his Cabinet post.

There was, at the time, no very great appreciation of what the man from Illinois would be able to provide in the way of leadership. Everywhere men figured that there had been some kind of miscarriage of party justice in the Republican ranks: Seward should have been the man of the new period, not this fellow Lincoln. Even the South figured it that way, and as the word circulated all over that the Auburn man was actually running Washington before Lincoln arrived, there were many—including William Henry—who decided he would continue to do so after Lincoln took office.

As the first month of administration advanced, William Henry went two or three times a day to the White House. There he gazed confidently at the tall man through his experienced and almost ancient eyes, with the philosophy of the whole world's politics in a way summed up inside of him and in his capacities. He was smaller than ever, with whitening hair, slits of eyes, careless clothes, a very very surpassing manner, and it may have been difficult for him to shield from the taller man the way he wore his attitude of natural political superiority.

Observing Lincoln on those frequent trips to the Executive Chamber, he wasn't impressed with what he saw. Even so he spotted the essence of Lincoln's character quicker than most, for he wrote to his friend, Charles Francis Adams, "The President has a curious vein of sentiment running through his thought, which is his most valuable mental attribute."

Lincoln was swamped at first in the detail of handing out jobs to Republicans who had worked hard for the victory; and he may have been dazed by the new role and the sudden responsibility. He was nevertheless intrigued by the way William Henry moved about in that calm manner while everyone else was harried: and because Lincoln could have a pliable and simple way with men, he gave the Auburnian the same impression of inexperience, rawness, even incapacity.

There were senators who believed Lincoln to be a kind of country bumpkin, "a romantic adventurer," a political accident, and they continued to look to William Henry for the real direction, and the Secretary of State, in the privacy of his new quarters, thought he had to live up to these expectations.

But at the outset, no two men contrasted more severely than these.... Here was William Henry, in the Cabinet sanctum, the great world traveler and cosmopolitan, professional carrier-on of the tradition of John Quincy Adams, friend of the great Easterners, suave, styled, expert and unruffled in a crisis, at home in the drawing rooms of the nation and the world, acquaintance of the late Marquis de Lafayette, legal colleague of the late Aaron Burr, himself touched by the most mystic chords of the American political tradition.

And here was Lincoln ... as in the upsetting incident of late March.

Charles Francis Adams arrived in Washington to get verbal instructions from the President for the carrying-out of his duties as Ambassador at the Court of St. James. William Henry had called him here: "Come and meet the President, we shall talk over the policies to be pursued," the Secretary wrote. "It is important you establish an accord with Mr. Lincoln as I have not, with ease, brought about your appointment, in the face of the President's desire to see William Dayton sent to England. It will be a grave and important moment for you, for the country."

The grave moment arrived.

William Henry ambled into the President's office on the second floor of the White House in his usual unimpressive way, with coat and trousers baggy and loose and shiny, and smoke trailing from his perpetual cigar, the fume rising to Adams' face; and "goddamits" interspersed his observations on State affairs. The New Englander moved in a stately way, about him the bearing naturally of courts and mansions. He had often been in this apartment a generation earlier, when his father John Quincy Adams was President, and a nostalgia was momentarily upon him as he gazed across the room that was about forty feet by twenty-five. His glance settled on the large white marble fireplace, with its big brass andirons and the high brass fender. He remembered that so distinctly. A wood fire burned and cords of wood were piled on one side. Beyond, the large windows opened on the beautiful lawn to the south, where he could see the unfinished Washington Monument. In Adams' mind this room was associated with neatness, order, dignity, even a bit of majesty.

A door opened, and there entered the big-featured man with the scraggly beard taking root. He was dressed in a long-skirted faded dressing gown, wearing slippers and coarse stockings, and he slouched a bit. He seemed very bony at the knees, and Adams tried not to betray a sense of upset as he gazed at what he conceived to be an apparition of sorts. If the President noticed some undue sensitivity, he was too busy a man to be concerned.

"Mr. President," said William Henry, "I present Mr. Adams, my friend and yours—and the country's."

They shook hands. Adams, still standing, spoke softly, eloquently, his thanks for the assignment, mentioned his resolve to commit himself at his highest and best, statesmanship and protocol burbling on while Lincoln slid into his chair listening in a kind of abstract way, as if something else were on his mind.

"Have a seat," the President chirped, and motioned to both to relax. He settled into a large armchair at a table on the west side of the room, near a window.

William Henry sat. Adams, in his chair, still murmured excitedly about the tasks ahead, policy, what he hoped to do; and yet it was all said in a moment or so, then Lincoln drawled:

"Well, Mr. Adams, you know this appointment don't come from me exactly...." Lincoln leaned forward, his left knee clasped by both hands.

Adams raised his distinguished eyebrows.

"If you feel obligated in any way," Lincoln said, "just thank the gentle-

344

man sitting right there," and the President pointed his long, boned index finger at his Secretary of State.

William Henry and Adams exchanged a quick glance. It wasn't news to Adams that his friend had interceded in his behalf but it seemed that the President was laboring the point.

"I wanted Dayton for the job," Lincoln rambled on candidly, looking the New Englander straight in his statesman's face. "But Seward here asked for so little and begged so hard to get this for you that, well, there you are...."

The President smiled faintly and wryly. He had said this without malice or point. He simply wanted Adams to know that he, Lincoln, understood full well that he was not naming the minister to St. James. Let Adams know he knew it.

The Chief Executive stretched his legs, and then mentioned to William Henry what was really on his mind.

"Governor, I've this morning decided that Chicago Post Office appointment." He seemed real interested in that, more than in the ambassadorship to England.

William Henry's small eyes widened and opened to their fullest. Here was Honest Abe again, unpredictable in so many situations, withholding much, either not ready or able to discuss foreign policy, and willing to send Adams abroad without a single instruction.

He nodded his head on the Chicago appointment.

The Ambassador to England wanted to ask what line he should take with the British. What about England staying out of American affairs? Deal with them softly or strongly? What?

But it was all left unsaid.

Soon the two tall men stood and they shook hands, and the short one, a little puzzled, puffed heavily on a new smoke.

The new Ambassador was astonished, displeased, upset, unimpressed. He was chagrined, he was embarrassed, and he felt violated.

"My God," he said to William Henry, as they left the office, "what are we in for? I have never never seen such a jackass. Never, never, never!"

Charles Francis Adams never forgot that moment.

Once more William Henry felt confirmed in his own impression that the man in the White House was no President—certainly not as he, William Henry, could be.

In this atmosphere, and at this moment, when William Henry thought so of himself, and thus of Lincoln, when his reputation was international and even somewhat Olympian, and the Illinoisian was merely lanky and green and raw and full of "I reckons," the Secretary of State—keen old bird that he was—proceeded to prove that in addition to all of these excellences and conditions that he stood for, he was also human. Not that he intended any such demonstration, or that he was interested in proving his humanity or fallibility, or anything else other than his supremacy. But out of his honest feeling that he was the big man of the hour and of the national crisis, and that nobody else could think things through as well as he, and out of what was very probably the admirable desire to preserve the Union over all else, he decided that he ought to tell Mr. Lincoln what had to be done next and who had to handle the thing.

So, on a Sunday afternoon, April 1st, as he paced up and down the interior of his soft-carpeted State Department quarters, a mood to write came over him. It was the Sabbath day, most things were closed down, and he could think well. He sat at his desk, and, with a newfangled steel-point pen that didn't work too well, he wrote thoughtfully and carefully over a large sheet of paper. He began with a title for this communication: "Some Thoughts for the President's Consideration."

His pen scratched out the notation that they were at the end of a month's Administration and there was no policy, either domestic or foreign. This wasn't anyone's fault, William Henry wrote, the patronage activity was upsetting, but it would be dangerous for the country for this to continue, it would bring scandal on the Administration, and the stream of applicants for office had to be hustled out of the way.

He had a ruling idea, he went on, that the question before the public should be changed from one of slavery to one of either Union or Disunion; get the thing out of partisan political considerations and make it a matter of land and country and patriotism; he would end the Fort Sumter question, as a means of changing the issue to Union, defend the navy in the Gulf, have the navy recalled from foreign stations and get set for a blockade and put Key West under martial law.

But beyond these considerations, there was another way to make the Union secure, and to prevent a split, and this was to demand explanations of Spain and France as to what their intentions were in the present divided state of affairs. Did they intend to intervene on our soil or stay out? He reached his main point now:

I would seek explanation from Great Britain and Russia, and send agents into Canada, Mexico and Central America to rouse a vigorous continental spirit of independence on this continent against European intervention, and if satisfactory explanations are not received from Spain and France, would convene Congress, and declare war against them ... But whatever policy we adopt, there must be an energetic prosecution of it. For this purpose it must be somebody's business

346

to pursue and direct it incessantly. Either the President must do it himself, and be all the while active in it, or devolve it on some member of his Cabinet. Once adopted, debates on it must end, all agree, and abide. It is not my especial province; but I neither seek to evade, or assume responsibility.

There it was, and he asked Fred to read it aloud. Fred did so, and thought it sounded fine; it certainly told that long fellow in the White House how to prevent the country from falling apart. Fred suggested he ought to rewrite the missive in his own younger hand so that Lincoln could read it faster, and so that they'd have the original in William Henry's own hand, for their own records. The Assistant Secretary of State rewrote; then he sent a messenger with the "Thoughts" at once to the White House.

The President sat at his creaky chair in the Executive Chamber and he read. He stirred in his seat as he got through the "Thoughts." Then he stood and he slapped the desk angrily. He could have split a rail, a gut, and a white hair or two. I better not tell Mary about this, he said to himself, or she won't let Little Bill come into the House, and that'll be the dickens. Now what the devil am I going to do with this fellow? He just don't abide by elections and appointments the way he should.

He rose angrily, moved about the room, his slippers silent on the crimson-and-white carpeting. How to handle this little man with the undoubted talents, who had the confidence of so many people, and the philosophic and practical background to rule a nation? He walked around the well-used furniture; its scraggly look had already caught the attention of the New York *Herald*'s correspondent. Mrs. Lincoln intended having the President's room scraped and re-papered, and fixing it up with new furniture. The only recent item was a few feet from the desk: it was a large rack holding maps of the country, in color and in black and white.

Abe moved about between the worn desks, chairs and tables, up and down the cavernous quarters, realizing that he wouldn't have anything more important to do today than handle this letter and his Secretary of State. He glanced about the room that William Henry would have liked to occupy, and in his sympathetic inner heart he could well understand it; half of the men in the Cabinet wanted to be in this office and to sit in his chair. He glanced over the envied spot and wondered for an instant whether it was so enviable.

He knew damned well that he fitted this room; he was tall and so were the walls; he looked up at the edges of the ceiling, where gilding and frescoes were badly in need of brightening.

The President stroked his beard, the beard he was growing because a

347

little girl told him to grow it in order to cover up his homeliness; it was just beginning to grow; maybe a beard would help in the distracting business of handling big ambitious men like Salmon Chase, Edwin Stanton and Seward. The only one who didn't want to run the White House, as yet, as far as he could see, was the little Secretary of the Navy, Gideon Welles, the New England fellow, a mere postmaster, who hadn't had quite as much big-time experience as the others in the Cabinet. Now, said Lincoln to himself, what would I do if I were William Henry Seward?

He decided that if he were Seward and he were not Lincoln, he'd have written a letter to Lincoln titled, "Some Thoughts for the President's Consideration." But if I were Lincoln instead of Seward, what would I do? And then, since that was easier, since he was Lincoln, and in a different position, he did what Lincoln would do if he were Lincoln.

It was as much Sabbath day—and a bit quieter in the White House for Lincoln—as it was for William Henry in the State Department. He could closet himself in his Chamber and find time to think clearly, too, on an off day like Sunday—and he decided to get this matter out of the way today. Once and for all! He wasn't too sure about the merits of some of the thoughts that Seward uttered in the way of domestic and foreign policy; they might be all right, and to his thinking many of these proposals already were under consideration, and the way it seemed to him, they *did* have a policy; he was elected President on the basis of that policy, and he at least knew where he was going, and nobody had accused him of compromise and concessions the way they had charged Seward; he wasn't going to let the slave question be abandoned, and he said so, and he was as much interested in preserving the Union as the other fellow.

What he didn't like was the last few lines which suggested that Seward could take over on the administration of these matters if the President thought he needed any help, or even needed a successor.

Lincoln had an imperious quality. So far he hadn't displayed it, but the time came, this Sabbath, when he must. It wasn't true that he was an unsophisticated man. He had gotten off to a start in politics at a younger age than William Henry. Nobody could be an Illinois lawyer, in court year in and year out, going to Congress, being a candidate for the Whig vice-presidential nomination in 1856, without knowing the score. It was merely that he'd never had a large and glorious place in public affairs. And perhaps he did speak with a little more of the idiom of the West and the vernacular of the street than did the cultured and erudite New York Stater. No, it wasn't lack of sophistication on his part; it was simple newness in a position of great import in an hour of profound crisis, and he was still a little numb with it all, trying to gather it between the fingertips of his mind, and groping to control many powerful personalities such as William Henry, and to use them for the country's good.

Nonetheless, the external look of a raw Westerner was in the one and the aspect of a sophisticated Easterner was in the other; and the actual situation prevailed of a Secretary who fancied himself Prime Minister, while the President knew perfectly well that he would be able to rule when he created for himself the chance.

On this Sabbath day, Lincoln saw the opportunity he wanted to take and to temper the driving spirit of the smaller, eminently gifted man. The White House rankled with the animosities of Mary Lincoln, who naturally knew and understood her husband's strength; she had told someone that William Henry was a "sneaky Abolitionist," and she didn't trust him; and she had kept after her husband to "show them" he was President.

Now it had come to him in simple written form, as a matter of record, and when it came to words and to writing he could handle himself as well as the next one. "I'll make a good Secretary of State out of him yet," he said to himself, because he needed a good one, and he wrote a reply that they did have a foreign policy, and a domestic line too, and he knew as well as the other that the important thing was to preserve the Union, and this had been stated in his inaugural address; he moved on to a point by point answer to William Henry's communication; he spoke of Fort Sumter, St. Domingo, other immediate matters.

Then, when he finished the letter he decided not to send it.

He took the "Thoughts" and he placed it with a sheaf of personal papers which were tied with a string and kept in his desk, just for his own use and record, and not for anything else; not for discussion, and not for release to others, nor to the press, but just a roll of papers that ought to be kept and not much done with.

Instead, he sent for William Henry.

"Cigar?" Lincoln asked the Secretary of State. He was very amiable.
"I will, thank you. You didn't learn that from my friend Weed, did you?"
"Governor, the cigar approach is practically national, by now."
They lit up.

Lincoln figured that a drink might be even more helpful. "Say, I'm tired and need a bit of a lift. I'll bet you do too."

He went out of the room and returned in a minute with a bottle of bourbon and two tumblers.

"I don't like to keep this here in the Executive Chamber," he said. "So many people come to see me, and there's temperance folks among them."

It was a little more familiarity than the President had yet shown to

William Henry, and the Secretary of State was suspicious. It put him in mind of something and he wondered what it was.

The President held his glass up in a mild token of a toast, and William Henry answered in the same half-lift of his glass, and they each sipped the hard drink.

"You don't miss being at court, I'll bet, hey Mr. Seward?"

That was it; Lincoln was being the lawyer this afternoon. That was dangerous; two lawyers sitting down to talk quietly, moderately, when there was actually a big cause of action between them over which they could be warring—that was difficult and dangerous. The President might be thinking of taking another one of those "tricks" he'd heard say the President liked to draw in the card game he played with the Cabinet members.

"No, I found law practice dull as hell. The damned stuff bored me nine hours out of ten."

Lincoln mused to himself that his Secretary was warden of an Episcopal church, but apparently the ritual life of the church and his sometime declamations about "higher law" didn't prevent him from cussing. He'd cussed every time he was in the President's presence so far, sometimes worse than this.

"I glanced at your notes, Mr. Seward. Some mighty fine thoughts in there. You express yourself real well."

William Henry didn't know what to say; Lincoln was passing the thing off, it seemed, not contemptuously, but politely and seriously. He lifted the bourbon to his lips.

"Sometimes I wish you and I saw a little more eye to eye on what to do about the Secesh." He quickly went on, "I don't blame you for how you feel about the English. Our kinfolk over there have been kind o' mean to us a couple times before."

William Henry perked. "Precisely, Mr. President. I can't imagine our having a situation of disunion here, and England staying out of our affairs. I think it's a matter of taking the offensive with them, before they surprise us somehow by interceding on the side of the Disunionists."

"I know that's what you think, Mr. Seward. And to tell you the truth, we wouldn't be the first country in the world to settle our problems at home by a little shooting match in some other part of the world."

"Precisely. The North and the South would get together right away, if we fell into difficulties with England or any other country."

"I believe you have a point there. The possibility of intervention is just about our greatest threat...."

William Henry nodded. This was the Secretary's big province and passion, and out of this nettle he hoped still to pluck the rose of national leadership.

"And I agree," Lincoln went on, "that we have to take a firm stand with those devils, and tell them off, and bluff them, and hit them hard, and make them understand they have to stay out—"

William Henry affirmed with an up and down motion of his head; he thought he was making headway with his foreign war thesis; while a second glass of bourbon was dulling him a bit.

"They certainly have been a pestiferous country for us folks," Lincoln said with a meaningful shake of his head.

William Henry remarked that the tradition of trouble with England was just about the biggest thing in the national past. And hadn't there been danger of war with England recently, in the 1840s, in the trouble over Oregon?; and war dangers with them since?; and he enumerated a few of the tense international situations. He bubbled now: there was a foreign-war party around currently, he said, not a big party, but there were important men who saw this as a way out, and a way to keep the States from falling apart; the slave question would be resolved before long anyway, it was plainly and simply on the roll of history for resolution at an early date; the slaveocracy was doomed to collapse sooner or later anyway. Why go into a war with the South, and take a chance of everybody in Europe coming across the ocean and tumbling into the land?

He's no doubt sincere, Lincoln said to himself.

"Well, it's your department as Secretary of State to think of such things and come up with ideas, Mr. Seward. That's what you're here for."

Then William Henry wondered whether he was hearing right, or whether he'd had too much to drink. For the President was saying, "We certainly have to send them strong notes and tell them what's what ... but that don't mean we want to knock the chip off their shoulder and actually fight 'em. I can't see that."

The Secretary could see it, and this time his head did not move in any direction.

Besides, Lincoln was saying, he'd come into office on a pledge not to let slavery expand, and there it was right now, the Secesh trying to do just that, to stand pat and even secede and maybe even threaten to spread their ways north. "I came in here, Mr. Seward, because I promised not to compromise on the question of extending slavery. Nothing else. If I stood away from that line, why, there wouldn't be any reason for me to be President, or for the folks to have nominated me, or then elected me. If we back away, all the work we've done is lost, and sooner or later we'd have to do it all over again. You wouldn't want to have to make all those speeches all over again that you made in the Senate on this slave question from 1850 till now, would you?"

The President didn't wait for a reply. In a quiet voice, like one lawyer saying to another that the case could be settled out of court or gone into with moderation or the action be postponed or just agreed upon somehow —in that kind of conciliation, in softness, he said that it appeared clear to him that the tug was on now, and it was better now than any time hereafter, and it just had to be faced, instead of being postponed, which a foreign war would do to it.

"Now, Mr. Secretary, you aren't the first one to ask me to shift ground from what I was elected on. Before I came here to Washington, people North and South tried to get me to step back from what our party platform said we stood for, but I can't do that and honestly sit here in this chair."

William Henry listened with pursed lips, taking no more drinks, no more puffs on his cigar. The cigar went out and the ashes dropped to the floor, and William Henry stared at the softly speaking figure before him, and he knew that he must listen with respect for it was the President of the United States speaking, and he was here in Washington by the President's invitation.

But he saw now that he was not called here this afternoon as much to speak as to listen. He sensed a power of decision he hadn't known was there till this minute. His upper lip trembled in its incessant uncontrolled manner, himself oblivious of the pulsating gesture that he couldn't feel. He was learning suddenly, clearly, unequivocally, that the gangly fellow was an engine of execution and will.

"Now as to the question about the issue before the country being changed from one of slavery to either Union or Disunion, I am under the impression, unless I am a fool, that this was clearly stated in the inaugural which you examined and you should be able to remember that. I don't see as you have brought in anything new here, Mr. Seward, though I will acknowledge that your attitudes on the need for foreign war represent your own independent views, which have never occurred to me...."

"As you say, Mr. Lincoln, it may be my function as your foreign affairs secretary to duly present such thoughts and any thoughts which I may believe to be of service to the country."

"...It certainly is, sir. And I'm mighty glad you have the integrity to say what you have in mind; I have always felt you were a very original man, and my admiration to you, Mr. Secretary, for being just that way. That's why I like having you as my Secretary of State." That was said with rising enthusiasm, and the President moved in his seat, and he smiled and he was all cordiality as he sipped another taste of bourbon through his lips.

William Henry sensed he was taking some kind of drubbing, he wasn't sure what; it was the man's down-country style of approach that was hard to handle.

The President, his knees crossed, his fingers toying with his glass, his voice gentle, rolled on as if he were talking about some law case in the circuit in Illinois, or talking horses to the town barber in Springfield. "Now the way I see it, Mr. Secretary, we got one big dickens of a proposition on our hands here with these states wanting to pull out, and it seems downright risky to me to be thinking of declaring war on England—Spain—France—Russia—the whole blessed world. Seems to me the way we ought to look at it is: One war at a time, Mr. Seward. *One war at a time!*"

Here the President broke into a kind of chuckle, and mildly slapped his thigh, and deliberately picked up the bourbon bottle and poured a little more into William Henry's glass, and he apologized, "I sure wish I had some champagne at hand here, because I don't know whether you like this stuff or not."

William Henry didn't like it. None of the stuff. But he saw he was dealing with a man who meant to be President of the country, whether he was yet or not. William Henry wasn't disrespectful; he just wasn't convinced.

The President sensed that he hadn't said all he needed to say to his ornery and too effervescent Secretary.

"Now about you being willing to take on all these affairs yourself with all these countries and your being willing to put the right shoulder to the wheel and see that it all goes all right, I'm appreciative, but you'll allow there may be more than one policy to go ahead on. It does seem to me that if we are going to go into anything so big as setting a match to other countries, I do think it ought to be a Cabinet matter, something for all the boys to talk over. I presume I'm entitled to have lots of advice in the case of a big program like you have cut out. And as to me doing it or somebody else, like say, yourself, I remark, Mr. Seward, that if this must be done, then *I* must do it!"

And as he said that his voice clipped in a momentary imperious way, and he seemed to be staring through the smoke and over the bourbon in a penetrating and final way.

"Certainly, sir," said William Henry, against the ropes. "I understand, Mr. President."

"Good, Mr. Seward—then we may have some further things to talk about in connection with your 'Thoughts' and I may want to give some more attention to these matters and maybe talk them over with the others."

It seemed to call for a very scant reply from William Henry.

"Yessir, I shall be happy to be of service in any way you wish."

He was on his feet, wiser, a little shocked and surprised, and he peered upward at the man who was a foot taller. Lincoln looked somewhat more definite than he had seemed before: and the Secretary of State went to his home on F Street to think and to think and to think.

Chapter Fifty-Two

THE LETTER THAT WASN'T BURNED

IN THE weeks immediately after Fort Sumter was fired upon William Henry continued to feel the force of the President. The President's rejection of those "Thoughts" that suggested there was someone else ready and willing to lead rankled in him. Grudgingly he was being made to realize that he wasn't in first place, and it came over him a little reluctantly and sadly that things had a meanness about them.

By mid-May something was taking place inside of him, primarily a realization of Mr. Lincoln's personal authority, loath though the Cabinet member was to recognize this. At that time he reached the age of sixty, and he felt prompted to write to Frances a letter curiously disconsolate, tinged with a mournfulness that he rarely expressed. It seemed a matter of regret to him, he wrote, that he had lived to reach this age under circumstances so trying and painful. He pitied himself, a rare indulgence: "A country relying so largely on my poor efforts to save it, had refused me the full measure of its confidence, needful to that end. I am a chief reduced to a subordinate position and surrounded with a guard, to see that I do not do too much for my country, lest some advantage may revert indirectly to my own fame...."

He had undertaken to organize a secret service to guard against the Secession fifth column in Government. It was a necessary, a dictatorial step, filled with power and the danger of error. He moved precipitately to make numerous arrests, to regulate passports, to halt the mails, and supervise the flow of telegrams that might aid the Disunionists—and he operated so vigorously that he roused the charge that he was running an inquisition, that he was too severe, he was a tyrant. So, quickly, he was removed from this area, and Secretary of War Stanton took over the thankless job of uncovering and restraining seditionists.

Yet in the course of his removal from these functions, a guard was actually placed about him. Did Lincoln order it? Did others in the Cabinet insist on it? Was this a Presidential rebuke, not too subtle, to the over-ambitious Secretary?

Whatever, William Henry hadn't yet fully learned how determined the Chief Executive was to rule his own Cabinet. Privately the President soothed him, talked with him, placated him, and continued the firm gentling process, toning his subordinate's ambitions. It was growing on William Henry by the hour that he faced a man who meant to be President, and who was President. And so, to Frances he wrote, "It is due to the President to say that his magnanimity is almost superhuman. His confidence and sympathy increase every day. But, but—let all this pass."

But it wouldn't pass, and it didn't pass until it was settled.

Lincoln had his eye closely on William Henry. The President was convinced that the little fellow was a powerhouse all to himself, and needed only to have his wheels set going in the right direction, and then he might become the most useful man in the Cabinet.

William Henry's dispatches to American ministers at embassies throughout the world took the positive tone that the Union was supremely confident, that the American purpose was to restore the Union, that any help to the insurrectionists would be interpreted by the Union Government as an act of hostility, as warlike, and would meet with a proper and true resistance. He advised the ambassadors to uphold the Government's course, to prevent the countries to which they were emissaries from injuring the Union by helping the Confederacy, and they must be prepared for war if they undertook to do so.

Actually it was a philosophy of boldness at a time when the Confederacy was wild with self-confidence and moves toward war.

All through May he was still hell-bent on the idea of foreign war, mostly because he felt it was inevitable. It was natural that Great Britain would side with the Confederacy, would want to see a sundered nation, would want to enter the conflict so as to make sure the country stayed divided: and thus reclaim what it had lost in 1776 and in 1812.

William Henry, as a historian and as a patriot, felt this in his bones: this was the great danger of the present crisis; all would be lost, he felt, unless he got the Cabinet to talk boldly against the Old World and to act boldly against it. He was unrelenting in this policy and he told Frances his fears: "They have misunderstood things fearfully in Europe. Great Britain is in great danger of sympathising so much with the South, for the sake of peace and cotton, as to drive us to make war against her, as the ally of the traitors. If that comes, it will be the strife of the younger branch of the British stock, for freedom, against the older, for slavery. It will be dreadful but the end will be sure and swift."

356

He was worried about the American soil. A battle seemed shaping up not far from Washington, and he didn't want to see fratricidal horror.

In New York, Thurlow Weed labored on two fronts: the war for the preservation of the Union, and the battle for the enrichment of Thurlow Weed.

The dictator had revenged himself on Horace Greeley a few months earlier by engineering the editor's defeat for a position in the Senate. When William Henry became a Lincoln aide, his Senate post was left open, and Greeley wanted it. But Weed, at a desperate caucus in the Governor's room at Albany, thwarted his old colleague, even though, as a result, a routine political hack, Ira Harris, went to the Senate.

"There," said Weed, "I got even with Greeley for what he did to Seward and me at Chicago."

Thereafter Greeley settled down to a steady carping attack on Lincoln and the Administration. Nothing ever quite satisfied him about the prosecution of the war.

Early in June, William Henry wrote to Frances a letter that she never thought he could write about anyone else in the land:

....the war is ostensibly prosecuted with vigor. But you have no idea how incessant my labors are to keep the conduct of it up to the line of necessity and public expectation.

Executive skill and vigor are rare qualities. The President is the best of us; but he needs constant and assiduous co-operation. But I have said too much already. Burn this, and believe that I am doing what man can do.

The letter never was burned, and he probably didn't really want it to be burned.

At about this time William Henry took over a big old roomy house on nearby Lafayette Square. It was a red-brick building, plainly and substantially built, but the interior was roomy, and many prominent Washingtonians and foreign ministers had lived here. It was sometimes called "the Clubhouse," and its principal parlors and living rooms were designated red, blue and green rooms, as at the White House.

William Henry had the place furnished, decorated with flags and flowers; he hired a staff of servants, and made ready to entertain statesmen, officers, Government heads, and their families. Frederick and his wife, Anna, lived with him, and he looked forward to a visit from Frances and his daughter. They and his youngest son, William Henry, Jr., were in Auburn.

There was actually no great departure from the domestic life he had been living for thirty or forty years: Frances was at Auburn most of the time, he rarely saw his daughter but wrote to her every few days, and he was really living intimately with the great mistress of his life, Politics.

Chapter Fifty-Three

THE RADICAL REPUBLICAN AND
THE WHIG

THROUGH the summer, Frances considered going to Washington, but she was fearful of the hot weather there, and inclined to postpone. Life on South Street was generally more congenial to her than the Washington whirl. Lazette was at home with her now, for Alvah Worden had died in 1856, after which the two sisters stayed together in old Judge Miller's house. There Lazette minded her weakened sister. A lifetime of rheumatics had about disabled Frances, and her best effort now was at her writing table, where she spent hours daily keeping in touch with absent family members.

And yet, by September, she was curious to see the Capitol during wartime, and she and Fanny made the trip there. She wanted to see the new house William Henry had moved into, and she was curious to meet the man who, her husband said, "is the best of us."

"After dinner Henry took Fanny to see the President," she wrote to Lazette. "Henry sleeps and eats well— I know he works too hard—yet I think his situation now is more congenial to his taste than his position in the Senate— I will give you the occupation of one day, which, with the addition of Cabinet meetings, will answer for others— He rises at seven, sometimes earlier, goes to the library or piazza, where he reads the morning papers, breakfast at eight—after breakfast a cigar, the papers or visitors until nine, when he and Fred go to the State Department where they remain until five o'clock— When they come home some of the family go for a drive with Henry, and the President goes at the same time, with his carriage— This occupies the time until seven, the hour for dining—always two or three gentlemen to dinner, which is always well-cooked and handsomely served— After dinner the time is occupied with visitors until he is allowed to go to bed— When there are Cabinet meetings other matters yield to them."

One evening, she and the President met at William Henry's fireplace, and they chatted of the rumors of battle on the other side of the Potomac, of the encampments about the city, and of the war and its causes and its progress.

The President detected Frances' independence of views; he was amused that she was much less the moderate than her husband, and more like the Radical Republicans who were giving him so much pressure in the Senate to hasten up the war, to liberate the slaves, to take other impatient and untimely steps.

Yet he was entertained by the respect that the Sewards showed for each other's attitudes. He admired a woman who could have a different set of thoughts than those of a husband as prominently placed as hers.

Frances had heard much of Mary Lincoln's reputation for acerbity of tongue. William Henry suggested to his wife that he wasn't popular with the First Lady, that her mistrust of him was deep-seated; Mrs. Lincoln remained unconvinced of the confident working relationship that was developing between him and the Chief. The Secretary of State suggested that Frances should be her usual gracious self when she met Mrs. Lincoln, and not be turned or provoked by anything that the President's wife might conceivably say.

When they did meet, it was cool, as Frances suspected it would be, and the two women never cultivated each other, and Frances returned to the privacy of her house on Lafayette Square, to the informal entertainments of their own evenings, to occasional talks with the President when he visited their house, and to the obscurity that, she felt, this time and the hour and her position required.

Not long after her first meeting with Mr. Lincoln, Frances wrote to Lazette of the social and political life, how she bypassed a ride in the President's carriage: "There were rumors of an engagement on the other side of the Potomac yesterday, but nothing serious resulted— The day was very warm— At five we all went for a drive—I was not very well, and preferred our own carriage with Fred and Anna— The others went with the President in his— We visited five different encampments but did not get out of the carriage— They were in the direction of Silver Springs— some infantry, some cavalry— What a multitude of horses there were, chiefly bay, and all well in appearance— One or two regiments were drawn up for evening parade, one going through some evolutions, others were cooking their suppers—the odor of coffee was very perceptible in the vicinity of the French camp— Picket guards were stationed all along the road— Do you remember the brick church on the hill? A fortification has been raised in front of it—I presume the church will be occupied as a barrack— The white tents and the camp fires were very pretty to look upon—but war is terrible in its consequences...

"There were guests at dinner but I was too tired to go to the table— I went into the parlor however in the evening to see General Scott who complimented me with a visit—it is the first he has made here since the war commenced— We talked about everything but the war— He said I was very brave to come at this time— It was rather ignorance than bravery, for I doubt whether I should have come had I known how imminent an engagement was— I came to my room, leaving the others in the parlor— I went to bed but slept little— I was up many times looking at the long line of army wagons going, going, going all day and all night toward the Potomac."

The rumble of army wagons went on all that night and the next day. Occasionally she heard a cannon fired from the other side of the river. Cavalry passed in the mid-morning, going across the river at Chain Bridge, and then infantry came on, and she watched the soldiers from her window. The infantry stopped briefly in front of the Clubhouse; they were singing and in good spirits, though they knew that a battle was coming shortly.— "Henry went out to see them— I felt an indescribable oppression in the reflection that many of them might not see the light of another day— Four picket guards were killed night before last— Still we hear of no battle."

That night she heard, for the first time, a strange and stirring song rising from the ranks of infantry still marching past their Washington residence—John Brown's body lies a-mouldering in the grave—and a deep chorus picked up the song— But his soul goes marching on—and the long line kept going, each column chanting the measure, as they kept time to it. The song they sang, it wasn't of Union now—it was of Abolition.

Late in the autumn, and just before Frances was ready to return to Auburn, the family were together in one of the lower rooms of the Clubhouse. Frederick and his wife, Anna, and Fanny listened to their elders disagreeing over war policy.

William Henry defended his moderate Whig's view of the national scene, and Frances pressed a sterner Radical Republican policy.

"My whole policy is based on the preservation of the Union—nothing else," he told Frances.

"Are you not interested in seeing the slaves emancipated?"

"I am, but not if it destroys the nation. Rather than see our country dismembered and overrun by the Europeans, I would see slavery persist awhile and go out later, as eventually and inevitably it must, because it is an extinct form of society anomalously prolonging itself."

"Henry, you know how I hate war; but I do not see how the Southern institution can be crushed without the military conflict that now occurs."

"I am as much committed to this conflict as anyone—but I wage it without hatred of my fellow Americans in the South. I have taken the position of talking boldly to the foreign countries because if they are not repelled by a strong stand on our part, they will be encouraged to intervene."

"But I think it omits the question of abolishing the slave institution."

"Slavery was doomed with the nomination of Lincoln and with his advent to office. I contend that it is only an incident in the national history. A hundred years from now, when there is no more slavery, it will be seen that slavery came and slavery went, but that the great effort was to preserve the Union."

"How serious is the menace of intervention?"

"As serious as it is possible. The monarchies of Europe fear to have our democracy rise. They fear a libertarian and equalitarian society. They would crush it if they would, to perpetuate themselves. The danger is that our conflict can easily spread into a world conflict—and I believe that some day there will be a world conflict, if not out of our own present crisis, then out of another—but the monarchies will and must challenge the rise of the democracies like ours. This is their opportunity—and my policy is directed at preventing that opportunity and making it possible for us to subdue the rebellion at home. Meantime, publicly I must appear to actually favor a foreign war as a panacea."

"This is bringing you into misunderstanding in the Cabinet and in the Senate."

"That is inevitable, but a Secretary of State must take many positions, publicly and privately, for the good of his country, without being able to make full explanations why certain steps and certain attitudes are at times necessary. Bluster has a part in foreign policy, but it must make its appearance in state papers as dignified demand, backed by the weight of right and history and of national strength."

"You are the Secretary, Henry. I only say that I would like to see one outcome of this great war—the abolition of the peculiar institution."

"Frances, if ever there is a proclamation of emancipation, you can be sure my name will be signed to it."

Chapter Fifty-Four

THE UNKNOWN SURRENDER OF
WILLIAM HENRY

D ID William Henry really want war with England or some other nation as a means of forestalling and avoiding war at home and reuniting the two sections?

For six months he succeeded in filling the international air with such possibilities, alternatives, misgivings, doubts—while the two sections girded at home.

Yet when one excellent opportunity to go to war with England presented itself, and even the Northern public seemed to want war with the motherland, William Henry backtracked smartly, and induced the rest of the Cabinet to his position.

The *Trent,* a British packet leaving Havana for England on November 8th, carried four Confederate insurgents. Two of them, James M. Mason and John Slidell, were appointed Confederate Commissioners to Great Britain. As the boat moved along the narrow Bahama Channel, a sloop of the American Navy, the *San Jacinto,* pursued the *Trent,* fired a shot across her bows, and prepared to board the English vessel.

Captain Charles Wilkes of the *San Jacinto* watched through spyglasses as his lieutenants boarded the *Trent,* and captured Slidell and Mason, and their secretaries.

The Confederates were brought back to the United States, and the *Trent* moved on to England.

When Captain Wilkes arrived in New York harbor with his quarry, a jingo spirit spread through the North. Slidell and Mason were notable proponents of the slave system, and Wilkes was heroized for capturing them.

But in England, when the *Trent* returned, and its Commander Williams reported to his Government how his ship had been boarded, the British military spine was touched. Lincoln was branded as a mediocrity and

William Henry was called a firebrand seeking war with all Europe. The British demanded of Washington to know whether Wilkes acted under Government orders: if he did, there'd be war. If not, they wanted an apology and the return of Slidell and Mason.

The incident touched American pride. Back down before the British? The general public couldn't bear the thought, and neither could most members of the Cabinet. Lincoln didn't want war with England, but he too didn't like to eat British crow.

It was William Henry's great opportunity to reveal what his full policy was, whether he really wanted foreign war, or only feared it, and whether he really believed war with England would unite the North and the South. He took two courses of action: he told a correspondent of the London *Times,* "We will wrap the whole world in flames! No power is so remote that she will not feel the fire of our battle and be burned in our conflagration." Apparently he wanted this kind of sentiment carried to the British; he wanted them to feel that the Union was ready for war.

But privately, in the Cabinet, he worked for the return of the pair of commissioners.

For two days the Cabinet debated what to do, and finally William Henry convinced his colleagues that it was a moment to backtrack. He seemed now to be the most ardent proponent of Lincoln's policy of one war at a time.

Even the President was reluctant to kowtow to the British, but when William Henry, at Lincoln's suggestion, drew a lengthy paper expressive of the American position and acknowledging error in capturing Slidell and Mason, and when this was dispatched to England, the crisis was past.

The rumor in the Senate now was that William Henry ran the White House, that he told the President what to do, and that the President did it.

Schuyler Colfax privately sympathized with the Radical Republicans, but as Speaker of the House his job was to moderate the sessions of the House impartially. Lincoln relied on Colfax to represent him well and fairly before the Senators, and so Colfax had ready access to the President. They went driving together occasionally and sometimes Colfax went to the theatre with Mr. and Mrs. Lincoln.

One night when they sat in the lower box at Glover's Theatre, and the play was on, and it chanced to be dull, and the voices on stage were not loud, the two men, in a lower whisper, talked over the war.

At length Colfax ventured the thought that the Radical Republicans were restive over the force that Seward was rumored to exert in White House affairs. This wasn't the first time the matter was presented bluntly to Lincoln; others had hinted and inquired; but the President replied affably, telling Colfax to be sure and tell his colleagues just what he was now about to tell him:

"Tell them they are entirely mistaken in supposing that Seward controls me, as they assume, in my official action. When subjects come before us, he argues them, instinctively and with great power, too, from the standpoint of what is the widest and most popular policy: while with me, my determination is to find out, and then to stand inflexibly, for the right.

"But I could not get along here at all without him and his counsel.

"He knows all about ancient and modern history—the Peloponnesian as well as Revolutionary War; he is familiar with great men in Europe, of whom I know but little; he can tell me all about etiquette, when I never went to dignity school in my life; and he writes all the speeches I make to the foreign ministers, for I wouldn't know what to say to them."

Colfax listened, and he remembered, and he told the senators—yet men went on believing what they wanted to believe.

Chapter Fifty-Five

THE MYTH OF WILLIAM HENRY'S PRIMACY

THURLOW WEED, in England in 1862, trying to help Charles Francis Adams in the object of keeping England away from American soil, pursued his private objects as well as working for the nation's good. He hadn't known what William Henry was going to do about the *Trent* case, he told a friend, but if he had he would have made three thousand pounds in investments. He owned property in Albany worth fifty thousand, real estate in New York, and he meant to get rich off the war as well as see the Union through to restoration.

In New York, that summer, Horace Greeley was rather ill. From time to time he suffered from a kind of brain fever that induced him to write weird letters. He had written one such in 1854 to William Henry. Now he dashed off another, this to Lincoln, begging him to halt the war. "If the Union is irrevocably gone, an armistice ought at once to be proposed. I do not consider myself at present a judge of anything but the public sentiment...." There were Union reverses on the military fields this season, and Greeley was sick and excited, but Lincoln himself opened this note, and when he read queer passages such as "do not fear to sacrifice yourself to your country," he wrapped it up in his special little round file with the red ribbon about it, and he put the growing sheaf of strange personal mail far back into his desk.

In Auburn, Frances and Lazette watched the progress of the war, and the summertime military losses were not heartening to the Secretary's wife. She wrote letters to her two sons, both officers, and each with regiments in the field. Major Augustus Seward was in the Southwest, and William Henry, Jr. led a regiment of Auburn soldiers; and they were training and preparing for battle. Frances was about fifty-seven now, and she was especially maternal toward her teen-age daughter. For young Fanny seemed deeply distressed by the great events in which her family were involved and by the blood that flowed in so many parts of the land. Frances tried to be light and pleasant when her daughter was about, but the child had grown in a time of tragedy and her sweetness was mingled with a deep vein of seriousness.

Frances waited for letters from William Henry—as she had all her life—and she would be willing now for him to leave his post and come to Auburn for a few weeks—and her notes were brief—and she tried to interest herself in small political acts of her own—helping to get pardons for prisoners she conceived to be deserving—and studying the course of the war—always studying the course of the war.

In the hot summer months she stayed in the garden about the big house, and she carried with her a disturbed feeling that while she breathed the soft air of a grape arbor and a peach orchard and flower beds, soldiers were dying—everywhere.

On one evening, during the long critical summer, William Henry and Lincoln sat at the fireplace in the Clubhouse. It had become the President's custom to drop in at his Secretary's almost every evening. There they reminisced about a lifetime of law practice and early-day politics, and the talks usually ended with discussions of the progress of the war. William Henry noticed that Lincoln's eyes seemed to have grown cavernous from worry; his beard had long since become full grown, and its darkness added to the starkness that had come into the President's face.

The Chief mentioned how they'd been losing battles in Virginia, how everywhere men were calling for peace, and how he didn't know what to do about the widespread dissatisfaction with General George McClellan.

"It seems to me, Mr. Seward, that if things go on like this, the Confederacy will capture the capital and the North."

"We need more men in the field, Mr. Lincoln, many more men."

"There is no doubt about it, and I meant to speak of this with you. Can I count on you to go to New York and try to raise a bigger army?"

"Certainly."

"Tell the governors when they confer that we need three hundred thousand men. Tell them of our crisis, will you do that, Mr. Seward?"

A few days later William Henry went to New York City. He told a governors' conference of the President's concern, and he afterward wired the President that the governors said they would comply. Out of these events, out of a fireside suggestion, came the lyric, "We are coming, Father Abraham, three hundred thousand more!"

They waited until Sunday, July 13th, to bury the infant son of Secretary of War Edwin Stanton. Now the funeral cortege, a dozen coaches of Cabinet members, their families, and a few Senatorial friends of Stanton, made its way through the dusty streets to a cemetery on the outskirts of the capital.

A white coach carrying a white casket went first. On its high box seat were two somber, black-dressed undertakers in tall black hats. Behind came Stanton's coach, and he was at the side of his wife, and with them sat other Stantons.

The third coach was the large roomy one of President Lincoln. With Lincoln, on one seat, sat Navy Secretary Gideon Welles, and opposite were William Henry, Frederick, and Frederick's pretty and youthful wife, Anna. She was somberly dressed in dark blue, wearing a white carnation, and she was silent as the men from time to time quietly talked.

William Henry looked out at the slovenly city, wondering when it would ever have the look of a true capital of a great nation, like London or Paris. So far the place was little more than a community where the big machines of Government operated. As he viewed and wondered, Lincoln's gentle words came to him:

"If the rebels do not soon cease their war on the Government and the Union, I believe we shall have to do something essential that I have been thinking about for some time."

"Yes, Mr. Lincoln?" William Henry inquired.

"I am thinking it may be necessary to emancipate the slaves by proclamation."

The cabinet men listened hard.

"I see no evidence that the rebels will cease to persist in their war on the Government. I know that what I speak of is a grave step, but I have given it much thought no matter how delicate the matter, and I have reached the conclusion that this is now a military necessity absolutely essential for the salvation of the Union."

He paused a minute. "This is the first time I have mentioned this to anyone, and I wish you gentlemen to frankly state how you feel about the proposition."

William Henry was momentarily halting in his answer. "Well, Mr. Lincoln, the subject involves consequences so vast and momentous that I should certainly wish to give this my most mature reflection before advancing any decisive answer...."

Lincoln picked up. "It seems to me that we must either free the slaves or ourselves be subdued. I see no other solution...."

"It seems so to me, right at this minute," William Henry concurred.

368

"My present opinion is that the measure is justifiable, and I think expedient and even necessary—yet I do wish we would consider this seriously before we act precipitately."

"Of course, Mr. Seward."

Gideon Welles agreed with William Henry that the matter should be thought about in detail before there was any too-swift action upon it.

The funeral procession rumbled on over the hot stones of the city pavements, and they reached the cemetery.

It was a new departure for President Lincoln. Until this time, whenever anyone mentioned the idea of slave emancipation, he emphatically put them aside. Lincoln and most other men agreed, till now, that slavery was a local matter, a matter for each state to decide for itself.

But now all was changed. The defeat of the Union armies at Richmond had sobered the President, and made his colleagues desperate for recourse. It was a time for extraordinary measures.

Actually he had moved quite rapidly toward this position: he had been in office only sixteen months.

And yet William Henry didn't believe in an Emancipation Proclamation —certainly not now. He felt that Lincoln was responding to the pressure of the Radical Republicans in Congress, some of whom saw the war as a liberation war first, and a war for the preservation of the Union secondly. There were Abolitionist Republicans, and William Henry wasn't one of them.

He told Frances that an Emancipation Proclamation was mere talk and paper and a seal, and that it wasn't real. It wasn't real if there were not a military situation to back it up and to make it real. It was a shriek of vengeance at the Confederacy rather than a true step. Only military successes now would be real and would bring true liberation for the slaves and restoration of the Union.

But the military successes weren't around. Beyond that, the Republicans took a defeat in the local elections of 1862; it was a no-confidence vote to the Lincoln Administration, and peace talk circulated as regularly as any other.

In the Senate, the Republicans decided that they needed to recoup their lost strength nationally. They continued to believe that William Henry made the main decisions, that he was truly the man behind the President; and in any case, this belief could now play into their hands. By getting him out of the Cabinet they could go to the people and say, "We can go ahead now, we have got rid of the man who is holding back the war."

It didn't matter that William Henry told anyone who asked, "There is but one vote in the Cabinet, and that is cast by the President."

The myth of William Henry, as a wartime premier, was now at its height, and only Lincoln could shatter it....

On the evening of Friday, December 19th, the President had a poor appetite for dinner. At table Mary asked him why he wasn't eating, and he said he was actually a bit hungry but he couldn't eat. He wished he could escape his present moment of distraction and eat, but he couldn't; he had a meeting soon with some senators, and it was on his mind.

"If you are going to get disturbed about every meeting you have you'll soon be in no condition for any meeting."

"I know that, Mother."

"You better eat, and let those senators go without, if anyone is not to eat."

But unable to dine any further, he excused himself, and strode back through the White House to his large office on the second floor.

Once there, he felt cool, the coals on the grates burned low; there were large piles of wood on each side of the fireplace, and he built up the blaze. The physical action made him feel better. He turned up the gaslights, and the room lightened a bit. Then he paced toward one of the large tapestry-decked windows; he looked out through the lace curtains beyond into the southern grounds. The sun had just set and there was nothing but the faint dying glow of day over the lawn and over the distant river.

In less than a half-hour, he was thinking, a committee of senators would be here. They had held a secret caucus, with the result that they wanted to get Seward out of the Cabinet, but Lincoln didn't feel as though he ought to let the Senate dictate to him how he dealt with his Cabinet, or who was in it: historically that was the President's prerogative. The insurgents were charging that the Cabinet wasn't unified, and that there was a backstairs power dominating him. A few days earlier there had been a military defeat at Fredericksburg; the senators were upset, so was everybody in the North whose heart was with the Union cause; but Lincoln had the feeling that they were now looking for a scapegoat. As a consequence of these developments, he now had on his desk William Henry's paper of resignation. He didn't want that, and he didn't want the Senate dictation. Moreover, he knew that behind the rebellion was the activity of Secretary of the Treasury Salmon Chase who wanted his own radical Abolitionist policy to determine the course of the war.

The President, having no one to advise him how to proceed in this crisis of Government and war administration, having to maneuver his way between a shaken split Cabinet on one side and a rebelling Senate on the other, decided that he was like a man in a card game, around a table with many players. He must now determine the play himself. So he had invited the Senatorial committee to call this evening.

Now, with all these pressures operating on him, feeling melancholy and uncertain what tonight's meeting would yield up, wondering whether he could keep his ship afloat or even stay on as captain himself, he waited in his office.

A little later, eight senators strode into the President's chamber, solemnly, like pallbearers, together hoping to carry out spiritually the present composition of the Cabinet. They knew by now that William Henry had resigned. They sat on the two black walnut sofas, by the walls, and on the black walnut chairs around the long black walnut table in the center of the room. Their chairman was the conservative Republican, Senator Jacob Collamer, of Vermont: a man of seventy-one, with great prestige in the Senate. The firebrand Charles Sumner, who hated William Henry, limped in on his cane. He used a cane for support ever since he was badly beaten on the Senate floor by Senator Preston Brooks of South Carolina. He was an orator, somewhat like Abolitionist Wendell Phillips; harsh, handsome, with a flourish of hair about the back of his head and down his face. Most of the others had similar but varying hairdo's, characteristic of the individuality of that time and the desire of the statesmen to look wise and unique and distinguished. Senator William Pitt Fessenden of Maine, a trenchant critic of the White House, who wanted to be in the Cabinet himself, sat at the table, severe and straggly-haired. There was also Senator Harris, the man who took William Henry's place in the Senate, a conservative who was more of a politician than a statesman. But the others, Senators Trumbull Grimes, Howard and Pomeroy, were of the group that came to be known, for their hardness, as Jacobins, men bent on an eye-for-an-eye and a tooth-for-a-tooth approach to the Lincoln Administration and toward the Confederacy.

"Gentlemen," said Lincoln, "I have summoned the Cabinet to meet with you so that we can go into this fully."

It was Lincoln's trump. They hadn't expected to meet with the men they were so critical of, and hoped to force out. Lincoln signaled to his secretary, Nicolay, to call the Cabinet. The members walked in, like another set of pallbearers, ready and willing to carry out the senators.

All but William Henry. He wasn't there, and he wasn't invited.

He wasn't there, but as the evening wore, it appeared that he was the one who was primarily there. As the exchange of views developed, all visualized at the side of the tall President the little aging man, with the big birdlike head, the wagging tongue and the cigar, the alternating amiable manner and the cutting voice, the imperious know-it-all gesturings, and the age of experience in back of him. William Henry was there all right, but as a ghost haunting the Cabinet and the Senate and the war effort itself, as the President "played cards" all evening with the senators and Cabinet members.

The President, addressing himself primarily to the Cabinet, at first read the resolution of the Senate caucus, and calmly stated that he believed that his Cabinet was unified; that though not all of his advisers agreed on all matters, still when a line of approach was once adopted, all acquiesced.

Senator Collamer presented the general view of the committee. It was one of those implications of Seward's premiership, but he didn't mention his name, and as he spoke, everybody could just about see the little white-haired, beak-nosed devil on Lincoln's sloping shoulder.

"Our committee represents an opinion that desires united counsels, combined wisdom and more energetic action," the committee chairman said. "It seems to us that if there is wisdom in the old maxim that there is safety in numbers, it would be better if the advisers near Mister President and chosen by you, and all of whom are more or less responsible, should be consulted on the great questions of the national welfare. The ear of the Executive should be open to all and you should have the minds of all."

The implication was sharp that he was listening to only one man: the little one of the invisible presence.

Senator Fessenden took strength from the approach of the committee chairman; he almost mentioned the Secretary of State's name, but not quite. "I feel that the whole Cabinet should consider and decide great questions," he hinted, "and no one in particular should absorb and direct the whole Executive action."

Suddenly the presentiment of William Henry leaped to the center of the black walnut table and dervished; for three senators dumped William Henry's name plump into the room. Sumner and Grimes and Trumbull were warm as they denounced him.

"I doubt his zeal for the conflict," Trumbull said.

"I doubt his sincerity," said Grimes.

"I don't think he is interested in the freedom of the slaves," said Sumner.

Cabinet man Blair, the Postmaster General, decided to change the tack. The issue here, he said, was that the Senate wanted to run the war jointly with the President and the Cabinet, to force a plural leadership on the nation, and take away from the centralization necessary in such a crisis. The senators were acting illegally!

Cabinet member Bates leaped to the defense of Blair. These senators had come in with a British-type proposal, he said, for tossing out the Executive or limiting its influence, or giving the Cabinet a vote of no confidence.

Lincoln had the thing going the way he wanted now; the Cabinet members fighting for their own lives against the men who would displace them; and he felt strengthened. But at the same time he was deferential to the senators and wanted no personal animus with them; they should be put down quietly if that was possible.

He thought it was time for each senator to state what he believed. Should Seward be dismissed? And would that exclusion make the Administration and the Union cause stronger? Here the senators divided, some saying yes, drop him; others not wanting to commit themselves. It was another breach that the President welcomed.

Lincoln addressed himself to his Cabinet members, one by one. Was there or was there not unity in the Cabinet? "I particularly would like to hear the view of Mr. Chase."

Chase was angry; he saw why the President had brought the Cabinet and Senate committee together.

"I would not have come here tonight if I had known I was to be arraigned!"

"You are not being arraigned," Senator Fessenden interrupted. "You are merely taking part in an informal session of inquiry like the rest of us. We of the Senate didn't ask for this joint session of Cabinet and Senate committee. This is no movement of ours, nor did we suspect or come here for that purpose."

Chase backtracked. "Well, matters of first importance usually come before the Cabinet," he said, "though perhaps not so fully as might be desired. Yes," he went on, to questioning, "there has been no want of unity in the Cabinet, but a general acquiescence in public measures."

The senators were embarrassed. The man who had incited them to revolt, to caucus and to draw a resolution and to go see the President, couldn't or wouldn't sustain their position.

The gremlin of William Henry danced all over the floor and leaped into the gaslight. The senators wanted to leave; they were restive, they moved about sheepishly, angry with Chase. The Secretary of the Treasury himself wanted to get out of the room. "I think members of the Cabinet should withdraw from this discussion," he said.

The Cabinet men filed out.

For a while the President was alone with the senators, and now he felt more composed, as if he had somehow partially stymied them. Each shook hands with the President respectfully, but the last to leave was Senator Trumbull, and he raised his voice: "The last time the Secretary of the

Treasury talked with me he sounded a great deal differently about these matters than he did here tonight."

So the senators parted from the Chief, but with the feeling that they had been made fools of, and their anger was with the Secretary of the Treasury.

Bright and early the next morning several Cabinet members converged on the President at his offices. He wasn't away from his breakfast table yet, so the callers, Chase, Stanton and Welles, were surprised each to see the other there so early in the day.

They gathered close to the fire, as the morning was cold; they were silent, they waited.

Lincoln entered. He too wondered at the full office so early in the day, but he took his cue from the others and hurried to the fireside to warm his hands.

Chase at once started burbling that the previous evening had been miserable for him; he was needlessly pained about it all, and it was a shock to his sensibilities. "In fact," he said, "I've prepared my resignation."

Lincoln looked pleased. "Where is it?"

"I have it here," Chase answered. He removed a paper from an interior pocket.

Lincoln reached eagerly. "Let's have it."

The President read the brief resignation; then, unable to keep his pleasure to himself—for he believed he saw in it the key to his current problems—he turned to faithful Gideon Welles. "That does it," he said. "This cuts the Gordian knot. I see my way clear!"

The Cabinet men couldn't understand his elation. In fact, Stanton was so upset by the eagerness with which the Chief accepted Chase's resignation that he promptly offered his own.

Lincoln's normally somber face was alight. He waved Stanton away. "Go back to your department, I don't want yours. This is the one I want—" and he looked at Chase with a triumphant gaiety. The Secretary of the Treasury was more despondent than ever that the President should be so happy about his resignation.

The Chief Executive turned to Welles, then back to Chase, and he told them that his trouble was ended, the case was clear, they could go back to their departments.

The Cabinet men gathered about the President at his desk. Why was he so elated? They couldn't understand it. Lincoln even reverted to some Springfield farm idiom. "I got a pumpkin at each end of the pole. Now I can ride."

Perplexed, his counselors left. How did Lincoln figure that Chase's resignation solved anything?

But a little later in the morning William Henry received a note from the President and Chase got the same message. The President said he wouldn't accept the resignation of either man. The services of both were needed by him, by the Government and by the people, for the further prosecution of the war.

By declining both resignations, the one from the moderate Seward, and the other from the radical Chase, Lincoln restored his Cabinet to its status before the Senate revolt. Chase, who really wanted to serve in the Cabinet, was quieted; William Henry was reassured.

The two men were back in his grip, each a little tamer, quieter, each knowing *he* was the President. He had singlehandedly licked the Senate insurgents and quieted his rumbling advisers. Now Lincoln could have his own type of Cabinet again, a coalition affair, with a radical wing and a conservative wing, and his control over his subordinates was reaffirmed.

William Henry was never more chastened. He had seen the Republicans of the Senate turn against him; his prestige was low everywhere, in Government and in the community; and he was again in the Cabinet by the grace of the tall man from the prairies. He was far from being a Prime Minister or a Premier, but he had the opportunity now to be a loyal supporter, and a closer friend.

Deep down nothing would ever shake his imperial belief in himself and in his abilities, but from now on it stayed in the dark, like a secret he cherished to himself, and noted in letters only to Frances.

And so one of the sharpest of the many internal dramas of government life during the war entered into another level of development. William Henry had passed from a subjective, dubious premiership that he managed at first to make halfway real, to a stage where he was now a devoted supporter.

William Henry discovered that his Chief was a supreme politician. For it was the great achievement of Lincoln's political diplomacy that he had formed a compound Cabinet made up of the warring personalities of his principal Presidential competitors and of others. Perhaps he was tactician enough to know that hostile personalities could be depended upon not to easily unite against him. Maybe he was clever enough to feel that a united Cabinet that perceived the situation all one way or the other, all compromise or all Radical Republican, would be a group hard to handle and might dominate him.

He had, after all, a better grounding in practical politics than even the experienced William Henry. The Auburn man left to Thurlow Weed most of the sordid details of coping with human nature on the political make. Lincoln, in Illinois, had to handle all such human intricacies by himself, and he came prepared to the Presidency with this facility; therefore, he could afford to use William Henry to the full, and receive from him whatever he had to offer, and generously pay tribute to him for what he secured. It was around this time, when William Henry made these discoveries, that he said of the Chief, "He has a cunning that amounts to genius." This was high praise from William Henry, who had some of that himself: so that when it all settled down and the solvents were in operation, there was this hard-knit reliance and exchange of confidence, the leadership of one and the support and counsel of the other, the attraction of two giants, the warmth of complementation: and the relationship now moved into one of fast friendship.

Chapter Fifty-Six

THE BATTLEFIELDS AS SEEN
FROM AUBURN

FRANCES, spending most of the wartime period at her house on South Street, was glad to be in Auburn, and not at the capital. Women who graced the White House had, none of them, been very happy, she mused. President Taylor's wife had never wanted him to be President, and Mrs. Taylor had said that his nomination was a plot to deprive her of his society and to shorten his life by unnecessary care and responsibility. It had been the same with Abigail Fillmore, wife of President Fillmore: Abigail had spent much of her time alone in a special room on the second floor of the White House. Frances doubted whether First Ladyship boded any good for Mrs. Lincoln: that woman seemed troubled in her exalted environment, out of her depth, not altogether happy in her tense job of caring for a man who had such great duties. Political life, Frances mused, robbed women of their husbands. When a man went to Washington and got caught up in a Cabinet round, it represented a kind of divorce from pure and real domestic life. Being in Washington as First Lady of the Cabinet was nonsense and unrewarding, she felt: let young Kate Chase have such dubious honors. For her the repose of South Street and the ever-continuing job of watching out for her children.

Besides, war or no war, she fretted, Henry was probably surrounded by women—younger ones, too—when he sought a letdown from political pressure. The Clubhouse was a gathering place for all Washingtonians, and people who came there to dine or to be entertained brought people. William Henry could never be lonely. It was unfortunate, she felt, that because of his littleness, he had a constant need to demonstrate his masculinity....

She recalled an hour in Washington early in 1852, when she and Lady Kossuth, the wife of Louis Kossuth, the Hungarian patriot, were together at their home. Kossuth was there to get aid for Hungary, then struggling against Louis Napoleon's invasion of his country, and William Henry was about the best friend that Kossuth found when he arrived. Kossuth traveled about, trying to enlist support for his people, as the representative at that moment of the best republican traditions in Europe, but he didn't make much headway. Frances watched William Henry and Kossuth, standing among a group of prominent Washingtonians, and she told Lazette at the time: "I wish you could have seen them, as I did, standing together, two slight forms among a crowd of large and strong men, talking of their hopes for the ultimate triumph of liberty—" The picture came back to her now: she saw the two again, both short, shorter than all those about, but philosophically bigger than the others. Yet it was the slightness of William Henry that gave him, in large part, the psychology that drove him and goaded him, and at last made him extend his energies so as he must impress women, as well as men—the handsomer the better.

Now, war crisis or not, he was entertaining his old friend Charlotte Cushman, perhaps the most celebrated Shakespearean actress of their day. He'd known her a long time, Frances reflected, too long, perhaps twenty or more years; they saw each other from time to time, and they corresponded. What might there be between her husband and the famous actress? She could hardly recall how far back William Henry seemed enamored of her as an actress, as a woman of culture, and just when and where their friendship had begun. He had always gone out of his way to attend any show she appeared in, and he'd write home that he saw her perform and she was wonderful; then gradually he seemed to make her acquaintance. It has always been easy for a rapprochement between notable entertainers and notable politicals, and by the 1850s they appeared to bump into one another at various places, and Charlotte seemed frequently to be in Washington. At the outset of the war Miss Cushman was in Rome and she wrote to him to ask about the progress of the war, but it was a note in which she iterated her faith in his words, his friendship, his politics—and faith, fidelity, these were the keys to William Henry, and Frances knew that whoever understood that faith was his central idea knew the heart of him.

And now, just now, Frances received a letter from him in which he said, "Miss Cushman and her niece are yet with us and I hope are enjoying their visit," as if he didn't see his friend at all, as if they just used the Clubhouse as a hotel. Frances had her doubts. Not that Miss Cushman wasn't civic-minded and a patriot, as much as anyone else. She had emerged from retirement to perform again to raise money for the Sanitary Commission—to help wounded soldiers: and whenever she was in Washington she was William Henry's guest. Well, all that she could do about this was to be cheerful about it, hope it was as platonic as it seemed, and write it off to the exigencies of having a famous husband with a roving eye. It had always been thus, she recalled. Hadn't he got up the back stairs of the White House in the Taylor Administration through entrancing the women in the Taylor household? And daily, everywhere, he was dined by politicians and their wives, and at one time or another he mentioned the name and something of his talk with every belle in Washington, every senator's daughter or niece or friend. She recalled the first one, Mrs. Albert Tracy, of Buffalo, a long time ago, the anti-Mason's wife: "I have been to Tracy's and I have seen a beauty," he wrote excitedly at the time, and Mrs. Tracy was a stunner, too. Ever since then he always had one Mrs. Tracy or another in his life.

She hoped these were perfectly proper relationships, but she wasn't sure and she had her doubts. In fact, one of the reasons for her constant invalidism was the gnawing feeling that Henry, no matter how strong his bond with her, simply roved while he was away. He wrote home of his female company very openly, disarmingly, and she learned to make little or no comment on this phase of his fortunes.

Forget it, she told herself, forget it. He's a little man but he's a big one too; there's a war on, and the battle of the sexes antedated the one on American soil right now, and it would outlast this one. Henry was a soldier in both wars.

Whatever, the measured tread of her own distressed life was in empathy now with the national crisis. An accord mounted in her with the tragic crisis all about, and perhaps, in a vicarious way, she and the world were more attuned; now conflict was everywhere, not alone in her womanly soul.

The marriage with William Henry—mainly by letter now—went on as it had so often before, in the quickly dashed notes she wrote to him, and through the replies he sent to her of what he was doing and thinking: "My dearest Henry— A man came today to cut down the poplars— I could not see him then but will soon— I do not wish to be here when they are cut down as I feel every stroke of the axe—what shall be done with the wood?— Mr. Day thinks the man takes it for pay— Your Own Frances."

And he would answer with some of the details of State, those that could go by mail without endangering anything: because impressing her that he was a statesman was an important part of the acknowledgment he expected. And he was proving it now, helping to hold Europe at bay while the President led the war. He knew, and she knew, that it was a great role for a man, dealing with the nations of the world during such a crisis, handling one by one troubles with Mexico, France, England, many other countries, posting the American ministers all over the globe, sharing military problems with the Chief.

Better to stay away from him, she reflected, keep the house ready for him when he would return. *June 6, 1863:* A petition has to be sent to the President from New York for the insane convict Muhl—a German—of whom I have written— The doctor hopes a pardon may be obtained and sent before Muhl is recommitted to the prison—as he is sure such a step will induce a return of insanity—the doctor also asks as an especial favor that the pardon may be transmitted through my hands—as he wishes to make some provision for the safety and comfort of Muhl before he is sent away— You will probably see the reasons for this— I wish the poor convict were to have another as humane physician as Doctor Hace has proved to be—

So the old concern for the ill in mind went on in the Miller-Seward family.

In Washington, William Henry, receiving her letters of June and July, 1863, took some satisfaction that Frances was spared the great tension that now played over the White House, for all sensed that tremendous military things were happening along the Rappahannock. He smiled as he read her brief note of *June 12th:*— Tell Fred that the distance from the house to the old asparagus bed is sixty feet.

But she had other concerns too, during the next few days. William Henry Jr. had been wounded and was out of the battle. *June 17th:* I wish I could gain from some other source the confidence with which you inspire me when I am with you— I need it in this disastrous time— The business of the Confederate army is bewildering by its rapidity—the loyalty of the people is now put to the test— God grant that it may not fail— Our boy will reach Washington this morning—but I cannot write to him— Pray write us of him as you can.

Frances studied the newspapers and waited for reports of battle in Pennsylvania, where Union and Confederate troops were massing, marching, countermarching in an indecisive way. Mostly she waited for word from William Henry, for sometimes he gave her private information she couldn't get in the press. In general she took confidence in his picture of how the war proceeded.

In these weeks there shaped up the great Pennsylvania battle: Gettysburg, Harper's Ferry, all those beautiful little places that she and William Henry and Fred visited way back in 1835 when they made a smooth, soft summertime trip down through the East and the South. Now, as rumors came of the gathering of troops in this region, she saw again the minutes and the days they had spent from May through September of that long-ago year. She relived the journey, seeing it in a strange way, however: the early idyllic land, they in a carriage going over it; but her revery had an overlay of a military character: for the same towns they had seen so long ago, the very route they took, with all of its bucolic character, now ran with American blood: "We are watching and waiting with utmost anxiety the result at Gettysburg—today we get no paper—as it is the fifth of July—we had none yesterday in this town— But Mr. Perry kindly sent me an extra containing Meade's report of Thursday— It is a fearful struggle which seems to me the turning point of the war—it is astonishing to see how indifferent and how ignorant the majority of the people appear—few seem to know that the life of the government is in danger—having no doubt that they and theirs are perfectly secure they act as they did in the time of Noah—apprehending no deluge that will overwhelm them—how painful it is to read the lists of killed and wounded, although I am informed of Mohammed that those killed in battle have an immediate reward in a future state—those who are fighting for their country and human rights— Henry, do you remember 1835 when you and Fred and I went over the very soil on which our men are now shedding their blood?— I have been thinking much on this— Perhaps it were better if I thought of other things, but I cannot disengage my thoughts—for I cannot believe that this is happening to all of us— Your Own Frances."

The farewells on South Street had been happy, as they ought on that May morning twenty-eight years earlier, with the warm sun opening up the village's lilac buds, and they were off in a full gallop, out of the driveway, fast along Genesee Street, and out on the dirt road headed for Aurelius. The wagon was light, but strong, a barouche; it had two seats and an extension top; in the front sat their colored driver, William Johnson, quite as well dressed as anyone they would meet along the way. Beside him sat small Fred, his hair all curly, though he hated curls and wanted his hair cut short; the curls flowed about his lace collar, there were bright brass buttons down the front of his white shirt, and his knee pants were of velvet: altogether a well-taken-care-of little boy.

The driver snapped the whip lightly over the two horses, Lion and the Doctor. He called out, lapping the reins, "Come on, Doc, *gee-ap,* Lion," while Fred mimicked him, and tried clucking his tongue and lips as Mr. Johnson did.

From then on the trip unfolded, she recalled, like an idyll set to music ...the incessant chatter about whatever they passed, the quaint bridges over the streams they crossed; in the greening fields the placid sheep, heads down, eating, soon ready for fleecing; the cows, statuesque, their jaws going, an occasional moo, and William Henry trying to imitate the moo sound, to the infinite amusement of Frances, with young Fred thereafter doing a better imitation.

For two days and nights they had wagoned southward, and on the third morning, at a little farmhouse in northern Pennsylvania, there was some letter writing while William Johnson prepared the horses. Then a breakfast of ham and eggs, and on down the west bank of the Susquehanna with, once more, the road hanging like a shelf over the river edge, and the party a hundred feet high over the water, and to the other side a cliff to a mountain's height: everywhere dense pine and laurel underbrush, and the pure smell of the open.

So, she recollected, the days stretched into a week of days till they came to Lycoming County, where there were wild-running creeks with rocky and rugged banks, and narrow straits and slim valleys, and steep mountains and gulches; and rocky passes gave up an ever-changing variety. They must be fighting in these regions now, she was thinking.

There was the night they stayed in the noisy hotel, with the reveling drunks downstairs, and they had to change rooms; and then, on deeper into the Pennsylvania hills, where, in the narrow passes, they heard wolves chasing deer, and they watched for rattlesnakes. From here, small villages, the whitewashed rose-covered fences, the homes neat and livable, June shrubs coloring the dwellings: Lewisburg, Cumberland, Liverpool, Littleton, and everywhere the MacAdam roads, taverns and short canals on the way into Harrisburg. *The III Corps was at Littleton, and officer Reynolds, about to die at Cemetery Ridge, scrawled off a note to the Corps Commander at Littleton, "Hurry on, in God's name, we must fight here."*

Frances recollected how at Harrisburg, William Henry said, "There is a stop I want to make here, Frances, someone I must see." *In this city soldiers drilled in the streets now with scythes and fowling pieces, for lack of muskets.*

"You hadn't mentioned it."

"No, but there's the matter of General Harrison for President—I want to see how our friends here feel about it."

"You promised me no politics on this trip—!"

"Just this one infidelity, Frances."

And, she recalled, they did stop for a few hours to speak with local Whigs. A few days later they reached southern Pennsylvania; and the look of the region was changing, a southern aspect tinging the northern towns. Negroes were in the streets at Carlisle, a village already famous as a stop on the Underground Railroad. *Longstreet was now going through Carlisle on his way to Gettysburg.*

The climate warmed. Everywhere in the fields there was a softer, fresher look of summer; peas growing, strawberry patches showing, cherry trees looking black in the trunk and heavily leafed, with light red cherries peering like bright eyes. The three sightseers turned down the Walnut Bottom Road, past vineyards, into pretty Chambersburg, a border town near Maryland. *Three Union spies in the streets of Chambersburg counted 90,000 of Lee's men here.* Everywhere, at the side of log cabins, there was a yard full of chickens, and chicken was served in each tavern at every meal, even chicken for breakfast; then through wheat country, fields of yellow: Boonesborough, Hagerstown, young Fred reveling in each village, pointing excitedly at the sights, the squares, the market places, the courtyards, all looking more southern, the mood slower. *They were holding Lee fast in the line that ran through Hagerstown.* In some places wastrels lounged at the corners: hot sun, very hot, was directly overhead, so that they had to put up the suntop on the coach and keep it over them all of the time; the draggy village of Shepherdstown, on the Potomac.

They crossed the river on a scow, Negroes propelling the craft by poles. On the other side they knew they had entered Virginia because they passed the first plantations with their sure signs: log huts for the slaves, large wheat and rye fields, travelers on horseback, and white men dressed a little more pretentiously than the colored. Deeper into Virginia, over wasteland, into a ravine with limestone rocks where the going was slow, and here the travel was no pleasure. Down into a valley, and it was the town of the federal arsenal waiting quietly for its historic moment later on. *Here, Milroy's depleted command, harassed by Lee down to 2,000 men, came to a tired halt.* They moved on in the great Appalachian Valley, through Charlestown and ancient Winchester, so that they felt they were within some huge natural theatre, going down the aisles and across the stage into new aisles and moving upon new stages. *The head of Lee's force was at Winchester now, and well below, in Washington, Lincoln and William Henry were trying to fathom how to snap off the head.*

So the scenes returned to Frances of an earlier day in the vales now red with fratricide. In the Blue Ridge Mountains they saw Wyer's Cave. It was cool in the interior, and they wandered in the subterranean chambers beneath the limestone roof, seeing the stalactites, and the grandest scene of all called Washington's Chamber, a colossal stone that rose in a way reminiscent of the founder. And once, they saw ten children being whipped down the road by a white man. The slaves, none more than nine or ten, were naked, they were fastened to a long rope, two by two, by their wrists; behind them came the master with the long lash hurrying the boys and girls along. He drove his herd of children to a horse trough where they drank; then to a nearby shed, where they lay on the ground and sobbed and moaned themselves to sleep. *They may yet be free*, she said to herself. *Henry's name is along with Mr. Lincoln's on the Emancipation Proclama-*

tion. Henry says that the paper is meaningless, save that there are military securities of it. Now perhaps they occur at Gettysburg.

It was early in July when they arrived at the capital, and here they set eyes on the unfinished city. The wide avenues, named for each state in the Union, were unoccupied and unpopulated. Great land spaces were everywhere; and dry summer dust and intense heat; but the capital buildings were a joy to Frances. There were days of seeing the buildings, the great mecca trip of all Americans, taken early by the Sewards, when the nation was young and the capital just a stripling lad with General Jackson in the White House. *Now Lincoln and William Henry waited in Washington for the word from Gettysburg. Together they peered at pinpoints on a large map spread out on the President's desk. The reports were that Lee was whipped and moving southward.*

Frances wrote her letters, watched the papers, waited for news from Washington, and tried not to think of the time when she and her husband and young Fred had made a true Currier-and-Ives journey over eastern America. For, over all this terrain where there was fighting now, little was left that was idyllic, and nostalgia was not an easy flower to pluck from these states, though Frances had tried. *July 15th, 1863*— I have been so sickened by details of the outrages committed in New York that I have had no heart to write or to do anything else— I have always apprehended the resistance to the draft—knowing how much hard feelings there was here—and hearing that it was so in New York—when I read General Seymour's speech it seemed to be an incitement to the people to resist their government— Our State is disgraced before the civilized world—if there is any civilization in the world, which I sometimes doubt— I heard Rit Morgan censuring the government for stopping the draft— I am glad if it has stopped temporarily until a sufficient militia force can be obtained to enforce it, for I surely believe that our town would follow the example of New York—we get no telegraph communication from New York—for weeks we hear nothing directly from Washington although we hear in a circuitous way that Lee has reached the Potomac.

William Henry was upset by his old friends, the Irish, in New York. He felt that the immigrant group which he had befriended, through his sponsorship of parochial school legislation, had let him down, and he told this to Frances once or twice. In the big city, the Irish, who felt they had no great stake in the war and hadn't come here to get involved in such a thing, had rioted—and hysteria spread everywhere, even to Auburn. *July 18th*— We had a disturbed and fearful week— While the scenes of

384

violence and blood have been passing at New York— William Beardsley says that your "Higher Law" influence is the occasion of the New York riot—but I will not repeat all the malicious stories I hear—it is enough to know that some of our neighbors would be willing to see the Irish execute their threats of destroying our place....

Chapter Fifty-Seven

YANKEE RICHELIEU

SO THE picture of William Henry in his wartime prime matured. They saw him as the short, aging, lean incarnation of a kind of devil-adviser, still reputed by many to be the power behind the throne, disrespected by some of his Cabinet colleagues for the airs of supremacy and agility which he wore, and like all Secretaries of State, more or less mistrusted, hated, despised by the general public. For America does not love its Secretaries of State, no matter how great the burden they carry, no matter how inventive they are with the impossibly complicated tasks of juggling the world on their shoulders.

Every instant of his life was a contention and a gamble, a gamble for the highest stakes in the land, and a fight to retain position or gain new ground. Those who disliked him said he was without principle, he was erratic, a master of intrigue, impertinent, fond of show and parade, sinuous, pliable, flexible, a Mephistopheles, complex, intricate, brilliant and cynical, a man without convictions, an opportunist, optimistic, debonair, a temporizer, a compromiser.

But those who swore by him and followed him said he was great, a man like Cicero or Pericles or Richelieu, erudite, philosophic, and a principled and a consistent Whig (a moderate), eloquent, farsighted, prophetic, a Gladstone, also amiable, smiling, friendly, generous, affable.

Still others who tried hard to penetrate him conceived him as a man born for the State, ambitious, desirous of leading and to be loved and honored by the people, and in return for which he would give great services and, if need be, his life; they beheld him as a dedicated public man, his outer mind and his inner mind given over to the idea of public service, the Government, the people, human society—and that he would do whatever and be whatever would serve to make him such a representative and symbol.

The secret of William Henry's growth was his grounding in American history. He had studied history as a lawyer studies law books. He knew the incidents and the precedents of our national history, he knew the political processes, the alternatives in the variety of situations; he knew where each Founding Father had stood on each question. He worked from the Constitution as a physician works from the blood, the organs, the anatomy. He knew the measures that had been debated and who debated them, and the outcome of the debates. He knew how Jefferson stood on every matter, and what Washington had said, and what happened to John Quincy Adams when he took such and such a view of such and such a matter. When a point of diplomacy arose, and he thought of it, his mind went searching for the prior experience of his nation in or near the issue at hand, and on the basis of what had once happened or nearly happened he now composed his mind. He had pored over the State papers and the national papers, the treaties, the domestic and the international law, the doctrines and the creeds and the dogmas, and, bearing in mind his own fundamental principles, which were similar to John Quincy Adams'—the ideas of Union, and Power, and Liberty—he made his moves.

That was why Lincoln liked and needed him. Lincoln needed a historian at his side, and he had one.

Frances knew that resolve was his central characteristic. Resolution. Inwardly, something ticking like a clock that must not run down made him resolve and renew resolve from minute to minute and by the hour and the day. A defeat was merely an opportunity to make new resolutions and push on; and a victory was a reinforcement of the truth of the validity of resolution, and it all became a mechanism within him pushing him out front, as a man taking breast strokes in the water constantly finds his head before his shoulders. That faculty and facility, of feeling resolution and making resolve his engine and his mechanism and his power, was in whatever he said, in his private words and in his letters, and in his manner of living, and his way of doing things. He was not so much "irresistible Seward," as some came to call him, but resolute Seward, resolved on an aim and a purpose in this brief walk-on that men called living, and he resolved to live and serve and be someone and be something—if not President, then something less, but whatever, to be it with resolution.

He moved about in a courtly way that might well move some to describe him as delicate to the point of effeminacy. In fact, Thurlow Weed did describe his friend's sensitivity as having a purity and delicacy of habit and character almost feminine, yet with these qualities enshelled in a casing of steel resolve. Beneath the offhand manner of cultural grace and amiable brilliance there was the hardboiled statesman used to political back rooms: he smoked, he drank, he swore, and he may have had an occasional extramarital female. Once in a letter to his daughter he spoke of her gentleness and her abilities and her fine mind, and he got off the cynical remark, "You already are wise beyond your years, and good beyond your sex." Apparently he had or could have his way with many of the opposite sex, and he didn't overly respect the way they were willing to dole out their virtue to a man of his eminence.

He probably had no more egocentricity than most of his other colleagues of the Cabinet and senatorial rank, but he concealed his vanity less than the others: he saw no evil in tooting his own horn, in feeling his own importance, and solemnizing over it. Others, just as ambitious, gave off a quieter air and more seeming restraint, but the bubbles of eminence rose in them as sharply as in William Henry.

He was often seen in the State Department wearing a dark-colored frock coat and light-colored trousers. He was still erect, despite the enormous number of hours he was bent over a desk writing, and he loved the fresh air and the out-of-doors, and whenever he could, he was in the garden inhaling heavily of the flower fragrances, and he enjoyed his coach rides about the city.

The dinner group each evening at his house was a perseverant feature of his Washington days. And the whist games, the exchange of views with some famous New Yorker, or a foreign diplomat like Baron de Stoeckl.

They were saying that he absorbed a steady flow of spirits, for a little fellow, and everyone in Washington regarded it as a rare chance to be invited to his house and to hear him scintillate about everything in the world. In him conversation found its true artist, and a thousand brilliant performances of the sort went out on unrecorded sound waves. At these dinners he absorbed champagne in particular, and if he bet anyone anything he'd bet "a basket of champagne." He'd stop to tell someone, anyone, a good yarn, and to pass it on to Abe Lincoln, who absorbed stories the way William Henry chewed up cigars.

For a time Thurlow Weed didn't believe Lincoln could get re-elected. The Radical Republicans fired as steadily at the Chieftain as the Unionists shot at the Confederacy. Always there was the dark hint of getting rid of the big lanky bumbling bumpkin in the White House; and Greeley, for one, always looked for somebody else to be President other than the man who was.

Lincoln felt morose about it all, and he often said that perhaps he ought to step down. He had always been aware of his anomalous entry to the Presidency when William Henry had such a clear right, and the big sentimental fellow was troubled by this.

One evening when they talked by William Henry's fireside, Lincoln said, "Mr. Seward, I think I'd like to see you as my successor in the next Administration. Then all those friends in our ranks who were so disappointed at Chicago in 1860 will find all made right at last."

"No," said William Henry, "that is all past and ended. The logic of events requires you to be your own successor. You were elected in 1860, but the Southern states refused to submit. They thought the decision made at the polls could be reversed in the field. They are still in arms, and their hope now is that you and your party will be voted down at the next election. When that election is held and they find the people reaffirming their decision to have you President, I think the rebellion will collapse."

As the battles of 1864 went on, as Grant and Sherman opened their broad campaigns, as Lincoln left military matters more and more in Grant's hands, as June passed, carrying with it the record of Cold Harbor, and in August, the action at Mobile; and in September, as Sherman reached Atlanta and Sheridan moved in the Shenandoah Valley, perhaps to many there was the handwriting on the wall, and it was all a matter of time.

In November Lincoln was re-elected. William Henry was in Auburn for a few days, during the campaigning, and he told his townsfolk that the war had created of Lincoln a figure beyond the pale of human ambition: "Henceforth all men will come to see him as you and I have seen him— a true, loyal, patient, and benevolent man. Having no longer any motive to malign or injure him, detraction will cease, and Abraham Lincoln will take his place with Washington and Franklin, Jefferson, Adams and Jackson, among the benefactors of the country and of the human race."

William Henry had traveled a long way in four years, from his first view of the tall man as an untalented incompetent, to his present view of him.

Time and circumstance had recomposed William Henry into one of those challenging and ever-recurring human types in the world of politics and human affairs who are remarkable in spite or because of the fact that they symbolize contradiction.

Of course he compromised; but he knew that compromise was a relationship of history and living, with as much natural right as the other planes of politics, radicalism, reaction, conservatism, liberalism. For he remained a Whig, a liberal-conservative, and he never fully became a Republican as others about him were Republicans.

Even the Constitution, he knew, was a compromise of liberal and conservative equations, for the honorable Bill of Rights brought up the liberal or people's side of national affairs, and the property amendments assured possessing classes of the protection of their rights: but it was compromise, and it was of the essence of the American form of living.

Compromise had forestalled civil war since 1820, and preserved it till recently; the late Henry Clay was a two-generation symbol of this because he had proposed that relatively operable course. Most of the world of law and the operation of the wheels of the administration of justice, in Government, was a compromise. Relations between men and women universally were based on compromise, and agreement after disagreement. Why then was it so awful, so foreign to the human ways? He didn't think it was.

As to the war itself he seemed to be an apostate. For this the Radicals found him unforgivable, and there were many, like the principled Charles Sumner of Massachusetts, who hated him for having once been such an ardent Abolitionist, and now, for representing the moderate and the restraining force in the war against the Southern states.

But William Henry had no hatred in him for the people of the South. None whatever. They were Americans and they belonged to the same nation; they came from the same stock; North and South issued primarily from Great Britain. To him it was a horrible thing that they had come to blows; and he regarded all of this as transitory and unfortunate and tragic, and every effort must be bent simply to resuming the fraternal arrangement, but without slavery.

In the much-edited first inaugural address of Lincoln, the famous moderating nationalist closing passage had originally been penned by William Henry. Lincoln polished the thought, but the idea itself embodied the crucial concept of Union, the uppermost and never-ceasing aspiration of the Secretary of State. Said Lincoln:

I am loath to close. We are not enemies, but friends. We must not be enemies. Though passion may have strained, it must not break our bonds of affection. The mystic chords of memory, stretching from every battlefield and patriot grace to every living heart and hearthstone all over this broad land, will yet swell the chorus of the Union when again touched, as surely they will be, by the better angels of our nature.

This was not sentiment or emotion: it was policy, the open door stretched across the border states, the door open for peace and restoration of the Union. In these lines lay the element and the readiness for agreement, for compromise. In this idea there was malice toward none and charity for all, a line of thinking and feeling that grew with Lincoln and became his grandest contribution; but because he was militant in his intention to prevent the spread of slavery, perhaps he did not have such nationalist sentiments as William Henry pressed upon him. And because of this he leaned intuitively to the Secretary's characteristic restraint. It was this sobering, moderating conservative influence that Lincoln knew he needed, and he secured it primarily from William Henry; for nearly all other pressures upon him were those of Radical and Abolitionist fervor, fanaticism and bitterness, and the vision of these of a conquered and occupied Confederacy.

Chapter Fifty-Eight

SO MUCH FOR ONE WARM HEART

THROUGH March the war and political events moved on in a muddy way, sputtering toward a finish; there was rampant hunger all over the South, and the Confederacy was demoralized; in the Capitol they were already discussing the nature of Reconstruction approaches, and, as if there were no war on, the Congress acted on building projects and national expansion westward. There was a sense of finality over the whole country; and the big military question was: would Lee, desperate in Virginia, stage one more big final defense, and could he, possibly, win some such big battle, or retreat into the pine hills and war on, guerrilla fashion, into the years?

Frances, far removed from the war scenes, could, like others, only speculate; until one day, early in April, she received a telegram. She opened it hurriedly; perhaps it was private news from her husband that the conflict was ended ... but instead, she tightened and blanched. One more blow atop a lifetime of hurts.... The wire from Frederick read: FATHER SERIOUSLY INJURED IN COACH ACCIDENT COME AT ONCE.

For thirty-four hours, the sixty-year-old Frances moved over the rails—a trip far beyond her strength—to the capital, and she arrived in time to find him with his face so swollen and discolored that she couldn't recognize him; his voice seemed changed, and he barely knew that she was at his side ... and it all set her heart to aching, and to ebbing.

On Tuesday afternoon, April 5th, William Henry, Frederick, Fanny and her young friend, Mary Titus, were driving along Vermont Avenue in the big Clubhouse carriage. Once more the statesman took into his nostrils the strong sour smell of the team of horses. The horse smell mingled with the odor of the spring flowers which had blossomed all over the capital, and bees helicoptered around the horses, the coach and the passengers. He felt pretty good these days because he believed the war was ending, and even this day he had received from Lincoln, witnessing the wind-up of hostilities at Richmond, a wire picturing how Lee's lines were crumbling.

In this mood and in this spring air, feeling jaunty, he settled into the enjoyment of the ride when, of a sudden, something startled the horses: the coach jerked forward and rolled backward on its springs, and the wagon tossed from side to side as the animals raced down the avenue and the girls screeched. Frederick tried to get hold of the bays, but he failed; and William Henry, an old hand at coach travel, sought to leap from the wagon, perhaps to grab the harness—so as to prevent the girls from being thrown and hurt—and he landed on the pavement hard.

They brought him home, and they put him to bed; he had a jaw broken on both sides, a dislocated shoulder, and great pain. He slid into delirium, and they didn't know whether he had the heart to survive the blow. The family doctor, Charles Verdi, stayed at the Secretary's bedside. William Henry lay swathed in bandages so that his face was about all covered, his head turbaned in white cloth; and he was comatose.

Four days later, Lincoln returned from Richmond. On board the *River Queen,* on Palm Sunday, steaming up the Potomac, he was thinking that the first thing he'd do on his return was go see his friend at the Old Clubhouse, for the word of the coach mishap had been wired to him. When he and his party of Mrs. Lincoln and Senator Charles Sumner docked, the senator and Mrs. Lincoln drove to the White House, but the President told the coachman, "Take me to the Old Clubhouse."

At the door Frederick told the Chief how the accident happened, at the same time guiding him up the staircase to the second floor room where William Henry lay, out of his coma and his delirium ended, but in great pain.

It was nighttime, the gaslights were low in the Secretary's room, members of the family hovered about; Frances shook hands with the President, and he expressed his sympathy. "He will be happy to see you, sir," she said, and she motioned the Chief Executive to her husband's side.

The bed was in the center of the room. William Henry lay on the edge of the bed, at the side nearest the wall; he was in such discomfort that he tried to keep his wounded arm from touching the bedclothes.

Lincoln strolled to the bedside, and for once he dropped the formality that always marked their relations, Mister President, Mister Secretary, Mister Lincoln and Mister Seward. "Hello, Bill."

Behind his bandages, and on the inside of him, William Henry smiled, but nothing of the sort showed on the exposed portion of his face. He could only whisper, "You are back from Richmond?"

"Yes, and I think we are near the end."

Frances, Frederick and Fanny quit the room; they called to the male

393

nurse, Sergeant Robinson, to come out with them, and they left the two men together.

The President was very tired and he wanted to have a long talk with William Henry. In a casual way he relaxed on the bed; he sprawled out on his stomach and he rested his head on his elbow so as to have their two heads close and neither have to talk too loud; and he told the injured man of the things he had seen at City Point, at Petersburg, and at Richmond.

He had actually witnessed a repulse of the rebels at one point and had earlier wired William Henry and Stanton of this, and now he gave the details. The war is ending about where it began, he said, on the same battlefields, in the same neighborhood; the Union troops had retaken Fort Stedman; and he had seen the dead and the dying in both uniforms, the blue and the gray, and he had seen enough, and it would be good when it was done.

He heard the wounded groaning on the fields and in the camp hospitals and he saw prisoners of war, and he was a little weary of all that he beheld. He told the Secretary of the kind telegram he had received from Secretary of War Stanton. The War Department head had chastised him for exposing himself to rebel bullets, but Lincoln told of it with amusement. He described how grateful the Negroes were: the ex-slaves had gathered about him in crowds, at one place, and he'd promised them that so long as he was President, no one would put a shackle to their limbs.

William Henry managed to move his head ever so slightly in a pained acknowledgment of what the President said. Lincoln drifted on for more than a half-hour of the sights and the scenes of Virginia.

At last, in the gaslight glow, it seemed to him that the Secretary of State might be feverish, or tired, or in deep pain, and he thought he heard the breathing of a man who had slipped into some kind of sleep.

He rose and he tiptoed to the door; outside, in the adjoining room the Sewards were about, and the attendants and the male nurse, and the household help, and they watched how the President silently lifted his finger to his lips in a gesture of silence, and let the Secretary sleep.

That was their last meeting.

He gained strength in the next few days, and he knew and the country knew that he'd recover, but it was slow, and he was still confined to bed. So, on April 14th, when Lincoln called a Cabinet meeting to discuss what steps must be taken to restore life to the country, now that Lee had surrendered to Grant at Appomatox, the Secretary of State couldn't be there. But Frederick was there in his place; and for several hours the Cabinet members talked over ideas for the reanimation of the country and the reopening of channels of communication between the North and the South. After the meeting finished, the President chanced to say that he'd been asked to go to the theatre this night, and would General Grant go with him? The General couldn't.

Frederick returned to his father's side and told him what happened, and the Secretary, through his pained jaw, managed to utter that perhaps they ought to issue a Thanksgiving Proclamation, and he murmured something about a communication to England. He seemed pleased with what Frederick reported about the meeting, and he drifted back into his injured quiet. The family kept watch about him, in shifts, first Frances, then Fanny, then Augustus, then Fred, then two invalided male soldier nurses; and the day wore on into evening, and about that time, Mr. Lincoln and Mary Lincoln went to the Ford Theatre.

Dr. Verdi returned to his home after dressing William Henry's injuries. It was late in the evening, and he no sooner arrived when a messenger came to his door and told him he was needed at the Secretary of State's again, and this time it was tremendously urgent.

The physician hurried back. He reached the door of the Seward residence, he went upstairs quickly, and at the head of the stairs he beheld the terrorized face of Frances. Her voice was agonized. "Look to Mr. Seward!"

The doctor turned to the room, and there William Henry lay on his bed with pallid face, half closed eyes; he was bloody, he looked dying and already like a corpse. As the doctor walked into the carpeted room his feet sank into pools of blood that washed around his shoes. He saw blood streaming from a long gash in the swollen cheek, and the cheek itself lay open and the flap of it hung loose on his neck.

"Quick, ice water!" the doctor called.

Soon he checked the hemorrhage and tried to determine the extent of the wound. The gash began at the high cheekbone and went to the neck in a semicircular form toward the mouth: it was about five inches long and two inches deep. The doctor feared the jugular was severed because the wound bled so much, but he found that this wasn't so.

Frances and Fanny stood by, paralyzed, waiting for the verdict whether the Secretary would live.

Suddenly Dr. Verdi looked up hopefully at the two women; then he addressed William Henry, who was conscious, "Mr. Seward, even in your misfortune I must congratulate you, the assassin has failed and your life is not in danger." Apparently an iron brace inside the Secretary's jaw, placed there because of the coach injuries, staved off and absorbed the stab of the knife.

The doctor no sooner finished sponging William Henry's face and replacing the flap of loose flesh than Frances remarked, "Come here, Doctor."

"What is it?"

"Come and see Frederick."

Somewhat surprised, the physician asked what was the matter with Frederick.

She whispered painfully, "He's badly wounded, I fear."

He followed Frances into an adjoining room where the Assistant Secretary of State bled profusely from the head. He looked ghastly, he couldn't talk, he smiled slightly with recognition of the family doctor, and he pointed to his head.

The doctor found a large wound somewhat above the forehead and a little to the left, and there was another gash farther back on the same side. The cranium was crushed in both places and the brain was exposed. Ice cubes put to the wounds soon stopped the bleeding, but the doctor suspected that these wounds might be fatal.

Frances stared at the doctor again, in the same haunted way, and he tried to encourage the mother, but he felt that his words were meaningless.

After the doctor bandaged Frederick and stood erect, he saw that same look upon Frances' face, and she murmured, "Come here," as her glance turned in another direction. "Come and see Augustus."

"For heaven's sakes, Mrs. Seward, what does this mean?"

He followed her into an adjoining room on the same floor and there he found Mrs. Seward's eldest son with two cuts on his forehead and one on his right hand. He would recover earlier than the others.

Had Frances, of the divided heart, led the doctor to each of her family in the order of her personal preference? Or in the order of their political importance? Or in the order of what she conceived to be the seriousness of the injury? No one would ever know. But perhaps the divisions of her heart had their own logic.

As Dr. Verdi turned to comfort Frances, she said, "Come and see Mr. Robinson."

The doctor stopped thinking about it all; he felt stunned, and he followed her mechanically into another room.

He examined Robinson, the invalided soldier nurse; he had a few superficial cuts, and the doctor treated them.

This time the physician turned to Frances and his look only asked if there were any more.

"Yes, one more," she said, answering the look.

In another room he came upon Mr. Hansell, another attendant; and he groaned, and said he was wounded in the back. The doctor found a deep wound at the spine, but he determined that this man too had had a miraculous escape.

On Saturday the nation had Andrew Johnson for President: on Sunday and Monday they were preparing for Lincoln's funeral; on Tuesday the President lay in state in the East Room; and by now the gloom over the country was universal, and the news reached all the civilized spots of the earth where cable could carry the message.

On Wednesday, early, a salute woke the capital to its most solemn day.

There was a clear sky that morning, and William Henry's new attendant thought it might be nice if his bed were shifted around so that he could see how the greening trees swayed against the blue.

But within his vision, through the window, there chanced to be also the upper portion of the War Department Building.

He saw that a flag flew at halfmast. Abruptly, things connected in his mind, what day it was now, and when he had been assailed by Paine, and it dawned on him that the President had not come to see him.

"Oh," he moaned, "the President is dead."

The attendant didn't know what to say; he had been cautioned to tell the Secretary nothing that would agitate him. But William Henry managed to utter through his pained mouth and his scathed cheek, "If he was alive he'd be the first to call on me, but he has not been here, and no messenger has come from him to find out how I am—and there is the flag at halfmast."

A little later, when the Secretary was tired and his vision not quite clear, he stared into the street where he saw a moving vagueness and heard a low drumming. It was a detachment of the Veteran Reserves, and they were carrying away from the White House the hearse that contained the Chief.

The witnessing of the assassination attempt apparently obliterated much of Frances' previous life. She was so filled with the scenes of that ugly night that, as the weeks went on, she could see little else, think of not much else, and she was unable to recall, with much interest, the things that had happened before that evening.

Weed had come to Washington in a hurry, and to him she described how the family and the nurses were gathered in the house when the conspirator arrived at the door; he had brushed past the colored houseman, and had met Frederick on the staircase: they clashed, and Paine struck the knife blows that laid the Assistant Secretary of State unconscious. Fanny's screams wakened the house; Robinson, the male nurse, tried to fight off the burly invader as he headed into William Henry's room; and, in his bed, the Secretary of State knew that an attempt was being made on his life. Augustus and Robinson couldn't hold back the madman, and he descended on the bed of the already stricken William Henry. Fanny was there trying to shield her father, and, with a great effort, William Henry rose and tried to defend his daughter; down came Paine's blows, cutting his throat on both sides, nearly severing one cheek from his face. William Henry fell to the floor, but the murderer still tried to get at him; he raced around the side of the bed, but Augustus and Robinson grabbed hold of him, and Paine turned his knife on the defenders. The room was now an abbatoir. Augustus, cut and bleeding, ran for his pistol, but the attacker made his way to the stairs and he cut his way downward to the street.

Now it all went on, like a repeating picture, in Frances' head, over and over this scene.

Her concern for her husband and son weakened her. To Thurlow Weed she said, "It seems as if I had two hearts, one throbbing for Henry, the other for Frederick."

That was, of course, the true Frances, of the divided heart.

During the next few weeks Frances wilted under the anxiety and the strain of caring for the wounded in her family, and as she wrote her letters to Auburn, she herself was abed: "The wearing anxiety I feel about Mr. Seward and Frederick consumes my strength."

The decline went on through May, while the others, remarkably, made recoveries. William Henry emerged from his bed a true battlefield casualty, with a battered and distorted face which he was now prepared to exhibit to the world; the long cheek scars, the healing jaw, the remnant of the gash near the jugular, the crippled shoulder, and the half-useless left arm and hand.

It was hard for Frances to see this, and yet she could write to Lazette: "But our calamities do not make us unmindful of the great loss our country has sustained in the death of our good President."

Late in May she watched from her windows the return of the great armies, the regiments passing by the hour in front of their house, brigades, divisions and corps, until her eyes were weary and her tired brain dizzy with so much, so very much of this war.

She wrote no more letters. For she could no longer get out of bed. There came over her what the medicine of that time called a "slow fever." She was withering—from the shock, the grief, the watching, the war, the lifetime—and on the 21st of June, Frances Seward died: the one victim of the assassin who had not been directly touched by his knife.

It was a time of mourning nationally, of all sorts, the North mourning Lincoln, the South bemoaning its loss of the war, of its slaves and of its soldiers; and in Auburn they mourned for the loss of Frances.

She was placed, for a time, in the garden where she had spent so many years, writing her letters, reading her books, tending her children when they were young, growing intellectually so that she came to measure up to the demands made upon her by her exacting husband.

There the local citizens took a last look at her, and then came the ceremonies described as "the largest assemblage that ever attended the funeral of a woman in America, outside the great seaboard cities." The war leadership of Washington and of New York railroaded to Auburn, and the citizens of that town came out, and the farmers of Cayuga County solemnly drove into the town; and round and about Fort Hill, and far down into Genesee Street, and all along South Street, there were soldiers, citizens, horses, vehicles, and an unusual quiet for such a large aggregation.

Everywhere they were saying the same thing: how it was her backing and counsel, as much as Weed's, that led William Henry to the position he occupied; how, if the Secretary had great influence on the war, it was in large part because she was the lawyer's counsel. One of the eminent writers of the day, George William Curtis, said, "Her influence will be forever felt in the tranquil wisdom and fidelity of her husband's service to humanity and his country."

They beheld the Sewards, Frances and William Henry, as a team, inseparable in their contribution.

It was over now, their love story, an American love, a Puritan affair perhaps, with its own fidelities and its own kind of trespasses, with their own love of America also involved in their private lives.

All over, except a little more waiting that Frances had to do....

Chapter Fifty-Nine

AMERICA DOES NOT LOVE ITS SECRETARIES OF STATE

D
URING the succeeding months, as William Henry resumed his
place in the State Department, he scrawled letters home daily
to Fanny. His daughter was upset by the events at Washington,
and she seemed content to stay at Auburn. Once, he wrote to her morbidly
that it seemed almost time for him "to leave this troubled stage." He had
been thrown by the news of the suicide of his long-time friend, Senator
Preston King. Why didn't King want to stay around to see the fulfillment
of his own work for the country and for the world? William Henry
couldn't figure it, and he was filled with gloom.

He told his daughter to go on gathering her mother's papers; they
would be precious some day. He had a mystical streak: he not only believed
that the soul was immortal, but so was the body; the echoes of the flesh
could go on being heard in eternity, and the voice of man whispered out
on some kind of literal physical plane or wave, and nothing ever ended,
really; nothing that was worth while going on, and he didn't doubt he
might get advice from Frances now. Every lawyer had to have his lawyer,
and she was his counsel. He wrote to Fanny, "I find myself every day and
night trying to recall your dear mother, and to extort from her some
counsel, or at least, to win some sympathy."

He had imaginary talks with Frances, and he fancied her replies: she
was prodding him, making him move faster on the question of Negro
suffrage, always trying to undo his conservative work with Reconstruction
matters. She censured him sharply. *What's the idea of vetoing the Radical
Republican policies?* she asked. *All that they want to do is make good the
purposes for which the war was fought, make sure the slaves are liberated
and get wages and become represented in Government.*—Now now, he
answered, leave the politics to me, Frances; you know, whatever you are,
you are no politician; we are just following out Mr. Lincoln's policy, and I
support Mr. Johnson because I believe he is doing what Lincoln would;

we don't have to beat them into the dust now that we're able to do it.— *Henry, think of those slaves, and stop being the professional conservative; don't forget your early Abolitionism.*— Frances, dear, have you forgotten? My name is on the Emancipation Proclamation, and *I* signed the thirteenth amendment, not all those hotheaded Stevenses and Sumners in the Congress; slavery is dead, I tell you, it's dead!— *Henry, I shan't argue with you any more, you know how I feel about these things, and know what a maverick you are sometimes; and don't get mixed up in any of Weed's financial schemes.*— Frances, such mistrust!— *Henry, you are only mortal!*

So the conversations failed: as hers, in an earlier day, imagined with him absent, also failed.

Once, years earlier, when Fanny was only thirteen, he wrote to her that she was fortunate to be born in so stirring a time, when such great issues faced the people, and when a generation was alive to deal for all time with such principles and meanings. It was so perilous a time, he said, that he did not know whether she would be spared to grow up and to live, or whether he would be spared to have, in his old age, a daughter. It was a gloomy, a foreboding note.

But no, he was wrong. She may not have been so fortunate. It was he who had the life of distinction and peril and wonder, and not his daughter; for, with her frail feminine character, her disposition so much like her mother's, exposed as she was to the storms of Washington, herself trying to absorb the shocks that her father received as a storm center, hearing of whole divisions of soldiers killed in battle, witnessing an assassination attempt—for a young woman it was too much; her mother's death was too much.

At home she pined and wore away. Life was too vast, too horrible to comprehend. It was all tragedy. Her mother died, perhaps of too much politics and too much living, and too much warring and too much caring. The same "slow fever" that overtook Frances now seized upon the girl. More and more she spent time in bed, and her body was weakened, her will weakened, and food did not nourish her. The great grim American world in which her father was such a power did not satisfy her need for peace and the quiet life which most people require and which a well-bred, growing and cultured girl should have.

Fanny died at the age of twenty-one, at Auburn; and when the news reached Washington, how Seward's losses continued, his wife and daughter both gone in so short a time, they felt a little pity for him, even if they didn't like the way he stood by Andrew Johnson, and encouraged the

President's moderation, and went over Johnson's speeches, and wrote some of his veto messages.

And yet, though his grief was consuming, and though he now asked himself from time to time, What is it all for?—the national, the personal bloodshed, the mystery of living and dying?—he rose each morning, after the night of doubt, and he hobbled to the State Department, and presented to the world the same confident face, the ever-smiling, ever-optimistic statesman's face.

Outside, abroad, in the halls of legislation, in most political circles, even in the streets, they had come to hate him, as it seems they come to hate all Secretaries of State in this country, conserving for these the wrath of all our national frustrations, our individual and collective failures, our State and national defeats.

They didn't call for William Henry's impeachment; no, he was impregnable there by now, a true elder statesman, the rock in Washington, for all currents to dash against and be dashed back—and a rock couldn't easily be moved; but they could move in on Johnson, and they did. William Henry was on a peculiarly high eminence now, a little immovable, his job to patch up the feuds in Johnson's Cabinet; he had the complete run of the Foreign Office, far more power in that area than he had with Lincoln; but he was rated now as a congenital conservative, and the word held contempt in it.

"Whist is a very sensible game, Henry Adams."

"It certainly is, Mr. Seward."

On the evening of March 29th 1867, the Secretary of State had his regular game of whist with youthful Henry Adams, the son of Charles Francis Adams and descendant of two Presidents. The old spiritual relationship of the Auburnian with the famous Adams family continued into the postwar generation, and at the moment this new and youngest Adams was about the closest companion of William Henry in the capital. Adams was only twenty-eight or nine, and during the war years he had been his father's secretary at the British court; now he was staying around Washington, and most of his evenings were passed at the Seward house.

Adams had a personal credo. He believed that life was an education for everyone, and that all men lived only to secure an education, in one form or another, and that there was nothing greater than the experience of education as the essence of the act of living. He studied the slouching, slender figure of the older man as they tossed their cards on the table: the disorderly white hair, the eyebrows white and shaggy, like caterpillars; and he listened as William Henry occasionally spoke in a coarse, offhand manner, the free talk of what went on among the personalities in the Cabinet.

They chanced this time to speak of the role of the predictable and the unpredictable in human events; William Henry ventured the forecast that Lincoln's reputation would soar to some immeasurable height, while the identity of most men then living would decline. The legend of the immolated President would mount and mount.

"I suppose," said the discerning Adams, "there are many disappointed men here in Washington and that the political field generally yields up a constant quota of frustrated competitors...?"

William Henry, who was almost President in the nation's greatest crisis, blurted, *"Speak to me of disappointment!"*

That ineffable note sank, like rain, into the absorbing earth of the younger man.

William Henry continued, mentioning an even profounder disappointment. "I feel that Providence dealt hardly with me in not letting me die with Mr. Lincoln. My work was done. I think I deserved the reward of dying there. How much better to have died than to prolong my life in the miserable business of patching up Johnson's Cabinet. It is a cruel and a very personal tragedy, Adams."

"I understand."

"You do? I wonder if anyone can."

Adams sensed a drowsiness over the old man; he didn't play with his usual interest. It occurred to Adams that if someone painted William Henry's face green, and his hair red, he would look like a macaw, a description of the Auburnian that was to become durable.

It is nine-thirty, Adams thought, time I left. He looked at the beaked nose, the sleepy eyes. "Mr. Secretary, this is the last hand tonight."

"As you please, Adams; I'm tired. I've been doing a lot of business with Baron De Stoeckl in recent weeks, and I'm really exhausted."

Chapter Sixty

A STATESMAN HAS TO HAVE
A LONG EYE

WILLIAM HENRY lay in the dark of the bedroom, this tall-walled green room in the Old Clubhouse. The fingers of his left hand moved slowly upward to the jagged scar on his throat. Fortunately, by day, his high, outflung white collar partially covered it so that, at the Department, nobody but himself and Frederick knew the twisted depth of the mark close to the jugular and the constant discomfort that stayed part of him. The jawbone ached, and it always ached; there had been no complete healing from the fall out of the coach two years earlier. He knew that he was a scarred, arthritic old man, sixty-six now, much hated, much misunderstood, though he had served the nation faithfully, and an inward emotion of the ingratitude of man swept through him. His mouth closed tightly on the thought. He'd keep that to himself. You had to play the game, thank the public, your colleagues, the whole nation, at all times. Never let on that you knew their envy, their hatreds, their pettiness. And above all, don't sink to the level of biting at them. Let them be the biters, the petty malefactors. Let them envy and keep muttering and wondering about his influence on Lincoln and the course of the war. And, stubborn and partisan as Johnson was, don't let them impeach him. There was enough ruction and death and ripping up of souls, from the war itself. Everybody had a gun—for everybody else. Just let this nation set the precedent of throwing one President out, they'd throw them all out afterward.

One satisfaction remained. There were only two more years of this. Then he could retire and try to forget. There was so much to forget. Out there they didn't know that a Secretary of State might have personal feelings, that to see his wife and only daughter go in a matter of months, to have to look at Frederick each day and see the wounds of the assassin still upon him as upon himself, to remember his close friend, Mr. Lincoln, as dead and gone too, to sense a nation more dead than alive now...he was tired. If only Paine had got him in the jugular. If only he'd died the same night Lincoln did. He'd be remembered then, Lincoln and Seward. But now, to live on, to patch up the fights in Andy's Cabinet, to drag through the daily wrangles and feel the envy of less experienced men, that was too much.

Just when he finally fell asleep, Caleb, the manservant, knocked on his door and called out, "Mist' Seward...Mist' Seward."

The old Secretary was breathing harshly.

The houseman, carrying an oil lamp, moved across the deep-carpeted floor to the bedside, and he called gently into William Henry's ear, "Mist' Seward...sorry to wake you..." then louder, *"Mist' Seward."*

The eyes opened, and William Henry saw close by the dark soft face of the servant, smiling as he held the lamp, and saying over and over, "The Baron done come...the Baron want to see you."

"Where's Frederick?" he asked, sitting up.

"He with the Baron, he sent me to wake you..."

"Tell them I'll be right out..."

"They in the yellow room, Mist' Secretary."

"Get some drinks out in a hurry, Caleb."

He climbed from the high fourposter; Caleb lighted two lamps on a bureau; the servant asked about the clothes Mr. Seward would wear, and the Secretary said he'd take care of that himself, just get word out to Baron De Stoeckl that he'd be along in a few minutes.

Perhaps the Baron had heard from the Emperor! Just get the Baron's signature on that treaty! The big dream of his life, almost as big a dream as a Northern victory in the great war, as big a dream as raising his own family for the country to be proud of; now, the last sharp victory, the one big single stroke that would rock the country and the world, the one that would make him forevermore the darling of the visionists to come, the world-dreamers of the future. Russian America—another land almost as big as the fields the nation had fought over for the past four years, and it'd be ours from now on! But there'd be hurdles, big ones, and now...if only Frances were alive to see this one, the deal that would one day make the United States of America safe from the whole East: an arm, a fist out to the potentates of the Pacific, saying to whatever powers could rise there, "We roll our strength to the shores of the Orient: we go no farther, but you come not east!"

There it was, in the outer room, in the high-paneled yellow room, where, for five days and nights, he and the Baron had wrestled over the price of the great boot of land up beyond, and the sense and roll of that exchange swept into his mind as he dressed, the long argument flashing again, the astute bargainer, envoy extraordinary of Czar Alexander, opposing himself who had been taught by the years how to swap horses—even when you were in midstream....

"But Baron, believe me I have no support in the Cabinet for this. I cannot possibly get you ten million...."

And answering him, the Minister, large, paunchy, overdressed, with the heavy beard down the side of his face, the bulky mustache and shaved chin; a high forehead that held inside the key to the cold snowland far and beyond Canada, the forehead that went on up into a patch of baldness; the man with the long coat and shiny patent leather boots, looking always meticulous, with the gold watch in his vest, and a tendency to hold one hand behind him, the left, as he gestured vigorously with the right, "But Mister Seward, need I tell you that England also wishes...."

"I know, we don't want England so close to us, and I mean to buy this land of you, Baron, but you must understand that Mr. Johnson has authorized me to go no higher than five million...."

A gesture from the Minister, as if he intended leaving; but he had no intention, William Henry knew. It was a case of where one was as anxious to buy as the other to sell.

"I too am limited," he said in that faint Russian accent that was too subtle for recording, for the Baron had been minister here for a long time and he had mastered our language and some of our ways. "You know the Emperor feels very friendly ... but five million..."

"Precisely. That is why I think I can swing this—now—but later perhaps never. Now is the time you must sell, Baron, now!—when our people feel so friendly toward your people and your Government."

The Baron warmed himself over some American whiskey while William Henry gently took a few sips of champagne. "Exactly, my friend. Exactly. You know what my Czar said only a few months ago."

"I know." Czar Alexander II had said, "The Russian and American people have no injury to forget or remember." And William Henry now echoed this, by way of answering the Baron ... "no injury to forget or remember."

They smiled. They nodded. In the backdrop of the large airy room Frederick hovered, not interfering in the slightest, almost concealing his presence, leaving the big negotiation to his father, even though he, Assistant Secretary of State, could have participated in what was supposedly a State matter. The bargaining had gone on for five days and evenings, from March 10th through March 14th—two weeks earlier—dicker and poke, give and take, the details of a treaty....

"Now, Baron De Stoeckl, if we are buying Russian America there is this question of the archives...."

"Yes?"

"We shall be inheriting a land that has been in your possession for nearly two hundred years..."

"Yes, of course."

"The history of that land shall then be part of our history...."

"But to be sure."

"Well, then, should you be wishing to return to your Czar these archives, these records of Bering, of the Russian American Company, of Baranof, their spats with England and with us, in short..."

/ "In short, you would like the archives, Mr. Seward?" The Baron was standing at the oblong mahogany table. His gesturing hand came to rest on the tablecloth, and the other, as usual, behind him. A bargaining point! Make the Americans pay for this!

The Baron seemed to reflect. His brown businesslike eyes roved along the yellow walls...how best to make this look difficult, and make this wily old statesman with the parrotlike head shed some scarce American gold....

"But, Mister Seward, the archives of one's own land, the record of one's past—these things are valuable. Historians...you know...need I tell you how, in politics, the casual documents of today become the live... the live..."

"Yes, of course, tradition. These papers represent tradition, the founding of the Orthodox Church in these hyperborean lands, how you enslaved the Aleuts." It was a sharp crack, nobody anywhere else had ever been able to enslave North American Indians except the Russian traders who had settled the frigid territory.

"As to slavery, Mister Seward..." The Baron gave William Henry a glance that carried with it a reference to the entire plantation South only now wrested from the hands of the slaveholders.

William Henry bypassed this dangerous current, and resumed, "What I mean, Baron, is, if we are to possess this remote body of snow and ice and..."

"And *gold!* Mister Seward. Let us be clear about that! There is *gold* in Alaska. You know this and I know this! My Czar knows this, and in Russia now there are newspapers which would like to denounce our move to sell this land and its potential riches! Your own geologists have found gold there, and yet we—we Russians—we *want* to negotiate with you, we *want* to sell this land."

There were, De Stoeckl said, in a subdued aside intended to be carefully noted, five hundred gold prospectors in the Russian American Territory at this moment.

William Henry, not yielding to this pressure, stayed silent. Inwardly he felt dismayed that his colleagues in the Cabinet, and the men in the Senate, even the whole American public, which had heard these reports, were indifferent. Sutter's Gold had spoiled them. They had all they needed here in the States. Russian America was far far away.

"You feel that *you* have pressures, Mister Seward. What makes you think we do not have a vigilant press in my country? You think it is easy for us to sell Russian America over the heads of *our* people? No more than it is for you to buy it over the heads of *your* people ... I have something to show you...."

He went into his briefcase. He fished around in a clumsy way for a document he had had no intention of displaying to William Henry, but the distinguished Secretary was clinching and scrapping, and he must defend the Emperor's interest.

"Mister Seward," he said, "I know you do not know my language, but you will permit me to translate, and you may trust to the accuracy of my rendition...."

He explained that he was reading a statement which was supposed to have appeared in *Golos,* which translated was *The Voice.* It was an expression, he said, of spokesmen on lower levels, outside the court, who were in violent protest against the effort to sell Russian America:

The sale of the colonies will deprive Russia of the region at precisely the time when numerous indications of the presence of gold have been discovered on colonial soil, the mining of which, assuming the reports are true, would bring in more in two or three years than the United States is prepared to pay for them.

William Henry tried not to show interest by any sign in the muscles of his face. But he raised his shaggy white brows when De Stoeckl asked, "Do you know what we had to do about this—so as you and I could proceed as we are doing this minute—?"

The Secretary's look asked what.

"We had to censor this opinion and prevent its appearance in *Golos.*"

William Henry stayed silent. It was not for him to tell the Russians how to run their press; only to make these transactions into a treaty. He paced the room. His flock of white hair shook, the white sideburns settled about his face. The Baron was arguing hard, but William Henry had the envoy against the wall too. Of course there was gold in Russian America, and perhaps other minerals. He knew it, Sumner knew it, the geologists knew it; untapped gold, and a bit of it had been taken out, but still the Russians must sell.

Yet the Baron talked as one whose back was not against a wall; he argued with a power and a pride. "You know and I know that Russian America is poorly garrisoned. Our handful of soldiers cannot hold it against the English. The English want it. They may *take* it. You know this and I know it! You want to buy. I want to sell. But I think you need to know, now, Mister Seward, the British will also buy—and they will pay *three* times what you can afford to pay." His right hand went down hard on the table and the drinking glasses tinkled.

"Still you will not likely sell to them," William Henry said, gambling, his slight frame no heavier than it was thirty years before, and he whirled about. "Because you no more want England on your shores than we do! Now let us be clear about this. You will sell and we will buy. We have in common much. We both fear England. So, what about the archives?"

"Mister Seward, I see that you are a great man to place reliance upon the historic record. I see this as a patriotic sentiment on your part. I suppose that if you get our territory you should get the records that go with it—and we shall so state in our treaty—but I do not retreat from the figure of nine million dollars as the minimum sales price."

"We shall do our best about the sales price, Baron De Stoeckl," William Henry swiftly offered. "Now here then, let me write the passage on the transfer of the archives as a point of the treaty, and you shall help me to formulate.

"Fred," said the Secretary, "will you write as I dictate?" and then turning to De Stoeckl, "—and you, Baron, feel free to reformulate and alter or concur, as you will."

Frederick sat at the table, a long sheet of paper before him, as the old statesman opened... "In the cession of territory and dominion made by the preceding article are included ... and government archives, papers, and documents..." Frederick's thick blue-leaded pencil moved silently over a preliminary paper, the indigo jottings to form later a true articles of agreement.

That had been on March 10th, and on the day and night of March 11th they resumed with the treaty and the haggling over the sales price in the same yellow room, only the one other person, Frederick, present, with occasionally the servant quietly entering, bringing food or drinks, or something to smoke. Outside it was cold late winter weather; and the house was insulated against the rumble in the streets. But here within the air was warm, spattered with the agreement and the difference of the two interests.

"Ah, but these buildings are very valuable," the envoy extraordinary argued, speaking of the property of the Russian American Company.

"I have never seen them, but I understand that they are little more than barracks."

"Barracks?" The Baron's paunch reacted. "I assure you they are well built. Strongly enough to shelter men in the coldest climate in the civilized world. Now then, I expect you to acquire these buildings. We cannot transport them to St. Petersburg..." they laughed... "but these structures have been built by Russian hands..."

"Russian hands?"

"Well, the local labor, and our Russian direction, and yes, some of our Russian labor power... but regardless... this is valuable property. There are many buildings. They are worth hundreds of thousands of dollars. They are serviceable. They will stand for a long time and they can be used in any way your colonizers wish to use them."

"I am sure of that."

"This represents the Czar's financing; that is, the money of the Russian people."

"Let us say the Emperor's money," William Henry said with respect, "the investment of the Russian American Company."

"Whatever you will... Russian buildings."

That settled it. Nothing could take value easily away from the buildings. They belonged to Russia and they must be ceded to America, and he must move up from his minimum of five million dollars.

"I rather imagine these buildings might bring... I probably could influence the President to go up a few hundred thousand dollars for all of this construction."

"Ah, Mister Seward, the Russian American Company's properties are worth millions. They are numerous. In these buildings the fur trade is conducted, and you can take over these structures and work through them to immediate profits—without the need of new construction. Believe me, the men who settled there studied the kind of working and living quarters that would be serviceable and lasting." He was selling like a real-estate man now, and William Henry was wondering whether he could get Andy Johnson to go as high as seven million, and get the Baron to come down that far. He looked troubledly at Frederick, and Frederick smiled at him, and it was encouragement, it was saying, "You can do it, Father."

He was reflective. His head nodded, and he said, "Baron, we have to do something about those buildings. That is very real property. Your representatives did build these structures and put money into them, and it is a matter somewhat special. We shall have to do something about this."

"Of course, of course," said the Emperor's envoy, seeing now again the light of a larger sum coming through, eight and a half, perhaps nine million. "Of course." There was, from each, an air of cordiality and earnest desire to agree.

William Henry walked to a corner of the yellow room, and from a square and vertical cabinet a few feet high he drew out a gold-topped cane. He must walk with it, here in the carpeted and insulated room. For he was energetic enough to move about, and excited by the negotiation, but yet decelerated enough to feel he needed physical bracing.

"I shall definitely speak to Mister Johnson in the morning," the Secretary promised. "I shall ask him to recognize the effort and the value of this property. It won't be easy. But I shall try. I promise you that, sir, I shall try to get another million for the property, more if I can get it...but as I told you," and then he went on, giving his guest the argument that always made the Baron weaken, and back down and fret: "You know, Baron, I am alone in this virtually. The people don't care, except in the Far West. In California, and the Washington Territory perhaps, they might like your Russian America, but the rest of the country doesn't care. I think it might even be hostile if and when we should be able to announce this. In the Cabinet, as you know, I have no support for this, nobody but Sumner, as he is my friend, and even he weakly, and of course, fortunately, Mister Johnson...well, he listens to me on this matter. He has more foresight than many of his critics credit him with."

"Mister Seward, I do not wish to interfere in matters of your own domesticity. But I know you are supporting Mister Johnson in his present difficulties and in his policy of reconciliation with the South. The public knows it. I feel you can urge him to see our point of view. Surely he is grateful for your support at a time when the Radicals wish to see him impeached. Does it seem unfair to me if...if I..."

"No, no. Say what you please. You are not interfering in a thing. The whole world knows they are trying to get Johnson out, and my position of support for him is known also to the whole world. Now I cannot trade on this too much, Baron. Not too much. It is worth something, but not too much. I can't force the man. I can only appeal. And then, even with him, you know, I have to overcome his reservations. He also believes that there is nothing up there but ice and snow and cold and wind and bears and..."

"And *gold*, Mister Seward, and protection against the British, and security for your nation's future...and one thing more, Mister Seward!"

"What is that, sir?" Seward had the greatest respect for De Stoeckl's

411

knowledge of the American political scene. The envoy was briefed on the background of everyone in the Cabinet and in any other highly prominent public life. De Stoeckl had his informants, his agents; he knew what was what.

"There is your own lifetime philosophy, Mister Seward!" De Stoeckl's eyes gleamed. He knew he was stabbing Seward in the belly with the strongest argument. "I know how long you have had your eyes on Russian America, Mister Seward—for a whole generation! You have been shouting for years that America would one day own Russian America. Manifest Destiny! You think I do not know you are the prime advocate of this philosophy? Today Russian America, tomorrow the West Indies, later South America, perhaps some day ..."

Abruptly, the Russian minister whipped another paper out of his briefcase. It was a letter signed by the Czar's minister of finance at St. Petersburg. "... Tell Mr. Seward that the Russian crown recognizes the Manifest Destiny of the United States."

That, the Baron thought, would please the Secretary, and he said, "When I got that letter I knew the time had come for these meetings."

William Henry was smiling; he had both hands atop the glistening gold of his cane, and he listened with pursed lips, answerless, like a man caught in what he is thinking.

"Yes," he said, softly. "I have quite a dream for my country."

"It is quite a *dream* indeed! Russian America may be your ultimate right, and I am trying to sell it to you, but when you expect to buy a whole empire *for two cents an acre,* I expect you to go to whoever you must go to and *fight* for it if you have to, and get us the reasonable figure we are entitled to! We may be weak militarily, and we are distinctly unprotected up there, but there are alternatives ... you know.

In a far corner of the room, Caleb hovered about a wine table, the glasses tinkled under the houseman's vitalized hands. "Lord, Lord, two cents an acre!" Frederick heard him murmur half aloud. "... If I only had three-four dollars to spare!"

William Henry struck with a hidden strength: it was hidden in his own black briefcase carelessly holding down a corner of the long map-strewn table. De Stoeckl had gone into his portfolio, to speak from a strength he found therein, so ...

He scrabbled among his papers.

"There are alternatives indeed, Baron. Do you know what the Hudson's Bay Company is up to now?" He was searching for something in the black bag.

"Well," said the Baron, laying himself wide open, "what are these mysterious alternatives that I, as Russian Minister, might not know about?"

He had asked for it.

"The English seem bent on forcing the Russian American Company to extend the agreement to let them stay around your territory—in a military way—imminently."

"A military way—imminently?"

William Henry plucked a thin newspaper, the *British Colonist*, out of the portfolio, and began to read:

If we cannot succeed in inducing the Russian American Company to cede that territory to us entirely, we must still get that shoreline into our hands, in one way or another.

"Let me see that, Mister Seward. What is the date of this? Where did you get it?"

The envoy read on:

Should the Sitka Administration, however, set its mind upon attempting to stop us, we shall resort to our naval power to protect the inviolability of the pact. A small number of English troops would be sufficient to render the Russian gryphon quite tractable. Our soldiery could swiftly put an end to the uncertain situation in that region. Should we meet with difficulty, we could very easily push back the boundaries of the Russian possessions. Since we have in our hands the area which is rich in gold, we should also possess its adjacent territory.

De Stoeckl acted surprised, even outraged. "Oh my, Mister Seward, what do you think of this? These English. You see ... you see ... Mr. Secretary ... they are the enemies of both of us."

"Of course they are, and we do not want the British up there any more than you wish to be deposed by them."

"Mr. Seward, I have not told you that during the war I kept a special file of what the British newspapers and governmental officials said about you and Mr. Lincoln...."

William Henry's brows raised.

"They called you a beast when they said Lincoln was a brute. They called Lincoln a brute when they said you were a demon. They named you a tyrant when they called Lincoln a demon. *You* were the evil genius behind him—"

The Baron's effort to flatter the Secretary or to appeal to William Henry's anti-English feelings, if he had any, did not evoke a response. For William Henry, who merely listened, the purchase of Alaska was actually a matter of domestic vision far beyond any wartime recriminations toward anyone: but the Baron kept tying the knot of Russian-American affinity.

"Perhaps," said William Henry, "we shall need to appeal to such sentiments as we take this matter to the people. Public feelings are very affable toward your nation. We shall long remember how the Emperor's ships steamed into New York Harbor during our dark days and stood like raised arms of warning to the British threat."

The Baron warmed over more of the Russian-American friendliness. When, a few months earlier, there had been an attempt to assassinate Czar Alexander II, the American expressions of sympathy with the Emperor had been received in a heartfelt way in the Kremlin, he said, and by this the British had learned of the deep accord of the United States with the Eastern mind.

Perhaps this interlude helped the Baron to recover position. He didn't mean to have his bargaining power shaken by the report of a military incitement. He shrugged, he disclaimed immediacy, he said it was a far cry from a newspaper threat to a military action.

"Ah yes, our position is imperiled ... but the Czar ... he does not care so much for a land so distant from our country. He thinks it is a monopoly we have in Russian America and he cabled me recently, 'The time for monopolies has come to an end.' All that he wishes is added compensation, something better than what you have been offering ... *something*."

There was a world in that *"something"* and there was a chance that if the Emperor of Russia didn't get his price, thought William Henry, the Baron might be so unwise that the Czar through his advisers might hold onto Russian America until the British did move in—and that might be trouble for the United States; because, could we have the British owning so much territory, having such a base between the Orient and the Occident, such a boundary extending from Canada almost to Siberia, and possessing in the future whatever geologically might come out of Russian America? For the British had already fought the Russians over that territory, and were besides rampaging all over the world, because war and conquest were bread and milk to the British. Nobody's move could be underrated. Worse still, the Russians might, desperate for money or a deal, and not to lose their possession by military means, actually sell to the English—and get *twenty* millions too!

These were the thoughts and moods that flashed between the men, these the considerations in the world of their time, as each played card after card, each wanting most seriously to do his part, one to buy and the other to sell; one to get the land for the least, the other to secure the most cash—both anxious to keep England out of it—each sniping, smiling, arguing, fencing, and mingling all of this with an occasional toast to a moment of agreement.

There were no guests in the Old Clubhouse at the time. The great thirty-room mansion that sat just north of the Treasury Annex was quiet, and no one was being admitted while the two statesmen haggled. At night the big cumbersome chandelier in the yellow room was lighted up, every candle alight, and the shades down, and the two men talked on, the blue pencils flying as they scribbled notes on sheets of paper, and interspersed their smiles of agreement with moments of pride and snappishness—for they were each guarding millions, and history, and it was no dicker at the grocery store or a haberdashery shop.

In the kitchen of the huge mansion the colored servants whispered that the Secretary was doing something big in there; it must be, because they was so deadset on keeping everybody away from them and letting nobody in, and they had to keep an eye on Frederick to see when he gave them the high sign for meals and snacks and such. They were saying, "I never seen it so noisy in here and so quiet at the same time. Ain't been anything secret-like like this goin' on ever since Commodore John Rogers got this here grounds from Henry Clay for a prize Andalusian jackass."

That was true; this big old spot had begun in a horsetrade of sorts, and now the biggest horsetrade in history was going on, with each trader looking over the shanks, the teeth, the tail, the knees, the pastern and the gait of the critter on the block. Here was the place where Calhoun and Clay lived while they were Cabinet members, and Taney when he was Chief Justice. But whichever, boardinghouse, salon, or rendezvous, the Old Clubhouse this week was having its most momentous hour.

William Henry raised the question of the Czar's troops at Sitka. How would their withdrawal be effected? The Baron was semi-apologetic about the garrison; this would be no paramount problem. It was not exactly a great army they had there, it was a matter of timing; but what did the Secretary propose?

"It seems to me," said William Henry, "the propitious time would be for your soldiers to leave as soon as ours arrive...."

The Baron reacted for an instant, as if that were somewhat precipitate.

"That is to say," the elder statesman went on, "I should suppose that a date might be set for the exchange of flags, ours to go up, yours to go down, and thereupon your soldiers embark."

Again the Baron reacted oddly, as though a lamentful note from a balalaika had struck in his mind, a regret, a sudden realization of something passing. The Baron gazed northward for an instant as if he could see the flag coming down, a weakening for the Emperor possibly, the vanishing of a triumph of Russian history—and this young land of Americans raising their red, white and blue.

Perhaps the old Secretary divined the thing that was in the envoy's mind. He didn't press it. He said, "Well, if that idea suits you..."

"I suppose," said the Czar's representative, still caught in the fantasy of the last moment of the passing of a territory, "that would be the only thing that could happen."

William Henry smiled. "It doesn't seem like a point that either of our Governments can make money on."

They laughed heartily.

Yet De Stoeckl seemed to reconsider. "I am not so sure of that," he said, recovering. "It may be that this is the very point at which *one* of us will begin to make money...." and the forefinger of his right hand appeared to point Seward-ward.

William Henry bypassed the thought, and he spoke again of the difficulties he believed he might face trying to get ratification. First there would be the hurdle of the Senate. "And then there is the House, where they always raise the very dickens about everything."

"There should be ways," the Baron ventured. William Henry didn't know what he meant, or acted as if he didn't know. "I think your force will carry the day, Mister Secretary. Your country has grown to place great reliance upon your leadership." Then, with a polished flattery and courtesy, he suggested, "In most European capitals it is still supposed that you are...shall we call it...the Prime Minister?"

"Then so much more their unawareness," the Secretary said quietly. "Be assured, my friend, Johnson *is* President. He is his *own* Prime Minister. That is why there is such a torrent of abuse against him now. He cannot be shaken—by me—or by anyone. Nothing stirs him but his own convictions."

He returned the matter directly to the most important real-estate transaction.

He felt that certain matters pertaining to the Indian and native question were still unresolved. Some of these Indians had been forced to embrace the Russian Orthodox Church, along with being embraced by slavery. Now then, were these people to be considered Christians, Indians, slaves, Catholics, people with rights in the departing Russian American interests, or candidates for American reconversion? To whom did their souls now belong? What could he suggest about all this?

"If you buy Russian America, you buy the right to rule the Russians who will remain, the Indians, the Eskimos, and you buy our slaves," the

Baron said, rather shruggishly, and he gestured with his right hand, a curleycue of dismissal of the question.

"Slaves? We are buying slaves?" William Henry was amused. He smiled. He looked at his son, and Frederick was smiling. The Sewards buying slaves! The Secretary and the Assistant Secretary galed into laughter.

He wheeled to his son. "Frederick, never breathe a word of it to the outside world! Your father is negotiating for the purchase of slaves!"

It was a remarkable irony, actually. He who had as United States Senator created a bulwark of antislavery sentiment in the land, making it possible in large part for the North to mobilize ultimately such forces as would defeat the Confederacy, and then to have participated intimately with Lincoln in the decision of Emancipation—he, Seward, was now buying Aleut slaves! *Indian* slaves at that! For the Indians nowhere else in North America had ever been enslaved.

He said, "When our flag goes up, if it goes up, if you sell and we buy, slavery in Russian America—which will then be called Alaska—ends automatically as of the moment of the raising of the American flag."

In the remaining days and nights of negotiation they went over the additional points. They drafted an article for each: the transfer of church property to the United States; the transfer of the Indian population to the United States; the right being granted to all Russians who so wished to remain, each to retain the private property which he owned, and according to each the right to worship as he pleased.

As the treaty points were hammered out, the selling price narrowed and met closer to the middle, for each point was worth money. William Henry went up to seven million, and De Stoeckl came down to seven million five hundred thousand. It seemed that they were moving toward as direct a split as could be made between five and ten. Still, on the fifth evening of the debate, the Secretary said he would not or he could not go higher than seven million.

"You know Mister Johnson is absolutely cool to this. I talked with him again this morning. He said the Senate would never ratify more than five million. He said he didn't like it." William Henry was emphatic as he said "didn't like it."

De Stoeckl seemed unaroused. He was used to this now, he was thinking. Seward, who had tried to compromise the North and South so that they would not go to war, was a man who knew how to move toward the middle. Let him ambivalate. There were trump cards the Baron could and would play. He always had the Emperor to fall back on even as Seward

417

could fall back on his cold Cabinet and the indifferent public and the troubled President, and a hesitant reliance on his personal friend, Senator Sumner, who was lukewarm to any ideas of expansion.

"Mister Seward," the Baron began, hushedly, moving about the soft-carpeted yellow room with a small show of the energy that characterized William Henry's movement, though it wasn't as becoming to the Russian to prance about for he was big, and he was paunchy, and a display of nervous energy seemed unsuited to him. "Very well. We started at five and ten, and now, with nearly all the articles agreed upon, there is this matter of another half-million dollars. It strikes me that you Americans drive a very stern bargain."

"How so?"

"What is a half of five?"

William Henry wondered whether he should parry the query addressed to him as a schoolmaster might ask it.

"I know that answer," he answered directly. "I really know what half of five is, but I cannot get more than seven millions for you. The President said he absolutely would take no responsibility for anything more than that. Beyond that lies the failure of ratification."

"So," said the Baron, "in America half of five is two!"

Frederick was close by and he grinned, then William Henry laughed, and the Baron guffawed.

"I think," William Henry reopened, "that there is something else that is unfinished. I think we should be comprehensive and clear in our final treaty points about this. . . . What disposition do we make of the lawsuits the Russian American Company now has with the English and some of our American fur traders and fishermen? Are we to take over the unfinished business of the Company?"

"This is a problem. But what else? If you buy our fair lady and marry her you buy her for better or for worse, her fortunes and her faults. I do not see what we can do. I suppose you should take over these suits, and a few debts, and they are yours along with the fur trade, the gold that you will find there, and the political value of the region."

The Secretary was doubtful. "I don't know. I am sure the Senate and the House won't like to have these details hanging on. I think we should get it all free and unencumbered. I really do."

Baron De Stoeckl was silent. Then, "Do you?"

"I do."

"Good, so I shall tell you how you can do this."

"Yes?"

"For exactly two hundred and fifty thousand dollars we shall take over all the suits, the remaining business hangover, the whole residue of the troubles with the fur traders and the fishermen, and give you Russian America free and clear."

"Baron De Stoeckl, I doubt whether those suits would cost you that much to settle."

"Ah, but they would, and the litigation, the time—the time and the parleys, and the courts—these may drag on for us for several years after we sell you the territory, if we should agree to hang onto these bad debts and legal troubles. The liquidation of the Russian American Company—it is an old institution—can be most complicated."

"You are asking more than I can possibly get!" William Henry sounded despairing.

"The Emperor is asking, not I! You are dealing with Czar Alexander II! I am merely the minister. I told you what he wanted! What am I to do? I am limited, simply limited, Mister Seward!" The envoy of Emperor Alexander was shrill.

It seemed that they had reached a stalemate. The talk simmered. Once more the food came on. They even settled into a half hour of whist. William Henry could whip everyone in Washington at that, but he played a gently losing game with De Stoeckl. De Stoeckl felt the Secretary's sensitivity with the cards, and once he said, "I wouldn't play that if I were you."

Then, as the interlude finished, William Henry said, "Baron, I am going back in to see Mr. Johnson in the morning. I will ask him for that final two hundred and fifty thousand dollars so that we in America will spell out half of five in the same way as you do. I shall try my level best!"

The large Russian, suave and able, with his excellent English, his better knowledge of American politics than most Americans had, and his superior knowledge of William Henry, saw the possibility of a better deal. "Do that! Try! I shall meantime stay in touch with the Czar!"

They bade good night.

William Henry and his son ushered Baron De Stoeckl to the door of the Old Clubhouse. Outside the Baron's coach had waited all evening, and the Sewards watched him walk down the long lane to the door of the coach, and again they waved good night.

The following day, the 14th, William Henry met again with the Baron, and he broke the news as solemnly as he could that seven million was the most he could secure the President's concurrence with. He simply could do no better. He seemed sad about it. He hoped it would be sufficient. Would not the Baron convey this to the Emperor? Would not the envoy personally try to understand the great handicaps under which he labored?

Understand the enmity of some men, the coolness and the jealousy toward him in the Cabinet, the mistrust of many Americans for his policy of land annexation, even the faint support of his closest colleague, Sumner? The same arguments over again, a man with his hands tied, he had worked a miracle of inner-White House politics even to get this far, there would be a great outcry, please carry the word back to the Emperor that this was the best opportunity.

Appealed to in that fashion, the Baron appeared to accede. Reserving his real thoughts to himself, he did however suggest that Seward complete the difficult task of securing Cabinet support for the tentatively agreed-upon treaty details. There was no anger or hurt or chagrin in his leave-taking. Perhaps he gave the impression that he did realize the handicaps under which the Secretary labored.

The next day a tentative draft of the treaty in its main outlines was shown to the Cabinet. They were an ambivalent group as they examined the points, wondered about the sales price, and suspected William Henry of philosophic purposes to which they could not easily or necessarily sub-scribe. From the earliest projections of the Manifest Destiny theory in America, there had been debate and opposition. He himself was much opposed to annexation by military means; and until now he had been opposed to national expansion even by purchase. Let our democratic ideas sweep the backward regions of the world, and we shall conquer from this strength alone, he argued. The fruit of liberal measures, an egalitarian political life, the common man en masse, a Walt Whitmanish concept of the age and of political program, these could win the world. Let democracy spread, no arms would be needed. But now—here—with this grand oppor-tunity, a few paltry millions, a mood of amity between two rising powers in the world, so then, retreat from one's position—buy! They didn't under-stand this, but they went along with it anyway. Only a few treaty details must be altered. He was by now the elder statesman of the nation: the eminent figure in Lincoln's Cabinet to stay on through Andy Johnson's Administration, fifty years of public service to his good and the nation's, so they could not easily stand athwart this demonstration of his personal will. Besides which, nobody questioned his patriotism and his faith in America and his desire to see only prosperity and decency tiding out everywhere.

During the next few days he worked to get a free hand at the White House, and with the Cabinet. He told the President that there were details which he must take care of himself without having to call sessions of the Cabinet as matters arose. It might even mean a few more dollars, in case

De Stoeckl mavericked—for the present figure was not exactly final. President Johnson, on the 18th, granted him full powers to act.

He wasn't surprised when, on the following day, he received a message that De Stoeckl wished to see him. He knew just about what was in the Baron's mind.

Once more the yellow room:

"Mister Secretary, you shall pardon me...."

"Yes, of course...."

"I hesitate to renege upon a point to which I have already more or less acceded, yet no treaty has been signed, it is my right...."

"Go on, Baron De Stoeckl."

"The sixth article of the treaty?"

"Yes?"

"The last point?"

"About the cession of Russian America without any encumbrances?"

"Precisely." He paused, he coughed, he had a bit of a cold because for these many days he had been tense. They would be the greatest days in the life of Baron De Stoeckl, his claim to an enduring doubt in Russia and eternal recognition as an unwitting benefactor in America.

"Ah, er-a-a," the Baron was rarely at a loss for words, for command, for poise. He never hesitated about bargaining, yet now he fumbled. He recovered to say this: "The Emperor feels—and I may say I agree—that the United States should inherit the bride's moles and warts as well as her beautiful snow-white bosom."

The figure of speech sent the Sewards into ardent gaiety. After the Secretary of State and his Assistant subsided once more into seriousness of purpose, the two tradesmen settled down into a new discussion of the litigation that still involved the Russian American Company, trouble with American and British merchants, claims by English fishermen, claims by prospectors and fur traders, boundary items. They could be nasty and prolonged.

"This will be a blow to Mister Johnson," William Henry said. "He was happy about the sale being clean and unfettered. He was reluctant about the seven million, yet he felt that the purchase, with everything cleared up, made such a high sum finally agreeable."

The Baron arose, he stood on all the steppes of Russia. He said simply, "That is my position, Mister Seward," and he bowed.

The Baron had gambled dangerously—either a break in the negotiations, or a more satisfactory sum. He knew that the treaty and the seven-million figure had been bandied about among the Cabinet members; they seemed amicable to a deal; and he couldn't imagine a complete backdown now. Actually the Emperor might have settled the whole business for five million —that had been the expectation years before when annexation had been discussed—but the Baron had many reasons for holding out. In St. Petersburg there was a government crisis stemming from a treasury deficit, and they needed money; perhaps the Baron hoped to be able to keep a smattering of the revenue here for himself, possibly he believed he would need to actually spend money to see the sale through Congress and through to a Treasury check; perhaps he was just an expert trader and gambler and he wanted the adventure (in addition to the cash) of a do-or-die arm's-length hassle with one of the world's shrewdest statesmen. Perhaps all these things; for in any case, he waited in his quarters at the Russian Embassy for the next move from the Secretary—and he stayed quiet. He didn't cable his Foreign Office for approval of the seven-million figure, nor mention to them the developed treaty. He just sat, and read the papers, and waited.

The envoy calculated perfectly.

President Johnson, having gone so far as to grant full powers of action to his Secretary, was not resistant to a last appeal by William Henry. The Secretary told him that two hundred thousand dollars would placate the Baron. "This will do it, Mister President, I am sure, and with it we send an ultimatum."

So it happened; as the Baron had stood on his hind legs in a last desperate grasp for another quarter million, likewise now he stood on his. On the 23rd, the Baron received this note:

With reference to the proposed convention I have the honor to acquaint you that I must insist upon that clause in the sixth article of the draught which declares the cession to be free and unencumbered by any reservations...must regard it as an ultimatum; with the President's approval, however, I will add two hundred thousand dollars to the consideration money on that account.

WILLIAM H. SEWARD
Secretary of State

Two days later the Czar's envoy sent a note to William Henry accepting the new arrangements. He told the Secretary he was cabling a summary of the treaty to the Russian Foreign Office, with a request for the Emperor's signature.

Then there were four more days of waiting...

Now, tonight, evening of March 29th, William Henry had his usual game of whist with Henry Adams. Adams had gone, and he retired early. With his diversity of thought, and his worn emotions, and amid all this,

422

musing also about what might become the greatest coup of his career, the addition of a whole hunk of planet to his own, his native land, he had slipped into sleep, and there had come Caleb whispering into his ear that the Russian was here.

The Secretary was alert and mental almost instantly; he switched swiftly from his nightclothes into a gray suit, the nearest suit that was handy. It was cold, and he put on a highnecked sweater; then, over these garments he added a gold-striped maroon robe that was warm; and, as his throat bothered him almost chronically, he swung a slight woolen scarf about his neck. He strode out into the yellow room, which was now made more brilliant than ever by all of the lighted candles and lamps and the orange blaze from the fireplace.

The short, rounding-shouldered William Henry moved, his greeting hand outstretched, across the room to the center. There the Baron stood, feet apart casually in a warmth and a beaming, the good news written in his stance. A paper waved in his hands, a cablegram, and William Henry glanced questioningly at the man and the paper.

"See, see," said Baron De Stoeckl, "from St. Petersburg—from Alexander —a cable!"

Seward anxiously took the paper from the Baron's hand:

BLESSINGS OF GOD AND THE EMPEROR ON
BOTH OUR NATIONS SELL FOR $7,200,000
ALEXANDER II

The two men shook hands, a firm, exciting grip. And in the same act, before their fingers unclasped, William Henry was commanding, "we must act tonight, we must sign the treaty tonight—or it may never take place!"

"Why?"

"The Senate adjourns tomorrow at noon. Our only chance of ratification is a jackrabbit movement in the Senate before the closing. Baron, you must call your staff together, and I must call mine!"

"If you say, if you feel ..."

"I do say! I do feel! We do it tonight. We complete the treaty this night at the State Department in the presence of your staff and mine, a formal treaty based on our notes of agreement. We *must!*"

"Then at once, Mister Seward!"

A few hours later, at four o'clock in the morning, March 30th, 1867, the treaty for the purchase of Russian America was signed by two names:

EDOUARD DE STOECKL
WILLIAM H. SEWARD

Chapter Sixty-One

FRANCES WAITS NO MORE

AFTER he bought Alaska, and he perceived, unexpectedly, that a portion of his dream of Manifest Destiny was an accomplished fact, he moved sharply to safeguard the soil by trying to acquire other islands, peninsulas and properties close to our shores. He had an eye on Lower California, where it runs, like a gorilla's arm, alongside Mexico; and on the sprinkle of islands called the West Indies; and he urged his Capitol colleagues to do something about these places now, when the nation's prestige was high; buy them, buy them, he urged, and he made strenuous efforts along that line before his term in office closed: but they'd had enough of him and his outward-moving goings-on. There was a year-and-one-half wrangle over Alaska in Congress, after his coup, and there had been charges of bribery and waste and error, and Washington was tired of such realty ventures, and so his other similar efforts were ashcanned.

But he was still one of the great guns of the nation, and so were Weed and Greeley. They were around, flailing their political arms over the land, all through the impeachment time, while the murders of Negroes went on in the South, as the Radical Republican surge in Congress rose like a wrath over the land and the Confederacy lay prostrate but trying to find new ways of fighting back.

Their women were gone: Frances, Catherine Weed and Mary Greeley. In that time women had it tougher than the men, and they didn't, as women usually would a century later, outlive their husbands. But the old warhorses of the national scene stayed in the shadows of the high councils, and from the shadows threw their weight and their punches. William Henry made no pretense at premiership to Johnson (he'd learned), but he ran the foreign policy, he encouraged Johnson's moderation, he was a power. Greeley had his eye on the Presidency: the need itched inside of him, a peculiar kind of American thing that ate up public man after public man; and Weed lay out in New York in a nice big house in Lower Manhattan, counting his securities, and if Greeley dared raise his political head again and aim it at the Capitol, Weed would snap it off if he could—and if they lived a thousand years they'd bleed each other.

Then, inevitably, at the close of 1868, William Henry's Government service ended forever....

He was home again, his life's work over, it seemed, and the big old South Street residence looked pretty good. He stood in front on the slate sidewalk and glanced over the yellow-brick place; it wasn't new any longer; it had been up a half century, and its style belonged to an earlier period. A thought of old Judge Miller came back to him: how the judge had loved this place and fathered it, and fathered those within it. Old Miller had driven a hard but wonderful bargain with him; made him move in, if he wanted to have the daughter; and now all that was gone: the father, the daughter; and the nation was emerging from a civil strife that the judge was spared having to see.

He sensed something of the passage of a time, from the fact that a great row of Lombardy poplars stood like soldiers between the sidewalk and the curb: they had been just young growing trees when he arrived here; now they were big and old like everything else. He stared at the two couchant lions carved in stone, at the entrance of the house; the black iron gates were the same, iron wore well; and the broad carriage way was well taken care of, graveled and smooth, and it circled back to the stone stables. Well, he'd spend some time here now, quietly—maybe stay on till he died.

But he was so discredited that, in fact, had he known how badly into disrepute he had fallen, even in his own home town, he might have died broken-hearted. The distaste for him seemed to stem from everything he had ever done: now they decided he had *never* been any good, neither as a governor, nor as a senator, nor as a lawyer; nor as a human being, nor as anything. His purchase of Alaska was a mischievous error; his policy of moderation toward the South was a damned compromise of an unforgivable sort; he had sold out. Every vilification lingered in the backdrops of his presence and his existence.

Soon after he returned, the young Republicans locally were preparing a meeting, to celebrate one cause or another, and they were looking around for a likely speaker. Somebody proposed Seward: but the young fellow who was running local politics at the moment said, "Who, that wretched old wreck of a man? That discredited hulk of nothing? Not him. Let's get someone with some value and a meaning in the community."

After weeks of resting on the porch, and strolling in the back yard, and musing of his long past, and dining with old friends, and lolling in his grape arbor, he suddenly decided he was rusting.

425

He'd be damned if he'd do that! Go stale? Wind up like a clod? Vegetate here like a grape? No, he had better things he could do!

Besides, it was tough to realize that he was such a denigrated figure after having done so much for the country. "To the best of my abilities, anyway," he said to himself, "and the Union is saved, we all saved it."

He decided that he would pull a last coup on the world. He knew that all over the world he was a prized man, highly regarded; that some of the gloss of the cause of the liberation was upon him too, as it should be; and if they didn't appreciate him at home, well, they might in Mexico, in France, in China, in India, in Egypt, anywhere in the world. He'd make a last journey—this time around the world. He'd have the plaudits of the planet in his ears one final time before he left the scene.

Arthritic, hobbled, but with his bright eye missing nothing of what the world yet had to offer, he coached and shipped and wheeled around the planet. His old bones ached, but he went on, taking the applause that the globe offered him while he still lived, no matter how much he might be forgotten a century later.

Wherever he went the sentiment traveled with him that he uttered in the Senate long before when Kossuth was in the land:

This republic is, and forever must be, a living offense to despotic power everywhere. The days of despotism are numbered. We do not know whether its end is to come this year, or next year, or the year after, in this quarter of a century, or in this half of a century. But there is to come, sooner or later, a struggle between the representative and the arbitrary systems of government. Europe is the field on which that struggle is to take place. True wisdom dictates that we lend to European nations struggling for civil liberty all possible moral aid to sustain them.

Frances was waiting for him; she had been dead five years, and she was thinking, This has been the longest wait of all, must he take this trip around the world, and procrastinate, and dawdle? His work is done, what is holding him up? Henry, globetrotting, could from time to time hear her voice and see her words in immortal blackberry ink:— You are so exasperating, Henry, and as I think of it, you always were— Believe me, from where I look out, little enough will be said of you a century from now, the century you are so worried about, the name you are so worried about, the country you are so concerned about—they will forget for there will be new Secretaries of State to attack and to vilify—and new men, ambitious, like you, and as I have been for you—will go on up to the same thankless desk, and try, and try, and try at the job where only failure seems always

426

the result—Stop fretting about your place in history, darling, and come to rest with—Your Own Frances.

On his return to America, while he was in New York, he and Weed were in a carriage going through Lower Manhattan.

"I suppose we should have done something more about Greeley than we did," Weed reflected.

"I suppose we should have," said William Henry. "If we had given him some office everything might have been different."

"Who was to know he craved office more than he loved anything else?"

"Who is to know what lies within any human?" William Henry asked.

The traffic sounds came to their ears: they heard the screech, the roar and the clatter of the elevated railways, in which Weed had financial interests; there was new construction everywhere, and the buildings rose taller, taller; trolleys passed over the newlaid rails, and the pedestrians carried the mixed ethnic look of a changing America.

They passed through a park, and there, of a sudden, William Henry spied a black sculptured head and bust of Abraham Lincoln.

He called out to the driver on the box, "Hold up, sir, please."

The horse and carriage halted.

The two white-headed men looked out of a side window at the long, worn, wrinkled features of the late Chief Executive: Lincoln's beard looked wise and full: he had entered the ages.

"That would be my statue there, and not Mr. Lincoln's, if you had put me up for the Presidency in 1856, Weed."

Weed emitted a sound like a moan.

"If you had run me for the Presidency in 1856, instead of Frémont, I think I would have been elected—and the history of the country would have been very different."

The old square-jawed dictator, with the shock of white hair, the large hunched shoulders and the rich black clothes—for he was now worth a million and a half dollars made on war contracts and other emoluments of the national crisis—shook his head sadly. How he wished the friend seated beside him had been in the White House.

The two old men stared at the bust of Lincoln, and Weed kept uttering the moaning sounds of his regret.

But William Henry looked beyond the statuary into recollections of the President whose right arm he had been, and he murmured: "No matter. Lincoln's face looks very well there."

427

They urged him to do his autobiography, and in the months remaining to him he began it.

Books! Books! The line from Ecclesiastes came to him—that of the making of books there was no end—so it had been thousands of years before, in the time of prophets before him, so it was now: perhaps it would be ever thus, men inspired to set on paper what they felt and saw and believed, and what they thought might be or ought to be, each conceiving in his own way the linking of truth and reality, some born to read, some to write, to speak, to probe the mysteries of the material universe, and Whatever May Lie Beyond That; and this drive had seized upon him early in life with such a force that once it nearly cost his life. He knew what it was to almost lay down his life for love of the truth to be found in a book. It came back to him how, as a boy of twelve, doing his farm chores, he took the cows home from the distant pasture, trying to read at the same time. It was twilight, a maroon glow over everything, the fields, the barns, the cows, and even over the book he held; yet he stumbled on, reading, the cows going on before, he the abstracted herdsman. Two or three young farm lads came along and they laughed at the spectacle; he tripped and caught himself in the weeds, and he paid no mind to it but regained his footing and went ahead, still seeing the print only. A sprinkling of small stones came his way, and a few hit him and others fell about him. But young William Henry wasn't impressed with that, for what he read interested him, so he simply turned around and walked backward, the cows going in the same direction as he, toward a small river; yet he could read, keep his eyes on his tormenters and drive the cows home, all in one. Stones kept coming his way, but he dodged them, and absorbed the words just as steadily as before. Yet he was moving off of the regular path away from the bridge, and he tumbled into the deep water. It was calm water, but deep; he didn't know how to swim, and it was lucky for him that his older brother had watched the whole performance. His brother had a hard time pulling out William Henry. For a while the young reader lay on the bank unconscious. The older brother shouted at him, pummeled him about the chest, until William Henry breathed properly again.

It was much risk, he recalled, for the contents of a book that probably was not very exceptional.

And so, now, he wrote a few thousand words each day, and he was weary throughout the writing. Perhaps working by pen, in the quiet grape arbor, seemed a too-tame way for the macaw of Washington to end his vivid days in this vivid time of our nation.

One of his neighbors asked him what he considered the most important measure of his political career. "The purchase of Alaska," he answered, "but it will take the people a generation to find it out." And yet, though he said this, and may have believed it, still it was perhaps because he wanted to justify himself in the face of a national feeling at that moment that his purchase was folly.

And yet, far beyond that claim—his name and Lincoln's were on the Emancipation Proclamation, no others. He had labored a lifetime to help produce that document of unequaled significance, even though moderation characterized the latter stages of his employment in behalf of that end. His name alone was upon the certificate of ratification of the Thirteenth Amendment, abolishing slavery, signed: WILLIAM H. SEWARD, *Secretary of State, December 18, 1865.* His name and his alone was signed to the certificate of ratification of the Fourteenth Amendment to the Constitution, making citizens of all former slaves, guaranteeing them equal rights with all others; his only: *Done at the city of Washington, this twenty-eighth day of July, in the year of our Lord one thousand eight hundred and sixty-eight, and of the independence of the United States of America the ninety-third: William H. Seward, Secretary of State.*

Perhaps no other man in Anglo-Saxon history, not even the enduring Lincoln, has his signature on so many historic documents; these and the forty treaties, and the Big Horsetrade of the Far North; documents into which William Henry poured his ink, his blood and his days.

He had, in the course of helping to fashion America, become a unique American himself, standing with ten or fifteen other eminent men of our land at the pinnacle; he had succeeded in his private aim of carrying on in the John Quincy Adams tradition of Union, Power and National Expansion; he had done all of this in spite of the fact that he was, at times, in alignment with a great money power and with powerful individuals who had not his integrity, nor his love for the truth and the community service.

Radical? Conservative? Revolutionist? Politician? Statesman? American?

What was he, as he rode out the storms that shook the nation, and as he prepared now to leave it?

An exotic in politics, William Henry brought splendor, showmanship, and the magic of the genie to his performance. Sometimes, from his bag of tricks, there leaped a full-fledged fiasco, but his failures appeared to set off his successes and to make them shine the more brilliantly. He was a master of surprise; and color, and the volatile elements of the unexpected and the unpredictable, were ever-present ingredients of his political broth. Bizarre, fabled in his own time, he was more like an Oriental than a Yankee or an Anglo-Saxon. He was as a Turk without a turban, or as a dervish of East India whose whirls were political. Our most unique statesman.

The writing of his autobiography went slower, and it was clear to him he'd never finish it: his arthritic hand moved in a tremble; he had a way of telling some of the personal details of his story and then, for page after page, drifting off into political comment about the nature of the Constitution, or a description of how the Government worked. He spent a few hours daily at the task; his sons and their children and the servants were never far away, to take care of his wants or to tell him that he had done enough and perhaps he ought to rest.

The last stage of the Weed-Seward-Greeley feud unfolded in these declining days of William Henry. The hidden Greeley emerged once more, this time as the rival of General Grant in the 1872 race for the Presidency. Apostasy had marked all of the Whig partners, and now the brand lay clearly on the forehead of the distinguished editor. He, the lifelong reformer and Republican, now ventured forth in the maverick role of Democrat, defender of the Confederacy, to oppose the prestige-heavy Grant. What made Greeley think he could defeat the conquering hero of the great conflict? For a while, in the early campaign, it did seem as though he had an important tide of favor in the land, but steadily the guns of the political season martialed against him: first, the editors of the nation turned against him; and then Weed pulled the stops, and leveled a long effective tirade against Greeley's lifetime of inconsistencies, and this helped brake his headway. William Henry told the newspapers, "I never stood in his way and I shall not do so now." But the Auburnian, between the paragraphs of his personal story, watched the press, and he learned, as the fall came on, that the man who most of all beat him for the Big Job was himself to be denied. As the defamation of Greeley went on, the word reached William Henry that an unhappy, a very wretched Greeley remarked that he didn't know whether he was running for the Presidency or the penitentiary.

Maybe all of this made dying a bit easier, a bit more peaceable for the old macaw of Washington, New York, Auburn, Albany, Florida, the Frontier, and of the coaches, the steamboats and the railroads.

Whatever their feuding or fussing, the three of them primarily built the stage onto which Lincoln walked.

One morning he sat up sharply, keenly upright in the fourposter, for he saw a letter large, welcoming, covering the wall of the room, the dream reading:

My dear Henry:
    I am waiting—
        Your Own Frances

He slept more and more, he took longer naps on the big green sofa in the library. All around him were books, law books, and new books of the war statesmen, their memoirs, the rush of Lincolniana had begun, each telling his part in the antislavery conflict.

Nearby was the big round globe of the world, the world over which he had just traveled, and part of which he had helped to change, he hoped, for the better ... he was tired ... perhaps even of the world.

The pen scratched along ... he reached one day the story of how he had come to be nominated Governor of New York State by the Whigs.... Then, the pen slipped away from his fingers, and his head nodded. Afterward, he lay on the sofa in the library, amid the memories of his crowded life, wondering whether he'd ever be able to write it all. The thought itself was fatiguing.

Inside him something incessantly yawned and stretched.

He lay for hours, then for days, weakening, on the green divan.

Frederick sent a telegram to Weed: WE THINK FATHER IS DYING.

On October 10th, 1872, when his strength was gone, and his sons were about him, he uttered his last three words:

Love one another.

William Henry lay in his coffin in the parlor of the house built by Judge Miller, a long beautiful room that was now a virtual museum of curiosities of the time. The relics of the age abounded in each corner, on each pedestal, from each shelf, from the mantelpiece, and it was this way in each room of the mansion. The oils of his forebears, showing them in the quainter costumes of an earlier time, between the colonial and the pre-Republican America, ornamented the Governor's final moments: old Judge Seward and Mary Seward looked down on the gifted son that they had given to America, that he might give to the land much of the character that it now possesses, especially its national democratic character. The pictures of statesmen of all countries, those he had dealt with while he held Europe at bay during the Lincoln years, were framed and they were suspended on the walls, along the staircase, in the hallways of the upper rooms, so that the whole house was a miniature of the world and its personages in the year 1872. Swords and guns descended from hooks nailed to the moldings: important letters in the hand of the distinguished of the world, of the Civil War time, were neatly framed, and displayed for his visitors to examine if they cared to do so. Statuettes, busts of Lincoln, of John Brown, of the Governor himself, and family portraits by the most sensitive artists of the day, filled each space on the rich walls. The sunlight came in and it illuminated the last hours of an American slumbering in a sea of his own Americana: the iron, the leather, the cotton, the glass, the colors. The visitors came, and they looked at him and went out: Governors, Cabinet men, politicians, statesmen, and townspeople; they noted the moment, the place, the things, and glanced finally at the reposed face, now so like an eagle's.

In the midst of this, as the fashionably dressed notables came and went, or sat and viewed, or hushedly whispered and held their hats, while family and friends hovered, as the lavish wreaths and costly flowered emblems piled ever higher about the bier, as undertakers and Episcopalian ministers stood by, and as they made ready to close the coffin, a small black woman quietly came through the front door, and glided gently to the foot of the coffin. There, tenderly, she placed a wreath of ordinary field flowers upon the statesman's feet; she glanced at his face an instant; then turned and walked out. It was the war woman, Harriet Tubman, who led soldiers on the field of battle in the Department of the South, and who saw William Henry from time to time before he died.

They carried him, with all these meanings that his life and death held, quietly up the hillside of Fort Hill Cemetery. They bore what was left of his brightness, and his weakness, his generosity and his vanity, across the autumn knolls now brown and red and russet with the dying year. The controversies that had racked the nation since the time of William Morgan and the fighting over parochial schools, the rescue of slaves, the ending of feudalism—all these fiery matters of community interest they now moved with, up the grassy hillside, to the plot where old Judge Miller had gone a quarter century earlier.

The weathers of the region, usually cold and windy, suspended their terrors that day, and warmth glowed over the hump of hill in the town's center. The sun was warm and round and white and low in the sky, as if it always showed that way, and the air was untroubled and soft—so unlike William Henry's days.

As if the mood everywhere were: forgiveness.

He was placed beside the earth of Frances.

As they said his farewell, someone in the family rested at the head of his grave a small white clay John Rogers figurine of Frances, a statuette of her seated in a chair writing a letter—perhaps her most characteristic attitude—looking serene in her outflared dress, universal with wisdom and love, and with a slight bend of her head that was her own.

They were side by side now, the antislavery and Radical Republican, Frances, and the Unionist and moderate Whig, William Henry.

This had been the longest wait of all for her; she had been waiting for him for seven years; but at last his affair with his mistress was over, and he was back home to his Lady, they were at peace, and this time he would stay.